Java™

Methods

An Introduction
to Object-Oriented Programming

Maria Litvin
Phillips Academy, Andover, Massachusetts

Gary Litvin
Skylight Software, Inc.

Skylight Publishing
Andover, Massachusetts

Skylight Publishing
9 Bartlet Street, Suite 70
Andover, MA 01810

web: http://www.skylit.com
e-mail: sales@skylit.com
          support@skylit.com

Library of Congress Control Number: 2001126002

ISBN 0-9654853-7-4

2 3 4 5 6 7 8 9 10   06 05 04 03 02

Printed in the United States of America

To our parents

Brief Contents

Contents

Preface

This book is written with two kinds of readers in mind: the complete novice and the person somewhat familiar with software development in Pascal, C++, or another programming language.

For the novice, *Java Methods* provides a solid introduction to object-oriented programming, an illustrated explanation of Java syntax, and some practice using library classes and packages for developing GUI (graphical user interface) applets and applications. While you may have to struggle a little with the details of syntax, you have the advantage on the conceptual level of a fresh, unprejudiced view of the object-oriented programming approach. It will be easy for you to embrace OOP without reservations and use Java in the most effective way.

For the reader who has done some programming in C++ or another language, the challenges are different. You are already familiar with the general elements of programming: program syntax, control structures, working with a compiler and other software development tools. If you are coming from C++, you will recognize declarations of variables, if-else statements, for, while, and do-while loops, classes, and many other elements of Java syntax. But when it comes to OOP, you'll need to combine your experience with the open mind of a beginner! For while it would be possible to emulate Pascal- or C-style programming in Java, that would completely miss the point.

Fortunately, OOP concepts are more straightforward than the terminology makes them appear. The notions of *objects* (entities that combine data elements and functions), *classes* (definitions of types of objects), *methods* (functions that handle certain tasks), *instantiation* (creating an object of a particular class), *inheritance* (one class extending the features of another class), *encapsulation* (hiding the implementation details of a class), *polymorphism* (calling correct methods automatically for specific objects disguised as more generic types), and *event-driven* applications (where the operating system, the user, or events in the program trigger certain functions) are actually quite intuitive and useful.

This book will teach Java and OOP through examples, exposing you to all three levels of the language — the syntax, the conceptual OOP level, and the intermediate layer of library classes and GUI tools — at once. Even for a novice, it would have been difficult and boring to learn the programming language syntax and control statements without meaningful examples and case studies. (You can't learn to swim in a bathtub.) Instead we have provided more realistic examples, examples that apply OOP concepts and use GUI components. Our presentation strives to balance the technical details with clear explanations of fundamental concepts.

The examples may be daunting at first. Keep in mind that you are learning Java using an <u>immersion</u> method. Expect to <u>see</u> a lot from the very beginning, but don't try to understand all or even most of it. Only the highlighted little bits may make sense to you as you begin; the whole picture emerges gradually as you go along. The code in the early chapters, which you'll have to accept on faith at first, will make total sense by the end of the book. You will also pick up proper programming style, an element not mandated by formal Java language specifications but essential for writing readable professional programs.

We approach the library classes and packages in the same way. Of course you could learn them from Java's exhaustive online documentation, but a faster method, for the beginner and professional alike, is to look at examples. We provide more or less realistic examples from the outset, so that an inquisitive student can use them to start writing his or her own little programs with graphics and GUI right away. By the time we get to the more formal discussion of graphics (in Chapter 14) and GUI components (Chapter 15), you have already seen most of them in action in a case study or lab. Our examples use Java's Swing package, currently the standard one used by professionals.

Still, with all the examples and case studies, we leave a lot of work to you. This is not a *Java-in-n-days* book or an *n-hours-to-complete* book. It is a book for learning essential concepts and technical skills at a comfortable pace, for acquiring a repertoire of examples to work from, and for consulting once in a while when you start writing your own Java programs professionally or for fun.

Working through this book will not make you a Java expert right away — but it will bring you to the level of an entry-level Java programmer with a better than average understanding of the fundamental concepts. Object-oriented programming was invented to make software development more accessible to beginners, and *Java Methods* is written in that spirit.

Without further delay, let us begin learning object-oriented programming in Java!

How to Use This Book

The *Java Methods* companion web site —

http://www.skylit.com/javamethods

— is an integral part of this book. It contains instructions on how to acquire and set up various Java development tools and documentation. It also has a downloadable version of all our student disk files (with the code for case studies, labs, and exercises), as well as appendices, web "footnotes," web links, errata, supplemental papers, and syllabi and technical support information for teachers.

✿ The web symbol indicates a "footnote" that is on the book's web site in the alphabetical list of "footnote" links.

🖫 The disk icon marks those programs in the book that are included on the student disk.

 This icon brings your attention to a lab exercise or a hands-on exploration of an example.

1.■, 2.◆ In exercises, a square marks an "intermediate" question that may require more thought or work than an ordinary question or exercise. A diamond marks an "advanced" question that could be treacherous or lead to unexplored territory — proceed at your own risk.

✓ A checkmark at the end of a question in exercises means that a solution is included on your student disk. We have included solutions to about half of the exercises. They can be found in the Solutions 🖫 folder on your student disk and on the book's web site. ✿solutions

A teacher's disk with solutions to all the labs and complete solutions to all the exercises is available free of charge to teachers who use this book as a textbook in their schools.

❖   ❖   ❖

(To a slightly different subject...)

This book presents as illustrations several complete or partial programs. They are presented only to provide realistic context for the discussion, as part of our "immersion" method of presentation, in which you learn to read programs before you start writing them. You are not expected to study or understand all the code completely until later. **We have highlighted the relevant elements in the code that need your immediate attention.**

How you use this book will depend on your background in computers. If you are familiar with computers and programming, you can glance quickly at Chapters 1 and 3 just to see if they fill any gaps. If you know HTML, you can skip Chapter 2 or just read Section 2.9 to see how Java applets are integrated into web pages. If you prefer to see technical details before concepts, feel free to skip Section 4.6 — you can return to it later, after Chapter 8. If you know C++, Chapters 5, 6, 7, and 11 will be easy for you. Do still look at them for the sake of the case studies and labs, which may cover broader concepts than the chapter headings imply. But make sure to read Appendix A, *From C++ to Java*, first.

The self-tests after Chapters 6 and 12 are in no way comprehensive; they only indicate the general level of problems you should be able to solve (perhaps with considerable effort) at those points in the book. Consider them milestones on your way to proficiency in Java.

We have provided `EasyReader` and `EasyWriter` classes to supplement Java's stream I/O classes. `EasyReader` lets you read numbers, characters, words, and strings from the console and from a text file. `EasyWriter` lets you write these data elements into a text file (or append data to an existing file). These classes are in the `EasyReader` 🖫 folder on your student disk. You can combine these two classes into a `com.skylit.io` package and install it properly, but it may be easier at first to simply copy one or both of them into your project folder. Each of these classes has a simple example in its source file, and a more detailed description is available in Appendix E✱ on the web. You can also generate standard HTML documentation from `EasyReader.java` and `EasyWriter.java` with *javadoc*.

The *Ramblecs* game developed in the case studies and labs in Chapters 4, 6, 11, 15, 16, and 17 is yours to play with and improve upon as long as it stays in shareware, its source code remains open, and it is not used for commercial purposes. A compiled applet is available in the `RunRamblecs` 🖫 folder on your student disk. Send your version of the game (preferably a link to your web site) to `ramblecs@skylit.com` if you believe it deserves to be entered in our *Annual Ramblecs Game* contest.

Acknowledgments

Our sincere thanks to Richard Kick from Hinsdale High School in Hinsdale, Illinois, Roger Frank from Ponderosa High School in Parker, Colorado, and Gerald Berry from Thomas Jefferson High School for Science and Technology in Alexandria, Virginia, for reading an early draft of this book. Rich gave us numerous astute comments and suggestions that were implemented in the final version and helped improve the book. Roger's comments helped us make the book more accessible, and his attention to detail saved us from several mistakes and inconsistencies. Gerry's general critique inspired us to restructure several chapters and add or clarify a few examples and case studies, leading to a more enjoyable book.

We are very grateful to David Levine of St. Bonaventure University, New York, for reading the final draft and suggesting important technical and stylistic improvements, and for his unwavering support and encouragement on our path from a concept to a finished book.

Our colleague Andy Cline from Phillips Academy and the students in Maria's Computer-300 (*Introduction to Programming and Computer Science*) class worked through the first eight chapters over the winter trimester. We thank them for their enthusiasm and their patience while working with an incomplete text and for catching a few mistakes, typos, and obscurities. Our thanks also to Michael Ashley-Rollman and Aaron Hsieh, Phillips Academy '01, for working independently and enthusiastically through the entire draft and making useful comments and suggestions.

We thank David Penner, the Mathematics Department chairman at Phillips Academy, for encouraging and supporting innovation in the computer science program. We are very grateful to Aleta Sousa, the director of the computer center at Phillips Academy, and to Mary Ellen Witman, the assistant director, who graciously shared a lot of their time and advice and helped install and maintain Java development environments.

Our special thanks to Margaret Litvin for her thorough and thoughtful editing of everything we write.

We thank all the colleagues and friends who encouraged us to write a Java book.

About the Authors

Maria Litvin has taught computer science and mathematics at Phillips Academy in Andover, Massachusetts, since 1987. She is an Advanced Placement Computer Science exam reader and, as a consultant for The College Board, provides C++ and Java training for high school computer science teachers. Prior to joining Phillips Academy, Maria taught computer science at Boston University. Maria is co-author of *C++ for You++: An Introduction to Programming and Computer Science*, one of the leading high school textbooks for Computer Science courses (Skylight Publishing, 1998) and the author of *Be Prepared for the AP Computer Science Exam* (Skylight Publishing, 1999). Maria is a recipient of the 1999 Siemens Award for Advanced Placement for Mathematics, Science and Technology for New England.

Gary Litvin has worked in many areas of software development including artificial intelligence, pattern recognition, computer graphics, and neural networks. As founder of Skylight Software, Inc., he developed SKYLIGHTS/GX, one of the first visual programming tools for C and C++ programmers. Gary led in the development of several state-of-the-art software products including interactive touch screen development tools, OCR and handwritten character recognition systems, and credit card fraud detection software. Gary is co-author of *C++ for You++*.

ch 001

An Introduction to Hardware, Software, and the Internet

1.1   Prologue

Have you ever opened that inconspicuous gray or black (or purple) box sitting on or beside your desk, with tangled wires snaking out of it in all directions? If you do, you might find a mostly empty box, with a power supply, a printed circuit board on the bottom connected by tape cables to a small disk drive and a couple of other devices neatly tucked away in their bays. And that's all. But it brings you an entire world.

The most important piece of a typical computer is the ***Central Processing Unit*** or ***CPU***. In a personal computer, the CPU is a microprocessor made from a tiny chip of silicon, sometimes as small as half an inch square. Immensely precise manufacturing processes etch a huge number of semiconductor devices, called ***transistors***, into the silicon wafer. Each transistor is a microscopic digital switch and together they control, with almost perfect precision, billions of signals — little spikes of electricity — that arise and disappear every second. The size of the spikes doesn't matter, only their presence or absence. The transistors in the CPU recognize only two states of a signal, "on" or "off," "high" or "low," "1" or "0," "true" or "false." This is called ***digital electronics***, as opposed to ***analog electronics*** where the actual amplitudes of signals carry information.

The transistors on a chip combine to form logical devices called ***gates***. Gates implement ***Boolean*** operations (named after the British mathematician George Boole, 1815-1864,[boole] who studied the properties of logical relations). For example, an ***AND*** gate takes two inputs and combines them into one output signal. The output is set to "true" if both the first <u>and</u> the second input are "true," and to "false" otherwise (Figure 1-1 (a)). In an ***OR*** gate, the output is set to "true" if either the first <u>or</u> the second (or both) inputs are true (Figure 1-1 (b)). A ***NOT*** gate takes one input and sets the output to its opposite (Figure 1-1 (c)).

These three basic types of gates can be combined to make other Boolean operations and logical circuits. Figure 1-2, for example, shows how you can combine AND, OR and NOT gates to make an ***XOR*** ("***eXclusive OR***") operation. This operation sets the output to "true" if <u>exactly</u> one of its two inputs is "true." In the late 1940s, John von Neumann,[neumann] a great mathematician and one of the founding fathers of computer technology, showed that all arithmetic operations can be reduced to AND, OR, and NOT logical operations.

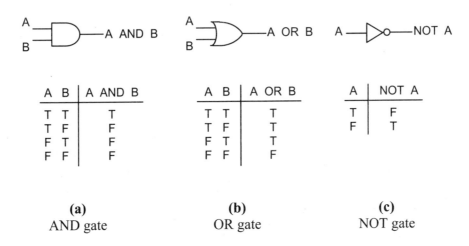

(a)	
AND gate	

(b)
OR gate

(c)
NOT gate

Figure 1-1. AND, OR, and NOT gates

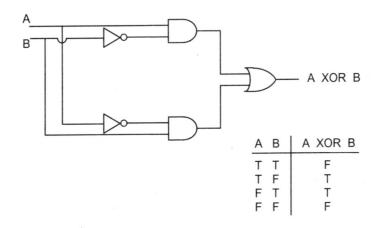

A	B	A XOR B
T	T	F
T	F	T
F	T	T
F	F	F

Figure 1-2. XOR circuit made of AND, OR and NOT gates

The microprocessor is protected by a small ceramic case mounted on a **PC board** (**Printed Circuit board**) called the **motherboard**. Also on the motherboard are memory chips. The computer memory is a uniform pool of storage units called **bits**. A bit stores the smallest possible unit of information: "on" or "off," "1" or "0." For practical reasons bits are grouped into groups of eight, called **bytes**.

One byte is eight bits.

There is no other structure to memory: the same memory is used to store numbers and letters and sounds and images and programs. All these things must be encoded, one way or another, in sequences of 0's and 1's. A typical personal computer made in the year 2000 has 64 to 128 **megs of RAM** (megabytes, i.e., millions of bytes, of Random-Access Memory) packed in a few SIMMs (Single In-Line Memory Modules).

The CPU interprets and carries out computer programs, or sequences of instructions stored in the memory. The CPU fetches the next instruction, interprets its operation code, and performs the appropriate operation. There are instructions for arithmetic and logical operations, for copying bytes from one location to another, and for changing the order of execution of instructions. The instructions are executed in sequence unless a particular instruction tells the CPU to "jump" to another place in the program. Conditional branching instructions tell the CPU to continue with the next instruction or to jump to another place depending on the result of the previous operation.

Besides the CPU, a general-purpose computer system also includes **peripheral devices** that provide input and output and secondary mass storage. In a notebook (laptop) computer, the "peripheral" devices are no longer quite so peripheral: a keyboard, a display, a hard drive, a CD-ROM or DVD drive, a fax/modem, a touch pad, a microphone, and speakers are all built into one portable unit.

CPU, memory, peripherals — all of this is called **hardware**. It is a lot of power concentrated in a small device. But to make it useful, to bring life into it, you need programs, **software**. Computer programs are also miracles of engineering, but of a different kind: **software engineering**. They are not cast in iron, nor even silicon, but in intangible texts that can be analyzed, modified, translated from one computer language into another, copied into various media, transmitted over networks, or lost forever. Software is to a computer as tunes are to a band: the best musicians will be silent if they haven't got music to play.

Take this amazing device with its software and connect it to the **Internet**, a network of millions of computers of all kinds connected to each other via communication lines of all kinds and running programs of all kinds, and you end up with a whole new world. Welcome to Cyberspace!

In the rest of this chapter we will briefly discuss

- Main hardware components: CPU, memory, peripheral devices
- What software is
- How numbers and characters are represented in computer memory
- What the Internet is

1.2   Hardware Overview

1.2.1   The CPU

What a CPU can do is defined by its instruction set and internal *registers*. The registers are built-in memory cells that hold operands, memory addresses, and intermediate results. Some of the registers are accessible to the programmer. The instruction set includes instructions for loading CPU registers from memory (RAM) and storing their values into memory, for logical and arithmetic operations, and for altering the sequence of operations.

Every computer has an internal "clock" that generates electrical pulses at a fixed frequency. All CPU operations and their component steps are synchronized with the clock's pulses; their duration is measured in *clock cycles*. The CPU's speed depends on the frequency of the clock. The Intel 8088 microprocessor in the original IBM Personal Computer, for example, ran at 4.77 Mhz (megahertz, or million pulses per second). Twenty years and a dozen computer generations later, CPU chips are pushing into the 1 or 2 Ghz range (1 Ghz, gigahertz, is equal to 1,000 Mhz).

A microprocessor CPU connects to RAM and to other devices through a set of parallel lines (wires printed on the motherboard) controlled by digital electronics, called a *bus*. A CPU may use a separate *address bus* for specifying memory addresses and a *data bus* for reading and writing memory values. Besides the internal clock speed, the computer's overall performance depends on the speed of the bus transfers and the width of the bus. The Mac 512k computer,[applehistory] introduced in September of 1984, had the Motorola MC68000 8-Mhz CPU and a 16-bit bus running at 8 Mhz, so it could carry 16 bits of data concurrently from memory to the CPU roughly at the same speed as the CPU could handle the data. The PowerMac G4 (the "Cube") released by Apple Computer, Inc. in the summer of 2000 has a 64-bit bus running at 100 Mhz.

1.2.2   Memory

Each byte of memory has a unique address that can be used to fetch the value stored in the byte or write a new value into it. A CPU does not have to read or write memory bytes sequentially: bytes can be accessed in any arbitrary order. This is why computer memory is called *random-access memory* or *RAM*. This is similar to a CD where you can choose any track to play, as opposed to a tape that has to be played in sequence. The size of RAM is measured in *kilobytes* (KB, or simply K) or *megabytes* (MB).

> A kilobyte is 1024 (2^{10}) bytes; a megabyte is 1024 x 1024 = 2^{20} = 1,048,576 bytes.

(Powers of 2 have a special significance in computer technology for a reason that will become clear shortly.)

In the early days, designers of personal computers thought 64K of RAM would suffice for the foreseeable future. An additional hardware mechanism, the *segment registers*, had to be added to the later versions of Intel's microprocessors to access a larger memory space, up to one megabyte, while maintaining compatibility with the old programs. But the one megabyte limit very quickly proved inadequate too. A 32-bit memory address bus allows programs to directly address four *gigabytes* (GB) of memory.

> One gigabyte is equal to 2^{30} = 1,073,741,824 bytes.

This should suffice for a while, but no one knows how long. (One gigabyte can hold roughly 250,000 pages of a text like this one.)

A small part of the computer memory is permanent non-erasable memory, known as *read-only memory* or *ROM*. A personal computer's ROM contains, among other things, the initialization code that *boots up* the *operating system* (that is, loads into memory the *boot record* or initialization code from the disk and passes control to it). Any computer program has to be loaded into memory before it can run. ROM solves the "first-program" dilemma — some program must already be running to load any other program into memory. The *operating system* is a program that has the job of loading and executing other programs. In a personal computer, ROM also contains the computer configuration program and hardware diagnostic programs that check various computer components. The ROM BIOS (Basic Input Output System) contains programs for controlling the keyboard, display, disk drives, and other devices. A special small memory — EPROM (Erasable Programmable ROM) — preserves system configuration data when the power is off.

1.2.3   Secondary Storage Devices

A computer's RAM has only limited space, and its contents are wiped out when the power is turned off. All the programs and data in a computer system have to be stored in secondary mass storage. The auxiliary storage devices include hard disks, floppy disk drives, CD-ROM drives, and other devices. A hard disk can hold several gigabytes; a CD-ROM can hold more than 650 MB (or up to 2 or 3 GB with data compression). Access to data on these devices is much slower than access to RAM.

> **An executable program has to be loaded from a hard disk, a floppy, or a CD-ROM (or from the Internet) into RAM before it can run.**

The operating system software organizes the data in secondary storage into *files*. A file may contain a set of related data, a program, a document, an image, and so on; it has a unique name. The operating system maintains a *directory* of file names, locations, sizes, dates and times of the last updates, and other attributes.

> **Thus a "file" is not a hardware but rather a <u>software</u> concept.**

When a program is running, it can read and write data directly to and from files stored on secondary storage devices.

1.2.4   Input and Output Devices

A personal computer receives user input through the keyboard and displays the output on the computer display (also called the *monitor*). In many programs the input is echoed on the screen as you type, creating the illusion that the keyboard is directly connected to the monitor. In fact these are two entirely different devices connected only through the CPU and the currently running program. The keyboard sends to the program digital codes that represent the pressed keys. The program captures these codes and takes appropriate actions, which may include displaying corresponding characters on the screen.

The screen is controlled by a *video adapter* and displays the contents of special video memory in the adapter, called *VRAM*. VRAM is addressable by the CPU and may contain codes, colors and attributes of characters when running in the text modes, or colors or intensities of individual *pixels* ("picture elements") in the graphics modes. The original IBM PC ran mostly in the text mode. You don't see the text mode much any more — everything is in graphics now, except diagnostic and configuration programs.

A *mainframe* computer (a very large multi-user computer) may have hundreds of terminals attached to it. The terminals send keystrokes and receive commands and display codes from the computer through digital transmission lines.

Printers, plotters, digitizing tablets, scanners and other devices receive commands and data from the computer in digital form and may send data or control codes back to the computer according to a specific communications protocol.

Network adapters and modems are essential for getting your computer connected to other computers. Network adapters and cables are used to connect several computers into a LAN (Local Area Network), which in turn may be connected to the Internet. Modems transmit digital information through telephone lines. A sending modem encodes bits of information into a sequence of electrical pulses that emulate signals obtained from different acoustic tones in a telephone. A receiving modem decodes the signal back into digital form.

Special data acquisition devices equipped with *A/D* (*analog-to-digital*) converters allow computers to convert an electrical signal into digital form by frequently sampling the amplitude of the signal and storing the digitized values in memory. *D/A* (*digital-to-analog*) converters perform the reverse transformation: they generate electrical currents from the digitized amplitudes stored in the computer. These devices allow the computer to receive data from all kinds of instruments and to serve as a universal control device in industrial applications and scientific experiments.

Input and output devices are connected to the computer via hardware *interface* modules that implement specific data transfer protocols. In a personal computer, the interfaces may be built into the motherboard or take the form of special adapter cards that plug into special sockets on the motherboard, called extension slots. Devices connected to the computer are usually controlled by special programs called *drivers* that handle all the details and peculiarities of the device and the data transfer protocol.

1.3   Software Overview

The term *software* refers to computer programs; it is also used as an adjective to refer to tasks or functions implemented through programs, as in "software interface," "software fonts," and so on. The line between hardware and software is not always clear. In the modern world microprocessors are embedded in many objects, from microwave ovens and VCRs to satellites. Their programs are developed using simulation tools on normal computers; when a program is finalized, it is permanently "burned" into ROMs. Such programs are referred to as *firmware*.

A modern computer not only runs individual programs but also maintains a "software environment." This environment involves several functional layers (Figure 1-3). The bottom layer in this environment comprises BIOS, device drivers, interrupt handlers — programs that directly support hardware devices and functions. The next layer is the *operating system,* a software program that provides computer access services to users and standard support functions to other programs. The top layer is software applications (word processors, Internet browsers, business, industrial, or scientific applications, games, etc.).

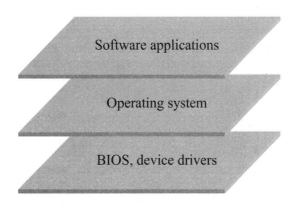

Figure 1-3. Software functional layers

The operating system loads programs into RAM from secondary storage and runs them. On a mainframe (a very large and powerful computer), the operating system allows multiple users to work on the computer at once through *time sharing*. In such a multi-user system, one user may be slowly editing a file or entering data on a terminal using only a small fraction of the available CPU time. At the same time another program may be doing "number crunching." A multi-user operating system allocates "time slices" to each program and automatically switches between them. The operating system prioritizes the jobs and swaps segments of programs in and out of memory as needed. A personal computer assumes one user, but contemporary users enjoy *multi-tasking* operating systems that let them keep several programs active concurrently (e.g., a word processor, an e-mail program, and a sound application for playing CDs).

The operating system also establishes and maintains a file system in secondary storage. Files are organized into a branching structure of directories and subdirectories. The operating system provides commands or utility programs for navigating through the directory tree.

Part of the operating system is a set of *routines* (sets of instructions, callable from other programs) that provide standard service functions to programs. These include functions for creating, reading, and writing files. The operating system *shell* provides a set of user commands, including commands for displaying, copying, deleting and printing files, executing programs, and so on. Modern operating systems use *GUI* ("Goo'-ee," *Graphical User Interface*), where commands can be entered by selecting items in menus or by clicking a mouse on an icon that represents a command or an object graphically.

The top layer of software consists of *application* programs that make computers useful to people. In the old days, application programs mostly performed calculations or processed files. If interaction with the user was required, it was accomplished via an unsophisticated text dialog: a computer would display questions (or *prompts*) in plain text and let the user enter responses, then print out the resulting numbers, tables, or reports. Such applications are called *console applications*. In a modern computing environment, users expect programs to have GUI. Menus, buttons and icons select different functions in the program; dialog boxes and text-edit fields are used to set options and enter data or text. The shift from console applications to GUI applications brought changes in the way programs are designed and written and brought about new software development tools and methodologies, such as *OOP* (Object-Oriented Programming), one of the main subjects of this book.

1.4   Representation of Information in Computer Memory

Computer memory is a uniform array of bytes that does not privilege any particular type of information. The memory can contain CPU instructions, numbers and text characters, and any other information that can be represented in digital form. Since a suitable A/D converter can more or less accurately convert any electrical signal to digital form, any information that can be carried over a wire can be represented in computer memory. This includes sounds, images, motion, and so on (but, so far, excludes taste and smell).

CPU instructions are represented in computer memory in a manner specific to each particular brand of CPU. The first byte or two represent the operation code that identifies the instruction and the total number of bytes in that instruction; the following bytes may represent the values or memory addresses of the operands. How memory addresses are represented depends on the CPU architecture, but they are basically numbers that indicate the absolute sequential number of the byte in memory. A CPU may have special *segment* registers and *index* registers that help calculate the actual address in memory for a specified instruction or operand.

The format for numbers is mostly dictated by the CPU, too, because the CPU has instructions for arithmetic operations that expect numbers to be represented in a certain way. Characters (letters, digits, etc.) are represented using one of the several character code systems that have become standard not only for representing text inside computers but also in computer terminals, printers, and other devices. The code assigns each character a number.

Fortunately, high-level programming languages, such as Java, shield computer programmers from the intricacies of how to represent CPU instructions, memory addresses, numbers, and characters.

Representing other types of information is often a matter of a specific application's design. A black-and-white image, for example, may be represented as a sequence of bytes where each bit represents a pixel of the image: 0 for white and 1 for black. The sequence of pixels typically goes from left to right along each horizontal line of the image and then from top to bottom by row. Other memory locations may hold numbers that represent the image dimensions.

1.4.1   Numbers

Integers from 0 to 255 can be represented in one byte using the binary (base-2) system as follows:

Decimal	Binary
0	00000000
1	00000001
2	00000010
3	00000011
4	00000100
5	00000101
6	00000110
7	00000111
8	00001000
. . .	. . .
252	11111100
253	11111101
254	11111110
255	11111111

If we use 2 bytes (16 bits), we can represent integers from 0 to $2^{16}-1 = 65535$:

```
      Decimal              Binary

         0            00000000 00000000
         1            00000000 00000001
         2            00000000 00000010
        . . .             . . .
      65534           11111111 11111110
      65535           11111111 11111111
```

In general, k bits can produce 2^k different combinations of 0's and 1's. Therefore, k bits used as binary digits can represent non-negative integers in the range from 0 to 2^k-1. A 32-bit memory address can identify $2^{32} = 4,294,967,296$ different memory locations. So if we want to be able to address each individual byte, 32-bit addresses cover 4 GB of memory space.

❖   ❖   ❖

CPUs perform all their arithmetic operations on binary numbers. A CPU may have instructions that perform 8-bit, 16-bit, or 32-bit arithmetic, for instance. Since it is difficult for a human brain to grasp long sequences of 0's and 1's, programmers who have to deal with binary data often use the ***hexadecimal*** (or simply "***hex***") representation in their documentation and programs. The hex system is the base-16 system, which uses 16 digits. The first ten digits are the usual 0 through 9, with the eleventh through sixteenth digits represented by the letters A through F. A byte can be split into two four-bit ***quads***; each quad represents one hex digit, as follows:

Decimal	Binary	Hex
0	0000	0
1	0001	1
2	0010	2
3	0011	3
4	0100	4
5	0101	5
6	0110	6
7	0111	7
8	1000	8
9	1001	9
10	1010	A
11	1011	B
12	1100	C
13	1101	D
14	1110	E
15	1111	F

Experienced programmers remember the bit patterns for the sixteen hex digits and can easily convert a binary number into hex and back. It is often convenient to use hex representation as an intermediate step for converting numbers from binary to decimal and back. For example:

$$700_{10} = 2 \cdot 16^2 + 11 \cdot 16 + 12 = 2BC_{16} = \underbrace{0010}_{2}\underbrace{1011}_{B}\underbrace{1100}_{C}{}_2$$

$$\underbrace{110}_{6}\underbrace{1101}_{D}{}_2 = 6D_{16} = 6 \cdot 16 + 13 = 109_{10}$$

The following examples show a few numbers represented in the decimal, hex, and 16-bit binary systems:

Decimal	Hex	Binary
0	0000	00000000 00000000
1	0001	00000000 00000001
12	000C	00000000 00001100
32	0020	00000000 00100000
128	0080	00000000 10000000
255	00FF	00000000 11111111
256	0100	00000001 00000000
32767	7FFF	01111111 11111111
32768	8000	10000000 00000000
65535	FFFF	11111111 11111111

For a software developer, knowing the hex system is a matter of cultural literacy. In practice programmers who use a high-level programming language, like Java, don't have to use it very often and there are calculators that can do conversions.

❖   ❖   ❖

What about negative numbers? The same bit pattern may represent an unsigned (positive) integer and a negative integer, depending on how a particular instruction interprets it. Suppose we use 32-bit binary numbers, but now we decide that they represent <u>signed</u> integers. Positive integers from 0 to $2^{31}-1$ can be represented as before. These use only the 31 least significant bits. As to negative integers, their representation may be ***machine-dependent***, varying from CPU to CPU. Many CPUs, including the Intel family, use a method called ***two's-complement arithmetic***. In this method, a negative integer x in the range from -1 to -2^{31} is represented the same way as the unsigned binary number $2^{32} - |x|$ where $|x|$ is the absolute value of x. For example, 21 and -21 will be represented as:

```
00000000 00000000 00000000 00010101 =  21₁₀
11111111 11111111 11111111 11101011 = -21₁₀
```

❖   ❖   ❖

Real numbers are represented using one of the standard formats expected by the CPU (or a separate floating-point arithmetic unit). Like scientific notation, this representation consists of a fractional part (mantissa) and an exponent part, but here both parts are represented as binary numbers. The IEEE (Institute of Electrical and Electronics Engineers) standard for a 4-byte (32-bit) representation uses 1 bit for the sign, 8 bits for the exponent and 23 bits for the mantissa. 127 is added to the exponent to ensure that negative exponents are still represented by non-negative numbers. This format lets programmers represent numbers in the range from approximately -3.4×10^{38} to 3.4×10^{38} with at least seven digits of precision. Figure 1-4 gives a few examples.

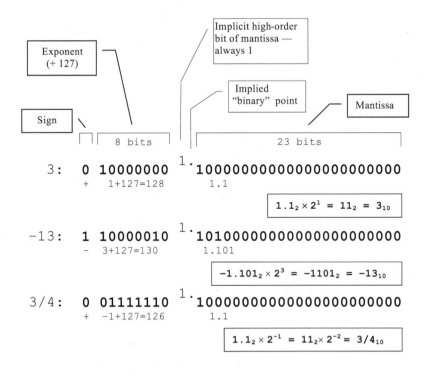

**Figure 1-4. IEEE standard representation of 32-bit
floating-point numbers**

1.4.2   Characters

Characters are represented by numeric codes. The two most common character codes are EBCDIC (Extended Binary Coded Decimal Interchange Code), used in IBM mainframes, and ASCII (American Standard Code for Information Interchange, pronounced as'-kee), used in personal computers, printers and other devices. Both of these use one byte per character. In the PC world, the term *ASCII file* refers to a text file (in which characters are represented in ASCII code), as opposed to a *binary file* that may contain numbers, images or any other digitized information. Normally you won't find EBCDIC-encoded data on a PC unless the file originated on a mainframe.

ASCII code proper defines 128 characters with codes from 0 to 127 and uses only seven bits of a byte. The second half of the code, from 128 to 255, is called *extended ASCII* and may vary from machine to machine. Codes from 33 to 127 represent "printable" characters: digits, upper- and lowercase letters, punctuation marks, and so on. 32 (hex 20) is a space.

The first 32 ASCII codes (0-31) are reserved for special control codes. For example, code 13 (hex 0D) is "carriage return" (CR), 10 (hex 0A) is "line feed" (LF), 12 (hex 0C) is "form feed" (FF) and 9 (hex 09) is "horizontal tab" (HT). How control codes are used may depend to some extent on the program or device that processes them. A standard ASCII table, including the more obscure control codes, is presented in Figure 1-5.

Internet documents use other character codes for foreign characters and alphabets, special symbols, and so on. Java programs are supposed to be very portable and platform-independent, so Java uses the Unicode standard ★unicode for encoding characters. Unicode uses two bytes per character. It includes ASCII codes as a subset, but generally can encode up to 65,000 characters, enough to encode the alphabets of most world languages and many special characters. Unicode has a provision to extend the character set even further, into millions of different codes.

Hex	0_	1_	2_	3_	4_	5_	6_	7_
_0	0 NUL	16 DEL	32 (SPACE)	48 0	64 @	80 P	96 `	112 p
_1	1 SOH	17 DC1	33 !	49 1	65 A	81 Q	97 a	113 q
_2	2 STX	18 DC2	34 "	50 2	66 B	82 R	98 b	114 r
_3	3 ETX	19 DC3	35 #	51 3	67 C	83 S	99 c	115 s
_4	4 EOT	20 DC4	36 $	52 4	68 D	84 T	100 d	116 t
_5	5 ENQ	21 NAK	37 %	53 5	69 E	85 U	101 e	117 u
_6	6 ACK	22 SYN	38 &	54 6	70 F	86 V	102 f	118 v
_7	7 BEL	23 ETB	39 '	55 7	71 G	87 W	103 g	119 w
_8	8 BS	24 CAN	40 (	56 8	72 H	88 X	104 h	120 x
_9	9 HT	25 EM	41)	57 9	73 I	89 Y	105 i	121 y
_A	10 LF	26 SUB	42 *	58 :	74 J	90 Z	106 j	122 z
_B	11 VT	27 ESC	43 +	59 ;	75 K	91 [	107 k	123 {
_C	12 FF	28 FS	44 ,	60 <	76 L	92 \	108 l	124 |
_D	13 CR	29 GS	45 -	61 =	77 M	93]	109 m	125 }
_E	14 SO	30 RS	46 .	62 >	78 N	94 ^	110 n	126 ~
_F	15 SI	31 US	47 /	63 ?	79 O	95 _	111 o	127 (NUL)

Figure 1-5. ASCII code used in personal computers and printers

1.5   The Internet

You basically need three things to make computers talk to each other:

1. A wire (or in more recent technology, a radio) link between them;
2. Hardware adapters at each *host* (the term used for a computer connected to a network), switches at the network junctions, and other hardware that controls the network;
3. A common language, called a *protocol*, so that the hosts can understand each other.

Of the three the protocol is probably the most important. Once a reliable and flexible protocol is designed, the hardware and the connections will somehow follow and fall into place. Actually a protocol standard defines hundreds, even thousands of distinct protocols that function at many different levels, or, as network designers say, layers. (Figure 1-6).

The protocols in the bottom layer deal directly with the hardware — the network technology itself and various devices that are connected to it: modems, switches, high-speed adapters, routers, and so on. These hardware protocols are constantly evolving due to changing and competing new technologies and standards set by manufacturers and professional organizations.

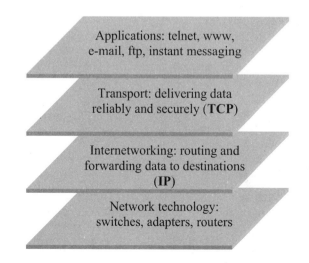

Figure 1-6.   TCP/IP protocols in layered network architecture

The next layer deals with routing and forwarding: how to make sure that the information from one host eventually reaches another host. These internetworking protocols must know about the general layout of the network (who is connected to whom), and be efficient and robust for reliable connections. The Internet's internetworking layer is called **IP** (the **_Internet Protocol_**).

The layer above internetworking, the transport protocol, is responsible for properly handling information from specific applications used on the network and for meeting the requirements of these applications: reliability, security, data compression, and so on. **TCP** (the **_Transmission Control Protocol_**) is the Internet's transport protocol. The **TCP/IP** combination is what really defines the Internet.

Finally, at the very top layer, there are protocols for network applications such as e-mail (using SMTP — Simple Mail Transfer Protocol), the World Wide Web (using HTTP — HyperText Transfer Protocol), file transfer (using FTP — File Transfer Protocol), instant messaging, remote terminal emulation (*telnet*), and other applications.

If we had to set a birth date for the Internet, it would probably be early September 1969 when the first computer network was tested. The network had only four nodes: University of California in Los Angeles (UCLA), Stanford Research Institute (SRI), University of California in Santa Barbara (UCSB), and the University of Utah in Salt Lake City. Here is how Dr. Leonard Kleinrock,[kleinrock] a computer science professor at UCLA and one of the pioneers, describes the event. Kleinrock and his group of graduate students hoped to log onto the Stanford computer and try to send it some data. They would start by typing "login" and seeing if the letters appeared on the remote terminal.

> We set up a telephone connection between us and the guys at SRI...We typed the L and we asked on the phone, "Do you see the L?" "Yes, we see the L," came the response. "We typed the O, and we asked, "Do you see the O." "Yes, we see the O." Then we typed the G, and the system crashed... Yet a revolution had begun.[firstlogin]

More precisely, the world's first instance of host-to-host, packet-switched data communications between networked computers had taken place.

The Internet has certainly made a lot of headway since, with millions of computers connected to it today and over 100 million users. By 2002, 165 million people are expected to be Internet users in the United States alone. The best way to explore the Internet, its history and use is certainly not through a book, but by getting online and browsing.[internethistory] A **_browser_** is a program that helps its user navigate through the Internet and presents the information that comes from the Internet back to the user. *Netscape Navigator* and *Internet Explorer* are the two most popular browsers. The information comes from the Internet in many different formats. The most common one is HTML documents — text files with embedded formatting tags in them. HTML is the subject of the next chapter, where we will learn to create "web pages," our own Internet documents. Other files use standard formats for representing images, sounds, and so on. A browser and its helper modules, called *plug-ins*, know how to handle different formats of data and show (or play) the data to the user.

In a matter of just a few years the Internet has become a vast depository of knowledge, information (and misinformation) of all kinds and from all sources. It would be very difficult to find anything in this ocean without some guidance. *Portals* are popular web sites that arrange a large number of Internet links by category and help users navigate to the subjects they need. *Search engines* are programs based on large Internet hosts that analyze and index the contents of web pages and find web sites relevant to the keywords a user enters.

1.6   Summary

Digital electronics represents information using two states: "on" or "off," "high" or "low," "1" or "0." Digital devices, called gates, implement simple logical operations on signals: AND, OR, NOT. All other logical and arithmetic operations can be implemented using these three simple operations.

The heart of a computer is a CPU (central processing unit) that can perform logical and arithmetic operations. An executable program is a sequence of CPU instructions in machine code. It must be loaded into RAM (random-access memory) before it can run. All instructions and data addresses are encoded in binary sequences of 0's and 1's. The CPU fetches instructions and data from RAM, interprets operation codes, and executes the instructions.

RAM is arranged into bytes; each byte is 8 bits; each bit can hold "1" or "0." The size of RAM is measured in kilobytes ($1 \text{ KB} = 2^{10} = 1024$ bytes) or megabytes ($1 \text{ MB} = 2^{20} = 1,048,576$ bytes) and may soon reach gigabytes (1 GB is over one billion bytes). The contents of RAM are erased when the power is disconnected.

Mass storage devices have larger memory capacity — several gigabytes — and they can hold the information permanently, but access to them is slower. Data in mass storage is arranged into files by the operating system software. The files are stored in a branching system of directories (represented as folders). The operating system also loads and runs applications, provides GUI (graphical user interface) to users, and provides system services to programs (such as reading and writing files, supporting input devices, etc.).

All kinds of information are represented in the computer memory as sequences of 0's and 1's. Integers are represented as binary numbers. Real numbers use standard floating-point binary representations. Characters are represented as their codes in one of the standard coding systems. The most common codes are ASCII and Unicode, a superset of ASCII that includes thousands of characters from virtually all world alphabets.

The Internet is a network of millions of computers connected in many different ways. The Internet is based on the TCP/IP (Transmission Control Protocol / Internet Protocol), which supports various network applications and controls information routing on the network. Higher-level protocols are used in Internet applications such as e-mail, the World Wide Web, file transfer, and remote terminal emulation. A browser is a program on your computer that processes your requests for Internet connections and delivers and displays the received Internet information, web pages in particular. The two most popular browsers are *Netscape Navigator* and Microsoft's *Internet Explorer*. Portals are popular web sites that list many Internet links, arranged by category. Search engines are Internet indexing services implemented on large hosts that collect and index information from the Internet and help you find web sites relevant to your requests.

Exercises

Section 1.1

1.   Mark T (true) or F (false) the output of each of the following circuits with the given inputs.

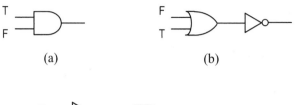

(a)   (b)

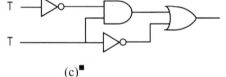

(c)▪

2.■   Let's say that two circuits are equivalent if they produce the same outputs for the same inputs. Draw a circuit equivalent to the one in Question 1.1-(b) using two NOT gates and one AND gate. ✓

3.◆   Simplify the circuit in Question 1.1-(c) to an equivalent one that has only two gates: one NOT gate and one AND gate.

4.   (a)■ Draw an alternative XOR circuit, different from the one in Figure 1-2, using two NOT gates, two OR gates, and one AND gate. ⋛ Hint: at least one of the inputs, A OR B, must be true AND at least one of the negated inputs, NOT A OR NOT B, must be true, too. ⋛ ✓

(b)◆ Draw a third XOR circuit using four gates: one OR gate, two AND gates, and one NOT gate.

Section 1.2

5.   Computer memory is called RAM because:

A. It provides rapid access to data.
B. It is mounted on the motherboard.
C. It is measured in megabytes.
D. Its bytes can be addressed in random order.
E. Its chips are mounted in a rectangular array.

6.   Mark true or false and explain:

(a)   One meg of RAM can hold exactly as much information as one meg on a floppy disk. _____

(b)   A factory-formatted floppy disk is split into a fixed number of files. _____ ✓

(c)   In personal computers the operating system resides in ROM. _____ ✓

7.   Find an old discarded computer, **unplug the power cord** and disconnect all other cables. Open the cover and identify the motherboard, CPU, RAM, serial and parallel ports (sockets for cable connectors), hard disk, CD-ROM, and other components and adapters, if present.

Section 1.3

8.   Identify the following entities or devices as part of a computer system's hardware (H) or software (S).

    (a)   Operating system   _____

    (b)   CPU   _____

    (c)   GUI (Graphical User Interface)   _____ ✓

    (d)   Modem   _____ ✓

    (e)   Bus   _____

    (f)   RAM   _____

    (g)■ File   _____

9.   Identify the operating system that is running on your current computer and some software applications installed on it: a word processor, an Internet browser, a spreadsheet program, e-mail, an image processing application, games, and so on.

Section 1.4

10.   Mark true or false and explain:

    (a)   Only data but not CPU instructions can be stored in RAM. _____

    (b)   In ASCII code each character is represented in one byte. _____ ✓

    (c)   16-bit binary numbers can be used to represent all non-negative integers from 0 to $2^{16}-1$. _____

    (d)   Programs stored in ROM are referred to as "firmware." _____

11.   What is the maximum number of different codes or numbers that can be represented in

    (a)   3 bits?   _____ ✓

    (b)   8 bits?   _____

    (c)   2 bytes?   _____

12.   An experiment consists of tossing a coin 10 times and its outcome is a sequence of heads and tails. How many possible outcomes are there?

13.   Assume that these binary numbers represent unsigned integers in the usual way, with the least significant bit on the right. Write the decimal value and the hex representation of these binary numbers. Example:

Binary	Decimal	Hex
00001000	8	08
00011100	28	1C

(a)   00000010   _____   _____
(b)   00000111   _____   _____
(c)   10000000   _____   _____
(d)   00001011   _____   _____ ✓
(e)   11000011   _____   _____
(f)   11110101   _____   _____

(g)▪   00000101 10010010

_____   _____ ✓

14.   How much memory does it take to hold a 512-by-512 gray-scale image with 256 levels of gray? ✓

15.   When a printer runs out of paper, the eight-bit printer status register of the parallel interface adapter gets the following settings: bit 7 (leftmost bit), "BUSY," is set to 1; bit 5, "PE" ("paper end"), is set to 1; and bit 3, "ERROR," is set to 0. Bit 4 is always 1 when a printer is connected, bit 6 is 0, and bits 0-2 are not used. Write the hex value equal to the setting of the printer status register when the printer runs out of paper, assuming that bits 0-2 are 0.

16.▪   Design a method for representing the state of a tic-tac-toe board in computer memory. Can you fit your representation into three bytes? ✓

17.   (a)   Using the ASCII table in Figure 1-5, write the ASCII codes for the following characters in decimal, hex and binary:

	Decimal	Hex	Binary
'A'	_____	_____	_____
'a'	_____	_____	_____
'Z'	_____	_____	_____
'z'	_____	_____	_____

(b)   Note that the binary representations of the ASCII codes for the lower and upper case of the same letter differ only in one bit. Write the binary and hex representations of a byte where that bit is set to 1 and all other bits are set to 0.

18.◆   In the game of *Nim*, stones are arranged in piles of arbitrary size. Each player in turn takes a few stones from any one pile. Every player must take at least one stone on every turn. The player who takes the last stone wins.

Games of this type often have a winning strategy. This strategy can be established by tagging all possible positions in the game with two tags, "plus" and "minus," in such a way that any move from a "plus" position always leads to a "minus" position, and from any "minus" position there is always a possible move into some "plus" position. The final winning position must be tagged "plus." Therefore, if the first player begins in a "minus" position, he can win by moving right away into a "plus" position and returning to a "plus" position on each subsequent move. If, however, the first player begins in a "plus" position, then the second player can win, provided he knows how to play correctly.

In the *Nim* game, we can convert the number of stones in each pile into a binary number and write these binary numbers in one column (so that the "units" digits are aligned on the right). We can tag the position "plus" if the number of 1's in each column is even and "minus" if the count of 1's in at least one column is odd. Prove that this method of tagging "plus" and "minus" positions defines a winning strategy. Who wins starting with four piles of 1, 3, 5, and 7 stones — the first or the second player? What's the correct response if the first player takes five stones from the pile of 7?

19.◆ The table below is called a ***Greco-Roman square***: each of the three Latin letters occurs exactly once in each row and each column; the same is true for each of the three Greek letters; and each Latin-Greek combination occurs exactly once in the table:

Aγ	Bα	Cβ
Bβ	Cγ	Aα
Cα	Aβ	Bγ

Substitute the digits 0, 1 and 2 for A, B, C and for α, β, γ (in any order). Convert the resulting base-3 numbers into decimal (base-10) numbers. The base-3 system uses only three digits: 0, 1, and 2. The numbers are represented as follows:

Base 3	Decimal
0	0
1	1
2	2
10	3
11	4
12	5
20	6
21	7
22	8
100	9
. . .	. . .

Add 1 to each number. You will get a table in which the numbers 1 through 9 are arranged in such a way that the sum of the numbers in each row and column is the same. Explain why you get this result and find a way to substitute the digits 0, 1, and 2 for letters so that the sum of numbers in each of the two diagonals is the same as in the rows and columns. What you get then is called a ***magic square***. Using a similar method, build a 5 by 5 magic square.

Section 1.5

20.   What does TCP stand for?

  A.   Telnet Control Program
  B.   Transmission Control Protocol
  C.   Transport Compression Protocol
  D.   Telephone Connectivity Program
  E.   None of the above

21.   Are the following entities or devices hardware (H) or software (S)?

  (a)   Host   _____ ✓
  (b)   LAN   _____
  (c)   Browser   _____
  (d)   Search engine   _____ ✓
  (e)   Router   _____
  (f)■   TCP/IP Adapter   _____ ✓

22.   Find and explore the home pages of some Internet and World Wide Web pioneers.

<h1>Chapter 2</h1>

Designing Web Pages with HTML

2.1   Prologue

HTML, or HyperText Markup Language, is a simple tool for formatting documents, especially web pages. Since Java applets run on web pages, it is important for us to get at least a basic idea how web pages are created and how to run applets from HTML files.

The term *hypertext* refers to a text fragment or document in which certain words or phrases act as "hot links": when you "touch" such a link (click on it with a mouse or literally touch it on a touch screen) it takes you to a specified place — in the same text, in another document on your computer, or, with the Internet, to a document on a computer halfway around the world. This powerful method of viewing and browsing through information is possible only with computers. In 1987, Apple Computer, Inc. released a Macintosh software application called *HyperCard* that popularized the hypertext concept and gave non-programmers a tool for creating hypertext applications.

Markup implies that the text is formatted by means of embedded commands or "*tags*." Marked-up text is called **HTML source**. A program that can interpret HTML files looks at the tags and renders the document on the screen or in a printout according to the formatting commands in the document (and also according to the capabilities of a particular monitor or printer). For example, if you wanted a word or a phrase to appear in italics, you would mark that phrase with an opening `<i>` tag and a closing `</i>` tag in the HTML source, as in:

```
The term <i>hypertext</i> refers to
```

It will be interpreted and shown as

> The term *hypertext* refers to

HTML documents can be created using a general-purpose text editor or word processor. One approach is to first put all the textual information in, spellcheck the text, then add HTML tags. You can also take an existing document, say in *MS Word* format, save it as "text only," then add HTML tags to it.

> **HTML files usually have the extension .html or .htm. If you are using a text editor or a word processor to write them, make sure you save documents as "text only" type but give the saved file name the .html or .htm extension.**

HTML files can be interpreted by different programs, but primarily by Internet browsers (*Netscape Navigator*, Microsoft's *Internet Explorer*, and other browsers[browsers]). As HTML evolves and new browser releases appear, the HTML standard is by and large controlled by the most popular browsers and also by the World Wide Web Consortium (W3C[w3c]), which coordinates development of new technologies for the web. Other programs, including some word processors, can interpret HTML, too. But if you use a simple text editor (e.g., *Notepad* in *Windows*) to create HTML documents, then you have to use a web browser to see how the final document will look, going back and forth between the editor and the browser to make adjustments and see the results. Specialized web authoring tools can generate HTML documents automatically in a WYSIWYG ("What-You-See-Is-What-You-Get," pronounced "wee-zee-wig," just like it looks) manner. Then you can make minor adjustments by editing the HTML source.

HTML was conceived in late 1980's by Tim Berners-Lee,[bernerslee] a computer scientist at CERN, an international high-energy physics research center in Switzerland. Berners-Lee was looking for a universal format that would allow users to create documents without specialized software or word processors, keep the formatting overhead in documents small, and allow the documents to travel over a network as ASCII text. The formatting commands also had to be suitable for displaying the same document on a variety of computers with different display capabilities: from simple text terminals to fancy graphics devices. In the early 1990s HTML quickly became the standard for the emerging network of computers that supported http (HyperText Transfer Protocol) — the network now called the *World Wide Web*.

> **A *web page* is basically an HTML document. A *web site* is a collection of related web pages and supporting files, such as images, audio clips, MP3 files, PDF (Portable Document Format) files, plain-text files, and so on, usually located on the same *host* (computer connected to the network).**

It may sound disappointing, but HTML is not a programming language and designing web pages in HTML is not programming. Although HTML tags can be viewed as commands or instructions of a sort, HTML has no facility for implementing algorithms, a process considered to be the key characteristic of programming. (Algorithms are explained in Chapter 3.) Writing an HTML file is more like formatting text in a word processor. If you want your web pages to perform more sophisticated tasks, you have to program these tasks in a programming language to be used in conjunction with HTML.

One such language is JavaScript, a rather limited programming language specifically designed for adding some action to web documents. Its primary use is for validating and processing data that come from online forms embedded in web pages. For example, when you type your address and credit card information into a form on a web page, JavaScript functions may be used to check that the required fields are filled with reasonable values and that the credit card number is valid. JavaScript shares some syntactic elements with Java, but the similarity ends there. JavaScript deals primarily with objects embedded in web documents (such as fields in a form) and lacks the capabilities required for writing general-purpose programs. We do not go into HTML forms or JavaScript in this book.

Java, on the other hand, is a complete high-level programming language that can be used for programming anything: from little web applications, or "applets," to large software systems. ***Applets*** are small Java programs written for the Internet. HTML allows you to incorporate applets into a web page. HTML has also become a useful tool for creating software documentation and help systems. For example, a utility for Java developers, called *javadoc*, automatically generates HTML documentation files from Java programs.

Naturally you can find many HTML tutorials and reference guides on the web.☜htmltutorials But you can also learn from any web page: if you choose the `View source` menu option in your browser, you will see the document as a plain-text document with embedded HTML tags. Go to any simple web page and try it.

In this chapter we will learn the following HTML features:

- The main structural elements of an HTML document
- Text layout (headings, paragraphs)
- Text formatting (font attributes, colors)
- Hyperlinks
- Using lists
- Embedding images into HTML documents
- Using tables
- Embedding Java applets into HTML documents

2.2   Example

Figure 2-1 shows an example of a simple HTML document and Figure 2-2 shows its appearance in a *Netscape Navigator* window. Note the following features:

1.   Each HTML tag is enclosed in angular brackets, `<...>`. Many opening tags have a corresponding closing tag that starts with a slash (as in `<xyz> - </xyz>`). Some closing tags, especially for the new paragraph mark `<p>`, may be omitted. Some tags, like `<img>`, do not use a closing tag.

2.   HTML tags are <u>not</u> case-sensitive. Some people use all caps to make the tags stand out more, others use lower case.

3.   Unless overridden by special tags, HTML interpreters ignore line breaks and whitespace characters (spaces, tabs, etc.) in the original document, replacing each whitespace sequence with one space. HTML interpreters basically treat the whole document as one long line of text. Special tags such as `<p>` (new paragraph), `<br>` (line break), and tags marking lists and tables control how the lines of text appear on the screen.

4.   The whole document is enclosed between `<html>` and `</html>` tags that identify the type of the document for the browser.

5.   The rest of the document is split into two parts: the "head" (enclosed between `<head>` and `</head>`) and the "body" (enclosed between `<body>` and `</body>`).[*]

6.   Some tags may have attributes. For example, the `<h2>` tag that marks a header line (of the second rank) may have an attribute that centers the heading in the window:

```
<h2 align="center">
```

The `<hr>` ("horizontal rule") tag that makes a horizontal line may have optional attributes for the line width, "size" (thickness), and color:

```
<hr width="80%" size="3" color="#0000A0">
```

---

[*] More formal HTML specification calls the opening tag and the closing tag and everything in between *a tag*, and defines formally which other tags may occur inside a given tag. In this terminology, an HTML document consists of one `html` tag, which contains `head` and `body` tags. Thus this terminology stretches the common use of the word "tag" a bit.

```
<html>

<head>
<title>Winter Track</title>
<meta name="Keywords" content="Andover, Winter Track, Athletics">
</head>

<body>
<h2 align="center">Girls' Winter Track</h2>

<center>
<table width="95%" cellpadding="10">
<tr>
<td width="50%">
Lead by captains Lucy Greene and Sean Scott, Indoor Track
completed another winning season studded by many brilliant
individual performances.  Rain, snow, sleet, or storm,
the girls practiced since early December under the cover of
the Case Memorial Cage and consequently took the lead over
competitors early on.  Phillips Academy ran against local
schools Haverhill, Tewksbury, Andover High School, Central
Catholic, and Chelmsford, falling only to the Tewksbury team.

</td>
<td valign="center" width="50%">
<img src="wintertrack.jpg" alt="Winter track meet"
     width="233" height="235">
</td>
</tr>
</table>

<p><i>By L.G.</i>.

<br><br>

<hr width="80%" size="3" color="#0000A0">
<a href="athletics.html">Back to Athletics</a>
<hr width="80%" size="3" color="#000080">
</center>

</body>
</html>
```

Figure 2-1. `Ch02\wintertrack.html` 💾

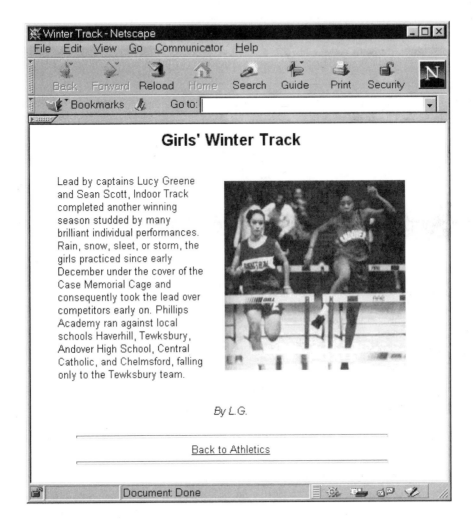

**Figure 2-2.   The HTML document from Figure 2-1 as it
appears in *Netscape***

In general, attributes have the form `attribute="value"`. Some attributes (such as `src` in `<img>`) are required, while others (such as `alt`, `width` and `height` in `<img>`) are optional.

7. Certain characters, such as >, <, &, and ", cannot be used directly in HTML documents because they are reserved for HTML commands. They are represented by "escape sequences" such as `&gt;`, `&lt;`, `&amp;`, and `&quot;` in the HTML source. An escape sequence starts with an ampersand (`&`), ends with a semicolon, and has a standardized abbreviated name of a character in between. Escape sequences are also used for characters that are not on the keyboard, such as `&copy;` for the copyright symbol. You can find a complete list of special characters on the web.☆htmlescapes

2.3   Document Structure Tags

HTML document structure is shown in Figure 2-3. The three main tags that help establish a document's structure are `<html>`, `<head>`, and `<body>`. As we mentioned above, the `<html>` tag is the outermost tag that identifies the document as an HTML document. The `<head>` ... `</head>` tag isolates information <u>about</u> the document itself rather than information to be displayed in the document. The head can contain `<title>`, one or several `<meta>` tags, and a few other tags. The `<title>` tag defines the document's title as it will be displayed in the browser window's title bar when you open the document. It is also used as the bookmark description when visitors bookmark your page in their browser, so it is important to choose a meaningful and descriptive title. For example, "Alphabetical Listing of HTML Tags" is a better title than "Tags."

An optional `<meta>` tag can list just about any information about your document. Its `name` attribute tells what information is included and its `content` attribute lists the information. You can write, for instance,

```
<meta name="my dog's name" content="Tessie">
```

but this may be not very relevant. A more conventional use is to enter the author's name and a few keywords to help web search engines find the page. For example,

```
<meta name="author" content="Mark Taggit">
<meta name="keywords" content="HTML, www, tutorial">
```

`<meta>` tags should not be viewed as just comments because they may be read by search engines. HTML has a special comment tag:

```
<!-- any text -->
```

that can be used to explain the source or modifications. You can also temporarily disable pieces of HTML text and commands by surrounding them with a comment tag.

```
<html>

<head>
<title>title text</title>
<meta name="author" content="...">
<meta name="keywords" content="...">
</head>

<body attributes>
...
<address>
...
</address>
</body>   .

</html>
```

Figure 2-3.   HTML document structure

The information displayed in the document is placed between opening and closing `<body>` tags. The `<body>` tag may have some optional attributes that redefine the default text color, background color or background image, colors for active and followed links, and other attributes. For example,

```
<body text="coral" bgcolor="antiquewhite">
```

displays "coral" text on an "antiquewhite" background.

You can find a complete list of HTML colors (with samples) on the web;[htmlcolors] of course, all common color names are included. You can also specify color as a # sign followed by six hex digits — two hex digits (i.e., a value from 0 to 255) for the intensity of each of color's red, green, and blue components.   For instance, `"#FFFFFF"` represents white and `"#000080"` represents dark blue.

```
<h1>The Biggest Heading</h1>
<h2>A Smaller Heading</h2>
<!-- and so on >
<h6>The Smallest Heading</h6>
<p>One paragraph
<p>Next paragraph</p>
One line<br>
Next line
<blockquote>
Indented text
</blockquote>
<pre>Preformatted <u>text</u></pre>
<xmp>Preformatted <u>text</u> with no
interpretation of tags</xmp>
```

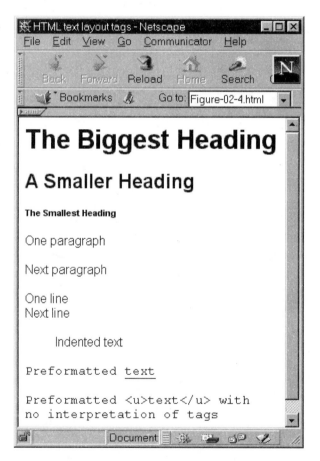

Figure 2-4. HTML text layout tags

It is customary to close the body of the document with an `<address>` tag that lists (in italics) the name and address of the organization or person responsible for the web page, the last revision or copyright date, and so on. For example:

```
<address>
Copyright &copy; 2001 by Nasty Loops, Inc.<br>
<br>
This entire site is protected by copyright.<br>
All rights reserved.  By looking at this site, you agree
to be subject to the &quot;Terms and Conditions Governing
Use and Access to Nasty Loops Online.&quot;
</address>
```

(The Internet culture is open and free, and Internet users normally expect to see friendly sites with no complicated licensing terms or user agreements.)

2.4   Text Layout and Formatting Tags

The HTML tags useful for text layout are summarized in Figure 2-4.

`<h1>` through `<h6>` tags can be used to display document and section or subsection headings of different levels: from `<h1>` (the biggest font) to `<h6>` (the smallest). These headings do not have to be used in any particular order and, unlike in some word processors, do not automatically keep track of section or subsection numbers. The heading tags can include a horizontal alignment attribute. For example:

```
<h1 align="center">Welcome to eyesight.org</h1>

<h6 align="right">(If you can read this, your eyesight is 20/20)</h6>
```

The `<p>` tag marks the beginning of a paragraph, leaving a blank line above it. It, too, can include a horizontal alignment attribute for center, left, or right alignment of the whole paragraph. In most cases, the closing `</p>` tag can be omitted, but it is safer to put it in, especially if the paragraph is not left-justified.

The `<br>` tag marks the end of a line (in the displayed document, not in the source). For example, HTML source

```
<p>
An Internet poet named Braque
Had <br> tags all out of whack
```

will show up in a browser as:

An Internet poet named Braque Had
tags all out of whack

To display the lines properly, you need

```
<p>
An Internet poet named Braque<br>
Had &lt;br&gt; tags all out of whack<br>
```

Two <br> tags in a row create a blank line.

We should also mention here the helpful "non-breaking space" character . Normally, browsers and HTML interpreters eliminate all white space from the document, replacing any series of line breaks and spaces in the source with one space in the displayed document. A "non-breaking space" inserts a space that does not disappear from the displayed document. A series of   ... leaves some empty space when displayed. If used between words,   keeps these words on the same line.

The <blockquote> tag indents all text between <blockquote> and </blockquote> and inserts blank lines above and below the indented paragraph. It is used for paragraph quotes (or for any indented text).

The <center> tag centers all the text and other elements (tables, images, etc.) until the closing </center> tag.

The <hr> ("horizontal rule") tag makes a horizontal line. It may have the optional attributes width (length, usually in percents, relative to the width of the browser window), size (thickness), and color. For example:

```
<hr width="80%" size="3" color="#0000A0">
```

<pre> ... </pre> (preformatted text) and <xmp> ... </xmp> (sequence of literal characters) tags display the fragment of text between them using a fixed-width font and preserving all line breaks and spaces in the original text. This is useful for displaying fragments of computer programs, data files, and so on. The difference between the two is that <pre> interprets other HTML tags inside it. Therefore you have to use escape sequences in place of >, <, and & inside the <pre> tag. The <xmp> tag completely disables all HTML interpretation and shows the text exactly as it is in the source until </xmp>.

❖   ❖   ❖

The text attribute tags are summarized in Figure 2-5. They provide for bold, italicized, and underlined text, smaller and bigger fonts, and subscripts and superscripts. The `<code>` tag enables a fixed-width font and is used to display computer-related items (e.g., names of functions or variables in a computer program or HTML tags in an HTML tutorial). The `<cite>` tag is used for displaying names of books or articles. In fact it simply italicizes the text, just like the `<i>` tag, but it's better to use the tags according to their intended purpose. Similarly, the `<strong>` tag displays text in bold, just like `<b>`, but `<strong>` is more abstract, meaning highlighted text, while `<b>` just means bold. More recent HTML versions allow you to redefine the meanings of some tags using style sheets. For instance, `<strong>` may become red instead of bold.

```
<p> <b>Bold</b> <i>Italics</i> <u>Underlined</u>

<big>Big</big> <small>Small</small>

x<sub>1</sub> y<sup>2</sup>

<p> <code>Courier</code> <cite>Citation</cite>

<strong>Emphasis</strong>
```

> **Bold** *Italics* Underlined Big Small x_1 y^2
>
> Courier *Citation* **Emphasis**

Figure 2-5. HTML text attribute tags

The `<font>` tag with the `size` attribute allows you to choose a font size from 1, the smallest, to 7, the largest. You can also increment or decrement the current size by preceding the value with a plus or minus sign. The default font size is 3. The `color="value"` attribute sets a different color for the font. For example,

```
<font size="+2" color="blue">
```

increments the current font size by two steps and sets the color to blue. Font attributes remain in effect until the closing `</font>` tag.

2.5   Anchors and Links

It is the <a> tag that converts ordinary text into hypertext. This tag is used in two ways: it can define an "anchor" or a link. An ***anchor*** simply marks a particular location in the document. To define an anchor, use the <a> tag with a name attribute. For example,

```
<a name="sect2_5">
<h2 align="center">Section 2.5   Anchors and Links</h2>
```

The closing tag </a> is not required for an anchor.

Once an anchor is set, you can define hypertext ***links*** that send to this anchor. For example:

```
<p>The use of hypertext anchors and links is described
in <a href="#sect2_5">Section 2.5</a>.
```

In this HTML fragment the <a> tag with an href attribute indicates that the words "Section 2.5" are linked to the anchor sect2_5. A browser displays links in a color different from the rest of the text, and usually underlined. If you click on a link, the browser will take you to the position described in its href attribute. The # in front of sect2_5 indicates that it is an anchor and not a file name.

In general, a link can take you to any ***URL***. In Internet lingo, URL stands for ***Uniform (or Universal) Resource Locator*** and can represent a file (a web page) on the same computer (or as we say ***host***) or any Internet address. If you write

```
<p>The use of hypertext links and anchors is described
in <a href="tutorial.html#sect2_5">Section 2.5 of our tutorial</a>.
```

the link will take you to the file tutorial.html, presumably a different web page on the same web site as the current document, and position the display at the anchor "sect2_5" in it. If you omit the anchor, then the link will take you to the top of the other document. For example:

```
<p>The use of hypertext links and anchors is described
in <a href="tutorial.html">our tutorial</a>.
```

If your web site files are split between different directories, you should include the path for the file as part of the URL.

> **It is usually much better to use <u>relative</u> paths in URL links to documents on the same web site. A relative path defines the path going from the directory of the current document. A relative path <u>does not</u> begin with a slash.**
>
> **Use forward slashes in paths for compatibility with all systems.**

For example,

```
<p>The use of hypertext links and anchors is described
in <a href="courses/tutorial.html">our tutorial</a>.
```

The folder (directory) that holds the document containing the above lines has a subfolder, called `courses`, with the `tutorial.html` file in it. Here we go <u>down</u> one level in the directory tree. We can also go <u>up</u> one or several levels. For example:

```
<p align="center"><a href="../home.html">Back to the Home Page</a>
```

(`../` means go up one level, to the parent directory of the current directory.)

Finally, you can put into an `href` attribute the complete web address (URL) of a document on another web site. You can include an anchor in it if you wish. For example:

```
<p>A complete
<a href=
"http://developer.netscape.com/docs/manuals/htmlguid/index.htm#tags">
alphabetical listing of HTML tags</a>
is available in Netscape Communications' Reference Guide.
```

This will appear in a browser as

> A complete **<u>alphabetical listing of HTML tags</u>** is available in Netscape Communications' Reference Guide.

Don't forget the `</a>` tag after your "hot" text, or the whole rest of your document may show up as one big hyperlink.

URLs do not have to point only to HTML documents: they can point to any type of file or resource. Your browser will decide what to do with a file or resource based on its type. For example, it may call *Adobe Acrobat Reader* to display a PDF file, offer to download and save a zipped file on your computer's hard disk, or play music from an MP3 file. One particular URL that may be of interest has the form `mailto:` followed by an e-mail address. When you click on such a link, it brings up your e-mail program ready to send a message to the specified address. For example:

```
Report all problems with this web site to the
<a href="mailto:webmaster@nastyloops.com">webmaster</a>.
```

This will appear in a browser as

> Report all problems with this web site to the **webmaster**.

Note that URLs for your links are hidden on display and in printouts of your web page unless you repeat them explicitly in visible text. For example:

```
<p>A complete alphabetical listing of HTML tags is available in
Netscape Communications' Reference Guide at
<a href=
"http://developer.netscape.com/docs/manuals/htmlguid/index.htm#tags">
<code>
http://developer.netscape.com/docs/manuals/htmlguid/index.htm#tags
</code>
</a>.
```

> A complete alphabetical listing of HTML tags is available in Netscape Communications' Reference Guide at
> **http://developer.netscape.com/docs/manuals/htmlguid/index.htm#tags**.

Or

```
The best way to reach me at any time of day or night is
to e-mail me at<br>
<a href="mailto:emailaddict@coffeeshop.org">
emailaddict@coffeeshop.org</a>.
```

> The best way to reach me at any time of day or night is to e-mail me at
> **emailaddict@coffeeshop.org**.

2.6   Lists

HTML lets you put a list of items on your page. It supports three types of lists: an unordered (bulleted) list using the <ul> tag, an ordered (numbered) list using the <ol> tag, and a "definition list" of items with captions using the <dl> tag. These lists are illustrated in Figure 2-6.

```
<ul>
<li>Item 1</li>
<li>Item 2</li>
<li>Item 3</li>
</ul>

<ol>
<li>Item 1</li>
<li>Item 2</li>
<li>Item 3</li>
</ol>

<dl>
<dt>Item 1</dt>
<dd>Definition 1</dd>
<dt>Item 2</dt>
<dd>Definition 2</dd>
<dt>Item 3</dt>
<dd>Definition 3</dd>
</dl>
```

- Item 1
- Item 2
- Item 3

1. Item 1
2. Item 2
3. Item 3

Item 1
    Definition 1
Item 2
    Definition 2
Item 3
    Definition 3

Figure 2-6.   <ul>, <ol>, and <dl> tags for lists

For the <ul> tag, you can add the type attribute with the possible values "circle", "disc", or "square" which defines the shape of the bullet ('disk" is the default). In the <ol> tag, the type attribute may have the values "1" (default), "I", "i", "A", and "a", and it defines the style of numbers (regular numbers, upper- or lowercase Roman numerals, or upper- or lowercase letters). You can also change the starting number with the start="*value*" attribute. In both unordered and ordered lists each item is placed between <li> ("list item") and </li> tags. In a "definition list," the term is placed between <dt> and </dt> tags ("definition term") and the definition itself is placed between <dd> and </dd> tags ("definition description").

HTML lets you nest one list inside another (Figure 2-7). In this example we used indentation and blank lines in the source to make the source more readable. They do not affect the displayed page.

```
<h4 align="center">Java Programming Style</h4>

<ol>
<li>White space
  <ol type="A">
  <li>Use spaces around all operators,
  to the left of <code>(</code> and <code>{</code>
  and to the right of <code>)</code> and <code>}</code></li>
  <li>Use blank lines to separate meaningful segments
  of code</li>
  </ol>
</li>

<li>Names
  <ol type="A">
  <li>Use meaningful names for classes, methods and
  variables</li>
  <li>Use nouns for classes and verbs for methods</li>
  </ol>
</li>
</ol>
```

Java Programming Style

1. White space
   A. Use spaces around all operators, to the left of (and { and to the right of) and }
   B. Use blank lines to separate meaningful segments of code
2. Names
   A. Use meaningful names for classes, methods and variables
   B. Use nouns for classes and verbs for methods

Figure 2-7. Nested lists

2.7   Images

One picture is worth a thousand HTML tags. The two most common formats for images on the Internet are *GIF* (Graphics Interchange Format) and *JPEG* (Joint Photographic Experts Group) format. Both use image compression because image files can be quite large. Even with compression, downloading a large image from the Internet to your computer can take a long time. GIF file names have the extension .gif and JPEG files have the extension .jpg.

Images are incorporated into an HTML document using the <img> tag. This tag has many attributes of which the most important one, and the only one required, is the source of the image. It has the form `src="url"`, where *url* is a name of a file, usually somewhere on the same web site. For example,

```
<img src="wintertrack.jpg">
```

Other attributes are:

- `align` with values `"top"`, `"center"`, or `"bottom"`. Specifies vertical alignment of the image with respect to text in the same line and is useful for small images: icons, bullets, and so on.

- `alt="text"`. Specifies the text to display in place of the image when the image is not available for some reason. Some browsers also show this text inside a yellow label that appears when you position the mouse cursor over the image.

- `border="thickness"`. Specifies the thickness of the border. 0 means no border.

- `height="value"` and `width="value"`. Specify the dimensions of the image in pixels.

Height and width attributes are optional, but they allow the browser to reserve space for the image and continue loading the page while the image file is still on its way. If the specified dimensions are different from the actual image dimensions, the image is scaled, which may result in poor quality.

A more complete <img> tag with attributes may look like

```
<img src="wintertrack.jpg" width="320" height="100" border="0"
     alt="Girls winter track team">
```

There is no closing tag for <img>.

> **You can surround an image tag with `<a href="someURL">` ... `</a>` tags. Then the whole picture becomes a "hot" button that, when touched, will take the user to the specified URL.**

A more interesting trick is to make different areas in a picture active with different URLs attached to them. You can do this using a <map> tag with a list of areas in it. Each area can have its own URL, which is activated when that area is touched. The areas may include circles, rectangles, and polygons; you can define more complex areas by using several overlapping shapes with the same URL. An image can be tied to a particular map by adding a `usemap="#mapname"` attribute to the `<img>` tag. For example:

```
<img src="wintertrack.jpg" width="320" height="100" border="0"
     alt="Girls winter track team" usemap="#teammap">

<map name="teammap">
  <area shape="circle" coords="10,20,30"   href="Lucy.jpg">
  <area shape="rect" coords="60,20,85,40"  href="Sean.jpg">
  <area shape="polygon" coords="25,150,50,100,100,100,150,200"
                                     href="Melissa.html">
  < ... etc. >
</map>
```

In this example, the map "teammap" overlaps the picture. Presumably areas in the map outline faces in the photograph and when you click on an area, the browser opens a file with a bigger picture of that person. The coordinates are in pixels, with the origin in the upper-left corner of the image. A circle is described by the x and y coordinates of its center, and its radius. A rectangle is described by the coordinates of its two opposite corners. A polygon is described by the coordinates of its vertices.

2.8   Tables

The `<table>` ... `</table>` tags define a table in your document. You have to describe each row of the table separately using the `<tr>` ... `</tr>` ("table row") tags. Within each row you describe each individual table entry between the `<td>` ... `</td>` ("table data") tags.

Figure 2-8 shows HTML example of a table used to display a calendar for a month.

This calendar will look rather ugly (Figure 2-9 (a)): the day names in the heading row do not stand out and the numbers are not right-justified. The first problem is easy to fix: all you have to do is replace all the `<td>` tags with `<th>` ("table heading") tags in the first row:

```
<tr>
<th>Sun</th><th>Mon</th><th>Tue</th><th>Wed</th><th>Thu</th>
<th>Fri</th><th>Sat</th>
</tr>
```

```
<p><b>November 2001</b></p>

<p>
<table>
<tr>
<td>Sun</td><td>Mon</td><td>Tue</td><td>Wed</td><td>Thu</td>
<td>Fri</td><td>Sat</td>
</tr>

<tr>
<td></td><td></td><td></td><td></td><td>1</td><td>2</td><td>3</td>
</tr>

<tr>
<td>4</td><td>5</td><td>6</td><td>7</td><td>8</td>
<td>9</td><td>10</td>
</tr>

<tr>
<td>11</td><td>12</td><td>13</td><td>14</td><td>15</td>
<td>16</td><td>17</td>
</tr>

<tr>
<td>18</td><td>19</td><td>20</td><td>21</td><td>22</td>
<td>23</td><td>24</td>
</tr>

<tr>
<td>25</td><td>26</td><td>27</td><td>28</td><td>29</td><td>30</td>
</tr>

</table>
```

Figure 2-8. HTML document that uses a table to show a calendar

To fix the second problem add the `align="right"` attribute to each `<tr>` tag:

```
<tr align="right">
<th>Sun</th><th>Mon</th><th>Tue</th><th>Wed</th><th>Thu</th>
<th>Fri</th><th>Sat</th>
</tr>
  ... etc.
```

(a)

November 2001						
Sun	Mon	Tue	Wed	Thu	Fri	Sat
					1	2	3
4	5	6	7	8	9	10
11	12	13	14	15	16	17
18	19	20	21	22	23	24
25	26	27	28	29	30	

(b)

November 2001						
Sun	Mon	Tue	Wed	Thu	Fri	Sat
					1	2	3
4	5	6	7	8	9	10
11	12	13	14	15	16	17
18	19	20	21	22	23	24
25	26	27	28	29	30	

(c)

November 2001						
Sun	Mon	Tue	Wed	Thu	Fri	Sat
				1	2	3
4	5	6	7	8	9	10
11	12	13	14	15	16	17
18	19	20	21	22	23	24
25	26	27	28	29	30	

Figure 2-9. Formatting tables in HTML

You can use the `align` attribute with individual `<td>` and `<th>` tags; then they will override the alignment specified in `<tr>`.

With these changes the result looks a little better (Figure 2-9 (b)), but the column widths are still uneven and the heading is too close to the numbers. You can add an empty row after the first row to separate the day names from the numbers. To make it show up, put one non-breaking space in it. For example:

```
<tr><td> </td></tr>
```

To make the columns even, you can add the `cols="7"` and `width="300"` attributes to the `<table>` tag. These attributes set the number of columns and table's width in pixels. Unfortunately, not all browsers seem to understand the `cols` attribute. It may be safer to specify the width of each column by adding the `width` attribute to each `<td>` tag (at least in the first row of the table).

You can also specify the width of the table relative to the width of the browser window. For example: `width="30%"`. If you specify column widths for individual columns with percent values, the column widths will be set relative to the width of the whole table.

With these changes our calendar begins to look better (Figure 2-9 (c)). For a finishing touch, we might mark Thanksgiving on the 22nd. Let's make it "lightcoral" on a "lavenderblush" background (these color names come from the list of HTML-supported colors[htmlcolors]):

```
<td bgcolor="lavenderblush"><font color="lightcoral">22</font></td>
```

Working with tables is not easy because `<table>`, `<tr>`, and `<td>` tags have many attributes and `<td>` attributes can override the same attributes for the `<tr>` tag. On top of this, different browsers or versions of the same browser may support and interpret some of the attributes differently. So you have to be careful and test your page on different platforms. If your web page is for everyone, you should try to use safer proven methods.

On the other hand, tables are very powerful. HTML does not give you many tools for controlling page layout: tables are pretty much all you have. You can use tables for all kinds of things: side bars or horizontal bars with navigation links, narrow columns of text and multi-column text, text and picture insets, blocks of text with borders or color backgrounds, and so on. Lists, images, and applets may all be placed inside a table cell, and you can have tables within tables. Look at some web sites you like for examples of how tables are used.

The following attributes will add flexibility to your tables:

`<table>`
    `border` — border thickness in pixels; 0 means no border
    `cellspacing` — space between a table's cells
    `cellpadding` — additional space between data and the borders of the cell
    `hspace` and `vspace` — additional horizontal and vertical space around the table

`<tr>`, `<th>`, and `<td>`
    `align` (`"left"`, `"center"`, or `"right"`) — horizontal alignment
    `valign` (`"top"`, `"middle"`, or `"bottom"`) — vertical alignment
                                      (inside the cell)
    `bgcolor` — background color

You can also place a `<caption>` tag inside a table definition (but outside of all row definitions):

```
<caption align="..."> ... </caption>
```

The `align` attribute here can be "`top`" (top of the table, default) or "`bottom`".

2.9   Applets

Finally, you can add an *applet*, a little Java program, to a web page. This is done using an `<applet>` tag.

> **Applet tags can appear in more or less any place in your HTML document; a web page can run several applets or several copies of the same applet concurrently.**

The following example loads and runs the *TicTacToe* applet from the standard Java SDK-2 demo collection and provides a link to its source code, `TicTacToe.java`:

```
<html>
<head>
<title>TicTacToe v1.1</title>
</head>

<body>
<h1>TicTacToe v1.1</h1>
<hr>
<applet code="TicTacToe.class" width="120" height="120"
     alt="Can't run the applet, for some reason.">

Your browser is completely ignoring the &lt;APPLET&gt; tag!

</applet>
<hr>
<a href="TicTacToe.java">The source.</a>
</body>
</html>
```

The `code` attribute defines the applet name.

> **Applet file names are case-sensitive!**

The applet's file name in the `<applet>` tag has the `.class` extension, which is the standard extension for a Java class compiled into bytecodes (see Section 3.3).

The `codebase` attribute specifies a path to the directory (folder) that contains the applet's code. It can be the absolute path but more often it is the path relative to the location of your HTML file. You do not need to specify `codebase` at all (or you can put `codebase="."` for the current directory) if the applet's code is in the same folder as your HTML source. `codebase` may be case-sensitive, too, depending on the operating system. In the above example, the `TicTacToe.class` file happens to be in a folder called `TicTacToe` somewhere under `jdk1.3`. It is possible (although unusual) to have the code on a different host. Then you need to use the directory path for the full URL. For example,

```
codebase="http://java.sun.com/applets/jdk1.3/demo/applets/TicTacToe"
```

`width` and `height` attributes define the dimensions of the window in which you want the applet to run. More often than not these dimensions depend on the applet itself: few applets are written to be completely scaleable. Try to open the *TicTacToe* applet and play it with *width*=50 and *height*=50, and you'll see what happens.

You can use the `align` attribute with a value of `"left"` or `"right"` to align your applet with the left or the right margin of the web page. You can also use it with a value of `"top"`, `"middle"`, or `"bottom"` to place the applet within the current text line and align it with the top, middle, or bottom of the text.

The `alt` attribute tells the browser what message to display if the applet fails to run for whatever reason. You can also put any text between the `<applet>` and `</applet>` tags; this text will be visible only if your browser does not recognize the `<applet>` tag at all.

Occasionally an applet needs one or several parameters to run. You can set the values of parameters using `<param>` tags placed between `<applet>` and `</applet>`. The format for the `<param>` tag is:

```
<param name="anyName" value="anyText">
```

anyName is the parameter's name, defined by the programmer. It is used in the program to fetch the parameter's value. The value is a string of text; the program can convert it into a number, if necessary.

2.10 Summary

HTML stands for HyperText Markup Language. It is used to format documents, especially web pages. HTML uses formatting tags embedded in the text. The most commonly used tags are summarized in Figure 2-10.

```
<html>
<head>
<title>HTML Summary</title>
<meta name="author" content="Maria Litvin and Gary Litvin">
<meta name="Keywords" content="Web, HTML">
</head>

<body text="black" bgcolor="white">

<a name="top">
<h2 align="center">Summary</h2>

Lines wrap around automatically.<br> A new line
after a manual line break.
<p>A new paragraph starts here.

<blockquote>
The &lt;blockquote&gt; tag indents all text
between &lt;blockquote&gt; and
&lt;/blockquote&gt;
</blockquote>

<hr size="3" width="60%">
<b>Bold</b> <i>Italic</i> <u>Underlined</u>
<strong>Highlighted</strong> <cite>Citation</cite>
<code>Computer item</code>

<font size="7">Big</font>
<font size="1">Small</font>
<font color="red">Red</font>

<hr size="3" width="60%" color="#0000A0">

<p align="center">
<a href="#top">Back to Top</a> |
<a href="http://www.skylit.com">Home</a>

<br><br>
```

Figure 2-10 `summary.html` *Continued* ⇗

```
<center>
<table width="75%" cellspacing="5" cellpadding="5" border="3">

<tr bgcolor="cyan" valign="top" align="center">
<th width="60%">An image:</th>
<th width="40%">A Java applet:</th>
</tr>

<tr valign="top">
<td>
<p align="center">
<img src="carnation.jpg" alt="Carnation" align="center"><br>
Carnation
</td>

<td>
<p align="center">
Current time:<br>
<applet code="Clock2.class" codebase="c:/jdk1.3/demo/applets/clock"
      width="170" height="150" alt="Something is wrong!">

<param name="bgcolor" value="#ffffff">
Your browser does not recognize the &lt;applet&gt; tag!
</applet>

</td>
</tr>
</table>
</center>

<address>
<p align="right">from: Java Methods<br>
by Maria Litvin and Gary Litvin</p>
</address>

</body>
</html>
```

Figure 2-10. `Ch02\summary.html` 💾

Exercises

Sections 2.1-2.4

1.   Which of the following are valid HTML tags?

        `<u>, <small>, <sup>, <red>, <strong>`

2.   Choose one of the tags, `<pre>`, `<cite>`, `<blockquote>`, `<xmp>`, or `<hr>`,
        to accomplish each of the following tasks:

        (a) Indent all lines between the opening and closing tags.
        (b) Put all text between the opening and closing tags in italics.
        (c) Stop processing all HTML tags between the opening and closing tags. ✓
        (d) Display a horizontal line.
        (e) Display the text between the opening and closing tags in a fixed-width
            font and show spaces and line breaks exactly as in the source, but apply
            formatting from HTML tags embedded inside.

3.   (a)   Create an HTML document with the phrase:

               HTML stands for **H**yper**T**ext **M**arkup **L**anguage.

               formatted as shown above.

        (b)   Make the background color blue and set the default text color to white
               for the whole document. ✓

4.   Show the following design on your web page using the `<hr>` tags:

5.   Create an HTML document that looks in a browser window as shown inside
        the box below. The first paragraph is text that fills the width of the browser
        window. It is automatically split into lines as necessary when the window is
        resized. The program segment should look exactly as shown.

                                                        Continued ➘

Console Output in Java

The `System.out` object is defined in each Java program. It has methods for displaying text strings and numbers in plain text format on the system display. For example:

```
public class Hello
{
   public static void main(String[] args)
   {
      System.out.println("Hello, World!");
   }
}
```

Hint: do not use `<br>` tags in the first paragraph — let the browser fill the lines.

6. A limerick is a five-line poem (usually funny or silly) with a particular rhythm and rhyming pattern.^{limerick} Finish the limerick on page 38 and put it into an HTML document, formatted as follows: ✓

An Internet poet named Braque
Had `<br>` tags all out of whack

\-

\-

\-

By \-\-\-\-\-\-\-\-\-\-\-\-\-\-

For example:

An Internet poet named Braque
Had `<br>` tags all out of whack
His non-breaking spaces
Would get out of places
But nested lists just blew his stack!

By Brenda Webb

7.   What happens when `<xmp>` ... `</xmp>` tags are embedded inside `<pre>` ... `</pre>` tags? Experiment with different browsers and report the results.

Sections 2.5-2.9

8.   The `<ul>` tag marks a bulleted list. Create your own bulleted list (e.g., a list of things to do) without using the `<ul>` tag. Find a collection of free icons on the web and choose one for your bullet. Then create a bulleted list using the `<blockquote>`, `<img>`, and `<br>` tags and, if necessary, non-breaking space characters.

9.   The `<ul>` ... `</ul>` or `<ol>` ... `</ol>` tags (without any `<li>` tags) can be used to indent text. Explore the differences between one `<ul>`, two `<ul>` tags next to each other, one `<blockquote>`, and two `<blockquote>` tags next to each other.

10.   Come up with a way to show a boxed number on your web page. For example:

11.   Create an HTML document that shows a partial list of Java reserved words, arranged in a table with three columns (see page 125).

12.▪   Find on the web a description and a solution to the *Eight Queens* problem. Create a web page that shows a chessboard with the solution on it using only text — no images. ⸲ Hint: use a table and set alternating background colors for its cells. ⸲ Add to your page links to a few web pages that describe the problem.

13.   (a)   Create a web page with a list of people from your class.
         (b)   Create a clickable e-mail directory for your class.

14.▪   Create a web page with text in the middle column and pictures to the left and to the right of it. The text should occupy 1/3 of the browser window width. The pictures should be centered vertically with respect to the text. ✓

15.■ Create a picture gallery for your friends, family, town, team, or band, or for your pet. Use a list or a table of clickable reduced pictures as an index for your gallery. You will need two versions of each picture: a large one and a reduced one. (Reduced pictures can be scanned at different resolution or created using any image editing program, such as Adobe's *Photoshop*.)

Section 2.10

16.♦ Create a personal web site consisting of at least two pages (HTML documents) with links among them. Use headings, images and tables.

$$ch \leftarrow 3$$

An Introduction to Software Development

59

3.1   Prologue

One of the first computers, ENIAC,✱eniac developed in 1942-1946 primarily for military applications, was programmed by people actually connecting hundreds of wires to sockets (Figure 3-1) — hardly a "software development" activity as we know it. (ENIAC occupied a huge room, had 18,000 vacuum tubes, could perform 300 multiplications per second, and used more than 180 kilowatts of electricity.) In 1946, John von Neumann developed the idea that a computer program can be stored in the computer memory itself in the form of encoded CPU instructions, together with the data on which that program operates. Then the modern computer was born: a "universal, digital, program-stored" computer that can perform calculations and process information.

Figure 3-1. Two technicians wiring the right side of ENIAC

(Courtesy of U. S. Army Research Laboratory)

Once program-stored computers were developed, it made sense to talk about programs as "written." In fact, at the beginning of the computer era, programmers wrote programs in pencil on special forms; then technicians punched the programs into punch cards✱punchcard or perforated tape. A programmer entering a computer room with a deck of punch cards was a common sight. Fairly large programs were written entirely in machine code using octal or hexadecimal instruction codes and memory addresses. It is no coincidence that the same word, "coding," is used for writing programs and encrypting texts. Programmers were often simply mathematicians, electrical engineers, or scientists who learned the skill on their own when they needed to use a computer for their work.

In those days computers and "computer time" (i.e., the time available for running programs) were very expensive, much more expensive than a programmer's time, and the high computer costs defined the rules of the game. For instance, only fairly important computer applications could be considered, such as military and scientific computations, large information systems, and so on. Programmers strove to make their programs run faster by developing efficient ***algorithms*** (the concept of an ***algorithm*** is described in Section 3.2). Often one or two programmers wrote the entire program and knew all about it, while no one else could understand it. Computer users were happy just to have access to a computer and were willing to learn cryptic instructions and formats for using programs.

Now, when computers are so inexpensive that they have become a household commodity, while programmers are scarce and expensive, the rules of the game have changed completely. This change affects which programs are written, how they are created, and even the name by which programmers prefer to be called — "software engineers." There is still a need, of course, for understanding and optimizing algorithms. But the emphasis has shifted to programmers' productivity, professionalism, and teamwork — which means using standard programming languages, tools, and software components.

Software applications that run on a desktop are loaded with features and must be very interactive and "***user-friendly***," (i.e., have an intuitive and fairly conventional user interface). They must also be ***portable*** (i.e., able to run on different computer systems) and internationalized (i.e., easily adaptable for different languages and local conventions). Since large teams may work on the same software project, it is very important that teams follow standard methodologies, and that the resulting programs be understandable to others and well documented. Thus software engineering has become as professionalized as other engineering disciplines: there is a lot of emphasis on knowing and using professional tools in a team environment, and virtually no room for solo wizardry.

A typical fairly large software project may include the following tasks:

- Interaction with customers, understanding customer needs, refining and formalizing specifications
- General design (defining a software product's parts, their functions and interactions)
- Detailed design (defining objects, functions, algorithms, file layouts, etc.)

- Design/prototyping of the user interface (designing screen layouts, menus, dialog boxes, online help, reports, messages, etc.)
- Coding and debugging
- Performance analysis and code optimization
- Documentation
- Testing
- Packaging and delivery
- User technical support

(And, in the real world:

- Bug fixes, patches and workarounds, updated releases, documentation updates, etc.)

Of course there are different levels and different kinds of software engineers, and it is not necessary that the same person combine all the skills needed to design and develop good software. Usually it takes a whole team of software designers, programmers, artists, technical writers, and specialists in quality assurance ("QA") and technical support.

In this chapter we will first discuss general topics related to software development, such as algorithms, high-level programming languages, and software development tools. We will discuss the difference between compilers and interpreters and Java's hybrid compiler + interpreter approach. Then we will learn how to compile and run simple Java console and GUI applications and applets and take a first look at the concepts involved in object-oriented programming.

3.2   Algorithms

We begin with a glimpse at algorithms because, historically, software development was largely viewed as understanding, designing, and implementing algorithms. A formal definition of an algorithm is elusive, which is a sure sign that the concept is fundamentally important.

An *algorithm* is a more or less abstract, formal, and general step-by-step recipe that tells how to perform a certain task or solve a certain problem on a computer.

The paradox of this definition, however, is that algorithms existed long before computers. One of the most famous, Euclid's Algorithm for finding the greatest common factor of two integers, dates back to about 300 BC. You may also recall the algorithm for long division of numbers, often used in the pre-calculator era. The question of whether computers have evolved the way they are to support the implementation of algorithms or whether algorithms (as they are understood now) gained prominence due to the advent of computers is of the chicken-and-egg category.

A method of performing a task or solving a problem can be described at different levels of abstraction. Algorithms represent a rather abstract level for solving problems. In computer applications, an analyst can describe a method in fairly abstract terms to a computer programmer. It helps if the analyst knows the capabilities of computers and the general principles of computer programming, but he or she does not have to know any specific programming language. In fact, an algorithm can be used without any computer by a person equipped with a pencil and paper. The programmer can then implement the algorithm in Java, C++, or any other programming language of choice.

Various tools and notations have been developed for describing and teaching algorithms. *Flowcharts*, for example, represent them graphically. The flowchart in Figure 3-2 (a) represents an algorithm for calculating $1^2 + 2^2 + ... + n^2$. Parallelograms represent input and output; rectangles represent processing steps; rhombuses, conditions checked. The arrow means "set to," so i $\leftarrow$ i+1 means "set i to the value of i+1" (i.e. increment i by one).

Another representation of an algorithm is called *pseudocode*. It uses operations similar to those defined in most programming languages, but without paying much attention to the specifics of a language; this produces a shorthand that all programmers, regardless of the language they use, can read and understand (Figure 3-2 (b)).

You can learn several general properties from this simple algorithm. First, its description is rather short. Potentially we could add up the squares of numbers from 1 to, say, 100 by brute force, making our "algorithm" quite long (Figure 3-3). But what good would it do to have a computer that could execute millions of instructions per second if we had to write every single one of these instructions separately! A reasonable algorithm folds the computation into one or several fragments that can be repeated multiple times. These repetitions, called *iterations*, may work with different values of variables but execute the same instructions. In the example in Figure 3-2 the algorithm iterates *n* times through three steps, incrementing *i* by one in each iteration.

(a)

(b)

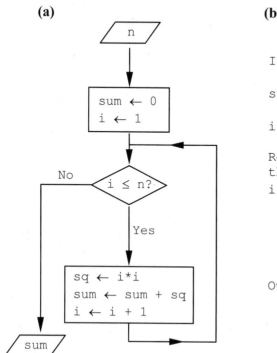

```
Input: n

sum ← 0

i ← 1

Repeat the following
three steps while
i ≤ n:

    sq = i*i
    sum ← sum + sq
    i ← i + 1

Output: sum
```

Figure 3-2. Flowchart and pseudocode for an algorithm for calculating $1^2 + 2^2 + ... + n^2$

```
sq = 1*1; sum ← sum + sq
sq = 2*2; sum ← sum + sq
sq = 3*3; sum ← sum + sq
sq = 4*4; sum ← sum + sq
...
  (and so on, every single line)
...
sq = 99*99; sum ← sum + sq
sq = 100*100; sum ← sum + sq
```

Figure 3-3. Brute-force "non-algorithm" for calculating $1^2 + 2^2 + ... + 100^2$

The second property of an algorithm is that it is rather general. The brute-force "algorithm" in Figure 3-3 works for *n*=100, but you have to change your program if you want it to work for, say, *n*=500. The algorithm in Figure 3-2, a "real" algorithm, works for any *n* without changing anything. The value of *n* serves as an input value for the procedure. The running time of a program based on this algorithm will be different for different *n*, but the length of the program text itself remains the same regardless of the value of *n*.

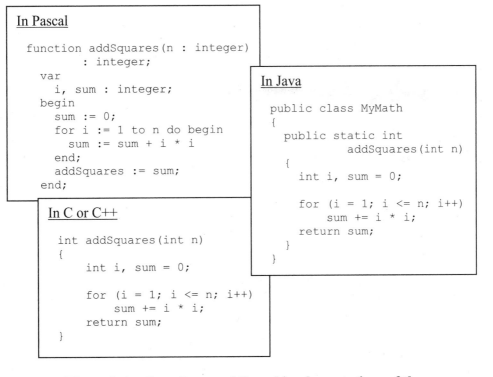

**Figure 3-4. C++, Java, and Pascal implementations of the
sum-of-squares algorithm**

The third property of an algorithm, as we have mentioned above, is that an algorithm is abstract: it does not depend on a particular programming language or computer system. Figure 3-4 shows how the same algorithm will be coded in Pascal and C++ functions and in a Java ***class*** with the `addSquares` ***method*** (in Java functions belong to "classes" and are called "methods").

Because algorithms are abstract, we can study their properties and compare them for efficiency without ever implementing them on a computer. For example, we can see that in the sum-of-squares algorithm in Figure 3-2 a multiplication operation will be executed *n* times. Multiplication is in general a more time-consuming operation than addition. A slightly more efficient version of this algorithm (Figure 3-5) can calculate the same result without any multiplications!

```
Input: n
k ← n + n
sum ← 0
sq ← 0
i ← 1
Repeat the following three
steps while i ≤ k:
    sq ← sq + i
    sum ← sum + sq
    i ← i + 2
Output: sum
```

Figure 3-5. A more efficient version of the sum-of-squares without multiplications

❖   ❖   ❖

Another powerful method for describing and implementing algorithms is recursion. A recursive solution describes a procedure for a particular task in terms of applying the same procedure to a similar but smaller task. A recursive solution also isolates very simple situations (the base case) when a computation is obvious and recursion is not required. For example, in the task of calculating $1^2 + 2^2 + ... + n^2$, recursive thinking would go like this: if $n = 1$ the result is simply 1; if $n > 1$, calculate the sum $1^2 + 2^2 + ... + (n-1)^2$, then add n^2 to it. The underlined phrase represents a recursive call to the same procedure for a smaller number, $n-1$.

To most people, though, this algorithm will seem totally unsatisfactory. They may ask, "Right, but how do I know how to calculate $1^2 + 2^2 + ... + (n-1)^2$? The algorithm does not tell me anything about that!" In fact it does, because the same rule applies to any input, and in particular to $n-1$. So to calculate $1^2 + 2^2 + ... + (n-1)^2$ you need to calculate $1^2 + 2^2 + ... + (n-2)^2$ then add $(n-1)^2$. And so on, until you get to 1, and you know the answer for $n = 1$.

```
public class MyMath
{
  public static int addSquares(int n)
  {
    if (n == 1)
      return 1;
    else
      return addSquares(n-1) + n * n;
  }
}
```

Figure 3-6.   Recursive method in Java for computing
$1^2 + 2^2 + ... + n^2$ **(not recommended for this task)**

Recursion may seem very tricky to an untrained eye, and some people never completely come to grips with it. But it is easy for computers: they handle recursion as a form of iterations, which however are hidden from the programmer. In high-level languages, such as Java, or C++, recursion is implemented in terms of functions calling themselves. In Java, for instance, the above recursive algorithm can be implemented as shown in Figure 3-6. Computers have a hardware mechanism, called the ***stack***, that facilitates recursive function calls. Some programming languages, such as LISP, almost always suggest the use of recursion in favor of explicit iterations. In Java, recursion is used in standard packages but programmers do not have to program recursive functions themselves very often. Still, it is very useful for understanding certain classic algorithms such as Mergesort (Section 12.8) or tree traversals.

Some people, once they understand it, find recursion so elegant that they are tempted to use it everywhere. Indeed, as Figure 3-6 shows, recursive solutions may be short and expressive. But they may be also more costly then iterative solutions in terms of running time and memory space, and in some cases this cost may become prohibitive.

3.3   Compilers and Interpreters

Computer programmers very quickly realized that the computer itself was the perfect tool to help them write programs. The first step towards automation was made when programmers began to use ***assembly languages*** instead of numerically coded CPU instructions. In an assembly language, every CPU instruction has a short mnemonic name. A programmer can give symbolic names to memory locations and can refer to these locations by name. For example, a programmer using Intel's 8086 assembly language can write:

```
index   dw    0         ; "Define word" -- reserve 2 bytes
                        ;  for an integer and call it "index".
        ...
        mov   si,index  ; Move the value of index into
                        ;   the SI register.
        ...
```

A special program, called the ***assembler***, converts the program written in assembly language into the ***machine code*** expected by the CPU.

Obviously, assembly language is totally dependent on a particular CPU; ***porting*** a program to a different type of machine would require rewriting the code. As the power of computers increased, several ***high-level*** programming languages were developed for writing programs in a more abstract, machine-independent way. FORTRAN (Formula Translation Language) was defined in 1956, COBOL (Common Business-Oriented Language) in 1960, and Pascal and C in the 1970s. C++ gradually evolved from C in the 1980s, adding OOP (object-oriented programming) features to C. Java was introduced in the mid-1990s and eventually gained popularity as a fully object-oriented programming language for platform-independent development, in particular for programs transmitted over the Internet. Java and OOP are of course the main subjects of this book, so we will start looking at them in detail in the following chapters.

A program written in a high-level language obeys the very formal ***syntax*** rules of the language. This syntax produces statements so unambiguous that even a computer can interpret them correctly. In addition to strict syntax rules, a program follows ***style*** conventions; these are not mandatory but make the program easier to read and understand for fellow programmers, demonstrating its author's professionalism (See Appendix B, *The 17 Bits of Style*).

❖   ❖   ❖

A programmer writes the text of the program using a software program called an ***editor***. Unlike general-purpose word-processing programs, programming editors may have special features useful for writing programs. For example, an editor may use colors to highlight different syntactic elements in the program or even have built-in tools for entering standard words or expressions common in a particular programming language.

> **The text of a program in a particular programming language is referred to as** *source code*, **or simply the** *source*. **The source code is stored in a file, called the** *source file* **or the** *source module*.

In compiled languages, such as COBOL, Pascal, or C++, a program is converted into machine language by a special software tool called a ***compiler***. The compiler is specific to a particular programming language and a particular CPU. It analyzes the source code and generates appropriate CPU instructions. The result is saved in another file, called the ***object module***. A large program may include several source modules that are compiled into object modules separately. Another program, a ***linker***, combines all the object modules into one ***executable*** program and saves it in an executable file (Figure 3-7).

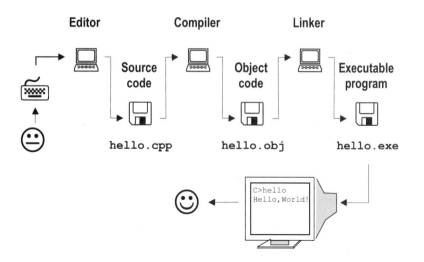

Figure 3-7.   Compiled language development cycle:
edit-compile-link-run

In an approach alternative to compiling, a program in a high-level language can be ***interpreted*** by a software tool called an ***interpreter***. The difference between a compiler and an interpreter is subtle but important. An interpreter looks at the high-level-language program, figures out what instructions it has to execute and executes them. But it does not generate an object-code file and does not save compiled or executable code. It is like a live concert as compared to a studio recording.

To better understand the difference between a compiler and an interpreter, consider a program that contains the statement:

```
R = P + Q;   // Set R to the sum of P and Q
```

A compiler when it sees this statement will *parse* the statement (analyze the structure and extract its elements) and then generate object code according to the following algorithm:

```
Generate and save an instruction that moves P into a register
Since the operation sign is '+', generate and save an
    instruction that adds Q to that register
Generate and save an instruction that moves the result from the
    register into R
```

In 8086 assembly language the resulting code may look like

```
mov ax, P      ; move the value of P into the AX register
add ax, Q      ; add the value of Q to the AX register
mov R, ax      ; move the contents of the AX register into R
```

An interpreter will also parse the statement and implement a similar algorithm, but instead of generating and saving the instructions it executes them right away:

```
Move P into a register
Since the operation sign is '+', add Q to that register
Move the result from the register into R
```

A particular programming language is usually established as either a compiled language or an interpreted language (i.e., is either more suitable or more often used with a compiler or an interpreter), but there is really no clear-cut distinction. BASIC, for example, was initially an interpreted language, but soon BASIC compilers were developed. C is a compiled language, but C interpreters also exist.

❖   ❖   ❖

Java uses a mixed compiler-plus-interpreter approach. A Java compiler first compiles the program into *bytecodes*, instructions that are pretty close to a machine language. But a machine with this machine language does not exist! It is an abstract computer, a *Java virtual machine*. Bytecodes are then interpreted on a particular computer by the Java interpreter for that particular CPU. A program in bytecodes is not object code because it is still platform-independent. It is not source code, either, because it is not readable by humans. It is something in between.

Why does Java use a combination of a compiler and an interpreter? There is no reason why a regular Java compiler couldn't be created for a particular type of computer. But one of the main purposes of Java is to deliver programs to users via the Internet. A *Java-enabled* browser (i.e., a browser that has a Java interpreter built into it) can run little Java programs, called ***applets*** (little "applications"). The applets already written and available free on the Internet with their source code are one of the reasons why Java has become so popular so fast. When you connect to a web site and see some action on your screen, it probably means your computer has received a Java applet and is running it.

Java designers had to address the key question: Should users receive Java source or executable code? The answer they came up with was neither. If users get source, their browsers must have a built-in Java compiler or interpreter. That would make browsers quite big and compiling or interpreting on the user's computer may take a long time. Also, software providers may want to keep their source confidential. But if users get executables, then web site operators must somehow know what kind of computer each user has (e.g., PC or Mac) and deliver the right versions of programs. It would be cumbersome and expensive for web site operators to maintain different versions of a program for all different platforms. There is also a security risk: What if someone delivers a malicious program to your computer?

Bytecodes provide an intermediate step, a compromise between sending source code or executables to users (Figure 3-8). On one hand, the bytecodes' language is platform-independent, so the same version of bytecodes can serve different users. It is not readily readable by people, so it can protect confidentiality of the source code.

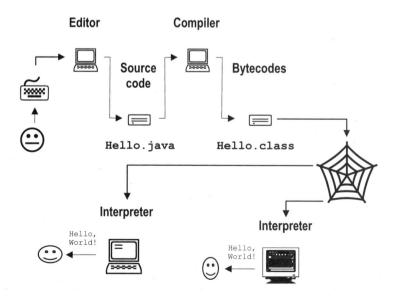

Figure 3-8. Java development and distribution through the Internet

On the other hand, bytecodes are much closer to the "average" machine language and they are easier and faster to interpret than "raw" Java source. Also, bytecodes interpreters built into browsers get a chance to screen programs for potential security violations (for example, block reading of and writing to the user's disks).

To speed up the loading of applets, a new software technology has emerged, called **JIT** (Just-In-Time) compilers. A JIT compiler combines the features of a compiler and an interpreter. While interpreting bytecodes it also compiles them into executable code. (To extend our music analogy, a JIT compiler works like a recording of a live concert.) This means an applet can be interpreted and start running as soon as it is downloaded from the Internet. On subsequent runs of the same applet, it can be loaded and run from its executable file without any delay for reinterpreting bytecodes.

Naturally, bytecodes do not have to travel through the Internet to reach the user: a Java program can be compiled and interpreted on the same computer. That is what we will do for testing Java applets and applications in our labs and exercises. We do not even have to use a browser to test applets: many development environments provide their own tools to run applets. The standard Java Software Development Kit (SDK) has a program, called *Applet Viewer*, that runs applets. *Applet Viewer* is a tiny HTML interpreter that understands the `<applet>` tag and skips all other HTML tags.

❖   ❖   ❖

Modern software development systems combine an editor, a compiler, and other tools into one ***Integrated Development Environment*** (***IDE***). The IDE has a convenient GUI — one mouse click on an icon will compile and run your program or applet. Modern programs may be rather complex, with dozens of different types of objects and functions involved. ***Structure analyzers*** and viewers, built into an IDE, create graphical views of source files, objects, their functions, and the dependencies between them. GUI ***visual prototyping and design*** tools help a programmer design and implement a graphical user interface.

Few programs are written right away without errors or, as programmers call them, ***bugs*** (Figure 3-9). Some errors violate the syntax rules of the language and are caught by the compiler or interpreter. Other bugs come from a programmer's logical errors or failures to handle certain data or conditions properly. It is not always easy to correct bugs just by looking at the source code or by testing the program on different data. To help with this, there are special ***debugger*** programs that allow the programmer to trace the execution of a program "in slow motion." A debugger can suspend a program at a specified break point or step through the program statements or CPU instructions one at a time. With the help of a debugger, the programmer can examine the sequence of operations and the contents of registers and memory locations while the program is running.

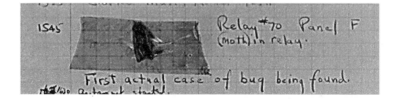

Figure 3-9. The term "bug" was popularized by Grace Hopper,[*hopper] a legendary computer pioneer, who was the first to come up with the idea of a compiler and who created COBOL. One of Hopper's favorite stories was the story of a moth that was found trapped between the points of a relay, which caused a malfunction of the Mark II Aiken Relay Calculator (Harvard University, 1945). Technicians removed the moth and affixed it to the log shown on the photograph.

3.4   Software Components and Packages

Writing programs from scratch may be fun, like growing your own tomatoes from seeds, but in the present environment few people can afford it. An amateur, faced with a programming task, asks: What is the most original (elegant, efficient, creative, interesting, etc.) way to write this code? A professional asks: What is the way to <u>not</u> write this code but use something already written by someone else? (A modern principle, but don't try it with your homework!) With billions of lines of code written, chances are someone has already implemented this or a similar task, and there is no point duplicating his or her efforts. Software is a unique product because all of its production cost goes into designing, coding and testing <u>one</u> copy; manufacturing multiple copies and reusing it is virtually free. So the real task is to find out what has been done, purchase the rights to it if it is not free, and reuse it.

There are many sources of reusable code. Extensive software packages come with your compiler. Other packages may be purchased from third-party software vendors who specialize in developing and marketing reusable software packages to developers. Still other packages may be available for free in the spirit of an "open systems" philosophy. And every experienced programmer has accumulated his or her own collection of reusable code.

Reusability of software is a two-sided concept. As a programmer, you want to be more efficient by reusing existing code. But you also want to write reusable code so that you yourself, your teammates, your enterprise, or the whole world can take advantage of it later. Creating reusable code is not automatic: your code must meet certain requirements to be truly reusable. Here is a partial list of these requirements:

- Your code must be divided into reasonably small parts or components (modules). Each component must have a clear and fairly general purpose. Components that implement more general functions must be separated from more specialized components.

- Your software components must be well documented, especially the interface part, which tells the user (in this case, another programmer) <u>what</u> this component does and how exactly to use it. A user does not necessarily always want to know <u>how</u> a particular component does what it does.

- The components must be robust. They must be thoroughly tested under <u>all</u> possible conditions under which the component can be used, and these conditions must be clearly documented. If a software module encounters conditions under which it is not supposed to work, it should handle such exceptions gracefully, giving its user a clue when and why it failed instead of just crashing the system.

- It should be possible to customize or extend your components without completely rewriting them.

Individual software components are usually combined into ***packages***. A package combines functions that deal with a particular set of structures or objects: a graphics package that deals with graphics capabilities and display; a text package that manipulates strings of text and text documents; a file package that helps to read and write data files; a math package that provides mathematical functions and algorithms; and so on. Java programmers can take advantage of dozens of standard packages that are already available for free; new packages are being developed all the time. At the same time, the plentitude of available packages and components puts an additional burden on the software engineer, who must be familiar with the standard packages and keep track of the new ones.

3.5 *Case Study:* Three Ways to Say Hello

A traditional way to start exploring a new software development environment is to write and get running a little program that just prints "Hello, World!" on the screen. In this case study we will do it using Java SDK and explore two other very simple console applications. Later, in Section 3.7, we will look at simple GUI applications and applets.

For now we will use the most basic set of tools, Java SDK (Software Development Kit) also known as JDK (Java Development Kit). SDK comes from Sun Microsystems, Inc., the makers and owners of Java. It includes a compiler, an interpreter, and the *Applet Viewer* program. SDK itself does not have an IDE (Integrated Development Environment) but many third-party vendors and various universities and other organizations offer IDEs for running Java. This book's companion web site has instructions for using several development environments and the **FAQs** (**Frequently Asked Questions**) about their installation and use. But here we want to get familiar with SDK itself, without any IDE.

Download (or obtain on a CD) Java SDK and install it on your computer. Read Sun's instructions for installing and configuring SDK under your operating system.

SDK tools are *UNIX*-style **command-line** tools, which means the user has to type in commands at the system prompt to run the compiler or the interpreter. For example, to compile a program `HelloWorld.java` under *Windows* you have to open the *MS DOS Prompt* window, move to the folder that contains your program (e.g., `Mywork`) using the `cd` (change directory) DOS command, and type:

```
C:\Mywork> javac HelloWorld.java
```

Our examples and commands in this section are for *Windows*. You need to set the path in the `autoexec.bat` file on your computer to include the folder that contains SDK tools. For example, if your SDK is installed in `C:\jdk1.3`, you need to add `C:\jdk1.3\bin` to the path. While you are at it, add the `doskey` command to `autoexec`, too. It allows you to repeat and edit previously typed commands using cursor keys — you will appreciate it as soon as you start typing long commands.

> **Create a work folder (e.g., `C:\Mywork`) where you will put the code you are working on. Back it up frequently to avoid losing your work and, when you finish a project, copy important source files from `Mywork` into more permanent folders.**

You can use any editor or word processor to enter Java source code. If you use a word processor, make sure you save Java source files as "Text Only." Word processors, such as *MS Word*, tend to attach the `.txt` extension to your file. The trick is to first choose `Save as type: Text-Only (*.txt)`, and only after that type in your file name with the correct extension (e.g., `HelloWorld.java`).

> **In Java, names of files are case sensitive.**

This is true even when you run programs in an *MS DOS Prompt* window. Make sure you render the upper and lower case correctly.

> **The name of the file that holds a Java class must be exactly the same as the name of that class (plus the extension `.java`).**

This rule prevents you from having two runnable versions of the same class in the same folder. Make sure you name the files correctly.

This case study involves three examples that are very simple console applications. Once you get the first program running, the rest should be easy.

1. Hello, World

In your editor, type in the following program (exactly as shown):

```
/*
 *  Hello World program
 */
public class HelloWorld
{
  public static void main(String[] args)
  {
    System.out.println("Hello, World!");
  }
}
```

> **The Java interpreter calls the `main` method in your class to start your program. Every application (but not applets) must have a `main` method, defined as in the above example:**
>
> **`public static void main(String[] args)`**

`System` is a class that is imported into all Java programs and provides a few system-level services. `System.out` is a data element in this class, an object that represents console screen output.

> **Examine what you have typed carefully and correct mistakes — this saves time.**

Save the text of your program in the file `HelloWorld.java`. Compile the program. The compiler executable file is called `javac.exe`, and the command to compile the `HellowWorld` file is

```
C:\Mywork> javac HelloWorld.java
```

If you have mistyped something in your source file you will get a list of errors reported by the compiler. This list may be quite long because a single typo can cause several errors. Verify your code against the one above, eliminate the typos, and recompile until there are no errors.

Type the `dir` (directory) command. You should see files called `HelloWorld.java` and `HelloWorld.class` in your folder. The latter is the bytecodes file created by the compiler.

Now run the Java interpreter to execute your program:

```
C:\Mywork> java HelloWorld
```

2. Greetings

A Java application can accept "command-line" arguments from the operating system. These are words (character strings separated by spaces) that the user can enter on the command line when he runs the program. For example, if the name of the program is *Greetings* and you want to pass two arguments to it, "Annabel" and "Lee", you can enter:

```
C:\Mywork> java Greetings Annabel Lee
```

If you are using an IDE, it usually has an option, a dialog box, where you can enter command-line arguments before you run the program.☆faqs

The following Java program expects two command-line arguments.

```java
/**
 *  This program expects two command-line arguments
 *  -- a person's first name and last name.
 *  For example:
 *  C> java Greetings Annabel Lee
 */
public class Greetings
{
  public static void main(String[] args)
  {
    String firstName = args[0];
    String lastName = args[1];
    System.out.println("Hello, " + firstName + " " + lastName);
    System.out.println("Congratulations on your second program!");
  }
}
```

Enter this program in your editor and save it in the file `Greetings.java`. Compile and run this program with two command-line arguments: your first and last name.

3. More Greetings

Unfortunately, Java does not have an easy way to read console (keyboard) input from the user. We have developed our own class, called `EasyReader`, that does that. This class is available on your student disk and on the book's companion web site. To use `EasyReader` all you have to do is copy it into the same folder as your program. Now we can try a program that will prompt you for your name and then display a message. You can modify the previous program and save it in the file `Greetings2.java`.

```
public class Greetings2
{
  public static void main(String[] args)
  {
    EasyReader console = new EasyReader();
    System.out.print("Enter your first name: ");
    String firstName = console.readLine();
    System.out.print("Enter your last name: ");
    String lastName = console.readLine();
    System.out.println("Hello, " + firstName + " " + lastName);
    System.out.println("Congratulations on your third program!");
  }
}
```

Our `Greetings2` class refers to `EasyReader`. How does `javac` know what `EasyReader` is? When we compile `Greetings2` —

```
C:\Mywork> javac Greetings2.java
```

— `javac` looks for the file `EasyReader.class` in the same folder. If it can't find `EasyReader.class`, `javac` then looks for `EasyReader.java` and, if found, compiles it first. If `javac` cannot find either `EasyReader.class` or `EasyReader.java` it reports errors for those lines that refer to `EasyReader`.

3.6   Object-Oriented Programming

In von Neumann computer architecture, a program is a sequence of instructions executed by the CPU. Blocks of instructions can be combined into ***procedures*** that perform a certain calculation or carry out a certain task and can be called from other places in the program. Procedures manipulate some data stored elsewhere in memory. This way of thinking is suggested by the hardware architecture, and naturally it prevailed in the early days of computing. In this "procedural" programming, a programmer has an accurate picture of the order in which instructions might be executed and procedures might be called. In high-level "procedural" languages, one statement replaces a group of instructions and groups of statements are combined into functions, but the nature of programming remains the same: the statements are executed and the functions are called in a precise order imposed by the programmer. These procedures and functions work on data structures defined separately.

In the early days, user interface took the form of a dialog: a program would show prompts asking for data input, and display the results at the end, similar to the *Greetings2* program in the previous section. This type of user interface is very orderly — it fits perfectly into the sequence of a procedural program. When the concept of graphical user interfaces (GUI) developed, it quickly became obvious that the procedural model of programming was not very convenient for implementing GUI applications. In a program with a GUI, a user sees several GUI components on the screen at once: menus, buttons, text entry fields, and so on. Any of the components can generate an event: things need to happen whenever a user chooses a menu option, clicks on a button, or enters text. A program must somehow handle these events in the order of their arrival. It is useful to think of GUI components as animated objects that can communicate with other objects. Each object has a memory of its own to represent its current state. A completely different programming model is needed to implement this metaphor. ***Object-oriented programming*** provides such a model.

The OOP concept became popular with the introduction of Smalltalk,[*smalltalk] the first general-purpose object-oriented programming language with built-in GUI development tools. Smalltalk was developed in the early 1970s by Alan Kay[*kay] and his group at the Xerox Palo Alto Research Center. Kay dreamed that when inexpensive personal computers became available, every user, actually every child, would be able to program them; OOP, he thought, would make this possible. As we know, it hasn't quite happened. Instead, OOP first generated a lot of interest in academia as a research subject and a teaching tool, and then was gradually embraced by the software industry, along with C++ and later Java, as the preferred method of designing and writing software.

One can think of an OOP application as a simulated world of active objects. Each object may have its own "memory," which contains other objects. Each object has a set of ***methods*** that can process messages of certain types, change the object's state (memory), send messages to other objects, and create new objects. An object belongs to a particular class, and the functionality of each object, its methods, and the structure of its memory, are determined by its class. A programmer creates an OOP application by defining classes.

Two principles are central to the OOP model: *event-driven* **programs and** *inheritance.*

In an OOP program many things can be happening at once, and outside events (e.g. the user clicks the mouse or types a key, the application's window is resized, etc.) can determine the order of program execution. An OOP program, of course, still runs on sequential von Neumann computers; but the software simulates parallelism and asynchronous handling of events.

An OOP program usually defines many different types of objects. However, one type of objects may be very similar to another type. For instance, objects of one type may need to have all the functionality of another type plus some additional features. It would be a waste to duplicate all the features of one class in another. The mechanism of ***inheritance*** lets a programmer state that one class of objects ***extends*** another class. The same class may be extended in several different ways, so one ***superclass*** may have several ***subclasses*** derived from it. An application ends up looking like a branching tree, a hierarchy of classes. Classes with more general features are closer to the top of the hierarchy, while classes with more specific functionality are closer to the bottom.

Object-oriented programming aims to answer the current needs in software development: lower software development and documentation costs, better coordinated team development, making and using reusable software components, more efficient implementation of multimedia and GUI applications, and so on. Java is a fully object-oriented language that supports inheritance and the event-driven model. It includes standard packages for graphics, GUI, multimedia, events handling, and other essential software development tools.

3.7   *Case Study:* More Ways to Say Hello

In Section 3.5 we have learned how to run very simple console applications. These types of programs, however, are not what makes Java great: they can be easily written in other programming languages. Java's built-in support for GUI and graphics and its support for object-oriented programming are what distinguishes it from other languages. In this section we will consider four more examples: two applications, one with a simple GUI object, another with graphics, and two applets, one with graphics and one with animation. Of course at this stage you won't be able to understand all the code in them — we have the whole book ahead of us, and this is just a preview of things to come! Here you will only get a general idea of what is involved and see how the executable programs work.

1. A GUI application

In this program, HelloGui.java, we create a standard window on the screen and place a "Hello, World!" message on it. Our class <u>extends</u> the JFrame library class, which is part of Java's Swing package. Swing is a newer Java package for implementing GUI. It was introduced in the Java 2 release that we are using. We are lucky we can reuse JFrame's code: it would be a major, major job to write a class like this from scratch. We would have to show the title bar and the border of the window and support resizing of the window and other standard functions. JFrame takes care of all of this. All we have left to do is add a label to the window's ***content pane*** — the area where you can paint graphics and place GUI components.

```java
import java.awt.*;
import javax.swing.*;

public class HelloGui extends JFrame
{
  public HelloGui()    // Constructor
  {
    super("Hello World with GUI");    // Set the title
    Container c = getContentPane();
    c.setBackground(Color.white);
    c.setLayout(new FlowLayout());
    c.add(new JLabel("Hello, World!"));
  }

  public static void main(String[] args)
  {
    HelloGui window = new HelloGui();
    window.addWindowListener(new ExitButtonListener());
    window.setSize(300, 100);
    window.show();
  }
}
```

Figure 3-10. `Ch03\HelloGui\HelloGui.java` 💾

Our HelloGui class is shown in Figure 3-10. In this program, the main method creates one new object, which we called window. The type of this object is described as HelloGui, that is, window belongs to the HelloGui class. This program uses only one object of this class. main then sets window's size (in pixels) and shows it on the screen. The class has a ***constructor***: that is, a special method for constructing objects of this class. Constructors always have the same name as the class. Here the constructor calls the superclass's constructor to set the text displayed in the window's title bar and adds a label object to the window's content pane.

The code in Figure 3-10 is a little cryptic, but still we can see roughly what's going on. The most cryptic part is the

```
window.addWindowListener(new ExitButtonListener());
```

statement. The problem is that the JFrame class does not automatically enable the exit button that you normally use to close a window. With this button disabled it is not possible to exit your application gracefully. We have to supply the code to enable the exit button ourselves. For that purpose we have written another class, called ExitButtonListener. It uses Java's event model to call the System.exit method when the exit button is clicked. We will use this class whenever we have a GUI application. This class is quite short — only a few lines. (You can examine it on your student disk in the Ch03\HelloGui folder if you are curious what it looks like.)

When we compile HelloGui —

```
C:\Mywork> javac HelloGui.java
```

— the file ExitButtonListener.java will be automatically compiled first (if it has not been compiled earlier).

2. Hello, Graphics

We will now change our program a little to paint some graphics on the window instead of a text label. The new class, HelloGraphics, is shown in Figure 3-11. Each window object has a paint method that generates all the graphics contents for the window. paint is called automatically by the application's event manager whenever the window is opened, resized, or repainted. These events are reported to the application by the operating system. (An application can also trigger its own paint method at any point by calling the window's repaint method.)

By default, paint only paints the background of the content pane. Our class redefines paint to add a blue message inside a red box. paint receives an object of the type Graphics, traditionally called g, that represents the window's graphics context (its position, size, etc.). The graphics coordinates are in pixels and have the origin at the upper left corner of the window (the *y*-axis points down).

```
import java.awt.*;
import javax.swing.*;

public class HelloGraphics extends JFrame
{
  public HelloGraphics()  // Constructor
  {
    super("Hello World with Graphics");
    Container c = getContentPane();
    c.setBackground(Color.white);
  }

  public void paint(Graphics g)
  {
    super.paint(g);     // Call JFrame's paint method
                        //  to paint the background
    g.setColor(Color.red);
    g.drawRect(75, 25, 150, 50);  // draw a rectangle 150 by 50
    g.setColor(Color.blue);
    g.drawString("Hello, World!", 120, 50);
  }

  public static void main(String[] args)
  {
    HelloGraphics w = new HelloGraphics();
    w.addWindowListener(new ExitButtonListener());
    w.setSize(300, 100);
    w.show();
  }
}
```

Figure 3-11. `Ch03\HelloGui\HelloGraphics.java` 💾

3. Hello, Applet

The difference between an applet and a GUI application is really minor. Instead of extending `JFrame`, your applet's class extends `JApplet`, a Swing library class that represents applet objects. An applet does not need `main` because the browser (or *Applet Viewer*) automatically constructs the applet object. Instead of a constructor, your applet class uses the `init` method to initialize your applet. Figure 3-12 shows the `HelloApplet` class adapted from the `HelloGraphics` class.

As you can see, the code has become a little shorter. But we need an HTML file to run this applet. We will use a very simple one (Figure 3-13). Some of the information — the size of the window — has shifted from Java code into the HTML file. The title bar is no longer used because an applet does not run in a separate window — it is embedded into a browser's (or *Applet Viewer*'s) window. An applet does not have an exit button either (the browser's or *Applet Viewer*'s window has one).

Let us test our applet with SDK's *Applet Viewer* first:

```
C:\Mywork> javac HelloApplet.java
C:\Mywork> appletviewer TestApplet.html
```

Now try to open `TestApplet.html` in your browser. But first make sure your browser is Java-enabled and that you are running a newer release or have installed a special plug-in that supports Java 2 and Swing. ☆java2

```
import java.awt.*;
import javax.swing.*;

public class HelloApplet extends JApplet
{
  public void init()
  {
    Container c = getContentPane();
    c.setBackground(Color.white);
  }

  public void paint(Graphics g)
  {
    super.paint(g);      // Call JApplet's paint method
                         //   to paint the background
    g.setColor(Color.red);
    g.drawRect(75, 25, 150, 50);   // draw a rectangle 150 by 50
    g.setColor(Color.blue);
    g.drawString("Hello, World!", 120, 50);
  }
}
```

Figure 3-12. Ch03\HelloGui\HelloApplet.java 💾

```
<html>
<head>
<title>My First Java Applet</title>
</head>
<body>
<applet code="HelloApplet.class" width="300" height="100"
   alt="Java class failed">
Java is disabled
</applet>
</body>
</html>
```

Figure 3-13. Ch03\HelloGui\TestApplet.html 🖫

4. Hello, Action

And now, just for fun, let's put some action into our applet (Figure 3-14). Compile the `Banner` class and test it in the *Applet Viewer* or in your browser.

Look at the code for `Banner.java`. The `init` method in this applet creates a `Timer` object called `clock` and starts the timer. The timer is programmed to fire every 30 milliseconds. Whenever a timer fires, it generates an event that is captured in the `actionPerformed` method. This method adjusts the position of the message and repaints the screen. Try to resize the *Applet Viewer* window while this applet is running and see how the position of the "banner" changes. It is able to adjust the position properly because `actionPerformed` obtains the current dimensions of the content pane by calling its `getWidth` and `getHeight` methods each time the timer fires.

You might notice that unfortunately the animation effect in this applet is not very smooth: the screen flickers whenever the message moves. One of the advantages of Swing is that it can help deal with this problem. We will learn how to do it in later chapters.

```java
import java.awt.*;
import java.awt.event.*;
import javax.swing.*;

public class Banner extends JApplet
  implements ActionListener
{
  private int xPos, yPos;

  /**
   *  Called automatically when the applet is initialized
   */
  public void init()
  {
    Container c = getContentPane();
    c.setBackground(Color.white);
    xPos = c.getWidth();
    yPos = c.getHeight() / 2;
    Timer clock = new Timer(30, this);  // Fires every 30 milliseconds
    clock.start();
  }

  /**
   *  Called automatically after a repaint request
   */
  public void paint(Graphics g)
  {
    super.paint(g);
    g.drawString("Hello, World!", xPos, yPos);
  }

  /**
   *  Called automatically when the timer fires
   */
  public void actionPerformed(ActionEvent e)
  {
    Container c = getContentPane();
    xPos--;
    if (xPos < -100)
    {
      xPos = c.getWidth();
    }
    yPos = c.getHeight() / 2;
    repaint();
  }
}
```

Figure 3-14. Ch03\HelloGui\Banner.java 💾

3.8   Summary

An algorithm is an abstract and formal step-by-step recipe that tells how to perform a certain task or solve a certain problem on a computer. Flowcharts and pseudocode are two popular methods for describing algorithms. The same algorithm can be implemented in many different programming languages. A meaningful algorithm usually folds the task into one or several fragments that can be repeated multiple times with different values of variables. These repetitions are called iterations. Another method of reducing large tasks to small programs is recursion. Recursion describes a task in terms of performing a similar smaller task.

In the modern development environment, programmers usually write programs in one of the high-level programming languages such as C++ or Java. A program written in a high-level language obeys the very precise syntax rules of that language and must also follow stylistic conventions established among professionals. A software program called the compiler translates the source code for a program from the high-level language into machine code for a particular CPU. A compiler creates object modules that are eventually linked into an executable program. Instead of compiling, a program can be interpreted by a software tool called an interpreter. An interpreter does not generate an executable program but instead executes the appropriate CPU instructions immediately.

Java takes a mixed compiler-interpreter approach: the source is compiled into code (called bytecodes) for a non-existent "virtual machine." Bytecodes are still independent of a particular CPU, but are much closer to a machine language and are easier to interpret than "raw" Java programs. A Java interpreter installed on a specific computer then converts the bytecodes into instructions for that specific CPU.

An IDE (integrated development environment) combines many tools, including an editor, a compiler and a debugger, into a one package with a convenient GUI.

The software development profession has evolved from an individual artisan craft into a highly structured engineering discipline with its own methodology, professional tools, and conventions. Modern applications are built out of standard reusable components from available packages. Programmers strive to produce and document new reusable components that meet the reliability, performance, and style requirements of their organization.

One can think of an OOP application as a simulated world of active objects. Each object has a set of methods that can process messages of certain types, send messages to other objects, and create new objects. A programmer creates an OOP application by defining classes of objects. Object-oriented programming is widely believed to lower software development costs, help coordinate team projects, and facilitate software reuse.

Exercises

Sections 3.1-3.2

1. Name several important steps in a fairly large software project.

2. Draw a flowchart and write pseudocode for an iterative algorithm that calculates $1 + \dfrac{1}{2^2} + \dfrac{1}{3^2} + ... + \dfrac{1}{n^2}$ for any given n. (This sum converges to $\dfrac{\pi^2}{6}$ as n increases.) ✓

3.■ Draw a flowchart and write pseudocode for an iterative algorithm that calculates $1 - \dfrac{1}{2} + \dfrac{1}{3} - ... + (or\ -) \dfrac{1}{n}$ for any given n. $\dfrac{1}{k}$ is added to the sum if k is odd and subtracted from the sum if k is even. ⸮ Hint: multiply $\dfrac{1}{k}$ by a factor that is equal to 1 or -1 before adding it to the sum. Flip the sign of the factor on each iteration. (This sum converges to the natural logarithm of 2.) ⸮

4.■ Design an iterative algorithm that, given two positive integers m and n, calculates the integer quotient and the remainder when m is divided by n. Your algorithm can use only +, −, and comparison operations for integers. Show your algorithm in pseudocode or draw a flowchart. ✓

5.■ Recall that $1 + 3 + ... + (2p - 1) = p^2$ for any integer $p \geq 1$. Using this property, come up with a simple iterative algorithm that finds out whether a given number is a perfect square. Your algorithm can compare numbers and use addition but no other arithmetic operations. Show your algorithm in pseudocode or draw a flowchart.

6.■ In a bag of n coins, one is radioactive. In one trial we are allowed to measure radioactivity of any pile of coins. Describe an efficient recursive algorithm for finding the radioactive coin in the bag. How many trials are needed to find the radioactive coin in a bag of 1000 coins using your algorithm? ✓

Sections 3.3-3.4

7. Which of the following are the advantages of using a high-level programming language, as opposed to a machine language? Mark true or false:

    (a) It is easier to write programs. _____
    (b) It is easier to read and understand programs. _____
    (c) Programs run more efficiently. _____ ✓
    (d) Programs can be ported more easily from one hardware platform to another. _____

8. Name four commonly used programming languages besides Java.

9. Mark true or false and explain:

    (a) The operating system compiles source files into executable programs. _____

    (b) Each modern computer system is equipped with a compiler. _____ ✓

    (c) The compiler analyzes the source code and translates it into machine language by generating appropriate CPU instructions. _____

10. Which program helps programmers create and modify source code?

    A. Editor
    B. Compiler
    C. Linker
    D. Interpreter
    E. None of the above

11. What is a debugger used for? ✓

    A. Removing comments from the source code
    B. Running and tracing programs in a controlled way
    C. Running diagnostics of hardware components
    D. Removing syntax errors from C++ programs
    E. Removing dust from the computer screen

12. True or false: a modern IDE combines an editor, compiler, debugger, and other software development tools with GUI. _____

13. Describe the differences between a compiler, a JIT compiler, and an interpreter.

Section 3.5

14. (a) Replace the forward slash in the first line of the HelloWorld program (Ch03\Hello\HelloWorld.java ▦) with a backslash. Compile your program and observe the result.

(b) Remove the first three lines altogether, compile and run your program. What is the purpose of the /* and */ markers in Java programs?

15. ▪ The Java program below expects one command-line argument: a positive integer. It converts the entered string into an integer and stores it in a variable *n* of the int type. The program then calculates

$$1 + \frac{1}{2^2} + \frac{1}{3^2} + \dots + \frac{1}{n^2},$$ estimates π from it (as explained in Exercise 2 above),

and displays the result.

```java
public class EstimatePi
{
  public static void main(String[] args)
  {
    int n = Integer.parseInt(args[0]);
    int k;
    double sum = 0, sq, pi;

    for (k = 1; k <= n; k++)
    {
      sq = k * k;
      sum += 1 / sq;
    }
    pi = Math.sqrt(6 * sum);
    System.out.println("Pi estimate for n = " +
                       n + " is " + pi);

  }
}
```

Enter this program and save it in the EstimatePi.java file. Run this program with different command-line arguments (e.g., 100, 1000) and compare the result with the actual value of π.

16. Write, compile, and run a short Java program *HelloNTimes* that accepts two command-line arguments, a name and an integer *n*, and displays the line "`Hello, <name>!`" *n* times. For example,

```
C:\Mywork> java HelloNTimes Sunshine 3
```

displays

```
Hello, Sunshine!
Hello, Sunshine!
Hello, Sunshine!
```

Hint: using the cut and paste features in your program editor, combine some code from the program `Greetings` (from Section 3.5) with some code from `EstimatePi` in Question 15. ✓

17. (a) Write a program that prompts the user to enter an integer and displays the entered value times two. For example:

```
C:\Mywork> java DoubleInput
Enter an integer: 5
2 * 5 = 10
```

The `EasyReader` class has a method `readInt` that reads an integer from the console. For example:

```
EasyReader console = new EasyReader();
...
int n = console.readInt();
```

Use

```
System.out.println("2 * " + n + " = " + (n + n));
```

to display the result.

(b) Remove the parentheses around `n + n` and test the program again. How does the + operator work for text strings and for numbers?

Sections 3.6-3.8

18.   Name the two concepts that are central to object-oriented programming.

19.■   Modify *HelloApplet* (`Ch03\HelloGui\HelloApplet.java` 🖫) to show a white message on a blue background. ⸔ Hint: there is a graphics method `fillRect` that is similar to `drawRect`, but it draws a "solid" rectangle, filled with color, not just an outline. ⸕ ✓

20.◆   Modify the *Banner* applet (`Ch03\HelloGui\Banner.java` 🖫) to show a solid black box moving from right to left across the applet's window.

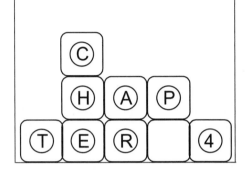

Java Classes, Objects, and Events: A Preview

4.1   Prologue

The following preview has been approved for all audiences!

In this chapter we will take a simple applet and discuss in general terms how it is put together and how it works, without going too deeply into the details of its code. Our goal is to get familiar with classes, objects, and their methods, and to get a glimpse of the way events are handled in Java programs. We will focus on the overall structure, leaving the details for later. This is only a preview — you don't really want to know the whole story right away, do you?! For now, be prepared to face some Java code that you might not be able to understand quite yet; in fact, it might look like a foreign language! As you work through this book and master that language, the details of Java syntax, control statements, and Swing will become clear to you. Meanwhile, just focus on the elements of code that we bring to your attention.

4.2   *Case Study:* the *Ramblecs* Applet

Figure 4-1 shows a run of the *Ramblecs* applet. Initially the applet appears as an empty window with a "Go" button at the bottom. When the user clicks on "Go," a cube with a letter on it appears at the top, falls down, and lands at the bottom of the window. Each time the user presses "Go," a cube with a new random letter falls down.

This may not seem like a very useful program. In fact it's only the first sketch for a computer game in which a player builds words from falling letter cubes. We have named it *Ramblecs*. In the final version of the game, a random letter is painted on each of the six faces of a cube. The player can rotate the cube and shift it to the left and right while it is falling. The landed cubes fill a "letter grid" and the objective is to make as many words as possible. Who knows: by the end of this book we might end up with a complete game!

The source code for the *Ramblecs* prototype consists of three files: `Ramblecs.java`, `LetterPanel.java`, and `FallingCube.java`. Copy these files from the

`Ch04\Ramblecs` ⊟ folder on your student disk into your work folder. Also copy `TestRamblecs.html`, an HTML file that runs this applet.

Compile the three source files using SDK's `javac` and run the applet in *Applet Viewer*, or set up and run a project in your favorite IDE. There are instructions*ide* on the book's companion web site for setting up projects in several development environments.

If you are using SDK, the following commands will compile all three classes and run *Ramblecs* in the *Applet Viewer*:

```
C:\Mywork> javac Ramblecs.java LetterPanel.java FallingCube.java
C:\Mywork> appletviewer TestRamblecs.html
```

> **If you are trying to run this applet in a browser, make sure you have a recent version of the browser or a plug-in that supports Java 2.***java2*

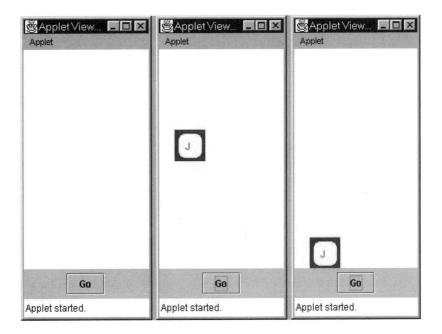

Figure 4-1. A first prototype for the *Ramblecs* applet

4.3   Classes and Objects

In the OOP model, a running program maintains a world of interacting objects. To write such a program you need to describe different types of objects: what they can do, how they are created, and how they interact with other objects. The definition of a particular type of objects is called a ***class***.

> **Any Java program consists of** *classes*. **A class is called a "class" because it describes a** *class of objects*, **their structure and behavior.**

So, what objects do we use in our *Ramblecs* applet? If you guessed the "Go" button and the falling cube, you are right — these two are the most obvious ones. The responsibility of the button is to trigger the cube's fall. The responsibility of the cube is... well, to fall. In the spirit of object self-sufficiency in OOP, it is also the cube's responsibility to draw itself at its current position — it should "know" how to do that.

Does our program create only one falling cube object or different cubes for each fall? This is a very good question. There is a lot of flexibility in how an OOP application is designed. Good design decisions may simplify the final code or make the program more efficient. In our *Ramblecs* applet either approach is possible: we could create a different cube object for each fall or we could use only one cube and simply reset its position back to the top and paint a new letter on it each time the "Go" button is pressed. In this case it's a little easier to use one cube object for all the "falls."

As far as the programmer is concerned, there is a big difference between the button object and the cube object. A button is a standard type of object that appears in many programs. Java's Swing package has a ***library class***, called `JButton`, that describes buttons. So you don't have to write your own class — you can just use the library class. You can customize the button a little when your program creates it by specifying what text (or icon — a little picture) is displayed on the button. We will see shortly (in Section 4.7) how you can tell your program what to do when the button is clicked. Java ***packages*** (also called ***class libraries***) contain hundreds of classes of all kinds, already written and tested: classes for graphics, images, math functions, GUI components, event handling, communications, multimedia, and so on.

The cube object is specific to our applet, so we have written a class that describes this type of object. We have named the class `FallingCube` and put its source code in the file `FallingCube.java`.

Are there any other objects in *Ramblecs* that you can think of? Well, the cube has to be painted on something: some kind of "canvas" or "panel." In our program we have named this object `whiteboard`. This object is less obvious. Not all the objects in a program need to be visible or touchable — some of them may be rather abstract. `whiteboard` is actually needed for two reasons. One is a general software design consideration; the other is a rather technical reason.

The design consideration is that we can assign to `whiteboard` the responsibility to create and control the falling cube.

> **In a well-designed OOP program, each object is responsible for its own clearly defined set of tasks. Objects must be tractable and not too complicated.**

It would be possible to make the falling cube control its own motion, but then the `FallingCube` class would become rather complex, and there would be too much interaction between different objects. It is a nice division of labor if `whiteboard` creates and controls the cube (Figure 4-2).

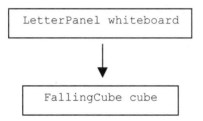

Figure 4-2. The `whiteboard` and the `cube` objects in *Ramblecs*

The technical reason for the `whiteboard` object is smoother animation. If you ran the *Banner* applet in the previous chapter (Section 3.7) you probably noticed some flicker when the message moved across the screen. That happened because each movement meant the whole window had to be repainted. One of the new features introduced in Swing is the ability to repaint not the whole applet window but individual components. `whiteboard` is the component that is repainted when the cube moves. `whiteboard` creates a `Timer` object that fires "pulses" with a specified frequency. Whenever a pulse is fired, `whiteboard` repaints its own background, then tells the cube to move and to draw itself in its new position. `Timer` is another example of a Java library class. By the way, `whiteboard` is not completely invisible: its background is set to white, but you could see it by setting it to some other color.

We have written a class that defines the type of objects to which `whiteboard` belongs. We have called this class `LetterPanel` and put its source code in the file `LetterPanel.java`. In OOP terminology, we say that `whiteboard` is an ***instance*** of the class `LetterPanel`. Luckily, we didn't have to write this class from scratch. Recall that the inheritance feature of OOP languages allows us to create a new class by extending an existing class. Swing has a class `JPanel` that defines "panels" — empty GUI components that are convenient for painting and for placing other GUI components on them. Our `LetterPanel` class extends `JPanel`:

```
public class LetterPanel extends JPanel
    <... etc. >
```

To complete the applet we need one more class that represents one object, the applet itself! If you were wondering who creates and displays `whiteboard` and the "Go" button, this is the answer. We have called this class `Ramblecs`, so its source file is `Ramblecs.java`. The only object of this class is created outside of our program, by the *Applet Viewer* or a browser. So we don't get a chance to name it and we will refer to this object simply as our "applet."

Our `Ramblecs` class extends the library class `JApplet` that implements an "empty" applet. We customize it by adding the features we need. A class derived from `JApplet` has one designated method, `init`, that is called automatically when the applet is started. The code in the `init` method creates a `JButton` object `go` and a `LetterPanel` object `whiteboard` and adds them to the applet's ***content pane*** — the visible area in the *Applet Viewer*'s (or a browser's) window that can hold other objects.

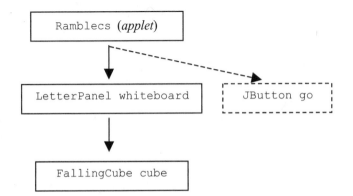

Figure 4-3. Objects and classes in the *Ramblecs* applet

Figure 4-3 shows how the three objects from three different classes that we have defined for the *Ramblecs* applet interact with each other. An arrow points from an object to another object that the first one creates or controls. Note that the `Ramblecs` class knows nothing about the `FallingCube` class, which is good: the less different classes know about each other the better. We have also included the `go` button in the picture, even though it belongs to a library class and such common objects are usually taken for granted.

Figure 4-4 shows our code for the `Ramblecs` class. You don't have to understand all the details at this point, but you can read it slowly and get a general idea of what's going on.

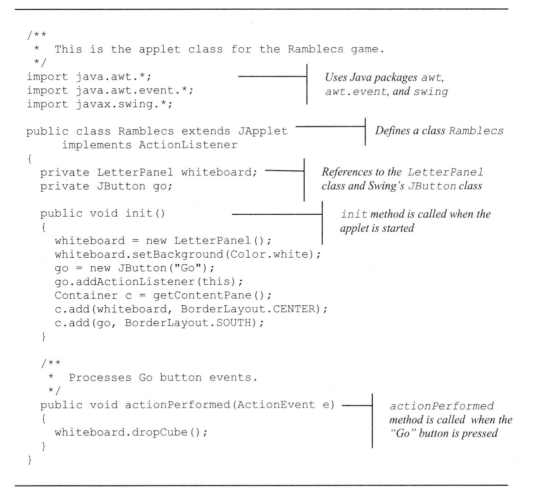

```
/**
 *  This is the applet class for the Ramblecs game.
 */
import java.awt.*;                          Uses Java packages awt,
import java.awt.event.*;                    awt.event, and swing
import javax.swing.*;

public class Ramblecs extends JApplet        Defines a class Ramblecs
     implements ActionListener
{
  private LetterPanel whiteboard;          References to the LetterPanel
  private JButton go;                      class and Swing's JButton class

  public void init()                       init method is called when the
  {                                        applet is started
    whiteboard = new LetterPanel();
    whiteboard.setBackground(Color.white);
    go = new JButton("Go");
    go.addActionListener(this);
    Container c = getContentPane();
    c.add(whiteboard, BorderLayout.CENTER);
    c.add(go, BorderLayout.SOUTH);
  }

  /**
   *  Processes Go button events.
   */
  public void actionPerformed(ActionEvent e)   actionPerformed
  {                                            method is called when the
    whiteboard.dropCube();                     "Go" button is pressed
  }
}
```

Figure 4-4. `Ch04\Ramblecs\Ramblecs.java`

4.4   Classes and Source Files

In Java each class is defined in a separate source file. The name of the source file must be exactly the same as the name of the class (including upper- and lowercase letters) with the extension `.java`.

There are exceptions to the one-class-per-file rule, but we will try to avoid them in this book.

For example, we have defined three classes for the *Ramblecs* applet — `Ramblecs`, `LetterPanel`, and `FallingCube` — and so its source code consists of three files: `Ramblecs.java`, `LetterPanel.java`, and `FallingCube.java`.

The location of Java files on your disk is very important: the Java compiler automatically tries to find source files for classes based on their names.

As you know, all files on your disk are arranged into a branching structure of *directories* and *subdirectories*. GUI operating systems, such as *Windows*, show directories as *folders*. A *directory* and a *folder* are basically the same thing. A *subdirectory* is a folder within a folder. A GUI operating system usually provides a tool for viewing the contents of folders, moving and copying files between folders, deleting files and folders, and so on. In *Windows*, for example, you may find it convenient to use *Windows Explorer* for these tasks.

The Java files for all the classes you create for a project should be located in the same folder.

It is easier to place the HTML file that runs the applet into the same folder, too (unless you want to include the `codebase=...` attribute in the `<applet>` tag; see Section 2.9). It is a good idea to keep all the files supplied to you on the student disk intact. That is why we asked you to make a temporary folder (e.g. `C:\Mywork`) and copy the four *Ramblecs* files there.

Java is case-sensitive: in a Java program, all words or names that differ in the upper or lower case even by one letter will be treated as different words.

It is not required by the Java syntax, but the convention is that names of all classes start with a capital letter (and names of objects start with a lowercase letter).

> **Java assumes that file names in your operating system are case-sensitive, too!**

The latter assumption is somewhat unusual: it is not used in other programming languages you might be familiar with. File names are indeed case-sensitive in *UNIX* and *Linux*. In *Windows* you are not allowed to have two files that differ only in the upper or lower case of letters. Still, if you name the source file for the `Ramblecs` class `ramblecs.java`, with a lowercase "r," and try to compile it —

```
C:\MyWork> javac ramblecs.java
```

— you will get this puzzling error message:

```
ramblecs.java:8: class Ramblecs is public, should be declared in a file
named Ramblecs.java
public class Ramblecs extends JApplet
              ^
1 error
```

At first, Java will certainly test your patience and your attention to detail.

If your source file has no syntax errors, the compiler will create a bytecodes file `Ramblecs.class` in the same folder as `Ramblecs.java`.

The code for the `Ramblecs` class refers to the `LetterPanel` class, so the compiler will try to find its definition in the same folder. First it will look for bytecodes, `LetterPanel.class`. If it cannot find `LetterPanel.class`, the compiler will look for the source file, `LetterPanel.java`, and if found, will try to compile it. If the compiler fails to find either `LetterPanel.class` or `LetterPanel.java` it will report an error:

```
C:\Mywork\> javac Ramblecs.java
Ramblecs.java:11: Class LetterPanel not found.
   private LetterPanel whiteboard;
```

"11" in `Ramblecs.java:11` refers to the line number where `LetterPanel` is mentioned.

> **A missing or misnamed file in a folder may be reported as an error when you compile another file.**

As you can see, there is a very close connection in Java between the names of classes and the names and locations of the files that define them. If you have programmed in C or C++, you will find this Java arrangement quite different. In C++, for example, one file can hold one or several classes; it can have any name you want and can reside in any folder. Working in Java forces you to keep track of precisely what your files are called and where they are located. A Java IDE can automate this process for you to some extent. Still, a Java programmer must know how to go into the folders (e.g., with *Windows Explorer*), examine their contents, copy and move files, and purge or rename unneeded files.

The `LetterPanel` class in turn refers to the `FallingCube` class, so the compiler will try to find it, too, and will compile `FallingCube.java` if necessary. So potentially you could compile all three classes with one command:

```
C:\Mywork\> javac Ramblecs.java
```

However, if you change `LetterPanel`'s or `FallingCube`'s source code, `javac` will not know about it and will not recompile the changed class when you recompile `Ramblecs.java`. It may be safer to recompile all the classes in the project explicitly. You can do it in three separate commands or in one command:

```
C:\Mywork> javac Ramblecs.java LetterPanel.java FallingCube.java
```

In an IDE, the equivalent of this recompilation would be to click on the "Build all" menu command to recompile all files in the project. Otherwise the IDE checks dates and times on your source and compiled files and recompiles only those files whose source has changed since the last compilation.

4.5   Imported Classes and Packages

As we have seen, using library classes from Java packages is essential to programming in Java. You can use objects of predefined types in your programs and you can extend library classes through inheritance, by ***deriving*** your class from one of the library classes.

> A *derived* **class (also called a** *subclass***) extends a** *base* **class (also called a** *superclass***).**

If you do not specify a base class, your class is automatically derived from a catch-all Java class called `Object`, which adds a few standard features to your class.

In the *Ramblecs* applet the `Ramblecs` class is derived from `JApplet`:

```
public class Ramblecs extends JApplet
    implements ActionListener
```

This class definition also says that `Ramblecs` ***implements*** the `ActionListener` ***interface***.

An *interface* **in Java is a formal specification, a list of specific methods.**

An interface only lists the methods and does not include any code for them. If a class implements an interface, that means it supplies all the methods required by that interface. Java packages include the definitions of many standard interfaces. The `ActionListener` interface requires only one method, `actionPerformed`.

In order to use Java library classes and interfaces in your program, you must first tell the compiler where to find them. This is done using the `import` statement.

The `Ramblecs` class, for example, imports three standard Java packages:

```
import java.awt.*;
import java.awt.event.*;
import javax.swing.*;
```

The first import is the ***awt*** (*Abstract <u>W</u>indowing <u>T</u>oolkit*) package, the second is the event-handling package, and the third is Swing.

Rather than importing a package a programmer can import individual classes from it. Import statements actually tell the compiler the full names of library classes you want to use. For example, `javax.swing.JButton` is the full name for `JButton`. In the technical lingo it is called the ***fully-qualified name***. As you know, in Java class names are associated with file names. The fully-qualified class name implies the location of the class file, its pathname. For example, `javax.swing.JButton` basically means "JButton.class is located in the `javax/swing` directory." (These paths are relative to the directory in which your Java library packages are installed.) By convention, the `java` directory contains all standard Java packages, and the `javax` directory contains newer Java extensions, such as Swing. In reality these folders and their contents are packed in `.jar` ("Java archive") files, so you won't actually find them on your disk. But "logically" they are there, and they may actually be present in some installations.

If you use the fully-qualified class's name everywhere in your program, then you don't need to import the class. The `import` statement

```
import javax.swing.JButton;
```

at the top of the program allows you to refer to `JButton` by its familiar "first" name. If '`*`' — the wildcard name — is used instead of a specific name, then you can use short names for all the classes in the package that is imported. For example,

```
import javax.swing.*;
```

tells the compiler fully-qualified names for all Swing classes and where to look for them. It is usually easier to import the whole package because you don't have to worry about specific library classes used in your code, especially if you keep changing your code.

> **One package, `java.lang`, is imported into all Java source files automatically. It defines classes that are fundamental to the language: `Object`, `String`, `Math`, `System` and several other classes.**

4.6 Fields, Constructors, and Methods

When you define a class of objects, you have to describe three things: the objects' structure, a way (or several different ways) of creating an object, and what these objects can do. The object's structure is defined by the data elements of the class, called *fields*. Fields may hold numbers, characters, strings of text, or other objects. Fields act as the "personal memory" of an object and the particular values stored in them determine the object's current state. Each object (instance of a class) has the same fields, but there may be different values stored in those fields.

A class's **constructors** define different ways of creating an object. The primary purpose of a constructor is to initialize the object's fields. A constructor may use a number of parameters that help to initialize the object with specified values. Different constructors use different numbers or types of parameters.

The behavior of an object, what the object can do, is defined by its **methods** — functions that perform certain tasks. "Method" is a term from object-oriented programming. It represents what an object of a particular type can do in response to a particular call or message.

As an example, let us consider the `FallingCube` class from the *Ramblecs* applet (Figure 4-5). The fields are usually declared at the top of a class, before all the other code. It is convenient to make a cube "remember" its own coordinates, `cubeX`, `cubeY`. If we had several cubes active in the program, each could remember its own coordinates. These values are represented by integers, Java's `int` type:

```
private int cubeX, cubeY;       // Cube coordinates (upper left corner)
```

A cube also remembers the letter written on it. (In our preliminary prototype, it's just one letter.) This is represented by a character, Java's `char` type:

```
private char randomLetter;      // Cube letter
```

`int`, `char`, and other ***primitive data types*** are discussed in Chapter 6.

```
/**
 *  Implements a falling letter cube for the Ramblecs game
 */
import java.awt.*;
                                           Fields
public class FallingCube
{
    private final int xLeft;        // Left margin for cubes
    private final int cubeSize;
    private int cubeX, cubeY;       // Cube coordinates (upper left corner)
    private int yStep;              // Distance (in pixels) to move down
                                    //   in one timer cycle
    private static final String letters = "ABCDEFGHIJKLMNOPQRSTUVWXYZ";
    private char randomLetter;      // Cube letter

    public FallingCube(int size)                  Constructor
    {
      cubeSize = size;
      xLeft = cubeSize / 2;
      yStep = cubeSize / 8;
      cubeX = -cubeSize;            // off the board --
      cubeY = -cubeSize;            //    not displayed
    }

    public void start()                             Method
    {
      int i = (int)(Math.random() * letters.length());
      randomLetter = letters.charAt(i);
      cubeX = 0;
      cubeY = -cubeSize;             // above the board for smooth entry
    }
```

Figure 4-5 `FallingCube.java` ***Continued*** ➡

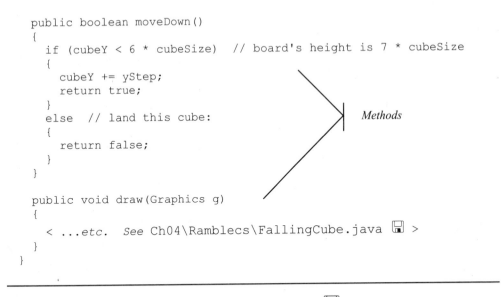

```
public boolean moveDown()
{
  if (cubeY < 6 * cubeSize)   // board's height is 7 * cubeSize
  {
    cubeY += yStep;
    return true;
  }
  else  // land this cube:
  {
    return false;
  }
}

public void draw(Graphics g)
{
  < ...etc.  See Ch04\Ramblecs\FallingCube.java 🖫 >
}
}
```

Methods

Figure 4-5. Ch04\Ramblecs\FallingCube.java 🖫

We have said that each object (instance of a class) has its own set of fields, but there is an exception: *static* fields are shared by all instances of the class. For example,

```
private static final String letters = "ABCDEFGHIJKLMNOPQRSTUVWXYZ";
```

declares a static field — a string of characters from which a random letter is chosen. (We will discuss strings in detail in Chapter 9.) It is declared `static` simply to save space in memory: when a program with many objects of the `FallingCube` type is running, they all will share the `letters` field. In fact, static fields are stored separately from instances of the class in a special memory space allocated for the class as a whole. The code for methods is not duplicated either: all instances of the same class share the same code for its methods.

The fields are usually followed by the class's constructor(s) and methods. In the code a method and a constructor look very similar: each of them has a header followed by the code within braces. The header includes the method's or constructor's name and a list of parameters in parentheses. But the name of a constructor is always the same as the name of the class.

The `FallingCube` class, for example, has only one constructor that takes one integer argument, the size of the cube. The cube's constructor saves the `size` argument, which is passed to it, in the cube's `cubeSize` field for future use; it also sets the cube's coordinates off the board so that the cube is not displayed until it is set in motion.

Constructors are not called explicitly, but they are invoked using the `new` operator. For example, the `LetterPanel` class has one constructor that takes no arguments; the `init` method in the `Ramblecs` class (Figure 4-4) creates `whiteboard` using that constructor:

```
whiteboard = new LetterPanel();
```

`init` also creates a `JButton` object:

```
go = new JButton("Go");
```

The programmer who wrote the above statement knows that the `JButton` library class has a constructor with one argument, the text to be displayed on the button. (`JButton` has another constructor that takes two arguments: the text and the icon to show on the button.)

An object may have fields that are objects of other classes. In that case, the class's constructor can construct the objects for its fields. Consider, for example, the `LetterPanel` class (Figure 4-6). It has fields `FallingCube cube` and `Timer t`. `LetterPanel`'s constructor creates `cube` and `t`:

```
public LetterPanel()
{
  cube = new FallingCube(CUBESIZE);
  t = new Timer(delay, this);
}
```

As we have seen, our `FallingCube` class has a constructor that takes one integer argument — the size of the cube — and this constructor is used here. You can find in Java documentation that the `Timer` class from the `java.lang` package has a constructor that takes two arguments: the time period (in milliseconds) between consecutive pulses, and the "action listener" object that will process these events, in this case `this` (the `LetterPanel` object that is creating the timer).

You don't need to worry about getting rid of objects after you create them. Java automatically disposes of all objects that are no longer needed, a process known as ***garbage collection***.

```
/**
 *  Implements a panel on which "letter cubes" fall
 *  in the Ramblecs applet
 */
import java.awt.*;
import java.awt.event.*;
import javax.swing.*;

public class LetterPanel extends JPanel
      implements ActionListener
{
  private FallingCube cube;
  private final int CUBESIZE = 40;
  private final int delay = 30;
  private Timer t;

  public LetterPanel()
  {
    cube = new FallingCube(CUBESIZE);
    t = new Timer(delay, this);
  }

  public void dropCube()
  {
    cube.start();
    t.start();
  }

  /**
   *  Processes timer events
   */
  public void actionPerformed(ActionEvent e)
  {
    boolean moved = cube.moveDown();
    if (!moved)  // "If not moved... "
    {
      t.stop();
    }
    repaint();
  }

  public void paintComponent(Graphics g)
  {
    super.paintComponent(g); // call JPanel's paintComponent
    cube.draw(g);
  }
}
```

Defines a class LetterPanel. The LetterPanel object will also capture timer events

Constructor

The dropCube method is called by actionPerformed method in the Ramblecs object

actionPerformed method is called when the timer fires

PaintComponent method redraws the background and the cube

Figure 4-6. `Ch04\Ramblecs\LetterPanel.java`

Methods define the functionality of an object. A method is basically a fragment of code that implements a certain task or computation and that is callable from other methods in the program. The same idea is used in all programming languages under different names: in Basic it may be a "subroutine," in Pascal a "procedure" or a "function," in C and C++ a "function." In Java it is a "method."

All objects in a class share the same set of methods. Therefore, as far as the programmer is concerned, he or she writes methods for the class. However, in a running program, a method is usually called for a particular object of the class (with the exception of *static* methods, discussed in Section 8.6).

Each method is designated `public` or `private`.

> **`public` methods can be called from any other class. `private` methods can be called only from other methods of the same class.**

The list in parentheses is the list of *parameters* of a method. When a method is called, the values of the *arguments* passed to the method become the values of parameters. If there are no parameters, empty parentheses are used.

> **A method is usually called for a particular object of a class.**

For example the statement

```
cube.start();
```

calls the `start` method for the `FallingCube` object `cube`. If we created two cubes, `cube1` and `cube2`, then we could use

```
cube1.start();
cube2.start();
```

To call the timer `t`'s `start` method we write:

```
t.start();
```

The names of two methods in `FallingCube` and in `Timer` are the same, `start`, but they perform very different tasks. There is no conflict in names because each call shows which object the method is called for: the method name is preceded by the object's name and a dot.

An object can also call its own methods. Then the object name is simply omitted, as in

```
repaint();
```

The `LetterPanel` class (Figure 4-6) shows three methods:

```
public void dropCube()
{
   ...
}

public void actionPerformed(ActionEvent e)
{
   ...
}

public void paintComponent(Graphics g)
{
   ...
}
```

`dropCube` is called by the applet object whenever you click the "Go" button. `actionPerformed` is called automatically whenever the timer, created by the `LetterPanel` object, fires a pulse. `paintComponent` is called automatically in response to each `repaint` request.

Since the `LetterPanel` class is derived from `JPanel`, it also inherits all `JPanel`'s methods. So `whiteboard` has all `JPanel`'s methods. You can see, for example, that `Ramblecs`'s `init` method calls `whiteboard`'s `setBackground` method:

```
whiteboard.setBackground(Color.white);
```

But we didn't write this method — it is inherited from `JPanel`.

4.7   Events

Java is uniquely suitable for programming *event-driven* applications. When you start the *Ramblecs* applet, a window opens on the screen with the "Go" button in it, and then... nothing happens until you click that button. How does your applet know that the button has been clicked? How does it know what to do when the button is clicked?

This functionality is achieved through a combination of operating system services and your program. The operating system monitors all mouse and keyboard events.

When it detects a mouse click somewhere inside your application window, it makes your application active. If your application is partially covered by other windows, the operating system brings it to the top and passes control of the keyboard to your application. Then the operating system places the event information into your application's *event queue*, telling your program, "Now take care of this event yourself."

Your program frequently checks whether there are any events waiting in the queue. In fact, your whole program works as one iterative cycle. On each iteration the program checks whether there are any events waiting and, if so, dispatches appropriate functions in response to different types of events. This type of application is called an *event-driven application*. Events may originate in the real world or come from other programs or be generated by other events in your program.

Java programs implement events handling through different event *listeners*. Listeners are objects that can be "attached" to buttons, menus, timers, and other objects. So one object generates events and another object "listens" to them. There are situations where an object is its own listener. In our program the `JButton go` generates events and the `Ramblecs` (applet) object listens to them and takes action. The statement

```
go.addActionListener(this);
```

tells the `go` button that `this` (the applet object) is its action listener. (A GUI object has a special field that holds a reference to its action listener. The `addActionListener` method sets that field. Because an object can have several action listeners, the method is called `add...` rather than `set...`)

According to its definition in Java, an `ActionListener` type of object must always have a public method called `actionPerformed`. Since we have attached the `Ramblecs` object to the `go` button, the `actionPerformed` method of the `Ramblecs` class is called whenever the "Go" button is clicked. In this case `actionPerformed` ignores the event information passed to it (it is not interested in where exactly on the button the click occurred or other specifics) and just calls `whiteboard`'s `dropCube` method:

```
public void actionPerformed(ActionEvent e)
{
  whiteboard.dropCube();
}
```

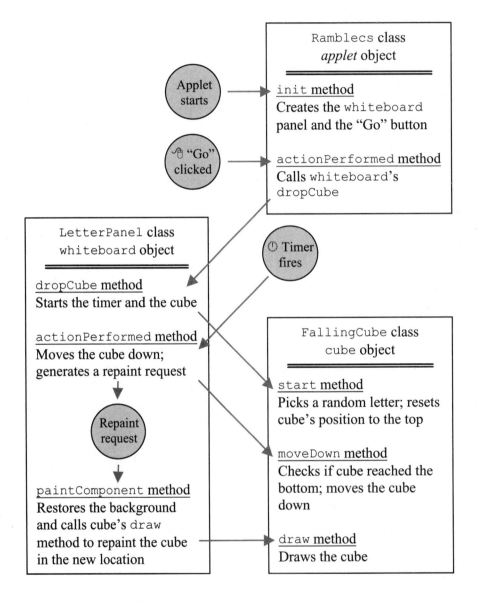

Figure 4-7. The *Ramblecs* applet: classes, objects, methods, and events

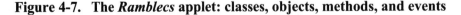

The `whiteboard` object is also a listener, but it "listens" for a different kind of events: it is attached to a `Timer` object and reacts when the timer fires a "pulse." The statement

```
t = new Timer(delay, this);
```

creates a timer with a 30-millisecond cycle (`delay` = 30) and attaches `this` (the `whiteboard` object that creates the timer) to the timer. `t.start()` starts the timer. Every 30 milliseconds the timer generates an event that automatically calls `whiteboard`'s `actionPerformed` method. This method tells the cube to move down and tells `whiteboard` to repaint itself. When the cube reaches the bottom, `actionPerformed` stops the timer.

Behind the scenes, your application processes all kinds of events. For instance, a call to the `repaint()` method generates a "repaint request" event which eventually triggers a call to the `paintComponent` method. The latter repaints `whiteboard` and the cube.

The `JApplet` class has its own event listener — a "window listener." If a window is moved or resized, the window listener sends a message that the window needs to be repainted. One particular event, loading the applet, triggers a call to the applet's `init` method and then opens the applet's window.

Figure 4-7 shows the interactions between `Ramblecs`, `LetterPanel`, and `FallingCube` objects, their methods, and the events that trigger them in more detail. We will learn more about handling different types of events in Java as we go along.

4.8   Summary

A Java program consists of classes. A class defines a certain type of objects. The source code for each class is stored in a separate file with the same name as the class and the extension `.java`. The names of classes and their files are case-sensitive. It's customary to place all your classes for the same project and an HTML file for testing your applet in the same folder.

Java classes are almost never written from scratch: they extend the functionality of classes provided in various Java packages. The `import` statements at the beginning of the source file tell the compiler where it can find the classes and packages that your class uses.

The data elements in a class, called fields, define the constants and variables available in each object of that class's type. They serve as the "personal memory" of an object. In OOP the data elements are usually all `private`, so only objects of this class have direct access to them. A class's constructor is used to create objects of the class. A constructor initializes the object's fields in a particular way. A constructor may take arguments that serve as parameters for creating the object. A class may have several constructors that differ in the number or types of their parameters. Any object must be created with the `new` operator before you can use it.

The functionality of a class — what it can do — is defined by its methods. A method accomplishes a certain task (much like a subroutine in Basic or a function in C or C++). It can be called from other methods of the same class or, if it is declared `public`, from methods of other classes. A method can take arguments as its "inputs" and can return a value as its result.

Java applications are mostly event-driven. Events can originate in the real world (e.g., a mouse click, a key pressed on the keyboard), in the operating system (e.g., a window resized, a program started or exited), or in your application itself (e.g., a timer fires). An object that generates events can have another object associated with it that "listens" to these events. A specific listener's methods are automatically called when events occur.

Exercises

Sections 4.1-4.5

1.   Mark true or false and explain:

    (a)   The name of a public class in Java must be the same as the name of its source file. _____
    (b)   The names of classes are case-sensitive. _____
    (c)   The names of source files are case-sensitive. _____ ✓
    (d)   The `import` statement tells the compiler which other classes use this class. _____ ✓

2.   Mark true or false and explain:

    (a)   The *Ramblecs* prototype code consists of three classes. _____ ✓
    (b)   A Java program can have as many classes as necessary. _____
    (c)   The `Ramblecs` class extends the `JApplet` class. _____
    (d)   A program can create only one object of each class. _____
    (e)   Every class has a method called `init`. _____ ✓

3.   Navigate your browser to Sun's web site

        `http://java.sun.com/j2se/1.3/docs/api/index.html`

        or, if you have the SDK documentation installed on your computer, open the file

        `<JDK base>\docs\api\index.html`

        (e.g., `C:\jdk1.3\docs\api\index.html`).

        (a)   Approximately how many different packages are listed in the API spec?

        (b)   Find `JApplet` in the list of classes in the left column and click on it. Scroll down the main window to the "Method Summary" section. Approximately how many methods does the `JApplet` class have, including methods inherited from other classes? 2? 12? 25? 250? ✓

Sections 4.6-4.8

4.   Explain the difference between public and private methods.

5.   Mark true or false and explain:

        (a)   Fields of a class are usually declared `private`. _____
        (b)   An object has to be created before it can be used. _____ ✓
        (c)   A class may have more than one constructor. _____
        (d)   The programmer names objects in his program. _____
        (e)   When an object is created, the program always calls its `init` method. _____ ✓

6.   Using the copy in your work folder, change the *Ramblecs* code to set `whiteboard`'s background color to yellow. Recompile and test the applet. ✓

7. (a) Examine the `Sign` class in `Ch04\Exercises\Sign.java` 🖫.
Which library class is `Sign` derived from? Is `setBackground` an
inherited method or `Sign`'s own method? Is `setMessage` an
inherited method or `Sign`'s own method? Is `message` a field of the
`Sign` class? What type of object is it? Is it public or private?

(b) The *Welcome* applet below, `Ch04\Exercises\Welcome.java` 🖫,
creates one `Sign` object, sets its background color to yellow and its
message to "Java," and adds the sign to the NORTH region of the
applet's "content pane."

```
public class Welcome extends JApplet
{
  public void init()
  {
    Container c = getContentPane();

    Sign sign1 = new Sign();
    sign1.setBackground(Color.yellow);
    sign1.setMessage("Java");
    c.add(sign1, BorderLayout.NORTH);
  }
}
```

Create an HTML file to test this applet.

(c) Modify the `Welcome` class above to add two signs: one with the word
"is" to the CENTER region and the word "Best" to the SOUTH region.
(If you'd like, also add panels of different colors to the EAST and WEST
regions.)

8. The applet below has a "Spring" button on a white background. Add
statements to change the applet's background to green when the button is
pressed. ✓

```
import java.awt.*;
import java.awt.event.*;
import javax.swing.*;

public class Spring extends JApplet
  implements ActionListener
{
  public void init()
  {
    JButton button = new JButton("Spring");
    button.addActionListener(this);
```

Continued ⇗

```
    Container c = getContentPane();
    c.setBackground(Color.white);
    c.add(button, BorderLayout.SOUTH);
  }

  public void actionPerformed(ActionEvent e)
  {
    < ... missing statements >
  }
}
```

9.■ (a) In the `Ramblecs` class, instead of adding the `whiteboard` panel directly to the CENTER region of the applet's "content pane," as in

```
    Container c = getContentPane();
    c.add(whiteboard, BorderLayout.CENTER);
```

we can first put it into a "box," then add the box to the content pane:

```
    Box b = Box.createHorizontalBox();
    b.add(whiteboard);
    Container c = getContentPane();
    c.add(b, BorderLayout.CENTER);
```

Make this change and test that the applet works as before.

(b) When we add several objects to a horizontal box, they are placed side by side. Change the `Ramblecs` class so that it creates two `LetterPanel` objects, `whiteboard` and `yellowboard`, and puts both of them in the box. How can you tell that the applet displays two different objects as opposed to the same object twice? Can the two boards have different background colors? ✓

(c) Change the "Go" button action to drop cubes on both boards at once.

(d) Change the "Go" button action to choose randomly the board where the cube starts falling when "Go" is pressed. ⸮ Hint:

```
    if (Math.random() < .5)
      ...
    else
      ...
```

⸮ How does the cube know on which panel it should fall? ✓

10.◆   (a)   Let's modify the `FallingCube` class to allow the cube fall at different horizontal positions. Presently the horizontal position of the falling cube is determined by the value of the `xLeft` field, which is set in its constructor:

```
xLeft = cubeSize / 2;
```

Add a second parameter to the constructor (say, `horzPos`), and set `xLeft` to `horzPos` instead of `cubeSize / 2`. In the `LetterPanel` class, add a second argument in the statement that creates the falling cube; the new argument should indicate the horizontal position of the cube. Make the cube's horizontal position equal `CUBESIZE` times 2. Test your modified applet in *Applet Viewer*; try reshaping its window while it is running.

(b)   Is there a way to adjust the horizontal position of the cube if the applet's window is reshaped while the cube is falling? Add a method to the `FallingCube` class to set the value of `xLeft`. For example:

```
public void setHorizontalPos(int x)
{
    . . .
}
```

⸸ Hint: you need to remove the keyword `final` in `xLeft`'s definition, because it is no longer a constant. ⸵

Make the cube stay in the middle of the board even if the applet's window is reshaped. ⸸ Hint: call `cube.setHorizontalPos` in `LetterPanel` each time before moving the cube down. `LetterPanel`'s `getWidth` method, inherited from `JPanel`, returns the current width of the panel. ⸵

(c)   Modify the `LetterPanel` class again to show two or three cubes (with different random letters on them) falling concurrently at different horizontal positions.

11.   (a)   The following applet (`Ch04\Exercises\Morning.java` 🔖) plays a "rooster" sound and sets the background to white when it starts. Create an HTML file to test this applet. Make sure the `roost.wav` file is in the same folder as `Morning.class` when you test the applet.

```java
import java.awt.*;
import javax.swing.*;
import java.applet.AudioClip;

public class Morning extends JApplet
{
  private AudioClip rooster;

  public void init()
  {
    rooster = getAudioClip(getDocumentBase(),
                                "roost.wav");
    rooster.play();

    Container c = getContentPane();
    c.setBackground(Color.white);
  }
}
```

(b)◆ Change the applet to play the sound every five seconds.

(c)◆ Change the applet to alternate the "rooster" sound with a "moo" sound and the white background with the black background every five seconds. (Find a free `moo.wav` file on the web.)

12.◆ Change the `FallingCube` class in the *Ramblecs* applet so that when the falling cube reaches the bottom of the window it starts moving up and when it reaches the top it starts moving down again.

≶ Hints: (1) Add a field `direction` and initialize its value to 1. Use

```java
cubeY += yStep * direction;
```

instead of

```java
cubeY += yStep;
```

Continued ➬

(2) Flip `direction`'s sign:

```
direction = -direction;
```

when the cube reaches the bottom and when it reaches the top. Set the initial top position of the cube to `yStep` instead of `-cubeSize`.

(3) Do not stop the timer — leave it running all the time. ∍

```
/**
 *
 */
```

Chapter 5

Java Syntax and Style

5.1   Prologue

In the previous chapter we discussed one Java applet, working through its general structure and the interactions between its objects and their methods. Unfortunately, there's much more than that to writing working Java code. The text of a program is governed by very rigid rules of syntax, and every symbol in your program must be in just the right place. A compiler can catch most syntax errors and give error messages that provide more or less comprehensible clues to what is wrong with the code. However, some errors may look like acceptable code to the compiler even as they completely change how the code works. Programmers have to find and fix "bugs" of this kind themselves. Then there are honest logic errors: you think your code works in a particular way, but actually it does something quite different. Java's run-time interpreter can catch some obvious errors (e.g., when you divide something by zero); but most errors just show up in the way your program works (or rather fails to work).

Besides producing working code, a programmer must also pay attention to the program's style, a very important element of software engineering. The style is intended to make programs more readable. Strictly speaking it is optional — the compiler doesn't care. But the people who have to read or modify your program do care a lot.

In the following sections we will take a more detailed look at Java's syntax and style. We will discuss the following topics:

- How plain-language comments are marked and used in programs
- What reserved words are
- How to name variables, objects, and methods
- Which requirements come from syntax and which come from style
- How program statements are grouped into nested blocks using braces.

In later chapters we will learn the specific syntax for declarations and control statements.

5.2   Using Comments

The first thing we notice in Java code is that it contains some phrases in plain English. These are ***comments*** inserted by the programmer to explain and document the program's features. It is a good idea to start any program with a comment explaining what the program does, who wrote it and when, and how to use it. This comment may also include the history of revisions: who made changes to the program, when, and why. The author must assume that his or her program will be read, understood, and perhaps modified by other people.

In Java, comments may be set apart from the rest of the code in two ways. The first format is to place a comment between /* and */ marks. For example:

```
/*  This is the main class for the Ramblecs game.
    Author: B. Speller  */
```

In this format, the comment may be placed anywhere in the code.

The second format is to place a comment after a double slash mark on one line. The compiler will treat all the text from the first double slash to the end of the line as a comment. For example, we can write:

```
if (!moved)  // "If not moved... "
```

or

```
// Draw the cube:
cube.draw(g);
...
```

> **Judiciously used comments are one of the most useful tools in the constant struggle to improve the readability of programs. Comments document the role and structure of major code sections, mark important procedural steps, and explain obscure or unusual twists in the code.**

On the other hand, excessive or redundant comments may clutter the code and become a nuisance. A novice may be tempted to comment each statement in the program even if the meaning is quite clear from the code itself. Experienced programmers use comments to explain the parts of their code that are less obvious. Self-explanatory code is better than well-commented obscure code (see Appendix B, *The 17 Bits of Style*, Bit 9).

Comment marks are also useful for ***commenting out*** (temporarily disabling) some statements in the source code. By putting a set of /*...*/ around a fragment of code or a double slash at the beginning of a statement, we can make the compiler skip it on a particular compilation. This can be useful for making tentative changes to the code.

❖   ❖   ❖

SDK supplies the *javadoc* utility program that generates documentation in HTML format automatically from special "documentation" comments in the Java source. A documentation comment must immediately precede an important element (a class, a method, or a field) in order to be processed by *javadoc*.

> **Documentation comments also use the /*...*/ comment delimiters, but in addition they have to be marked by a second * after the opening /* so that *javadoc* can recognize them.**

For example:

```
/**
 *  Reads the next character from a file (any character including
 *  a space or a newline character).
 *  @return character read or <code>null</code> character
 *  (Unicode 0) if trying to read beyond the EOF.
 */
public char readChar()
{
  ...
}
```

Note how HTML formatting tags may be embedded in a documentation comment to make the final HTML document look better. *javadoc* also understands its own special tags: @param describes a method's parameter, @return describes the method's return value, @precondition describes conditions that must hold when the method is called, @postcondition describes conditions that are true when the method is finished.

Any standard Java package is documented this way. Descriptions of Java library packages and classes in SDK's docs were generated automatically with *javadoc* from the documentation comments in their code. Some programmers write documentation comments even before the code itself.

5.3   Reserved Words and Programmer-Defined Names

In Java a number of words are reserved for a special purpose, while other words are arbitrary names given by the programmer. Figure 5-1 shows a list of the Java *reserved words*, loosely organized by category.

Primitive data types:	Storage modifiers:	Control statements:	Exceptions handling:
boolean	public	new	try
char	private	if	catch
byte	protected	else	finally
int	static	for	throw
short	final	while	throws
long		do	
float	Classes, inheritance:	switch	Not used in this book:
double		case	
void	import	default	continue
	class	break	package
Built-in constants:	interface	return	native
	extends		volatile
true	implements		transient
false	this		synchronized
null	super		instanceof
	abstract		

Figure 5-1. Java reserved words

Each reserved word is used only in a strictly prescribed way.

All reserved words use only lowercase letters.

Figure 5-2 shows fragments of the LetterPanel class with all the reserved words highlighted.

```java
/**
 *   Implements a panel on which "letter cubes" fall
 *   in the Ramblecs applet
 */
import java.awt.*;
import java.awt.event.*;
import javax.swing.*;

public class LetterPanel extends JPanel
      implements ActionListener
{
  private FallingCube cube;
  private final int CUBESIZE = 40;
  private final int delay = 30;
  private Timer t;

  public LetterPanel()
  {
    cube = new FallingCube(CUBESIZE);
    t = new Timer(delay, this);
  }

  public void dropCube()
  {
    cube.start();
    t.start();
  }

  /**
   *   Processes timer events
   */
  public void actionPerformed(ActionEvent e)
  {
    boolean moved = cube.moveDown();
    if (!moved)  // "If not moved... "
    {
      t.stop();
    }
    repaint();
  }

  public void paintComponent(Graphics g)
  {
    super.paintComponent(g); // call JPanel's paintComponent
    cube.draw(g);
  }
}
```

Figure 5-2. Reserved words in the `LetterPanel` class

In addition to reserved words, there are other standard names and words whose meaning normally does not vary. These include all standard package names and names of classes and methods from library packages. Examples include `java.awt`, `javax.swing`, `Object`, `String`, `Graphics`, `JApplet`, and so on. The names of methods from Java packages can be reused in your own classes, but you have to be very careful not to override inadvertently a library method when you derive your class from a library class.

> **A programmer gives names to his own classes, their fields and methods, and to variables inside methods. These names can use upper- and lowercase letters, digits, and the underscore character. No name may start with a digit. It is very important to choose names that are somewhat self-explanatory and improve the readability of the program.**

It is also desirable to follow some naming convention. For example, you might have noticed that in all the code you've seen so far, all names of classes start with a capital letter and names of methods and variables start with a lowercase letter. If a name consists of two or more words, all words starting with the second are capitalized.

> **Names of classes and objects usually sound like nouns, and names of methods usually sound like verbs.**

Names that are too short may be not expressive enough and names that are too long clutter the code and make it harder to read. Java style experts do not mind a small set of standard "throwaway" names for temporary objects that are used for a short time, such as

```
int i, k;
Container c;
String str, s;
```

and so on. But variables used throughout the program should get more meaningful names.

> **It is a common practice to give the same name to methods in different classes if these methods perform tasks that are similar.**

Names are discussed in more detail in Appendix B, *The 17 Bits of Style*.

5.4   Syntax vs. Style

Text within double quotes and end-of-line comments must be kept on one line. Aside from that, the compiler regards line breaks, spaces and tabs only as separators between consecutive words, and one space works the same way as 100 spaces. All redundant white space (any combination of spaces, tabs and line breaks) is ignored by the compiler. So our `Ramblecs` class from Chapter 4 could be written as shown in Figure 5-3. It would still compile and execute correctly. But although some people might insist that it makes as much sense as before, most would agree that it has become somewhat less readable.

```
import java.awt.*;import java.awt.event.*;
import javax.swing.*; public class Ramblecs extends
JApplet implements ActionListener{private LetterPanel
whiteboard;private JButton go;public void init(
){whiteboard=new LetterPanel();whiteboard.
setBackground(Color.white);go=new JButton("Go");
go.addActionListener(this); Container c=getContentPane()
;c.add(whiteboard,BorderLayout.CENTER);c.add(go,
BorderLayout.SOUTH);}public void
actionPerformed(ActionEvent e){whiteboard.dropCube();}}
```

Figure 5-3. `Ramblecs.java`: compiles with no errors

> **Arranging your code on separate lines, inserting spaces and blank lines, and indenting fragments of code is not required by the compiler — it is a matter of stylistic convention.**

More or less rigid stylistic conventions have evolved among Java professionals, and they must be followed to make programs readable and acceptable to the practitioners of the trade. But as we said before, the compiler doesn't care. What it does care about is every word and symbol in your program. And here programmers do not have much freedom. They can use comments as they want and they can name their classes, methods and variables. The rest of the text is governed by the very strict rules of Java *syntax*.

As opposed to English or any other natural language, programming languages have virtually no ***redundancy***. Redundancy is a term from information theory that refers to less-than-optimal expression or transmission of information; redundancy in language or code allows the reader to interpret a message correctly even if it has been somewhat garbled. Forgetting a parenthesis or putting a semicolon in the wrong place in an English paragraph may hinder reading for a moment, but it does not usually affect the overall meaning. Anyone who has read a text written by a six-year-old can appreciate the tremendous redundancy in natural languages, which is so great that we can read a text with no capitalization or punctuation and most words misspelled.

Not so in Java or any other programming language, where almost every character is essential. We have already mentioned that in Java all names and reserved words have to be spelled exactly right with the correct rendition of the upper- and lowercase letters. Suppose we inadvertently misspelled `paintComponent`'s name in the `LetterPanel` class:

```
public void painComponent(Graphics g)
{
  < ... code >
}
```

The class still compiles fine, but instead of redefining the `paintComponent` method inherited from `JPanel`, as intended, it introduces another method with a strange name that will be never called. When you run your applet, it does not crash, but you don't see any falling cubes either.

Not only spelling, but every punctuation mark and symbol in the program has a precise purpose; omitting or misplacing one symbol leads to an error. At first it is hard to get used to this rigidity of syntax.

> **Java syntax is not very forgiving and may frustrate a novice. The proper response is to pay more attention to details!**

The compiler catches most syntax errors, but in some cases it has trouble diagnosing the problem precisely. Suppose we have accidentally omitted the phrase `implements ActionListener` on Line 10 in the `LetterPanel` class.

```
         . . .
Line  9: public class LetterPanel extends JPanel
Line 10: // omitted by mistake: implements ActionListener
         . . .
Line 20:    t = new Timer(delay, this);
```

When we compile the program, the compiler can tell that something is not right and reports an error on Line 20:

```
C:\Mywork> javac LetterPanel.java
LetterPanel.java:20: cannot resolve symbol
symbol  : constructor Timer  (int,LetterPanel)
location: class javax.swing.Timer
    t = new Timer(delay, this);
          ^
1 error
```

But it doesn't know what exactly we meant to do or what exactly we did wrong (in the call to `Timer`'s constructor, `this` is supposed to be an `ActionListener` and we haven't defined it as one).

> **Notwithstanding the compiler's somewhat limited capacity to diagnose your syntax errors precisely, you can never blame the compiler for errors. You may be sure that there is <u>something</u> wrong with your code if it does not compile correctly.**

Appendix F☞ lists a few common compiler error messages and their causes.

Unfortunately, the converse is not always true: the program may compile correctly but still contain errors ("bugs"). Just as a spell-check program will not notice if you type "wad" instead of "was" or "you" instead of "your," a compiler will not find errors that it can mistake for something else. So it is easy to make a minor "syntax" or spelling error that conforms to all the syntax rules but happens to change the meaning of your code. For instance, in Java a semicolon marks the end of a statement. Suppose you want to calculate the sum of squares of all integers from 1 to *n* using the following loop:

```
int k, sum = 0;
for (k = 1; k <= n; k++)
{
  sum += k * k;
}
```

and you accidentally put an extraneous semicolon before the opening brace:

```
int k, sum = 0;
for (k = 1; k <= n; k++);
{
  sum += k * k;
}
```

The compiler doesn't care about your intentions or indentation; it will interpret your code as

```
int k, sum = 0;
for (k = 1; k <= n; k++);
sum += k * k;
```

You <u>think</u> your code will iterate *n* times through the statement within braces. Guess what: in fact it will iterate *n* times through nothing, an empty statement. As a result, it will set `sum` to $(n+1)^2$ rather than $1 + 2^2 + ... + n^2$.

> **Beginners can usually save a lot of time by carefully reading their code a couple of times <u>before</u> running it through the compiler. Get in the habit of checking that nothing is misspelled and that all semicolons, braces, and other punctuation marks are where they should be.**

5.5   Statements, Blocks, Indentation

Java code consists mainly of declarations and control statements. Declarations describe objects and methods; control statements describe actions.

> **Declarations and other statements in Java are terminated with a semicolon; statements can be grouped into blocks using braces { }. Semicolons are not used after a closing brace (except certain array declarations as explained in Chapter 10).**

Braces divide the code into ***nested blocks***. Figure 5-4 shows several blocks nested within each other. Statements inside a block are usually indented by a fixed number of spaces or one tab. In this book we indent statements inside a block by two spaces, which is a common Java style. A braced-off block is used to indicate that a number of statements form one ***compound statement*** that belongs in the same control structure, for example an ***iteration*** loop (`for`, `while`, etc.) or a ***conditional*** (`if`) statement. The outermost block is always the body of a class definition.

There are different styles of placing braces. One style is to place the opening brace at the end of the last line that precedes the block:

```
for (k = 1; k <= n; k++) {
  sum += k * k;
}
```

Others (including us in this book) prefer braces aligned one above the other:

```
for (k = 1; k <= n; k++)
{
  sum += k * k;
}
```

This way it is easier to see the opening brace. Just make sure you don't put, by mistake, an extra semicolon on the previous line.

```
private static int copyWords()
{
  String word;
  int count = 0;

  fileOut.println("RamblecsDictionary");
  while ((word = fileIn.readLine()) != null)
  {
    word = word.trim();
    int len = word.length();
    if (len >= minLength && len <= maxLength)
    {
      word = word.toUpperCase();
      fileOut.println(word);
      count++;
    }
  }
  return count;
}
```

Figure 5-4. Nested blocks, marked by braces, within a method

Another important way to improve the readability of your code is by spacing lines vertically. Make generous use of special comment lines and blank lines to separate sections and procedural steps in your code.

5.6   *Lab:* Correcting Syntax Errors

Figure 5-5 shows a Java applet that is supposed to let the user pick a color and display a colored disk when the "Draw" button is pressed. The code in Figure 5-5 has several syntax errors. Find and fix them. Do not retype the program — just copy ColorDisk.java 🖫 from the Ch05\Syntax folder on your student disk into your current work folder.

You might wonder, "How am I going to fix syntax errors if I have no idea what the correct Java syntax is?" Consider it an adventure game. Examine error messages generated by the compiler carefully and look for clues in them. For example, if the compiler tells you that a certain name is undefined, look at the line where that name is supposed to be declared. Compare that line with similar lines in the same program or in other programs in the book. Also check the spelling of the name.

Usually you should start working with the first error message. Do not panic if after fixing an error or two the total number of errors suddenly increases — this can happen if your compiler now understands your code better and sees other problems. Sometimes a compiler message may be misleading. For example, it may tell you "; expected" or ") expected" while in fact something else is wrong with your code.

When your program finally compiles, create an appropriate HTML file and test the applet. You will notice that it still has a bug that apparently slipped by the compiler because the syntax was acceptable. Instead of a disk, the applet shows only a quarter of a disk. The radius seems to be fine but the center is off. This is a tricky bug: fields that represent the coordinates of the center are accidentally redefined as local variables. Examine how fields are treated in the rest of the code and in other programs and fix the bug. Recompile and retest the applet.

```
import java.awt.*;
import java.awt.event*;
import javax.swing.*;

public class ColorDisk extands JApplet
    implements ActionListener
{
  private Color color = blue;
  private int radius = -1, xCenter, yCenter;
  private Container pane;
  private JButton button;

  public void init()
  {
    button = new JButton("Draw disk");
    button.add(ActionListener this);
    pane = getContentPane();
    pane.setBackground(Color.white);
    pane.add(button, Borderlayout.South);
  }

  public void actionPerformed(ActionEvent e)
  {
    Color pickedColor =
        JColorChooser.showDialog(this, "Pick a color" color);
    if (pickedColor != nul)
      color = pickedColor;
    int width = pane.getWidth;
    int height = pane.getHeight() - button.getHeight();
    radius = width / 4
    int xCenter = width / 2;
    int yCenter = height / 2;
    repaint();
  }

  public void paint(Graphics g)
  {
    superpaint(g);
    if (radius > 0)
    {
      g.setColor(Color);
      g.fillOval(xCenter - radius, ycenter - radius,
                                2 * radius, 2 * radius);
    }
  }
}
```

Figure 5-5. Ch05\Syntax\ColorDisk.java (with syntax errors) 💾

5.7   Summary

The text of a program is governed by rigid rules of syntax and style. The syntax is checked by the compiler, which does not allow a program with syntax errors to compile. The style is intended to make programs more readable and, even though the compiler does not check it, plays a very important role in producing readable, professional code.

Comments complement the program code, document classes and methods, and explain obscure places in the code. Comments can be also used to "comment out" (temporarily disable) statements in the program. Special "documentation" comments help the *javadoc* program automatically generate documentation in the HTML format.

A program's text contains reserved words, which are used for a particular purpose in the language, as well as some names determined by the programmer. Java is case-sensitive, so all words must be spelled with the upper- and lowercase letters rendered correctly. All reserved words use only lowercase letters.

A programmer gives names to classes, methods, variables, and constants, trying to choose names that make the program more readable. Names may contain letters, digits, and the underscore character. They cannot start with a digit.

Program code consists mostly of declarations and executable statements, which are normally terminated with a semicolon. The statements may be organized in nested blocks placed within braces. Inner blocks are indented in relation to the outer block.

Java syntax is not very forgiving and may frustrate a novice — there is no such thing as "just a missing semicolon."

Exercises

Sections 5.1-5.3

1. Name three good uses of comments.

2. Add *javadoc*-style comments to all three methods in the `ColorDisk` class from Section 5.6 (`Ch05\Syntax\ColorDisk.java` ▣).

3. Consider the *ColorDisk* applet.

   (a) Find the twelve different reserved words used in the `ColorDisk` class. ✓

   (b)▪ Identify the names of the packages, classes, methods, and constants that come from Java's libraries. Identify the twelve names chosen by the programmer of this applet. ⦃ Hint: some of them are rather unremarkable. ⦄ ✓

4. What happens if the name of the `init` method in the `ColorDisk` class is mistyped with a capital I? ✓

   A. A syntax error is reported.
   B. The class compiles but the applet reports a run-time error.
   C. The applet compiles and runs but shows a blank window.
   D. The applet compiles and runs as before.

Sections 5.4-5.7

5. Identify the following statements as referring to required Java syntax or optional style:

   (a) A program begins with a comment. _____
   (b) The names of all methods begin with a lower case letter. _____ ✓
   (c) Each opening brace has a matching closing brace. _____
   (d) All statements within a pair of matching braces are indented by 2 positions. _____
   (e) A closing brace is placed on a separate line. _____
   (f) A class has a blank line before each method declaration. _____
   (g) The word `IF` is not used as a name for a variable. _____ ✓

6.   Define "redundancy."

7.▪   In

```
if (pickedColor != null)
{
  color = pickedColor;
}
```

are the parentheses required by the Java syntax, or are they a matter of style? What about the braces? ✓

8.   Consider the *Banner* applet (with a "banner" moving across the screen) from Section 3.7 (Ch03\HelloGui\Banner.java 🖫). Add an extra semicolon in the `if` statement in the `actionPerformed` method:

```
if (xPos < -100);
{
  xPos = c.getWidth();
}
```

Try to compile and run the applet and explain the result. Why does it compile with no errors? Why is the message not moving across the screen?

9.   Restore line spacing and proper indentation in the following code: ✓

```
public boolean badIndentation(int maxLines) {int lineCount = 3;
   while(lineCount < maxLines) {System.out.println
(lineCount); lineCount++;} return true;}
```

10.   Mark true or false and explain:

(a)   The compiler recognizes nested blocks through indentation. _____   ✓
(b)   Each line in the program ends with a semicolon. _____
(c)   Text within double quotes cannot be split between two lines. _____   ✓
(d)▪   Adding spaces around a + sign or a parenthesis (that is not inside quotes) is a matter of style. _____
(e)♦   The order of methods and fields in a class definition is a matter of style and the programmer's choice. _____

```
int chapter = 6;
```

Data Types, Variables, and Arithmetic

6.1   Prologue

Java and other high-level languages let programmers refer to a memory location by name. These named "containers" for values are called ***variables***. The programmer gives variables meaningful names that reflect their role in the program. The compiler/interpreter takes care of all the details — allocating memory space for the variables and representing data in the computer memory.

The term "variable" is borrowed from algebra because, as in algebra, variables can assume different values and can be used in ***expressions***. The analogy ends there, however. In a computer program, variables are actively manipulated by the program. A variable may be compared to a slate on which the program can write a new value when necessary and from which it can read the current value. For example, the statement

```
a = b + c;
```

does not represent an algebraic equality, but rather a set of instructions:

1.   Get the current value of b;
2.   Get the current value of c;
3.   Add the two values;
4.   Assign the result to a (write the result into a).

The same is true for

```
a = 4 - a;
```

It is <u>not</u> an equation, but a set of instructions for changing the value of a:

1.   Take the current value of variable a;
2.   Subtract it from 4;
3.   Assign the result back to a (write the new value into a).

In Java, a statement

```
someName = expression;
```

represents an ***assignment*** operation that <u>evaluates</u> (finds the value of) the expression on the right side of the = sign and <u>assigns</u> that value to (writes it into) the variable `someName` on the left side of =. The = sign is read "gets the value of": "`someName` gets the value of *expression*." (If you want to <u>compare</u> two values, use another operator, ==, to mean "is equal to.")

> **Java supports several** *primitive data types* **of variables. A variable's data type is specified by the programmer depending on what kind of data it will contain. A variable of type `int`, for example, contains an integer value; a variable of type `double` represents a real number.**

In Java, values of primitive data types are <u>not</u> objects. This is a concession to more traditional programming languages, like C, from which Java borrows much of its syntax. Objects have data types, too: the data type of an object is its class. But `int`, `double`, and other primitive data types are not classes.

In Java, a variable that represents an object holds a ***reference*** to that object. A reference is basically the address of the object in memory. When an object is created with the `new` operator, that operator allocates memory space for the object and returns a reference to it. That reference can be saved in a variable and used to access the object. We'll explain references in more detail in Section 8.5.

In this chapter we explain the following concepts and elements of Java syntax:

- The syntax and placement of declarations for variables and constants
- Primitive data types
- Literal and symbolic constants
- Conversion of values from one type to another (*casts*)
- The *scope* of variables and symbolic constants
- Java's arithmetic operators

6.2   Declaring Fields and Local Variables

The fragments of code in Figure 6-1 show several ***declarations*** of fields in the `FallingCube` class and a constructor that sets their values (the complete class is shown in Figure 4-5 on pages 105-106). Fields are declared outside of any method, usually at the top of the class. But regardless of where they are placed, they are "visible" in all constructors and all methods of the class.

Usually all fields are declared `private`, which means they can be used only in the methods of their class and are not directly accessible to methods of other classes.

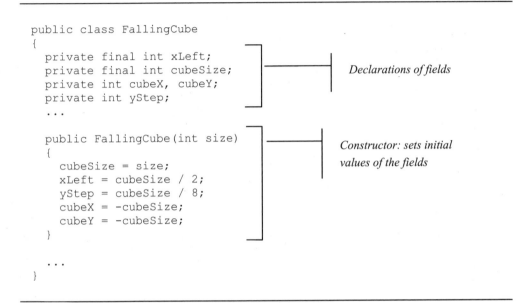

```
public class FallingCube
{
  private final int xLeft;
  private final int cubeSize;
  private int cubeX, cubeY;
  private int yStep;
  . . .

  public FallingCube(int size)
  {
    cubeSize = size;
    xLeft = cubeSize / 2;
    yStep = cubeSize / 8;
    cubeX = -cubeSize;
    cubeY = -cubeSize;
  }

  . . .

}
```

Declarations of fields

Constructor: sets initial values of the fields

Figure 6-1. A fragment from the `FallingCube` class

Note the following features in these declarations of variables and constants:

1. A declaration, like other Java statements, always ends with a semicolon.

2. A declaration must include the type of the variable and its name. For example:

    ```
    int cubeSize;
    char randomLetter;
    JButton go;
    LetterPanel whiteboard;
    ```

3. Several variables of the same type may be listed in one declaration, separated by commas. For example:

    ```
    int cubeX, cubeY;
    ```

4. A declaration may include an initialization that sets the initial value of a variable. For example:

```
int x = xLeft + cubeX;
int y = cubeY;
```

If a field is not explicitly initialized, Java provides a default value, which is 0 for fields of numeric types and `null` for objects. For example:

```
private int yStep;                  // yStep is set to 0
private LetterPanel whiteboard;     // whiteboard is set to null
```

5. A variable may be declared `final`, which means that its value, once assigned, cannot change. For example:

```
private final int CUBESIZE = 40;
```

So actually an initialized final "variable" is not really a variable but a constant. For a constant, its initial value is also its "final" value.

❖   ❖   ❖

In addition to fields, Java programmers use *local* variables. These are temporary variables that are declared <u>inside a method</u>. Once a method is finished, its local variables are thrown away.

For example, the `draw` method in `FallingCube` uses two local variables, `x` and `y`:

```
public void draw(Graphics g)
{
  int x = xLeft + cubeX;
  int y = cubeY;
  ...
}
}
```

The parameter `g`, strictly speaking, is not a local variable, but for all practical purposes it acts like one inside the method. The values of a method's parameters are set when the method is called and they can be used in the method's code like initialized local variables.

Local variables must be declared and assigned a value <u>before</u> they can be used. Local variables <u>do not</u> get default values.

The general format for a local variable declaration is similar to a field declaration:

```
sometype someName;
```

or

```
sometype someName = expression;
```

where `sometype` declares the type of the variable and `someName` is the name given by the programmer to this particular variable. The only difference with fields is that `public` or `private` cannot be used and that uninitialized local variables do not get default values.

A variable can be declared only <u>once</u> within its *scope* ("scope" refers to the space in the program where the variable is "visible" — see Section 6.5).

For example,

```
int x;
...
int x = xLeft + cubeX;
```

is a syntax error. Use either

```
int x;
...
x = xLeft + cubeX;
```

or

```
int x = xLeft + cubeX;
```

You might wonder: Why do we need local variables? Why can't we make them all fields? Technically it would be possible to use only fields, but a class is much better organized if variables that are used locally are kept local. In a good design, a field is a variable that describes a truly important, "global" aspect of its object. You don't want to use global variables for your temporary needs — just like you don't want to bring your own glass to every fast-food restaurant you go to.

6.3   Primitive Data Types

Java has the following eight *primitive data types* designated by reserved words:

```
boolean    byte
char       short
int        long
double     float
```

They are called *primitive* because variables of these types do not have the properties of objects (in particular, they do not have any methods).

> **Because variables of different types occupy different numbers of bytes in memory, we say they have different *sizes*.**

In Java (as opposed to some other languages, such as C++) each data type has a fixed size, regardless of the particular computer model or brand of Java interpreter. Table 6-1 summarizes the primitive types, their sizes, and the ranges of their values.

Type	Size (bytes)	Range
boolean	1	true or false
char	2	Unicode character set (with ASCII subset)
byte	1	from $-2^7 = -128$ to $2^7-1 = 127$
short	2	from $-2^{15} = -32,768$ to $2^{15}-1 = 32,767$
int	4	from -2^{31} to $2^{31}-1$
long	8	from -2^{63} to $2^{63}-1$
float	4	approx. from -3.4×10^{38} to 3.4×10^{38}
double	8	approx. from -1.8×10^{308} to 1.8×10^{308}

Table 6-1. Primitive data types

Although `float` and `double` can represent a huge range of numbers, their precision is limited to only about seven significant digits for the `float` and about twice as many for the `double`.

> **In this book we will work only with the `boolean`, `char`, `int`, and `double` primitive data types.**

The `boolean` type is discussed in Chapter 7.

6.4   Constants

Constants represent memory locations whose values do not change while the program is running. Your source code may include *literal constants* and *symbolic constants*.

Examples of <u>literal constants</u> are decimal representations of integers and real numbers, and characters in single quotes:

```
'y', 'H'              (chars)
7, -3                 (ints)
1.19, .05, 12.0, 3.   (doubles)
```

Character constants also include a special set of non-printable characters designated by *escape sequences* (the term derived from printer control commands). In Java, an escape sequence is a pair of characters: a designated printable character preceded by the "escape character," a backslash. An escape pair is placed within single quotes to designate one character constant.

Escape sequences include:

```
\n    newline
\r    carriage return
\t    tab
\f    form feed
\'    single quote
\"    double quote
\\    backslash
```

The most commonly used one is `\n` — "newline."

Escape pairs are also used in literal string constants (text within double quotes) — see Chapter 9. For example:

```
System.out.print("\nDon\'t let me down\nDon\'t let me down\n");
//                   ^^    ^^              ^^    ^^         ^^
```

❖   ❖   ❖

Symbolic constants are usually represented by initialized `final` variables. For example:

```
    private final int delay = 30;
    private final int CUBESIZE = 40;
```

(Sometimes, programmers write names of symbolic constants using all capital letters for better visibility.)

The general form of a symbolic constant's declaration is

```
    [optional modifiers] final sometype someName = expression;
```

where `sometype` is a data type followed by a name of the constant and its value. A constant may be also initialized to some expression.

In Java a constant doesn't have to be initialized right away in its declaration: its "final" value can be set in a constructor.

For example:

```
    private final int cubeSize;
    ...

    public FallingCube(int size)
    {
      cubeSize = size;
      ...
    }
```

It may seem, at first, that symbolic constants are redundant and we can simply use their literal values throughout the program. For example, instead of writing

```
    private final int delay = 30;
    ...
    t = new Timer(delay, this);
```

we could simply write

```
t = new Timer(30, this);
```

However, there are several important reasons for using symbolic constants.

> **The most important reason for using symbolic constants is easier program maintenance. If the program is modified in the future and the value of a constant needs to be changed, a quick tweak to the constant declaration will change the constant's value throughout the program.**

Consider, for instance, the code that we put together for drawing a letter cube:

```
public void draw(Graphics g)
{
  int x = xLeft + cubeX;
  int y = cubeY;

  g.setColor(Color.red);
  g.fill3DRect(x, y, cubeSize-1, cubeSize-1, true);
  g.setColor(Color. white);
  g.fillRoundRect(x + 5, y + 5, cubeSize - 10, cubeSize - 10,
                            cubeSize/2 - 5, cubeSize/2 - 5);
  g.setColor(Color.darkGray);
  String s = String.valueOf(randomLetter);
  g.drawString(s, x + cubeSize/2 - 6, y + cubeSize/2 + 5);
}
```

Surely we could write the same code with specific numbers plugged in for cubeSize equal to 40:

```
  ...
  g.setColor(Color.red);
  g.fill3DRect(x, y, 39, 39, true);
  g.setColor(Color. white);
  g.fillRoundRect(x + 5, y + 5, 30, 30, 15, 15);
  g.setColor(Color.darkGray);
  String s = String.valueOf(randomLetter);
  g.drawString(s, x + 14, y + 25);
  ...
```

At a first glance it might seem simpler. But if we needed to adjust the size of the cube, we would have to change all these numbers. Luckily in this case all the statements that depend on the size are grouped together, so they are not too hard to find. It could be much worse: they could be scattered around. But still, a programmer who is making the change would have to figure out what all these numbers mean and recalculate them.

Another advantage of symbolic constants is that they may make the code more readable and self-explanatory if their names are chosen well. The name can explain the role a constant plays in the program, making additional comments unnecessary. `cubeSize` above is a good example.

It is also easier to change a symbolic constant into a variable if a program modification requires it.

If necessary, you can declare a <u>local</u> constant within a method. For example,

```java
public void draw(Graphics g)
{
  final int offset = cubeSize / 8;
  int x = xLeft + cubeX;
  int y = cubeY;
  ...
  g.fillRoundRect(x + offset, y + offset,
      cubeSize - 2*offset, cubeSize - 2*offset,
      cubeSize/2 - offset, cubeSize/2 - offset);
  ...
}
```

Symbolic constants, like variables, are declared with a particular data type and are defined only within their scope (explained in the next section). This introduces more order into the code and gives the compiler additional opportunities for error checking — one more reason for using symbolic constants.

On the other hand, there is no need to clutter the code with symbolic names assigned to universal constants such as 0 or 1, or

```java
final int semiCircleDegrees = 180;    // pedantic
final int daysInWeek = 7;
```

if these numbers inherently belong in the code and never change.

6.5   Scope of Variables

As we have discussed above, each method in a class can have its own local variables, while the fields of a class can be used in all its methods. The question of where a variable is visible and can be used relates to the subject of *scope*.

In Java a variable is defined only within a certain space in the program called the *scope* of the variable.

Scope discipline helps the compiler perform important error checking. If you try to use a variable or constant outside its scope, the compiler detects the error and reports an undefined name. The compiler also reports an error if you declare the same name twice within the same scope.

The scope of a field extends throughout the class, including all its methods.

The scope of a local variable extends from its declaration to the end of the block in which it is declared.

A local variable exists only temporarily while the program is executing the block where that variable is declared. When a program passes control to a method, a special chunk of memory (a *frame* on the system *stack*) is allocated to hold that method's local variables. When the method is exited, that space is released and all local variables are destroyed.

As we mentioned earlier, local variables in Java do not have to be declared at the top of a method but may be declared anywhere in the method's code. But declarations inside nested blocks can lead to elusive bugs. We recommend that at first you avoid declaring local variables inside nested blocks unless you know exactly what you are doing.

Java allows you to use the same name for a field and a local variable, with the local variable taking precedence over the global one. This may lead to hard-to-catch errors if you inadvertently declare an identically named local variable that overrides the global one. You've already had to deal with a bug of this kind in the lab in Section 5.6.

This possible overlap of names is a good reason to give a class's fields <u>conspicuous</u> names.

x, y, or a are bad choices — they should be saved for temporary, throwaway local variables. cubeX, cubeY, and cubeSize are better names for fields.

Many programmers use a particular prefix in all field names to make them stand out. For instance they might write myCubeX and myCubeY instead of cubeX and cubeY. Others prefer to use a this-dot prefix with the name. this is a reserved word that refers to the object whose method is running. For example, you can use this.cubeX, this.cubeY instead of just cubeX and cubeY. It is largely a matter of taste.

> **It is perfectly acceptable to use the same name for local variables in different methods.**

In fact, this is a good practice when the variables represent similar quantities and are used in similar ways. But <u>never</u> try to economize on declarations of temporary local variables within methods by making them fields. Everything must be declared where it belongs.

6.6   Arithmetic Expressions

> **Arithmetic expressions are written the same way as in algebra and may include literal and symbolic constants, variables, the arithmetic operators +, –, *, and /, and parentheses.**

The order of operations is determined by parentheses and by the ranks of operators: multiplication and division are performed first (left to right), followed by addition and subtraction. The multiplication operation requires the * sign — it cannot be omitted. You can also use the minus symbol for negation. For example:

```
x = -(y + 2*z) / 5;
a = -a;               // Negate a
```

Java also has the % operator for integers:

```
    a % b
```

which is read "a modulo b," and means the remainder when a is divided by b. For example, 31 % 7 is equal to 3, and 365 % 7 is 1. This operator is handy for computing values that change in a cyclic manner. For example:

```
int minsAfterHour = totalMins % 60;
int dayOfWeek = (dayOfWeekOnFirst - 1 + day) % 7;
int lastDigitBase10 = x % 10;
```

It is also used to check whether a number is evenly divisible by another number. For example:

```
if (k % 2 == 0) ... // if k is even ...
```

The % operator has the same rank as * and /.

❖   ❖   ❖

Java allows programmers to mix variables of different data types in the same expression. Each operation in the expression is performed according to the types of its operands, and its result receives a certain type.

> **The type of the result depends only on the types of the operands, not their values. If the two operands have the same type, the result of the operation automatically gets the same type as the operands.**

This principle goes back to the C language and has serious consequences, especially for division of integers. If you write

```
int a = 7, b = 2;
System.out.println(a / b);
```

you will see 3, and not 3.5 as you might expect. The reason is that both a and b are integers and therefore the result of a/b must be also an integer. If it isn't, it is truncated to an integer (in the direction towards 0). So 7 / 2 is evaluated as 3 and -7 / 2 as -3.

> **If you want to get a true ratio of two `int` variables, you have to convert your `ints` into `doubles`. This can be done using the *cast* operator, designated by the target type in parentheses.**

For example:

```
double ratio = (double)a / (double)b;
```

The above statement is basically equivalent to introducing two temporary variables:

```
double tempA, tempB;
tempA = a;
tempB = b;
double ratio = tempA / tempB;
```

But casts do it for you.

The general syntax for the cast operator is

```
(sometype)variable
```

or

```
(sometype)(expression)
```

> **Note that the "same type" rule applies to all intermediate results of all operations in an expression.**

If you write

```
int a = 7, b = 2;
double ratio = a / b;  // Too late!
```

`ratio` still gets the value of 3, because the result of `a / b` is truncated to an `int` before it is assigned to `ratio`. Similarly, if you write

```
int degreesCelsius = 5 / 9 * (degreesFahrenheit - 32);  // Error!
```

`degreesCelsius` will be always set to 0 (because `5 / 9` is evaluated first and its result is 0).

If the two operands have different types, the operand of the "smaller" type is *promoted* (i.e., converted) to the "larger" type. (`long` is "larger" than `int`, `float` is "larger" than `long`, and `double` is the "largest"). Therefore, in the above example you could use only one cast:

```
double ratio = (double)a / b;
```

or

```
double ratio = a / (double)b;
```

The other operand will be promoted to a `double`. But trying to cast the resulting ratio would cause the same problem as above:

```
double ratio = (double)(a / b);
                        // Error: the result of a / b is already
                        //   truncated!  The cast is too late!
```

> **Your code will be more robust and better documented if you indicate explicit type conversions using the cast operator, where necessary, rather than relying on implicit type conversions.**

But you don't need to use casts with literal constants — just choose a constant of the right type. For example:

```
double volume = 4.0 / 3 * Math.PI * Math.pow(r, 3.0);
```

computes the volume of a sphere with the radius r (which is equal to $\frac{4}{3}\pi r^3$).

Sometimes you may need to use a cast in the opposite direction: to convert a "larger" type into a "smaller" one, such as a `double` into an `int`. For example:

```
int pointsOnDie = 1 + (int)(Math.random() * 6);
// 0.0 <= Math.random() < 1.0
```

The `(int)` cast truncates the number in the direction of 0, so `(int)1.99` is 1 and `(int)(-1.99)` is –1.

If you want to round a `double` value to the <u>nearest</u> integer, add .5 to a positive number or subtract .5 from a negative number first, and then cast it into an `int`. For example:

```
int pieChartDegrees = (int)((double)count / totalCount * 360 + .5);
```

or

```
int pieChartDegrees = (int)(360.0 * count / totalCount + .5);
```

6.7   Compound Assignment and Increment Operators

Java has convenient shortcuts for combining arithmetic operations with assignment. The following table summarizes the ***compound assignment*** operators:

Compound assignment:	Is the same as:
a += b;	a = a + b;
a -= b;	a = a - b;
a *= b;	a = a * b;
a /= b;	a = a / b;
a %= b;	a = a % b;

For example, the following statement:

```
cubeY += yStep;
```

is the same as:

```
cubeY = cubeY + yStep;
```

The += form may seem cryptic at the beginning, but, once you get used to it, it becomes attractive — not only because it is more concise, but also because it emphasizes the fact that the same variable is being modified. The latter form immediately gives away an amateur.

❖   ❖   ❖

Another shortcut is the set of special ***increment/decrement*** operators.   These operators are a shorthand for incrementing or decrementing an integer variable by one:

Increment/ decrement:	Is the same as:
a++;	a = a + 1;
a--;	a = a - 1;
++a;	a = a + 1;
--a;	a = a - 1;

Increment and decrement operators may be used in expressions. That is where the difference between the a++ and ++a forms and between the a-- and --a forms becomes very important.   When a++ is used, the value of the variable a is incremented after it has been used in the expression; for the ++a form, the value of the variable a is incremented before it has been used in the expression. This can get quite confusing and hard to read. For example:

```
a = b + c++;   // Too much!
```

Consider using a++ and a-- only as a separate expression. Avoid ++a and --a altogether, and avoid using ++ and -- in arithmetic expressions.

6.8   *Case Study:* Speed Gauge

In this case study we will add a numerical and graphical display for the speed of falling cubes in the *Ramblecs* applet, introduced in Chapter 4 (Figure 6-2). Later this will help us add different levels of play where the cubes fall slower or faster. Meanwhile, we will practice a little Java arithmetic and OOP design.

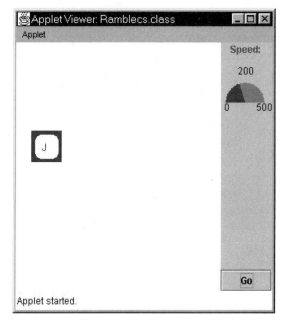

Figure 6-2.   *Ramblecs* applet with the speed gauge

The first question we must answer is where to put the gauge. Potentially we could draw it somewhere on `whiteboard`, the same panel where the falling cube is painted. This solution, however, is unsatisfactory for two reasons. First, the `LetterPanel` class may become too long and complicated. It would acquire responsibilities for two unrelated things: controlling and painting falling cubes and painting the speed gauge. Second, the `paintComponent` method would be painting too many things and it could become too slow for smooth animation.

A much better solution is to paint the gauge on a separate panel. We can move the "Go" button to that panel, too and call it the "control panel." To do that we need to define a new class, which we will call `ControlPanel`. We'll derive `ControlPanel` from `JPanel` because a panel is a good place to put buttons and to paint things. We'll create one object of this class, called `controlpanel`, and add it to the content pane of the applet's window. This way each panel, whiteboard and controlpanel, will have its own responsibilities and will be repainted separately only when necessary. We redefine ControlPanel's paintComponent method to paint the gauge on the panel.

We are also trying a different layout: we will place controlpanel vertically to the right of whiteboard (in the east region of the content pane). We will discuss details of different layouts in Chapter 15. The Ramblecs class will no longer have to worry about the "Go" button (a rather lowly responsibility for the "top-level" class derived from JApplet). Instead, controlpanel will create the "Go" button and listen to its action events itself. Now our applet's code consists of four classes: Ramblecs, ControlPanel, LetterPanel, and FallingCube (Figure 6-3).

The modified code for the Ramblecs class is shown in Figure 6-4. Note that when controlpanel is created, whiteboard is passed to it as an argument:

```
controlpanel = new ControlPanel(whiteboard);
```

This is necessary because controlpanel needs to know what exactly it controls. More specifically, it needs to know whose dropCube method to call when "Go" is clicked.

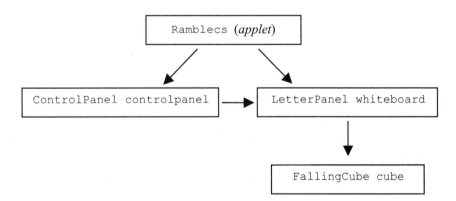

Figure 6-3. *Ramblecs* classes and objects after adding
ControlPanel

Figure 6-5 shows the code for our ControlPanel class. We have provided a constructor for it that takes one argument, a reference to a LetterPanel object, and a field where that reference is stored for future use. We gave that field the same name, whiteboard (although we could have used a different name).

```
/**
 *  This is the applet class for the Ramblecs game.
 */
import java.awt.*;
import javax.swing.*;

public class Ramblecs extends JApplet
{
  private ControlPanel controlpanel;
  private LetterPanel whiteboard;

  public void init()
  {
    whiteboard = new LetterPanel();
    whiteboard.setBackground(Color.white);
    controlpanel = new ControlPanel(whiteboard);
    Container c = getContentPane();
    c.add(whiteboard, BorderLayout.CENTER);
    c.add(controlpanel, BorderLayout.EAST);
  }
}
```

Figure 6-4. `Ch06\Ramblecs\Ramblecs.java` 🖬

```
/**
 *  Implements control panel for the Ramblecs applet
 */
import java.awt.*;
import java.awt.event.*;
import javax.swing.*;

public class ControlPanel extends JPanel
  implements ActionListener
{
  private LetterPanel whiteboard;
  private JButton go;
  private final int avgSpeed = 200, maxSpeed = 500;

  ControlPanel(LetterPanel lpanel) // Constructor
  {
    whiteboard = lpanel;
    setLayout(new BorderLayout());
```

Figure 6-5 `ControlPanel.java` *Continued* ➮

```java
    add(new JLabel("    Speed:        "), BorderLayout.NORTH);
    go = new JButton("Go");
    go.addActionListener(this);
    add(go, BorderLayout.SOUTH);
  }
  /**
   *  Processes Go button events.
   */
  public void actionPerformed(ActionEvent e)
  {
    whiteboard.dropCube();
  }


  /**
   *  Control panel's drawing method
   */
  public void paintComponent(Graphics g)
  {
    super.paintComponent(g);

    final int xGauge = 6, yGauge = 50;
                 // Coordinates of the upper left corner
                 // of the rectangular extent area into
                 // which the full circle of the gauge is inscribed
    final int size = 50;
                 // Width and height of the extent area
    // Draw the numeric speed display
    int speed = avgSpeed;
    g.setColor(Color.black);
    g.drawString(Integer.toString(speed),
                          xGauge + size/2 - 10, yGauge - 10);

    // Draw the gauge:
    int degrees = (int)(180. * speed / maxSpeed);
    g.setColor(Color.blue);
    g.fillArc(xGauge, yGauge, size, size, 0, 180);  // full semicircle
    g.setColor(Color.red);
    g.fillArc(xGauge, yGauge, size, size, 180 - degrees, degrees);
          // slice on the left side: from 180 - degrees to 180.

    // Draw the numbers below for 0 and maxSpeed:
    g.setColor(Color.black);
    g.drawString("0", xGauge - 2, yGauge + size/2 + 10);
    g.drawString(String.valueOf(maxSpeed),
                 xGauge + size - 11, yGauge + size/2 + 10);
  }
}
```

Figure 6-5. `Ch06\Ramblecs\ControlPanel.java` 🖫

We have also included a `JButton` field `go` that holds a reference to the "Go" button and two `final int` fields, `avgSpeed` and `maxSpeed`, that define the initial setting for the speed and the range for the speed (in some rather arbitrary units).

The first statement in `paintComponent` —

```
super.paintComponent(g);
```

— calls `JPanel`'s default `paintComponent` method, which we have redefined in our class. `super` stands for "superclass." This is necessary because we want to paint the background and all the components placed on the panel (e.g., the "Go" button) before we proceed with our own additional drawing.

The `paintComponent` method uses three local constants, `xGauge`, `yGauge` and `size`, and two local variables, `speed` and `degrees`. For now `speed` is set simply to `avgSpeed`, but eventually we will add methods to ask `whiteboard` about the current speed setting and to change it.

Copy `Ramblecs.java` and `ControlPanel.java` 🖫 from the `Ch06\Ramblecs` folder on your student disk to a temporary folder. Also copy `LetterPanel.java` and `FallingCube.java`, which have not changed, from the `Ch04\Ramblecs` folder. Compile all four classes and run the applet to see how it looks now. Use the updated `Ch06\Ramblecs\TestRamblecs.html` file that makes the applet wider.

The speed gauge is a blue semicircle with one red sector. We use the graphics method `fillArc` to draw it. We call `fillArc` twice: first we draw a complete blue semicircle, then a red sector on top of it. In general, the `fillArc` method can be used to fill not just a circular, but any oval arc. The position and size of the arc are defined by an imaginary box into which the oval that contains the arc is inscribed. The first two arguments are the coordinates of the upper left corner of the box, the next two are the width and the height of the box. The fifth argument is the arc's starting angle in degrees; and the sixth is the number of degrees in the arc, going counterclockwise. We have to calculate that number for the red sector using arithmetic operations and a cast:

```
int degrees = (int)(180. * speed / maxSpeed);
```

If we needed more precision, we could round the result instead of truncating it:

```
int degrees = (int)(180. * speed / maxSpeed + .5);
```

6.9   *Lab:* Pie Chart

Figure 6-6 shows an applet that takes a poll for the election of a school president. The results are shown as numbers for each of the three candidates and as slices on a pie chart.

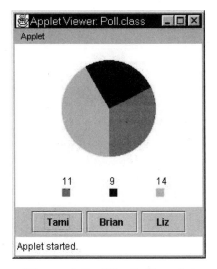

Figure 6-6.   The *Poll* applet

The partial code for this applet is shown in Figure 6-7.

Your task is to supply the missing code in the countToDegrees method, which takes a count of votes (for a particular candidate) and the total number of votes submitted and returns the size of the corresponding pie chart slice in degrees. Also fill in the blanks in the paint method by adding statements to draw the blue and green slices of the pie.

Copy Poll.java ⊞ from the Ch06\Poll folder on your student disk into your work folder and fill in the missing statements in the paint and countToDegrees methods. ⸨ Hint: in paint use the same variables degrees and from for all three pie slices. Increment from and compute degrees appropriately for the next slice. ⸩ Compile and test your applet.

```
/**
 *  Implements an applet with a pie chart
 *  that shows interactive polling results for three candidates
 */
import java.awt.*;
import java.awt.event.*;
import javax.swing.*;

public class Poll extends JApplet
    implements ActionListener
{
  JButton button1, button2, button3;
  int count1, count2, count3;

  public void init()
  {
    setName("Poll");

    button1 = new JButton(" Tami");
    button1.setToolTipText("Vote for Tami");
    button1.addActionListener(this);

    <... etc.  See Ch06\Poll\Poll.java 🖫>

  }

  /**
   *  Processes button events
   */
  public void actionPerformed(ActionEvent e)
  {
    JButton button = (JButton)e.getSource();

    if (button == button1)
      count1++;
    <... etc.  See Ch06\Poll\Poll.java 🖫 >

    repaint();
  }
```

Figure 6-7 `Poll.java` *Continued* ⇗

```java
/**
 *  Displays the numbers and the pie chart
 */
public void paint(Graphics g)
{
    super.paint(g);

    <... etc.  See Ch06\Poll\Poll.java 💾 >

    // Display pie chart
    int total = count1 + count2 + count3;
    if (total == 0)
        return;

    final int size = 4*xStep, x = 4*xStep - size/2;
    y = 20;
    g.setColor(Color.lightGray);
    g.fillOval(x, y, size, size);

    int degrees, from = -90;
    degrees = countToDegrees(count1, total);
    g.setColor(Color.red);
    g.fillArc(x, y, size, size, from, degrees);
    < ... missing statements >
}

/**
 *  Converts the count as a fraction of the total into
 *  the size of the pie slice in degrees.
 */
private int countToDegrees(int count, int total)
{
    return < ... missing expression >
}
}
```

Figure 6-7. `Ch06\Poll\Poll.java` 💾

6.10 Summary

Variables are memory locations, named by the programmer, that can hold values. Fields are variables declared outside of any method of a class. These variables are "visible" in all the class's constructors and methods. Local variables are temporary variables declared inside one of the methods or constructors.

Variables must be declared before they can be used. The declaration of a variable includes the data type of the variable, its name, and an optional initial value. Several variables of the same type may be declared in the same declaration:

```
[optional modifiers] sometype name1, name2, ...;
[optional modifiers] sometype name1 = expr1, name2 = expr2, ...;
```

Fields and local variables that never change their values are declared with the keyword `final`, usually with initial values; they are actually not variables but constants. Declarations of symbolic constants have the form

```
[optional modifiers] final sometype someName = expression;
```

Java has `byte`, `int`, `short`, and `long` primitive data types for representing integers of various sizes. We will always use `int`, which represents integers in the range from -2^{31} to $2^{31}-1$. Real numbers are represented by the `float` and `double` types. We will always use `double`. `char` represents single characters. The `boolean` type is discussed in Chapter 7.

Arithmetic expressions are written the same way as in algebra and may include literal constants, variables, the arithmetic operators +, -, *, /, and %, and parentheses. A multiplication sign * cannot be omitted.

The result of an arithmetic operation has the same type as the operands. If the operands have different types, the operand of the "smaller" type is automatically promoted to the "larger" type (e.g., an `int` may be converted to a `double`). Java provides a cast operator that explicitly converts a variable or constant from one data type into another.

It is a programmer's responsibility to make sure the values of variables and all the intermediate and final results in arithmetic expressions fit within the range of the chosen data types, and that these types satisfy the precision requirements for computations.

Exercises

Sections 6.1-6.5

1.   Which of the following lines are syntactically valid declarations of fields? Of local variables?

    (a)   `int hours, double pay;` _____ ✓
    (b)   `private double dollarsAndCents;` _____ ✓
    (c)   `char mi; int age;` _____
    (d)   `private final int year = 365, leapYear = year + 1;`
    _____
    (e)   `char tab = '\t', newline = '\n', a = 'a';` _____
    (f)   `public final double pi = 3.14159;` _____

2.   Mark true or false and explain:

    (a)   Each variable must be declared on a separate line. _____
    (b)   The scope of a variable is the largest range of its values. _____
    (c)   `i` is always a stylistically bad name for a variable because it is too short. _____
    (d)   Local variables in different methods of the same class may have the same name. _____ ✓
    (e)   The same name can be used for an `int` and a `double` local variable in the same method. _____
    (f)   If a local variable in a method and a field have the same name, the compiler reports a syntax error. _____ ✓

3.   Name three good reasons for using symbolic constants as opposed to literal constants.

4.   Which one of the following statements prints a backslash on the screen?

    A.   `System.out.print('\b');`
    B.   `System.out.print('\\');`
    C.   `System.out.print(\bs);`
    D.   `System.out.print(\);`
    E.   `System.out.print(\\);`

5.   Choose the right word: the scope of a variable is determined when the program is _____ (*compiled / executed*). ✓

Sections 6.6-6.9

6.   What is the output from the following statements?

     (a)   `System.out.print(5 / 10);` ✓
     (b)   `System.out.print(1 / 2 * 10);`
     (c)   `System.out.print(1.0 / 2 * 10);` ✓
     (d)   `System.out.print(1 / 2.0 * 10);`
     (e)   `System.out.print(13 % 5);`

7.   (a)   Assuming:

```
double rate = 1.058;
int balance0 = 100, balance = balance0 * rate;
```

     what is the value of `balance`? ✓

     (b)   Assuming:

```
int miles = 98, gallons = 5;
double gasMileage = miles / gallons;
```

     what is the value of `gasMileage`?

8.   Remove as many parentheses as possible from the following statement without changing the result:

```
count += (((total/pages) - 5) * words - 1);
```

9.   Find and fix a bug in the following statements:

```
final double g = 16.0;
double t = 35.5;
System.out.print ("The travel distance is ");
System.out.println (1 / 2 * (g * t * t));
```

10.   If `double` x has a negative value, write an expression that rounds x to the nearest integer.

11.   Given

```
int a, b, c;
```

write expressions that calculate the roots of the equation $ax^2 + bx + c = 0$ (assuming that the two real roots exist) and assign them to two `double` variables $x1$ and $x2$. Use a temporary variable to hold $\sqrt{b^2 - 4ac}$ in order not to compute it twice. ✓

12.■   Find a bug in the following code fragment:

```
double a, b;
int temp;

System.out.print("Enter two real numbers: ");
...
// Swap the numbers:
temp = a;
a = b;
b = temp;
...
```

✓

13.■   Write an expression that, given a positive integer n, computes a new integer in which the units and tens digits have swapped places. For example, if $n = 123$ the result should be 132; if $n = 3$ the tens digit is zero and the result should be 30. ✓

14.◆   An integer constant `dayOfWeek1` has a value from 0 to 6 and represents the day of the week for January 1st (0=Sunday, 1=Monday, etc.). A variable `day` has a value from 1 to 31 and represents a day in January. Write an expression that calculates the day of the week for any given value of `day`. For example, if `dayOfWeek1`=0 (January 1st is a Sunday) and `day`=13 (January 13th), then `dayOfWeek`, the day of the week for January 13th, should get a value of 5 (Friday).

15.◆ `curHour` and `curMin` represent the current time and `depHour`, `depMin` represent the departure time of a bus. Suppose all these variables are initialized with some values; both times are between 1 p.m. and 11 p.m. Fill in the blanks in the following statements that display the remaining waiting time in hours and minutes:

```
int _____ =

        _____ ;


System.out.println( _____ +

    " hours and " +  _____ +

    " minutes.");
```

16.■ A binder weighs 1 lb. 5 oz. (One pound is 16 ounces). An empty shipping carton weighs 1 lb. 9 oz. and can hold up to 12 binders. The shipping costs include $1.44 for each full or partial carton plus $0.96 per pound or fraction of a pound plus a $3.00 service charge.

Fill in the blanks in the following method that calculates the shipping costs for a given number of binders:

```
public double computeShippingCost(int nBinders)
{
   int nCartons = (nBinders + 11) / 12;

   int totalOunces = _____ ;

   int lbs = _____ ;

   return _____ ;
}
```

17. The *BMI* applet computes a person's body mass index (BMI). BMI is defined as the weight, expressed in kilograms, divided by the square of the height expressed in meters. (One inch is 0.0254 meters and one pound is 0.454 kilograms.) A fragment of the *BMI* applet with some omissions is shown below. The complete code is on the student disk in `Ch06\Exercises\Bmi.java` 🖫.

```
...
public class Bmi extends JApplet
  implements ActionListener
{
  JTextField inputLbs, inputInches, displayBmi;

  public void init()
  {
    JLabel labelLbs = new JLabel("Weight (lbs):",
                                 SwingConstants.RIGHT);

    < ... etc.  See Ch06\Exercises\Bmi.java 🖫 >

    c.add(p, BorderLayout.CENTER);
    c.add(go, BorderLayout.SOUTH);
  }

  public void actionPerformed(ActionEvent e)
  {
    int lbs = Integer.parseInt(inputLbs.getText());
    int inches = Integer.parseInt(inputInches.getText());
    double bmi = calculateBmi(lbs, inches);
    DecimalFormat df = new DecimalFormat("00.0");
    displayBmi.setText(df.format(bmi));
  }

  private double calculateBmi(int lbs, int inches)
  {
    < ... missing code >
  }
}
```

Supply the missing code for the `calculateBmi` method, which takes a weight in pounds and height in inches as arguments and returns the body mass index.

18.▪   Write a method

```
public int convertToHumanAge(int dogYears)
```

that converts a dog's age to the corresponding human age. Assume that a dog's first year corresponds to a human age of 13. After that every three years in a dog's life correspond to sixteen years in human life. The method returns the corresponding human age, rounded to the nearest integer. Write a console Java application using the `EasyReader` class to test your method (or, if you prefer, convert the GUI from the *BMI* applet in Question 17 into a dog-to-human-age converter). ✓

Figure R-1 shows the *Rainbow* applet. This "rainbow" is made of four overlapping semicircles. The three visible rings have red, green, and magenta colors (corresponding to the color constants `Color.red`, `Color.green`, and `Color.magenta`). The center of the rainbow is in the middle horizontally and 2/3 of the way down vertically in the applet's content pane.

Follow the instructions below and fill in the blanks in the applet's code. This code, `Rainbow.java` 🖫, is shown in Figure R-2, and is available in the `Rainbow` folder on your student disk.

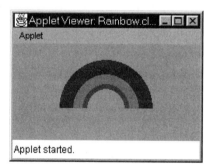

Figure R-1. The *Rainbow* applet

```java
import java.awt.*;
import javax.swing.*;

public class Rainbow extends JApplet
{
  // Declare skyColor
  // _____

  public void init
  {
    Container c = getContentPane();
    c.setBackground(Color.white);
  }

  public void paint(graphics g)
  {
    super.paint(g);
    Container c = getContentPane();
    int width = c.getWidth();
        height = c.getHeight();

    // Declare and initialize integer variables xCenter, yCenter
    // that represent the center of the rainbow rings
    // _____

    // Declare and initialize the radius of the large semicircle
    // _____

    g.setColor(Color.red);

    // Draw the large semicircle:
    // g.fillArc( ... );
    // _____

    // Declare and initialize the radii of the small and medium
    // semicircles and draw them
    // _____

    // Calculate the radius of the innermost (sky-color) semicircle
    // so that the width of the middle (green) ring is the
    // arithmetic mean of the widths of the red and magenta rings.
    // Draw the sky-color semicircle.
    // _____
  }
}
```

Figure R-2. `Rainbow\Rainbow.java` (with syntax errors) 💾

1.   Copy the `Rainbow.java` and `TestRainbow.html` files to your work folder.

2.   Add a comment with your name at the top of the file.

3.   Find and fix three syntax errors in `Rainbow.java` so that it compiles with no errors.

4.   Add to the `Rainbow` class a declaration of a `private final` field `skyColor` of the type `Color` initialized to `Color.cyan` (the color of the sky). In the `init` method, set the applet's background to `skyColor` rather than white.

5.   In the `paint` method, declare <u>local</u> integer variables `xCenter` and `yCenter` that represent the coordinates of the center of the rings and initialize them to 1/2 width and 2/3 height (down) of the content pane, respectively. (Recall that the origin of graphics coordinates in Java is at the upper left corner of the content pane with the *y*-axis pointing down.) Do not plug in fixed numbers from the applet's dimensions because then your applet will not be scalable — instead use the variables `width` and `height` provided in the code.

6.   Declare a local variable `largeRadius` that represents the radius of the largest (red) semicircle and initialize it to 1/4 of the content pane's width.

7.   Recall that `g.fillArc(x, y, size, size, from, degrees)` (with all integer arguments) draws a sector of a circle. `x` and `y` are the coordinates of the upper left corner of the square into which the circle is (logically) inscribed; `size` is the side of the square (and the diameter of the circle); `from` is the starting point of the arc in degrees (with 0 at the easternmost point of the horizontal diameter), and `degrees` (a positive number) is the measure of the arc, going counterclockwise. Add a statement to `paint` to draw the largest (red) semicircle. Test your applet using `TestRainbow.html` 🖫.

8.   Add statements to display the medium (green) and the small (magenta) semicircles. The radius of the small semicircle should be 1/4 of the height of the content pane. The radius of the medium one should be the geometric mean (the square root of the product) of the big and small ones, rounded to the nearest integer. (Recall that a call to `Math.sqrt(x)` returns the value of square root of x, a `double`.) Retest your applet.

Continued ➮

9. Add statements to display the innermost semicircle of the background ("sky") color to complete the rainbow. Use the `skyColor` constant for this semicircle's color. Choose the radius of the innermost semicircle in such a way that the width of the middle (green) ring is the arithmetic mean of the widths of the red and magenta rings.

10. Test your applet and try to resize it to see the limits of its scalability.

You can find a solution in `RainbowSolution.java` ⬚ in the `Rainbow` folder on your student disk.

if (chapter == 7)

Boolean Expressions and
`if-else` Statements

7.1   Prologue

Normally control flows sequentially from one statement to the next during program execution. This sequence may be altered by several types of control mechanisms:

1. Calling a method
2. Iterative statements (loops)
3. Conditional (`if-else`) statements
4. `switch` statements
5. Exceptions

In this chapter we will study the `if-else` statement, which tells the program to choose and execute one fragment of code or another depending on some condition. We will also take a look at the `switch` statement, which chooses a particular fragment of code out of several based on the value of a variable or expression.

The `if-else` control structure allows ***conditional branching***.   Suppose, for instance, we want to find the absolute value of an integer. The method that returns an absolute value may look as follows:

```
public static int abs(int x)
{
  int ax;

  if (x >= 0)      // If x is greater or equal to 0
    ax = x;        //    do this;
  else             // else
    ax = -x;       //    do this.
  return ax;
}
```

Or, more concisely:

```
public static int abs(int x)
{
  if (x < 0)       // If x is less than 0
    x = -x;        //    negate x;
  return x;
}
```

There are special CPU instructions called ***conditional jumps*** that support conditional branching. The CPU always fetches the address of the next instruction from a special register, which in some systems is called the Instruction Pointer (IP). Normally, this register is incremented automatically after each instruction is executed so that it points to the next instruction. This makes the program execute consecutive instructions in order.

A conditional jump instruction tests a certain condition and tells the CPU to "jump" to a specified instruction depending on the result of the test. If the tested condition is satisfied, a new value is placed into the IP, which causes the program to skip to the specified instruction. For example, an instruction may test whether the result of the previous operation is greater than zero, and, if it is, tell the CPU to jump backward or forward to a specified address. If the condition is false, program execution continues with the next consecutive instruction.

In high-level languages, conditions for jumps are written using relational operators such as "less than," "greater than," "equal to," and so on, and the logical operators "and," "or," and "not." Expressions combining these operators are called *logical* or *Boolean* expressions. The value of a Boolean expression may be either true or false.

In the following sections we will discuss the syntax for coding if-else and switch statements, declaring boolean variables, and writing Boolean expressions with relational and logical operators. We will also briefly discuss two properties of formal logic, known as *DeMorgan's laws*, that are useful in programming. We will talk about *short-circuit evaluation* in handling multiple conditions connected with "and" and "or" operators. Then we will use a case study to illustrate and practice the basics of object-oriented design and implementation methodology: how to define the classes and objects needed in an application, how to divide work among team members, and how to test parts of a project independently from other parts.

7.2 if-else Statements

The general form of the if-else statement in Java is:

```
if (condition)
   statement1;
else
   statement2;
```

where *condition* is a logical expression and *statement1* and *statement2* are either simple statements or *compound statements* (blocks surrounded by braces). Parentheses around *condition* are required. When an if-else statement is executed, the program evaluates the condition and then executes *statement1* if the condition is true and *statement2* if the condition is false.

The else clause is optional, so the if statement can be used by itself:

```
if (condition)
    statement1;
```

When if is coded without else, the program evaluates the condition and executes *statement1* if the condition is true. If the condition is false, the program skips *statement1*.

7.3   boolean Data Type

Java has a primitive data type called boolean. boolean variables can hold only one of two values: true or false. boolean, true, and false are Java reserved words. There is not much sense in declaring boolean constants because you can just use true or false. You declare boolean variables like this:

```
boolean aVar;
```

Boolean expressions are made of boolean variables, relational operators, such as >, and logical operators. You can assign the value of any Boolean expression to a boolean variable. For example:

```
boolean over21 = age > 21;
```

Here over21 gets a value of true if age is greater than 21, false otherwise. This is essentially the same as

```
boolean over21;

if (age > 21)
  over21 = true;
else
  over21 = false;
```

but much shorter.

7.4   Relational Operators

Java recognizes six relational operators:

Operator	Meaning
>	greater than
<	less than
>=	greater than or equal to
<=	less than or equal to
==	is equal to
!=	is not equal to

The result of a relational operation has the boolean type. It has a value equal to true if the comparison is true and false otherwise.

Relational operations are frequently used in conditional statements. For example:

```
if (x > y)
   max = x;
else
   max = y;
```

Note that in Java the "is equal to" condition is expressed by the == operator, while a single "=" sign means assignment. Be careful not to confuse the two.

Relational operators are applied mostly to primitive numeric data types. The == and != operators can also be applied to characters. For example:

```
if (gender == 'F')
{
   System.out.print("Dear Ms. ");
}
else
{
   System.out.print("Dear Mr. ");
}
```

Avoid using `==` and `!=` for `double` or `float` variables and expressions because floating-point arithmetic is imprecise. For example, in

```
15.0 / 3.0 == 5.0
```

the numbers on the left and right may be very close but not exactly equal due to rounding errors.

❖   ❖   ❖

> **If you apply the `==` and `!=` operators to <u>objects</u>, then instead of comparing the <u>values</u> of two objects you will be comparing two <u>references</u> to them (i.e., their addresses). This is a source of nasty bugs.**

For example, in the statements

```
String fileName;
...
if (fileName == "applet.html")
   ...
```

the `==` operator compares the addresses of the `String` object `fileName` and the `String` object that represents a literal string `"applet.html"`. Their addresses are most likely different, even though their current <u>values</u> may be the same. As we'll explain in Chapter 9, you have to use `String`'s `equals` method to compare string values, as in

```
if (fileName.equals("applet.html")) ...
```

or

```
if ("applet.html".equals(fileName)) ...
```

However, occasionally it is useful to compare references to objects, for example if you want to know which object (e.g., a button) caused a particular event.

7.5   Logical Operators

Java has two binary logical operators, "and" and "or," and a unary logical operator, "not." They are represented by the following symbols:

Operator	Meaning
&&	and
||	or
!	not

The expression

    condition1 && condition2

is true if and only if <u>both</u> condition1 <u>and</u> condition2 are true.

The expression

    condition1 || condition2

is true if condition1 <u>or</u> condition2 (or both) are true.

The expression

    !condition1

is true if and only if condition1 is false.

The following code:

```
boolean match;
...
if (!match)
   ...
```

works the same way as:

```
boolean match;
...
if (match == false)
   ...
```

The results of the logical operations `&&`, `||`, and `!` have the `boolean` data type, just like for the relational operations.

The "and," "or," and "not" operations are related to each other in the following way:

Boolean expression	has the same Boolean value as:
not (*p* and *q*)	not *p* or not *q*
not (*p* or *q*)	not *p* and not *q*

For example, "not (fun and games)" is the same as "not fun <u>or</u> not games (or neither)."

These two properties of logic are called ***De Morgan's laws***. They come from formal logic but they are useful in practical programming as well. In Java notation, De Morgan's laws take the following form:

> **`!(p && q)` is the same as `!p || !q`**
> **`!(p || q)` is the same as `!p && !q`**

A programmer may choose either of the equivalent forms; the choice depends on which form is more readable. Usually it is better to distribute the `!` ("not"). For example:

```
if (x >= 0 && x < 5)
```

is much easier to read than:

```
if (!(x < 0 || x >= 5))
```

7.6   Order of Operators

In general, all unary operators have higher precedence then binary operators, so unary operators, including `!` ("not"), are applied first. You have to use parentheses if `!` applies to the entire expression. For example:

```
if (!cond1 && cond2)
```

means

```
if ((!cond1) && cond2)
```

rather than

```
if (!(cond1 && cond2))
```

All binary arithmetic operators (+, *, etc.) have higher rank than all relational operators (>, <, ==, etc.), so arithmetic operators are applied first. For example, you can write simply:

```
if (a + b >= 2 * n)            // Ok!
   ...
```

when you mean:

```
if ((a + b) >= (2 * n))        // The inside parentheses are
   ...                          //   optional
```

Arithmetic and relational operators have higher rank than the binary logical operators && and ||, so arithmetic and relational operators are applied first. For example, you can write simply:

```
if (x + y > 0 && b != 0)       // Ok!
```

as opposed to:

```
if ((x + y > 0) && (b != 0))   // The inside parentheses are
                                //   optional
```

When && and || operators are combined in one logical expression, && has higher rank than || (i.e., && is performed before ||), but with these it is a good idea to always use parentheses to avoid confusion and make the code more readable. For example:

```
// Inside parentheses not required, but recommended for clarity:
if ((x > 2 && y > 5) || (x < -2 && y < -5))
   ...
```

The rules of precedence for the operators we have encountered so far are summarized in the table below:

Highest	! (unary)- (cast) ++ --
↕	* / %
	+ -
	< <= > >= == !=
	&&
Lowest	||

In the absence of parentheses, binary operators of the same rank are performed left to right, and unary operators right to left. If in doubt — use parentheses!

7.7   Short-Circuit Evaluation

In the binary logical operations `&&` and `||`, the left operand is always evaluated first. There may be situations when its value predetermines the result of the operation. For example, if *condition1* is false, then the expression *condition1 && condition2* is always false, no matter what the value of *condition2* is. If *condition1* is true, then *condition1 || condition2* is always true.

If the value of the first (left) operand in a binary logical operation unambiguously determines the result of the operation, the second operand is <u>not</u> evaluated. This rule is called *short-circuit evaluation.*

If the expression combines several `&&` operations at the same level, such as

        condition1 && condition2 && condition3 ...

the evaluation of conditions proceeds from left to right. If a <u>false</u> condition is encountered, then the remaining conditions are <u>not</u> evaluated, because the value of the entire expression is false. Similarly, if the expression combines several `||` operations at the same level,

```
condition1 || condition2 || condition3 ...
```

the evaluation proceeds from left to right only until a <u>true</u> condition is encountered, because then the value of the entire expression is true.

The short-circuit evaluation rule not only saves program execution time but is also convenient in some situations. For example, it is safe to write:

```
if (y != 0 && x/y > 3)
    ...
```

because x/y is not calculated when y is equal to 0.

> **Java also provides bit-wise "and" and "or" operators that normally work on <u>integers</u> and operate on individual bits. These operators are denoted as & and | (as opposed to && and ||). Unfortunately these operators also work on booleans, and they <u>do not</u> follow the short-circuit evaluation rule. This is really confusing and a source of bugs.**

Make sure you use && and || unless you are indeed working with individual bits. Bit-wise operators are explained in Section 16.3.

7.8   if-else-if and Nested if-else

Sometimes a program needs to branch three or more ways. Consider the *sign(x)* function:

$$sign(x) \;=\; \begin{cases} -1, & \text{if } x < 0 \\ \;\;0, & \text{if } x = 0 \\ \;\;1, & \text{if } x > 0 \end{cases}$$

The *sign(x)* method can be implemented in Java as follows:

```
public static int sign(int x)      // Correct but clumsy code...
{
  int s;

  if (x < 0)
    s = -1;
  else
  {
    if (x == 0)
      s = 0;
    else
      s = 1;
  }
  return s;
}
```

This code is correct, but it looks cumbersome. The x < 0 case seems arbitrarily singled out and placed at a higher level than the x == 0 and x > 0 cases. Actually, the braces in the outer else can be removed, because the inner if-else is one complete statement. Without braces, the compiler always associates an else with the nearest if above it. The simplified code without braces looks as follows:

```
public static int sign(int x)      // Correct, but still clumsy...
{
  int s;

  if (x < 0)
    s = -1;
  else
    if (x == 0)
      s = 0;
    else
      s = 1;
  return s;
}
```

It is customary in such situations to arrange the statements differently: the second if is placed next to the first else and one level of indentation is removed, as follows:

```
public static int sign(int x)      // The way it should be...
{
  int s;

  if (x < 0)
    s = -1;
  else if (x == 0)     // This arrangement of if-else is a matter
    s = 0;             //   of style: structurally, the second
  else                 //   if-else is still nested within the
    s = 1;             //   first else
  return s;
}
```

This format emphasizes the three-way branching that conceptually occurs at the same level in the program, even though technically the second if-else is ***nested*** in the first else.

A chain of if-else-if statements may be as long as necessary:

```
if (condition1)
{
   ...                  // 1st case
}
else if (condition2)
{
   ...                  // 2d case
}
else if (condition3)
{
   ...                  // 3d case
}

...
...

else if (conditionN)
{
   ...                  // N-th case
}
else  // the "else" clause may be omitted
{
   ...                  // otherwise
}
```

This is a rather common structure in Java programs and usually quite readable. For example:

```
if (points >= 90)
   grade = 'A';
else if (points >= 80)
   grade = 'B';
else if (points >= 70)
   grade = 'C';
else if (points >= 60)
   grade = 'D';
else
   grade = 'F';
```

Or:

```
if (x < lowerLimit)
{
  x = lowerLimit;
}
else if (x > upperLimit)
{
  x = upperLimit;
}
```

A different situation occurs when a program requires true hierarchical branching with nested `if-else` statements, as in a decision tree:

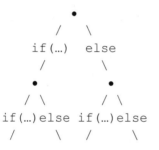

Consider, for example, the following code:

```
// Surcharge calculation:
if (age <= 25)
{
  if (accidents)
    surcharge = 1.4;   // Premium surcharge 40%
  else
    surcharge = 1.2;   // Surcharge 20%
}
else
{    // if age > 25
  if (accidents)
    surcharge = 1.1;   // Surcharge 10%
  else
    surcharge = .9;    // Discount 10%
}
```

Here the use of nested `if-else` statements is justified by the logic of the task.

When `if-else` statements are nested in your code to three or four levels, the code becomes intractable. This indicates that you probably need to restructure your code, perhaps using separate methods to handle individual cases.

Nested `if`s can often be substituted with the `&&` operation:

```
if (condition1)
   if (condition2)
      statement;
```

is exactly the same (due to short-circuit evaluation) as

```
if (condition1 && condition2)
   statement;
```

but the latter form is usually clearer.

7.9   Common if-else Errors

1. Extra semicolon:

```
if (condition);     // Compiled as:  if (condition) /* do nothing */;
   statement1;      //                  statement1;
```

2. Missing semicolon before else:

```
if (condition)
   statement1       // Syntax error caught by the compiler
else
   statement2;
```

3. Omitted braces:

```
if (condition)     // Compiled as: if (condition)
   statement1;     //                 statement1;
   statement2;     //              statement2;
```

4. "Dangling" else:

```
if (condition1)     // Compiled as: if (condition1)
   if (condition2)  //              {
      statement1;   //                 if (condition2)
else                //                    statement1;
   statement2;      //                 else
                    //                    statement2;
                    //              }
```

7.10 *Case Study and Lab:* Rolling Dice

In this section we will implement the *Craps* applet. "Craps" is a game played with dice. A player rolls two dice and counts the total number of points on them. If the total is 7 or 11, the player wins; if the total is 2, 3 or 12, the player loses. If the total is anything else, the player has to continue rolling. The total, called the "point," is remembered, and the objective now is to roll the same total as "point." The player keeps rolling until he gets either "point" or 7. If he rolls "point" first, he wins, but if he rolls a 7 first, he loses. You can see why this game was chosen as a lab for if-else statements!

Our team was asked to design and code a *Craps* applet for the web page of the "Casino Night" charitable event planned in our company. Three people will be working on this project. I am the project leader, responsible for the overall design and dividing the work between us. I will also help team members with detailed design and work on my own piece of code. The second person, Aisha, is a consultant; she specializes in GUI design and implementation.

The third person is you!

You can run the compiled *Craps* applet on your student disk to see how the final product will look. Use the TestCraps.html 🖫 and .class files in the Ch07\RunCraps folder. When you click on the "Roll" button, red dice start rolling on a green "table." When they stop, the result (win or loss) is added to the total or "point" is shown on the display panel (Figure 7-1). The applet allows you to play as many games as you want.

Let's begin by discussing which objects are needed for this applet. One approach may be to try making objects in the program represent objects from the real world. Unfortunately, it is not always clear what exactly is a "real world" object. Some objects may simulate tangible machines or mechanisms, others may exist only in "cyberspace," and still others may be quite abstract and exist only in the designer's imagination.

Here we need one object that represents the applet as a whole. Let us call its class Craps. As usual, we will derive this class from the JApplet class in Java's Swing package:

```
public class Craps extends JApplet ...
```

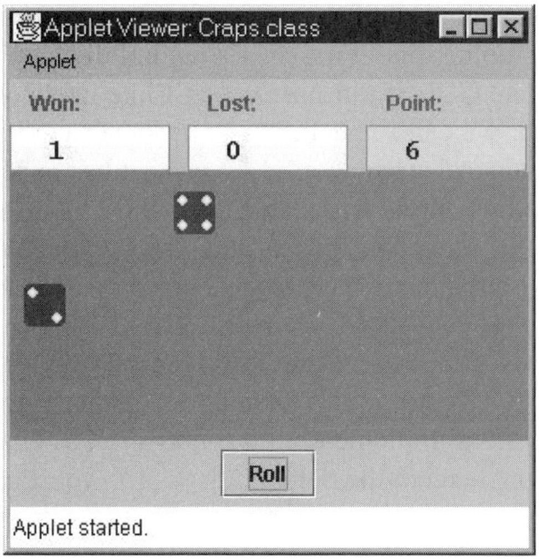

Figure 7-1.   The *Craps* applet

The `craps` object will be responsible for GUI and in general will hold our applet together. Aisha, as our GUI expert, will implement the `Craps` class when she has time.

We also need one object that will control the two rolling dice and report the sum of the points on the dice back to the `craps` object when the dice stop rolling. Let's call the class for this object `CrapsTable` and the object `table`. The `CrapsTable` class will be derived from Swing's GUI component `JPanel` because we have to repaint `table` separately for a smooth animation effect:

```
public class CrapsTable extends JPanel...
```

I like animations, so I will work on the `CrapsTable` class myself. As I start thinking about it, I realize that it will be cumbersome to keep track of the positions and speeds of two dice in one object. It would be much easier to have a separate object for each rolling die. Also my `CrapsTable` class would be too big if it tried to do everything. I like my classes to fit on one or two pages max. Besides, rolling dice can be reused in other games. So I decide to define another class, `RollingDie`, and let my `table` object create and manage two `RollingDie` objects, `die1` and `die2`.

Finally, someone has to implement the rules of the game itself. In this project we will separate the implementation of the rules of the game from the GUI. There are many good reasons for doing this. First, it is a natural division of labor. Second, we might need to change the GUI (if our boss doesn't like its "look and feel") but leave the game alone. Third, we can reuse the game in other applications. For example, we might use it in a statistical simulation of *Craps* that has to run quickly and doesn't need a fancy GUI at all. Fourth, Aisha and I know only the general concept of the game and are not really interested in learning the details. And fifth, we have a beginner on our team (you) and we have to give you a manageable piece of work.

So we will need a class CrapsGame and one object of that class. Let us call this object game. (game is a "conceptual" object, not something that can be touched. That won't prevent us from implementing it in Java.) The CrapsGame class won't be derived from anything (except the default, Object), won't use any Java packages, and won't process any events:

```
public class CrapsGame
{
    . . .
}
```

Figure 7-2 summarizes my general design, the interaction between objects and classes, and the division of tasks among us.

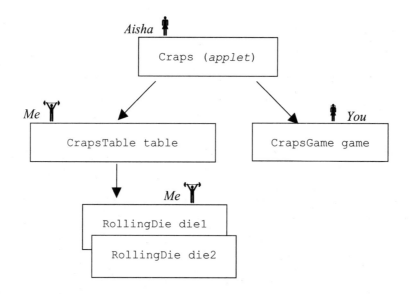

Figure 7-2. The classes and objects in the *Craps* applet

Now we have to agree on some details. Aisha's class `Craps` will hold the applet together; we have to decide what she needs from us. Basically she needs to be able to tell me that the "Roll" button was clicked and that I should roll the dice. My class, `CrapsTable`, will provide a method `rollDice()` that Aisha can call:

```
    table.rollDice();
```

When the dice stop rolling, I have to report that fact and the point total back to Aisha. Her `Craps` class will provide a method for this:

```
    public void processRoll(int pts)
    {
      . . .
    }
```

Then she needs to pass the points to you, since you are handling the game details. Your class `CrapsGame` will have a method for that:

```
    result = game.nextRoll(pts);
```

`nextRoll` returns the result of the roll: 1 if the player wins, −1 if he loses, and 0 if the game continues. The `game` object has a private field `point` that holds the "point" value. `nextRoll` sets the value of the `point` field to the point value, or to 0 if the current game is over. Initially `point` is 0, and it is reset to 0 after each game to get ready for the next one. Your class will provide an "accessor" method `getPoint` to let Aisha get the value of `point` from you, so that she can display it on the display panel.

We are ready to start the work. The only problem is the time frame. Aisha's completion date is unpredictable: she is very busy, but once she gets to work she works very fast. My task can be rather time-consuming. I will try to arrange a field trip to Las Vegas to make some videos of rolling dice. But most likely our boss won't approve that and I'll have to settle for observing rolling dice on the carpet in my office. Meanwhile you are anxious to start your part.

Fortunately Aisha has found an old test applet to which you can feed integers as input. She added a few lines to it to call `nextRoll` and `getPoint` and display their return values (Figure 7-3). She called her temporary class `CrapsOne`. Now you don't have to wait for us: you can implement your class independently. You won't see any dice rolling for now, but you will be able to test your class thoroughly.

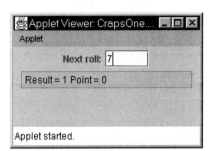

Figure 7-3. The preliminary applet for testing CrapsGame

```
public class CrapsGame
{
  private int point = 0;        // = 0 is optional: it's the default

  /**
   *  Calculates the result of the next dice roll in the Craps game.
   *  @param pts the total number of points on two dice.
   *  <code>result</code> is set to 1 if player won, -1 if player lost,
   *  0 if player continues rolling.  <code>point</code> is set to the
   *  saved total if the game continues, 0 if the game has ended.
   */
  public int nextRoll(int pts)
  {
    int result;

    < ... missing code:
       calculate result and set point appropriately;
       do not use other return statements. >

    return result;
  }

  public int getPoint()
  {
    return point;
  }
}
```

Figure 7-4. Ch07\Craps1\CrapsGame.java 💾

1. Copy the CrapsOne.java, CrapsGame.java, and TestCrapsOne.html 🖫 files from the Ch07\Craps1 folder on your student disk to your work folder. Fill in the blanks in the CrapsGame class (Figure 7-4) and compile and test it with the CrapsOne applet provided.

2. After you get the CrapsGame class to work, also test it with the *Craps Stats* application, which quickly runs the game multiple times and counts the number of wins. It is not an applet but a stand-alone application. Note how we <u>reuse</u> here the CrapsGame class that you have written for a different program.

   Copy CrapsStats.java 🖫 from the Ch07\Craps1 folder. You also need the ExitButtonListener.java file from the Ch03\HelloGui folder. You can run *Craps Stats* from your IDE or using Java SDK's compiler and interpreter:

   ```
   C:\Mywork> javac CrapsStats.java
   C:\Mywork> java CrapsStats
   ```

   Compare your simulation result with the theoretical probability of winning in *Craps,* which is 244/495, or about 0.493. If you run 1000 trial games, the number of wins should be between 462 and 524.

7.11 The switch statement

There are situations when a program must take one of several actions depending on the value of some variable or expression. If the program has to handle just two or three possible actions, you can easily use if-else-if statements:

```
int x = expression;      // Evaluate the expression
                         //   and save its value in x
if (x == valueA)
{
    // Take action A
    statementA1;
    statementA2;
    ...
}
else if (x == valueB)
{
    // Take action B
    statementB1;
    ...
}
```

Continued ➥

```
    ...
    ...

    else if (x == valueZ)
    {
        // Take action Z
        statementZ1;
        ...
    }
    else
    {
        // Take some default action
        ...
    }
```

(*valueA*, *valueB*, ..., and *valueZ* are integer constants.)

When the number of possible actions is large, the use of if-else-if becomes cumbersome and inefficient. Java provides a special mechanism, the switch statement, for handling such situations. Its general form is:

```
    switch (expression)
    {
      case valueA:        // Take action A
        statementA1;
        statementA2;
        ...
        break;

      case valueB:        // Take action B
        statementB1;
                ...
        break;

      ...
      ...

      case valueZ:        // Take action Z
        statementZ1;
        ...
        break;

      default:            // Take some default action
        ...
        break;
    }
```

valueA, *valueB*, ... , *valueZ* are integer or character literal or symbolic constants. When a switch is compiled, the compiler creates a table of these values and the associated addresses of the corresponding "cases" (code fragments). When the switch is executed, the program first evaluates *expression* to an integer. Then it finds it in the table and jumps to the corresponding case. If the value is not in the table, the program jumps to "default." The break statement at the end of a case tells the program to jump out of the switch and continue with the first statement after the switch. switch, case, default, and break are Java reserved words.

Note the following properties of the switch statement:

1. The expression evaluated in a switch must have an integral type (integer or char). In most programs it is really not an expression but simply one variable, as in switch(x).

2. Each case must be labeled by a literal or symbolic constant. A case cannot be labeled by a variable or an expression that is not constant.

3. The same action may be activated by more than one label. For example:

```
case '/':          // both '/' and ':' signify division
case ':':
  < ... statements >
  break;
```

4. There may be a break in the <u>middle</u> of a case, but then it must be inside an if or else, otherwise some code in that case would be unreachable. Such a break tells the program to jump out of the switch immediately. For example:

```
case '/':
  ...
  if (y == 0)
  {
      cout << "*** Division by zero ***\n";
      break;     // Jump out of the switch
  }

  < ... other statements >

  break;          // Jump out of the switch
```

5. The default clause is optional. If not specified, the default action is "do nothing."

6. It is a common mistake to omit break at the end of a case.

> **The `switch` syntax does not require that each case end with a `break`. Without a `break`, though, the program <u>falls through</u> and continues with the next case. This feature may lead to annoying bugs, and programmers usually take special care to put a `break` at the end of each case.**

Unusual situations, where a programmer intentionally allows the program to "fall through" from one case to the next, call for a special comment in the code.

7.12 *Case Study and Lab:* **Rolling Dice Continued**

By this time you have finished your `CrapsGame` class and Aisha has found the time to put together a GUI for it. I myself have gotten bogged down with my `CrapsTable` and `RollingDie` classes, trying to perfect the animation effects. Meanwhile, not to stall Aisha's testing, I have written a "stub" class `CrapsTable` to provide a temporary substitute for the actual class I am working on. A stub class has very simple versions of methods needed for testing other classes. This is a common technique when a programmer needs to test a part of the project while other parts are not yet ready.

Figure 7-5 shows my temporary stub class. In my stub class I have included a temporary version of the `rollDice` method that simply calls `Craps`'s `processRoll` method with a random sum of points. Aisha also asked me to add a `boolean` method `diceAreRolling` which will tell her not to call `rollDice` again while the previous roll is still in progress. In the stub class, `diceAreRolling` simply returns `false`. In return I asked Aisha to pass me a reference to her applet object when she constructs a new "craps table" because I need it to call her `processRoll` method. We forgot to discuss this earlier.

You're certainly welcome to take a look at Aisha's GUI implementation (Figure 7-6), but no one has time right now to explain to you how it works.

❖   ❖   ❖

```
public class CrapsTable
{
  private Craps craps;

  public CrapsTable(Craps applet)
  {
    craps = applet;
  }

  public void rollDice()
  {
    int pts1 = (int)(6 * Math.random()) + 1;
    int pts2 = (int)(6 * Math.random()) + 1;
    craps.processRoll(pts1 + pts2);
  }

  public boolean diceAreRolling()
  {
    return false;
  }
}
```

Figure 7-5. Temporary "stub" class `CrapsTable.java`

```
import java.awt.*;
import java.awt.event.*;
import javax.swing.*;

public class Craps extends JApplet
    implements ActionListener
{
  private CrapsTable table;
  private CrapsGame game;
  private JPanel display;
  private JTextField wonText, lostText, pointText;
  private int wonCount, lostCount;

  public void init()
  {
    display = new JPanel(new GridLayout(2, 3, 10, 0));

    display.add(new JLabel("     Won:"));
    display.add(new JLabel("     Lost:"));
    display.add(new JLabel("     Point:"));
```

Figure 7-6 `Craps.java` Continued ➪

```
                < ... etc.  See Ch07\Craps2\Craps.java 💾 >

    table = new CrapsTable(this);
    table.setBackground(Color.green);

                < ... etc.  See Ch07\Craps2\Craps.java 💾 >

    game = new CrapsGame();
  }

  public void actionPerformed(ActionEvent e)
  {
    if (!table.diceAreRolling())
      table.rollDice();
  }

  public void processRoll(int pts)
  {
    int result;

    result = game.nextRoll(pts);


    if (result > 0)
    {
      wonCount++;
      wonText.setText("   " + wonCount);
      pointText.setText("");
      pointText.setBackground(Color.darkGray);
    }
    else if (result < 0)
    {
      lostCount++;
      lostText.setText("   " + lostCount);
      pointText.setText("");
      pointText.setBackground(Color.darkGray);
    }
    else
    {
      pointText.setText("   " + game.getPoint());
      pointText.setBackground(Color.yellow);
    }
  }
}
```

Figure 7-6. Ch07\Craps2\Craps.java 💾

Since you are done with your part, I thought you could help me out with my RollingDie class. I've made a lot of progress on it, but a couple of details remain unfinished.

I have coded the constructor, the roll method that resets my die and starts it rolling, and the avoidCollision method that does not allow one die to overlap with another. I have also provided a simple accessor method getPoints that returns the number of points on the stopped die and the boolean method isRolling that tells whether my die is moving or not. But I am still working on drawing a rolling and a stopped die. I took what is called ***top-down*** approach with ***step-wise*** refinement, moving from more general tasks to more specific. First I coded the draw method in general terms:

```
public void draw(Graphics g)
{
  if (xCenter < 0 || yCenter < 0)  // this die is off the table
    return;
  else if (isRolling())
  {
    move();
    drawRolling(g);
    xSpeed *= slowdown;
    ySpeed *= slowdown;
  }
  else
    drawStopped(g);
}
```

Note how I used the if-else-if structure to process three situations: my die is off the table, it is still moving, and it is stopped. My draw method calls the more specialized methods drawRolling and drawStopped. I am still working on these, but I know that each of them will call an even lower-level method drawDots that draws white dots on my die.

```
private void drawRolling(Graphics g)
{
  . . .
  drawDots(g, x, y, randomPoints());
}

private void drawStopped(Graphics g)
{
  . . .
  drawDots(g, x, y, points);
}
```

I have started `drawDots` (Figure 7-7) and am counting on you to finish it. (Naturally, it involves a `switch` statement.) Meanwhile I will finish `CrapsTable` and we should be able to put it all together.

```java
private void drawDots(Graphics g, int x, int y, int points)
{
  int x1, x2, x3, y1, y2, y3, dotSize;

  g.setColor(Color.white);

  dotSize = dieSize / 4;
  int step = dieSize / 8;
  x1 = x + step - 1;
  x2 = x + 3*step;
  x3 = x + 5*step + 1;
  y1 = y + step - 1;
  y2 = y + 3*step;
  y3 = y + 5*step + 1;

  switch (points)
  {
    case 1:
      g.fillOval(x2, y2, dotSize, dotSize);
      break;

    < ... missing code >

  }
}
```

Figure 7-7. A fragment from `Ch07\Craps2\RollingDie.java`

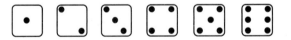

Figure 7-8. Dots configuration on a die for the `drawDots` method

Copy the `RollingDie.java` file from the `Ch07\Craps2` folder on your student disk into your work folder and fill in the blanks in its `drawDots` method. Figure 7-8 shows the desired configurations of dots on a die. Collect all four classes for the *Craps* applet: `Craps.java` and `CrapsTable.java` (from the `Ch07\Craps2` folder), CrapsGame.java (your solution from the lab in Section 7.10), and RollingDie.java. Compile them, and run the applet from the provided TestCraps.html file.

7.13 Summary

The general form of a conditional statement in Java is:

```
if (condition)
    statement1;
else
    statement2;
```

where *statement1* and *statement2* can be either simple statements (terminating with a semicolon) or compound statements (a block of statements within braces). *condition* may be any Boolean expression.

Conditions are often written with the relational operators

<	less than
<=	less than or equal to
>	greater than
>=	greater than or equal to
==	is equal to
!=	is not equal to

and the logical operators

&&	and
||	or
!	not

It is useful for programmers to know two properties from formal logic called *De Morgan's laws:*

```
!(p && q)  is the same as  !p || !q
!(p || q)  is the same as  !p && !q
```

Use the

```
if...
else if...
else if...
...
else ...
```

structure for multiway branching, and use nested if-else for hierarchical branching.

The general form of a switch statement is

```
switch (expression)
{
  case valueA:        // Take action A
    statementA1;
    statementA2;
    ...
    break;

  case valueB:        // Take action B
    statementB1;
    ...
    break;

  ...
  ...

  default:            // Take the default action
    ...
    break;
}
```

where *valueA*, *valueB*, etc., are integer or character literal or symbolic constants. The switch evaluates *expression* and jumps to the case labeled by the corresponding constant value, or to the default case if no match has been found. A switch can be used to replace a long if-else-if sequence.

Exercises

Sections 7.1-7.5

1.   Fill in the blanks to create a method that returns the value of the larger of the integers x and y (or either one, if they are equal): ✓

```
public static int max(int x, int y)
{
    _____

    _____

    return _____ ;
}
```

2.   Consider the three circuits in Question 1 for Chapter 1 (page 20). A Java expression equivalent to Circuit (a) is `a && b` (assuming that the two inputs are the values of `boolean` variables a and b). Write Java expressions equivalent to Circuits (b) and (c). ✓

3.■   Invent three ways to express the XOR ("exclusive OR") operation in Java (i.e., a Boolean expression that involves two `boolean` variables and that is true if and only if exactly one of the two variables has the value `true`).
      ≷ Hint: one of the possible solutions involves only one (relational) operator. For other solutions see Figure 1-2 on page 3 and Question 4 for Chapter 1 (page 21). ≷

4.   Which of the following expressions are equivalent (i.e., have the same value for all possible values of the variables a and b) to `!(a || !b)`?

      A.   `a || !b`
      B.   `!a || b`
      C.   `!a && b`
      D.   `!a && !b`
      E.   `a && !b`

5.   Simplify the following expressions (open as many parentheses as possible) using De Morgan's Laws:

      (a)   `!((!x || !y) && (a || b))` ✓
      (b)   `if (!(x == 7) && !(x > 7)) ...`

Sections 7.6-7.10

6.   Remove as many parentheses as possible without changing the meaning of the condition:

(a)   `if ((((x + 2) > a) || ((x - 2) < b)) && (y >= 0))` ✓
(b)   `if (((a >= b) && (a >= c)) && ((a % 2) == 0))`

7.   Simplify the following statements:

(a)   ✓
```
boolean inside = !((x < left) || (x > right) ||
    (y < top) || (y > bottom));
```
(b)
```
boolean no = (ch[0] == 'N' && ch[1] == 'O') ||
             (ch[0] == 'n' && ch[1] == 'o') ||
             (ch[0] == 'N' && ch[1] == 'o') ||
             (ch[0] == 'n' && ch[1] == 'O');
```

8.   Given an integer variable x, write a Boolean expression that evaluates to `true` if and only if the decimal representation of the value of x ends with exactly two zeroes. ✓

9.   Rewrite the following condition to avoid a possible arithmetic exception error:

```
if (Math.sqrt(x) < 3 && x > 7) ...
```

10.   Write a Boolean expression that evaluates to `true` if and only if the values of three integer variables a, b, and c form a geometric sequence (i.e. $a, b, c \neq 0$ and $a/b = b/c$). ⸮ Hint: recall that comparing `double` values for exact match may not work — use integer cross products instead. ⸮

11.■   Write a method

```
public static boolean isLater(
        int month1, int day1, int year1,
        int month2, int day2, int year2)
```

that returns `true` if the first date is later than the second and `false` otherwise. Test your method using the provided console application Dates (Ch07\Exercises\Dates.java 🖫), which prompts the user to enter two dates, reads the input using the `EasyReader` class, and displays the result of the comparison. ✓

12.▪ Write a `boolean` method `isLeapYear(int year)` that returns `true` if
`year` is a leap year and `false` otherwise. A leap year is a year that is evenly
divisible by 4 and either is not divisible by 100 or is divisible by 400. For
example, 2000 and 2004 are leap years, but 2003 and 2100 are not.

13.▪ Fill in the missing code in the `totalWages` method, which calculates the
total earnings for a week based on hours worked and the hourly rate. The
pay for overtime (hours worked over 40) is 1.5 times the regular rate. For
example, `totalWages(45, 12.50)` should return 593.75.

```
public double totalWages(int hours, double rate)
{
  double wages;

  < ... missing code >

  return wages;
}
```

Add your code to the `Wages.java` 🖫 applet, available in the
`Ch07\Exercises` folder, and test it.

14.▪ Priority mail costs $3.50 for one pound or less, $3.95 for over one pound but
not more than two pounds, and $1.20 for each additional pound (or fraction)
above two pounds. First Class mail costs 34 cents for the first ounce and 21
cents for each additional ounce (or fraction), up to 13 ounces, after which
Priority rates apply. For example, Priority Mail for 5 oz costs $3.50 and for
4.5 lbs — $7.55; First Class mail for 3.5 oz costs $.97 and for 15 oz —
$3.50. Supply the missing code for the following method:

```
private final char FIRSTCLASS = 'F', PRIORITY = 'P';
/**
 * @param ounces the weight in ounces
 * @param mailType the type of service
 *    ('F' for first class or 'P' for priority)
 * @return the required postage for a letter or package
 */
double calculatePostage(double ounces, char mailType)
{
  < ... missing code >
}
```

Add your code to the `Mail.java` 🖫 applet, available in the
`Ch07\Exercises` folder, and test it.

15. ■   Write the method

```
public Color bestMatch(int r, int g, int b)
```

The method's arguments represent the red, green, and blue components of a color. If one of the components is greater than the other two, bestMatch returns that component's color (Color.red, Color.green, or Color.blue). If two components are equal and greater than the third, then bestMatch returns their "composite" color, Color.yellow, Color.magenta, or Color.cyan (for red-green, red-blue, and green-blue, respectively). If all three components are equal, bestMatch returns Color.gray.

16. ◆   t1 and t2 are the playing times of two CDs, and t is the length of a tape (all in minutes). Write a method that takes these integer numbers as arguments and figures out the longest combination of CDs that fits on a tape. The method should return 3 if both CDs fit together, the CD number (1 or 2) corresponding to the longest CD that fits by itself (1 if the CDs have the same length), or 0 if neither CD fits on the tape. Your method is allowed to have only one return statement.

```
public int findBestFit(int t1, int t2, int t)
{
  < ... missing code >
}
```

Adapt the applet from Question 14 to test your code.

Sections 7.11-7.13

17.■   Finish the poem:

        One, two, buckle your shoe;
        Three, four, shut the door;

and write a console Java application that displays the appropriate line of your poem:

```
Enter a number 1-10 (or 0 to quit): 1
Buckle your shoe

Enter a number 1-10 (or 0 to quit): 2
Buckle your shoe

Enter a number 1-10 (or 0 to quit): 6
Pick up sticks

Enter a number 1-10 (or 0 to quit): 0
Bye
```

Use a `switch` statement.

18.◆   Finish the applet in `Ch07\Exercises\Rps.java` 🖫 that plays the "Rock, Paper, Scissors" game. You need to supply code for the `nextPlay` method. Use nested `switch` statements.

```
Chapter chapter8 =
      new Chapter(8);
```

Methods, Constructors, and Fields

8.1   Prologue

As we have seen in the previous examples, a class definition includes *methods*, *constructors*, and *fields*.

A method is a mechanism, a kind of black box, that knows how objects of a certain type carry out a particular task. You do not necessarily want to know how a method accomplishes its task (unless you have to program the method yourself).

A description of a task may use some parameters. For example, if the task is to calculate the square root of a number, you need to know the number. If the task is to add a button to a control panel, you need to know what button. Values passed to a method as parameters are called *arguments*, as in algebra. Some methods do not need any parameters. A method either returns a value (e.g., the square root of the number) or completes a task (e.g., adds a button to the control panel), or both.

From a pragmatic point of view, methods are self-contained fragments of code that can be called as often as needed from different places in your program. When a method is called, its arguments are copied to an agreed-upon place where the method can fetch them (e.g., the system stack). When the method has finished, it returns control to the place in the program from which it was called. That return address was also saved in a place accessible to the method (e.g., the same system stack) when the method was called. If the method returns a value, it places that value into an agreed-upon location where the caller can retrieve it (e.g., a particular CPU register).

In addition to methods a class may have several *constructors*, which are essentially methods for building objects of that class type. Like methods, constructors can take arguments, but they never return any values. The primary task of a constructor is to initialize the fields of the newly constructed object.

In this chapter we will take a more systematic look at methods and constructors. We will discuss the following topics:

- The syntax for defining methods and constructors
- Giving different methods in a class the same name (overloaded methods)
- Creating objects using constructors and the `new` operator
- Passing arguments to methods and constructors

- Returning values from methods using the `return` statement

- Static (*class*) and non-static (*instance*) fields and methods

- `public` and `private` fields and methods

After getting familiar with the above features of classes we will examine a complete class, `Fraction`, that uses most of them, and then work together on the *Snack Bar* applet where you will have to supply the missing code for the `Vendor` class.

8.2   Defining Methods

A method is always defined inside a class. When you define a method you need to give it a name, specify the types of its arguments,[*] and assign them names so that you can refer to them in the method's code. You also specify the type of its return value:

```
public [or private]
returntype methodName(sometype1 argName1, ..., sometypeN argNameN)
```

This declaration is called the method's **header**. *returntype* can be any primitive data type (e.g., `int`, `double`, `boolean`, `char`, etc.) or any type of object defined in Java or in your program (e.g., `String`, `Color`, `FallingCube`, `RollingDie`, etc.). *returntype* can also be `void` (a reserved word) which means that this method performs some task but does not return any value. The arguments can be of any primitive type or any type of objects, too. The order of arguments is important. A method may have no arguments at all, only empty parentheses.

Common Java style for naming methods is to choose a name that sounds like a verb and to write it starting with a lowercase letter. If the name consists of several words, subsequent words are capitalized. If a method returns the value of a field in an object, its name usually starts with `get...`, and if a method sets the value of a field, this method's name starts with `set...`, as in `getWidth()` or `setText(...)`. Following these conventions will help other programmers understand your code.

---

[*] In more precise terminology, *arguments* are the items that are passed to the method in a call, while *parameters* (or *formal parameters*) are the variables that represent arguments inside the method's code. We will often refer to both as *arguments* to keep it simple.

```
public class Poll extends JApplet
    implements ActionListener
{
  ...
  public void init()
  {
    ...
  }

  /**
   *   Processes button events
   */
  public void actionPerformed(ActionEvent e)
  {
    ...
  }

  /**
   *   Displays the numbers and the pie chart
   */
  public void paint(Graphics g)
  {
    ...
  }

  /**
   *   Converts the count as a fraction of the total into
   *   the size of the pie slice in degrees.
   */
  private int countToDegrees(int count, int total)
  {
    ...
  }
}
```

Figure 8-1.   The methods in the `Poll` class (`Ch06\Poll\Poll.java` 🖫)

As an example, consider the four methods defined in the `Poll` class that you helped to complete in the lab in Section 6.9 (Figure 8-1).   The first method, `init`, is declared as `void` because it does not return any value.   It does not take any arguments either.   The second method, `actionPerformed`, is also `void`, but it takes one argument.   The type of its argument is `ActionEvent` and the name of the argument is simply `e`, a common short name for an event.   The third method, `paint`, is again `void`.   Its argument has the type `Graphics` and is named `g`, a conventional short name for a `Graphics` object.   The fourth method, `countToDegrees`, is declared as an `int` method because it returns an integer value to the caller (the number of degrees in a slice of a pie chart). It takes two `int` arguments: `count` and `total`.

If a method's arguments have the same type, you still need to explicitly state the type for each argument. For example, the following won't work:

```
private int countToDegrees(int count, total)
                              //   ^ Syntax error!
```

You need:

```
private int countToDegrees(int count, int total)
```

❖   ❖   ❖

After you specify the method's name, its return type, and its arguments with their types, you need to supply the code for your method, called its ***body***. This is placed within braces following the method's header. The code uses Java operators and control statements and can call other methods.

The names of parameters (such as `count, total` above) matter only inside the method's body. There they act pretty much as local variables. You cannot use these same names for local variables that you declare in that method.

8.3   Overloaded Methods

It is not surprising that methods in different classes may have exactly the same names. Since a method is always called for a particular object (or a particular class), there is no confusion. For example:

```
cube.start();     // calls start in FallingCube class
t.start();        // calls start in Timer class

String s = String.valueOf(1.5);
                  // converts 1.5 into a string
Fraction f = Fraction.valueOf(1.5);
                  // converts 1.5 into a fraction
```

A more interesting fact is that two methods of <u>the same class</u> may also have the same name, as long as the number or the types of their arguments are different.

> **Methods within the same class that have the same name but different numbers or types of arguments are called *overloaded* methods.**

A method can have any number of overloaded versions as long as their argument lists are different. For example, in

```
public class SomeClass
{
  ...
  public int fun(int a)
  {
    ...
  }

  public int fun(double b)
  {
    ...
  }

  public double fun(int a, double b)
  {
    ...
  }

  ...
}
```

`SomeClass` has three different methods, all called `fun`. The code may be completely different in each of these methods. Overloading allows you to use the same method name for the tasks that sound similar. For example, the same name `print` is used for the methods of the `System.out` object that display a `char`, an `int`, a `double`, or a string.

The compiler knows which one of the overloaded methods to call based on the types of the arguments passed to it. In the above example, if you call `fun(1)`, the first overloaded method will be called, because `1` is an integer, but if you call `fun(1.5)`, the second overloaded method will be called because `1.5` is a `double`. If you call `fun(1, .99)`, the third version of `fun`, `fun(int, double)`, will be called. If there is no exact match between argument types in a call and available overloaded versions of a method, the compiler will make a reasonable effort to convert one or more arguments into something acceptable to one of the versions. For example, if you call `fun(1, 2)` the compiler will call `fun(1, 2.0)`. If an appropriate method is not found and a reasonable conversion is not possible, the compiler reports an error. For example, if `s` is a `String`, and you call `fun(s)`, the compiler reports something like "method `fun(String)` not defined in class `SomeClass`." (The compiler also reports an error if there is no exact match for argument types but more than one overloaded method can handle them.)

Note that the <u>names</u> of the formal parameters in the method definition do not distinguish overloaded methods. Only the <u>types</u> of the parameters matter. For example,

```
public int fun(int a, double b)
{
   ...
}
```

and

```
public int fun(int x, double y)
{
   ...
}
```

cannot be defined in the same class.

The return type alone cannot distinguish two methods either. For example,

```
public int fun(int a, double b)
{
   ...
}
```

and

```
public double fun(int a, double b)
{
   ...
}
```

cannot be defined in the same class.

> **When you are designing a class, be careful not to have too many overloaded versions of a method because they may get confusing and cause bugs.**

8.4   Constructors

Constructors essentially work like methods for building objects of a class. Like methods, constructors may take arguments of specified types.

> **A constructor always has the same name as the class. Constructors do not return any types of values, and have no return type, not even `void`.**

Constructors, like methods, are defined inside the class definition. Their main task is to initialize all or some of the new object's fields. Fields that are not explicitly initialized are set to default values (see Section 6.2).

Consider, for example, the constructor in the `FallingCube` class in the *Ramblecs* applet (`Ch04\Ramblecs\FallingCube.java` 💾):

```
public class FallingCube
{
  ...
  public FallingCube(int size)
  {
    cubeSize = size;
    xLeft = cubeSize / 2;
    yStep = cubeSize / 8;
    cubeX = -cubeSize;        // off the board
    cubeY = -cubeSize;        //    not displayed
  }
  ...
}
```

The name of this constructor is `FallingCube`, the same as the class. No return type for the constructor exists. This constructor takes one `int` argument, called `size`. The constructor assigns the value of `size` to a `FallingCube` object's field `cubeSize`. It also initializes a left border position for the cube, the speed of the cube (the number of pixels to move down in each timer cycle) and the coordinates of the cube. These are set to negative values (to indicate that it shouldn't be painted until we set it in motion).

❖   ❖   ❖

If a class has more than one constructor, then they are by definition overloaded and must differ in the number or types of their arguments. For example, consider a class `Fraction` that represents a regular fraction with an integer numerator and denominator:

```
public class Fraction
{
  private int num;
  private int denom;
  ...
}
```

It would be reasonable to provide at least two constructors for the `Fraction` class: we might want to construct a fraction from an integer, or from two integers, its numerator and denominator:

```
public class Fraction
{
  private int num;
  private int denom;

  public Fraction(int n)
  {
    num = n;
    denom = 1;
  }

  public Fraction(int n, int d)
  {
    num = n;
    denom = d;
    reduce();
  }

  . . .
}
```

We may also consider a ***copy constructor***, which constructs a fraction equal to the given one.

```
public class Fraction
{
  . . .

  public Fraction(Fraction other)   // Copy constructor
  {
    num = other.num;
    denom = other.denom;
  }

  . . .
}
```

(A more common way of making copies of objects in Java is to provide for your class a `clone` method, which returns a reference to a new object, a replica of its argument. We don't want to go into cloning in this book.)

Constructors can call the object's other methods, even while the object is still "under construction." For example, one of `Fraction`'s constructors above calls `Fraction`'s reduce method, which is presumably provided elsewhere in the class.

❖   ❖   ❖

You don't have to define any constructors for a class. If a class doesn't have any constructors, the compiler supplies a *default constructor*. The default constructor does not take any arguments; it allocates memory for the object and initializes its fields to default values (numbers to zeroes, `boolean` fields to `false`, and references to `null`).

If you define at least one constructor for your class, then the default constructor is <u>not</u> supplied automatically.

It is often desirable to supply or override the default constructor by writing your own constructor that takes no arguments. For example, the default constructor for the `Fraction` class would initialize both `num` and `denom` to 0 — an invalid fraction. It may be better to set the default fraction to a valid fraction. For example:

```
public class Fraction
{
  ...
  public Fraction()
  {
    num = 0;
    denom = 1;
  }
  ...
}
```

❖   ❖   ❖

Normally constructors should prevent programs from creating invalid objects. For example, the constructor

```
public Fraction(int n, int d)
{
  num = n;
  denom = d;
}
```

assumes that the program never tries to construct a fraction with the denominator equal to 0. But it would be better to check for that condition in the constructor's code and report an error if it occurs:

```java
public Fraction(int n, int d)
{
  if (d == 0)
  {
    System.err.println(
        "Fraction construction error: denominator is 0");
    num = 0;
    denom = 1;
  }
  else
  {
    num = n;
    denom = d;
    reduce();
  }
}
```

8.5   Creating Objects Using Constructors

When you declare a variable of a primitive data type, such as `boolean`, `int`, `double`, the variable holds a value of the corresponding type. The situation is different for a variable of some class type that represents an object. When you declare a variable of a class type — as in

```java
private JButton go;
private LetterPanel whiteboard;
private RollingDie die1, die2;
Fraction f;
```

— such a variable holds a *reference* to an object of the corresponding type. You can think of a reference simply as the object's address in memory. In the above declarations the five references are not explicitly initialized: they do not yet refer to valid objects. Your program can eventually assign valid references to these variables.

Your program creates a new object (with the exception of literal strings and initialized arrays, explained in Chapters 9 and 10) using the `new` operator and one of the constructors of this object's class. An object needs some memory space to store its fields; `new` borrows this memory from a pool of free memory, available to your program. This technique is called *dynamic memory allocation*. After memory is allocated, one of the class's constructors kicks in: it initializes the object's fields and may perform other preliminary tasks, if necessary. `new` returns a <u>reference</u> to the memory block allocated for the object, and you can assign this returned reference to a variable that will represent this object in your program.

The syntax for calling the `new` operator is:

```
someName = new ClassName(<arguments>);
```

where `someName` is the name of your variable and `ClassName(<arguments>)` invokes one of this class's constructors.

For example, in the previous section we discussed four constructors of the `Fraction` class:

```
public Fraction()
public Fraction(int n)
public Fraction(int n, int d)
public Fraction(Fraction other)
```

These constructors provide four different ways to create a `Fraction` object:

```
Fraction f1, f2, f3, f4;

f1 = new Fraction();        //          0 / 1
f2 = new Fraction(3);       //          3 / 1
f3 = new Fraction(2, 3);    //          2 / 3
f4 = new Fraction(f3);      // copy of f3, i.e. 2 / 3
```

As usual, a declaration of a reference variable and its initialization can be combined in one statement. For example:

```
Fraction f5 = new Fraction(99, 100);
```

When an object is no longer needed in your program (i.e., no one refers to it any more), the ***garbage collection*** mechanism releases the object's memory and returns it to the communal memory pool.

> **It is crucial to initialize a reference before using it. The `new` operator is one way for doing this.**

(Another way is to set it to a reference returned from a method, as we'll see in Section 8.8. With the exception of literal strings and initialized arrays, objects are always created with `new`, either in one of your methods or in one of the library methods that you call.) If you start using an object's methods and fields through an uninitialized reference, your program will report a `null` reference exception.

But make sure you do not declare a reference variable twice:

```
Fraction f6;
...
Fraction f6 = new Fraction();   // Syntax error!
```

Sometimes you can create an anonymous temporary object "on the fly," without ever naming it. For example:

```
display.add(new JLabel("     Won:"));
```

This is basically the same as:

```
JLabel temp = new JLabel("     Won:");
display.add(temp);
```

But after we add this label to the `display` panel, we don't have to keep track of it any longer, so we don't have to bother naming it.

8.6   Static Fields and Methods

We have already mentioned in Section 4.6 that a Java class may have two kinds of fields: regular (non-static) fields and *static* fields. Non-static fields (also called *instance variables*) may have different values in each object (instance) of a class. Each object has its own set of memory locations for holding the values of non-static fields. Static fields (also called *class variables*) are shared by all objects of the class. There is <u>only one</u> set of memory locations for holding the values of static fields (they are stored separately from all objects). Static fields are declared with the keyword `static`.

The word "static" may seem to imply that the values of static fields are constant. In fact it has nothing to do with constants. Static fields are called "static" because their memory is not dynamically allocated: memory for static fields is reserved even before any objects of the class have been created.

Those methods that access and manipulate only static fields are called *static* or *class methods* and are declared with the keyword `static`.

Static methods are not allowed to access or set any non-static fields or to call any non-static methods of the same class.

So static methods serve the class as a whole, not its individual objects.

```
import < ... >

public class RollingDie
{
  private static final double slowdown = .97,
                             speedFactor = .04,          Static fields
                             speedLimit = 2.;            (class constants
                                                          and variables)
  private static int tableLeft, tableRight,
                     tableTop, tableBottom;

  private final int dieSize = 24;          Non-static fields (instance variables) hold
  private int xCenter, yCenter;              different values for different objects
  private double xSpeed, ySpeed;
  private int points;

  public static void setBounds(int left, int right, int top, int bottom)
  {
    tableLeft = left;
    tableRight = right;
    tableTop = top ;
    tableBottom = bottom;                     Static methods
  }                                           (class methods)

  public static int randomPoints()
  {
    return (int)(6 * Math.random()) + 1;
  }

  public RollingDie()          ——          Constructor
  {
    xCenter = -1;
    yCenter = -1;
  }

  public void roll()          ——            Non-static method
  {                                         (instance method)
    < ... >
    xSpeed = width * (Math.random() + 1) * speedFactor;
    ySpeed = height * (Math.random() -.5) * 2. * speedFactor;
    < ... >
  }

  < ... other methods >
}
```

Figure 8-2. Fragments from Ch07\Craps2\RollingDie.java 🖫

For example, sqrt, random, and other methods in Java's Math class are declared static because they do not access or manipulate any non-static members of the Math class. (Math.random returns a pseudo-random number $0 \leq x < 1$.) In fact, the Math class doesn't have any non-static members, and Math objects are never created because all such objects would be identical! So the Math class exists in name only; all Math methods are static. Another example of such class is System. It has a few static fields (such as System.out) and static methods (such as exit, which quits the application, and currentTimeMillis, which returns the current time in milliseconds) but objects of the System class cannot be created.

These examples are a little extreme — more typical classes have some non-static fields and may also have some static fields. If a class has a mix of static and non-static fields, it is also likely to have a mix of some ***class methods*** (static methods) and some ***instance methods*** (non-static methods).

As an example, consider the RollingDie class in the *Craps* applet from Section 7.10 (see Figure 8-2). The two dice in the applet may have different positions and may have different speeds, and can also show different numbers of points. Therefore, all variables that hold these values are <u>non-static</u> <u>instance</u> variables. On the other hand, both dice share the same constants that help to model how they slow down and stop. These fields (slowdown, etc.), are declared static. The two dice also roll on the same "table," so the boundaries of the table (tableLeft, tableRight, etc.) are static variables, too.

The RollingDie class has two static methods: setBounds and randomPoints. setBounds sets the boundaries of the "table" for <u>all</u> the dice. randomPoints is a "public service" method that returns a random integer in the range from 1 to 6. It is used to paint random numbers of dots on moving dice but has nothing to do with any particular object of the class. Neither of these two methods is allowed to touch the instance variables.

The constructor, on the other hand, initializes instance variables, such as the initial position of the die. Theoretically, a constructor is allowed to set static fields, too, but it doesn't make much sense to do that because normally you don't want to affect <u>all</u> class objects while constructing one of them.

Instance methods can access and change both static and non-static fields.

In the RollingDie example, instance methods access the motion constants and the table boundaries (to make sure a die doesn't fall off the table) but do not change them. In other situations, instance methods can change static fields. This happens when a static field is used to collect totals or statistics for a class as a whole. For example, in the *Snack Bar* case study (Section 8.12) a static field is used to accumulate the total amount of sales from all vending machines. It is incremented by the instance method that implements a sale for a particular machine.

> **Another use of static fields is to represent symbolic constants.**

For example, we have used the `Color` class with its `public static final` fields `red`, `blue`, `green`, and so on. These fields are static because there is no need to duplicate them in different objects of a class. Similarly, the `Math` class has `double static` constants `PI` (for π) and `E` (for e, the base of the natural logarithm).

8.7   Calling Methods and Accessing Fields

You have probably noticed from earlier code examples that the syntax for calling methods in Java is different in different situations. Sometimes a method name has a prefix that consists of an object name with a dot:

```
whiteboard.dropCube();
cube.start();
result = game.nextRoll(pts);
display.setText(str);
```

Sometimes the prefix is a <u>class</u> name with a dot:

```
y = Math.sqrt(x);
s = String.valueOf(randomLetter);
```

Sometimes there is no prefix at all:

```
degrees = countToDegrees(count1, total);
drawDots(g, x, y, randomPoints());
repaint();
```

Our discussion of static and non-static methods in the previous section immediately gives us a clue why some methods are called with a class name prefix and others with an object name prefix. A static method belongs to the class as a whole and doesn't deal with any instance variables. Such a method can be called by simply using the class's name and a dot as a prefix to the method's name, as in

```
x = Math.random();
ms = System.currentTimeMillis();
```

When we call a <u>non-static</u> method, we call it for a particular object. The object for which the method is called becomes in effect an implicit argument passed to the call. This argument is not in the list of regular arguments — it is specified by the object's name and a dot as a prefix to the method's name, as in

```
int pts1 = die1.getPoints();
int pts2 = die2.getPoints();
craps.processRoll(pts1 + pts2);
```

This syntax signifies the special status of this argument: the object for which the method is called. While the method is running, the reference to this object becomes available to the method and all other methods of the same class under the special name this. this is a Java reserved word. this acts like a field of sorts and its value is set automatically when an instance (non-static) method is called or a constructor is invoked.

When a constructor or an instance method of a class calls another instance method for the same object, strictly speaking the latter should be called with the prefix this. When a method calls a static method of the same class, strictly speaking it should be called with the class name as a prefix. Java made these prefixes optional and often they are omitted. That's when you see method calls without any prefixes. For example,

```
degrees = countToDegrees(count1, total);
```

is the same as

```
degrees = this.countToDegrees(count1, total);
```

Or

```
drawDots(g, x, y, randomPoints());
```

is the same as

```
this.drawDots(g, x, y, RollingDie.randomPoints());
```

These syntax rules are summarized in Table 8-1.

A method calls `anyStaticMethod` of `OtherClass`	`OtherClass.anyStaticMethod(...)`
A method calls `anyInstanceMethod` of `otherObject`	`otherObject.anyInstanceMethod(...)`

A method calls `anyStaticMethod` of the same class	`anyStaticMethod(...)`
	or
	`MyClass.anyStaticMethod(...)`

A method calls `anyInstanceMethod` of the same object	`anyInstanceMethod(...)`
	or
	`this.anyInstanceMethod(...)`

Table 8-1.   Syntax for calling static and non-static methods

❖   ❖   ❖

Similar syntax rules apply to accessing <u>fields</u>. A static field (class variable) is accessed by adding the class's name and a dot as a prefix to the field's name. For example: `Color.blue`, `Math.PI`. A non-static field of another object is accessed by adding the object's name and a dot as a prefix. For example:

```
public Fraction(Fraction other)  // Copy constructor
{
  num = other.num;
  denom = other.denom;
}
```

An object's methods and constructors can refer to the same object's fields simply by their name. The prefix `this` for non-static fields and a class name prefix for static fields are optional. We could write for the sake of symmetry:

```
public Fraction(Fraction other)  // Copy constructor
{
  this.num = other.num;
  this.denom = other.denom;
}
```

But we prefer the first, simpler version.

Sometimes the prefix `this` is used to distinguish the class's fields from a method's or constructor's arguments. For example, in the code for the constructor

```
public Fraction(int n, int d)
{
    num = n;
    denom = d;
}
```

we used the names `n` and `d` for the parameters to avoid clashing with `num` and `denom`. Alternatively we could write:

```
public Fraction(int num, int denom)
{
    this.num = num;
    this.denom = denom;
}
```

Another style is to give all fields names with a distinct prefix of your choice. For example:

```
public class Fraction
{

    // Fields:
    private int myNum, myDenom;

    public Fraction(int num, int denom)
    {
        myNum = num;
        myDenom = denom;
    }
    . . .
```

`this` is also used for passing "this" object (whose method is running) to another object's method or constructor. For example,

```
    clock = new Timer(delay, this);
```

invokes `Timer`'s constructor with two arguments. The first argument is the time interval between consecutive firings of the timer (in milliseconds); the second is an `ActionListener` object. `this` means that the same `CrapsTable` object that is creating a new `Timer` will serve as its "action listener": it will capture `clock`'s events in `CrapsTable`'s `actionPerformed` method.

8.8　Passing Arguments to Methods and Constructors

When a method is called or a constructor is invoked, its arguments of primitive data types (`int`, `double`, etc.) can be any expression that has a value of the appropriate type: a literal or symbolic constant, a variable, or any expression that uses arithmetic operators, casts, and/or calls to other methods. For example,

```
craps.processRoll(die1.getPoints() + die2.getPoints());
```

is equivalent to the sequence:

```
int pts1 = die1.getPoints();
int pts2 = die2.getPoints();
int sum = pts1 + pts2;
craps.processRoll(sum);
```

The former form is preferable because it is shorter and just as readable. But if an expression gets too complicated, it is better to compute it in smaller steps.

> **Arguments of primitive data types are <u>always</u> passed "*by value.*"**

If a variable of a primitive type is passed to a method as an argument, its value is <u>copied</u> into some location (e.g., the system stack) that is accessible to the method.

Suppose you wrote a method to increment its argument:

```
public static void increment(int k)
{
  k++;
}
```

You test it somewhere in your program —

```
int n = 0;
MyMath.increment(n);
System.out.println("n = " + n);
```

— but nothing happens: the value of n remains 0. The reason is that k in the method is not the same variable as n passed as the method's argument: it is a <u>copy</u> that has the same value. You increment the copy but the original remains unchanged.

Some other languages (Pascal, C++) have special syntax that allows programmers to pass variables to functions "***by reference.***" In these languages, when you pass "by reference," a reference to (address of) the original variable is passed to the function and so there is a way to write a method similar to the one above that would work. But not in Java: primitive types are <u>always</u> passed to methods <u>by value</u>. This limits your freedom but helps you avoid bugs.

❖   ❖   ❖

Exactly the opposite happens with arguments that are objects of some class type (such as `String`, `Color`, `RollingDie`, `Fraction`). Recall that objects are created with the operator `new`, which returns a reference to a memory location occupied by the object. So objects in fact exist somewhere, but we receive only references to them (their addresses). When you pass an object to a method, <u>a copy of the reference</u> to the original object is passed. The method can reach and manipulate the data and methods of the original object through that reference. For example:

```
public void avoidCollision(RollingDie other)
{
  ...
  other.move();
}
```

Here `other` is a reference to another moving die that was passed to the method as an argument. `other` holds the address of the original. Therefore `other.move()` will indeed move the other die.

In other programming languages (e.g., C++), a programmer has an option of passing an object to a function by value. This is occasionally useful if the function needs to work with a temporary copy of the object and leave the original unchanged. Not so in Java.

> **In Java, objects are always passed to methods and constructors as references.**

8.9   `return` Statement

A method that is not `void` returns something to the caller. What is returned depends on the return type of the method. If the return type is a primitive type (`int`, `double`, etc.) then the method returns a value. For example:

```
public class Fraction
{
  ...
  public double getValue()
  {
    return (double)num / (double)denom;
  }
  ...
}
```

The return value here is of the type `double`. This value can be used in assignments and expressions. For example:

```
Fraction f = new Fraction(2, 3);
double x = f.getValue();
```

The returned value is specified in the `return` statement in the method's body:

```
return <expression>;
```

expression must be of the method's specified return type or something that can be converted into it.

If a method's return type is `boolean`, it must return a Boolean value: `true` or `false`. The return expression in a `boolean` method can include a constant (`true` or `false`), a `boolean` variable, or a `boolean` expression. For example:

```
public static boolean inRange(int x, int a, int b)
{
  return a <= x && x <= b;
}
```

This is the same as

```
public static boolean inRange(int x, int a, int b)
{
  if (a <= x && x <= b)
    return true;
  else
    return false;
}
```

but shorter.

❖   ❖   ❖

> A `return` statement tells the method what value to return to the caller and immediately quits the method's code and passes control back to the caller.

A method can have several `return` statements, but all of them except one must be placed inside a conditional statement (or, perhaps, inside a case in a `switch`):

```
if (...)
  return <expression1>;
...
return <expression2>;
```

Otherwise a method will have some "unreachable" code that is never executed because it is positioned after an unconditional `return`.

> A `void` method can also have a `return`, but without any value, just as a command to quit the method.

For example

```
... void someMethod(...)
{
  ...
  if (...)
    return;
  ...
}
```

❖   ❖   ❖

> A method can also have a return type of some class. That means the method returns a <u>reference</u> to an object of that class.

Usually such a method constructs and initializes a new object and sets its fields in a particular way and then returns a reference to the new object. For example, suppose we want to provide an `add` method in the `Fraction` class that takes this fraction, adds another one to it and returns a new fraction that is their sum:

```
public class Fraction
{
   ...
   public Fraction add(Fraction other)
   {
     int newNum = num * other.denom + denom * other.num;
     int newDenom = denom * other.denom;
     Fraction f = new Fraction(newNum, newDenom);
     return f;  // return a reference to a newly created fraction
               //   -- the sum of this and other.
   }
   ...
}
```

This method can be called as follows:

```
Fraction f1 = new Fraction(1, 3);
Fraction f2 = new Fraction(1, 6);
Fraction f3 = f1.add(f2);
       // f3 refers to a new fraction that represents the
       //   sum created by the add method
       //   (here the sum is equal to 1/2)
```

Note that the add method does not change either this fraction or the other. Instead it creates a new one, sets it to their sum, and returns a reference to it. The local variable f inside add is destroyed after the method finishes its work, but not the new fraction itself. A copy of f that refers to the new fraction is returned to the method's caller and assigned to f3.

We will encounter objects returned from methods again when we deal with String objects. For example, a String object has the substring(m, n) method, which copies the characters at positions m, $m+1$, ..., $n-1$ into a new string and returns (a reference to) the new string, leaving this string unchanged.

8.10 Public and Private Fields and Methods

As we have seen, every field and method in a class is declared as public or private. These keywords tell the compiler who can call a method and who can access a field.

These access rules are not complicated:

1. Any method or constructor has access only to the <u>public</u> constructors, methods, and fields of <u>another</u> class.

2. Any non-static method or constructor has access to <u>all</u> (public and private) constructors, methods, and fields of <u>its own</u> class.

3. Any static method has access to all (public and private) <u>static</u> methods and fields of <u>its own</u> class.

The purpose of private members of a class is to limit the access of a class's ***clients*** (users) to its objects. That way the hidden inner mechanics of the class (its private fields and methods) can change without any changes to the rest of the program. This makes program maintenance easier.

In OOP, fields are almost always private. The usual practice is to make all fields private but, if necessary, to provide special "get" methods, called ***accessors***, that return the values of private fields, and "set" methods, called ***modifiers***, that update private fields.

For example, although a `CrapsTable` object has itself created two dice, `die1` and `die2`, it cannot directly access their private fields `points`. An attempt to do so causes a syntax error:

```
craps.processRoll(die1.points + die2.points); // Syntax error
```

It has to call the accessor method instead:

```
craps.processRoll(die1.getPoints() + die2.getPoints());
```

Some methods of a class may be useful only to the objects of this class, but not to the class's clients. It makes sense to declare such methods private. For example:

```
private int countToDegrees(int count, int total)
                    // needed only inside the Poll class
private void reduce()
                    // useful only inside the Fraction class
```

Making all of a class's fields private and making the helper methods private assures that the class can be completely described to outsiders by its constructors and public methods. These constructors and public methods describe everything the class and its objects can do for clients. The rest of the information about the class is hidden inside. This concept is known in object-oriented design as ***encapsulation***.

8.11 *Case Study:* Fraction **Put Together**

Now, equipped with all this new knowledge, we can put together a complete class with constructors, private fields, public and private methods, and even a static method. Since we have talked so much about the Fraction class, let us finish and test it. We already have four constructors for it, the getValue method, and the add method. We still have to provide a private method reduce. Let's base it on Euclid's Algorithm for finding the greatest common factor of two positive integers, briefly mentioned in Section 3.2. We will make the gcf method that implements it a separate public static method in case someone else ever wants to use it. We will use a recursive implementation in gcf just to demonstrate that a method can call itself.

We also want to include a public method toString that converts a Fraction object into a string convenient for printing. The return type of this method is String. Every Java class has a toString method; if you don't write your own, then your class inherits toString from Object, which returns a string with some technical information about your object. We'll redefine it for Fraction to build a string with the numerator and denominator and a slash between them.

As an illustration of static methods, let us include a static method valueOf that takes a decimal value (with up to five places after the decimal point) and returns an equivalent simple fraction. As we have seen in examples, such valueOf methods are not uncommon in various library classes.

Our complete Fraction class is shown in Figure 8-3.

As a lab exercise, add the multiply method to the Fraction class. Then write a console application that declares and initializes a couple of fractions and displays their sum and product. You can use the toString method to display the result. For example:

```
f3 = f1.multiply(f2);
System.out.println(f1.toString() + " * " +
                    f2.toString() + " = " + f3.toString());
```

Also test the getValue and valueOf methods. For example:

```
double x = .375;
Fraction f = Fraction.valueOf(x);
System.out.println(f.toString() + " = " + f.getValue());
```

```java
public class Fraction
{
  private int num;
  private int denom;

  // Static methods
  // ==============

  public static Fraction valueOf(double x)
  {
    int n = (int) (x * 10000 + .5);
    int d = 10000;
    return new Fraction(n, d);
  }

  /**
   *  Returns the greatest common factor of two positive integers
   *  Precondition: n > 0, d > 0
   */
  public static int gcf(int n, int d)
  {
    if (n <= 0 || d <= 0)
    {
      System.err.println("Fraction.gcf precondition failed" + n + ", " + d);
      return 1;
    }

    int r = n % d;

    if (r == 0)
      return d;
    else
      return gcf(d, r);
  }

  // Constructors
  // ============

  public Fraction()
  {
    num = 0;
    denom = 1;
  }

  public Fraction(int n)
  {
    num = n;
    denom = 1;
  }

  public Fraction(int n, int d)
  {
    if (d == 0)
    {
      System.err.println("Fraction construction error: denominator is 0");
```

Figure 8-3 `Fraction.java` *Continued* ➪

```java
      num = 0;
      denom = 1;
    }
    else
    {
      num = n;
      denom = d;
      reduce();
    }
  }

  public Fraction(Fraction other)   // Copy constructor
  {
    num = other.num;
    denom = other.denom;
  }

  // Public methods:

  public Fraction add(Fraction other)
  {
    int newNum = num * other.denom + denom * other.num;
    int newDenom = denom * other.denom;
    Fraction f = new Fraction(newNum, newDenom);
    return f;
  }

  public double getValue()
  {
    return (double)num / (double)denom;
  }

  public String toString()
  {
    return num + "/" + denom;
  }

  // Private methods:

  private void reduce()
  {
    if (num == 0)
    {
      denom = 1;
      return;
    }

    if (denom < 0)
    {
      num = -num;
      denom = -denom;
    }
    int q = gcf(Math.abs(num), denom);
    num /= q;
    denom /= q;
  }
}
```

Figure 8-3. Ch08\Fraction\Fraction.java 💾

8.12 *Case Study and Lab*: *Snack Bar*

When Java was first conceived by James Gosling[gosling] at Sun Microsystems in the early 1990s, it was supposed to be a language for programming embedded microprocessors — chips that control coffee makers and washers and VCRs. As it turned out, that was not Java's destiny. The language might have been completely forgotten, but the advent of the Internet and the World Wide Web gave it another life.

In a tribute to Java's early history, let's implement an applet that simulates a set of vending machines in an automatic snack bar. As you will see in this case study, Java is a very convenient tool for such a project. Our vending machines will be quite simple: each machine can sell only one product. The user "deposits" quarters, dimes, or nickels into a machine, then presses the red button and "receives" a soda or a snack and change. When one of the machines is empty, you can call "service." After a concession operator enters a password ("jinx"), all the machines are refilled with "merchandise" and emptied of "cash." Figure 8-4 shows a snapshot of this applet. You can play with it using the compiled Java files on your student disk in the Ch08\RunSnackBar folder.

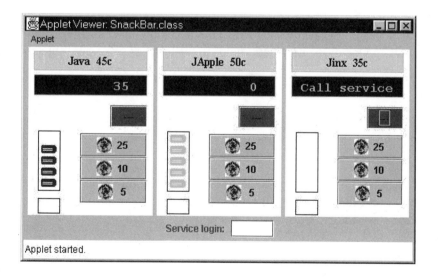

Figure 8-4. The *Snack Bar* applet with three vending machines

We begin as usual by identifying the classes involved in this project. One class, called SnackBar, is as usual derived from JApplet and represents the applet itself. It constructs and displays a number of vending machines (in this case three) and handles service calls with a password login. A fragment of this class is shown in Figure 8-5.

The second class, called VendingMachine, represents a vending machine. SnackBar's init method creates three instances of this class — three machines. VendingMachine declares and creates the necessary display fields and buttons for a machine, handles events generated by these buttons, and displays the results of these events. This is where event-driven OOP is at its best: we can create three almost identical machines and let each of them process its own events automatically without any confusion. A user can "deposit coins" in random order into each of the three machines, and our program will sort out all the events correctly.

Note that the SnackBar class actually knows very little about its vending machines: only how to construct them and that they need service or reloading once in a while (i.e., that they have a constructor with three specific arguments and that there is a static method service and a method reload). This is good OOP design: each object knows only what it really needs to know about other objects.

The complete VendingMachine class code is included on your student disk in the Ch08\SnackBar 🖫 folder. If you examine VendingMachine's code, you will notice that a vending machine is really not the entire machine, but only its front panel, the GUI. One of the non-static fields in this class is a vendor object:

```
    private Vendor vendor;
```

This object is created in VendingMachine's constructor:

```
    vendor = new Vendor(price, FULL_STOCK);
```

It is the machine's vendor that actually handles sales and keeps track of cash and inventory. For example, when the user "deposits" 25 cents into a machine, the machine calls its vendor's addMoney method:

```
    vendor.addMoney(25);
```

If the user presses the red "sale" button, the machine calls its vendor's makeSale and getChange methods:

```
        trayFull = vendor.makeSale();
        int change = vendor.getChange();
```

```
import java.awt.*;
import java.awt.event.*;
import javax.swing.*;

public class SnackBar extends JApplet
                      implements ActionListener
{
  private static final String MY_PASSWORD = new String("jinx");
  private VendingMachine machine1, machine2, machine3;

  public void init()
  {
    Color brandColor1 = new Color(130, 30, 10); // r, g, b
    Color brandColor2 = new Color(255, 180, 0);
    Color brandColor3 = new Color(90, 180, 0);
    machine1 = new VendingMachine("Java", brandColor1, 45);
    machine2 = new VendingMachine("JApple", brandColor2, 50);
    machine3 = new VendingMachine("Jinx", brandColor3, 35);

    <... etc.  See Ch08\SnackBar\SnackBar.java ⊟ >

  }

  /**
   *  Password field: user strikes <Enter>
   */
  public void actionPerformed(ActionEvent e)
  {
    JPasswordField password = (JPasswordField)e.getSource();
    String word = new String(password.getPassword());
    password.setText("");
    if (MY_PASSWORD.equals(word))
    {
      VendingMachine.service();
      machine1.reload();
      machine2.reload();
      machine3.reload();
    }
    else
    {
      JOptionPane.showMessageDialog(this,
        "Login failed", "Login failed", JOptionPane.ERROR_MESSAGE);
    }
  }
}
```

Figure 8-5. Ch08\SnackBar\SnackBar.java ⊟

And when a machine needs to know whether there is any stock left, it calls its vendor's getStock method:

```
if (vendor.getStock() > 0)
   . . .
```

As in our *Craps* applet in Chapter 7 and for the same reasons, we once again separate the GUI part from the number crunching. We try to define the Vendor class in rather general terms so we can reuse it in different situations: it can represent not only a mechanism of a vending machine, but a cash register, an online store, any kind of vendor. In fact, Vendor objects are so general they don't even know what they sell, only its price!

Figure 8-6 shows the three classes involved in the SnackBar applet: SnackBar, VendingMachine, and Vendor. The SnackBar object is the applet itself. It "knows" about the features of a vending machine and creates three of them, but it is not aware of "vendors" behind them. Each vending machine creates and utilizes its own vendor object. Even though all vendors have the same name, there is no confusion because each vending machine knows its own vendor.

As you have probably guessed, it will be your job to implement the Vendor class from the written specifications (Figure 8-7).

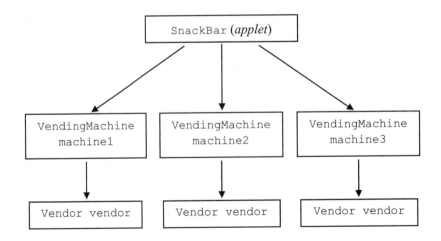

Figure 8-6. *Snack Bar* **applet's classes and objects**

```
/**
 * Class Vendor implements a vendor of items of a single type.
 * Carries out sales transactions and keeps track of total sales
 * for all vendors.
 */

public class Vendor
{
  private static double totalSales = 0.;
                  // total sales from all vendors (in dollars)
  < ... missing fields >

  /**
   * Returns the total amount of sales from all vendors
   * and zeroes out totalSales.
   * Arguments:
   *   None
   * Return:
   *   double total amount of sales from all vendors
   */
  ... getTotalSales ...
  {
    < ... missing code >
  }

  /**
   * Constructor
   * Arguments:
   *   int price of a single item in cents
   *   int number of items to place in stock
   */
  ... Vendor ...
  {
    < ... missing code >
  }

  /**
   * Sets the quantity of items in stock.
   * Arguments:
   *   int number of items to place in stock
   * Return:
   *   None
   */
  ... setStock ...
  {
    < ... missing code >
  }
```

Figure 8-7 `Vendor.java` *Continued* ➴

```
/**
 *  Returns the number of items currently in stock.
 *  Arguments:
 *    None
 *  Return:
 *    int number of items currently in stock
 */
... getStock ...
{
  < ... missing code >
}


/**
 *  Adds a specified amount (in cents) to the deposited amount.
 *  Arguments:
 *    int number of cents to add to the deposit
 *  Return:
 *    None
 */
... addMoney ...
{
  < ... missing code >
}


/**
 *  Returns the currently deposited amount (in cents).
 *  Arguments:
 *    None
 *  Return:
 *    int number of cents in the current deposit
 */
... getDeposit ...
{
  < ... missing code >
}


/**
 *  Implements a sale.  If there are items in stock and
 *  the deposited amount is greater than or equal to
 *  the single item price, then adjusts the stock, updates the
 *  total sales, and calculates and sets change and returns true.
 *  Otherwise refunds the whole deposit (into change) and
 *  returns false.
 *  Arguments:
 *    None
 *  Return:
 *    boolean successful sale or failure
 */
... makeSale ...
{
  < ... missing code >
}
```

Figure 8-7 `Vendor.java` *Continued* ➴

```
/**
 *  Returns and zeroes out the amount of change (from the last
 *  sale or refund).
 *  Arguments:
 *    None
 *  Return:
 *    int number of cents in the current change
 */
... getChange ...
{
  < ... missing code >
}
}
```

Figure 8-7. `Ch08\SnackBar\Vendor.java`

Each `Vendor` object can sell only one kind of item at one specified price. The vendor operates by collecting payment from a buyer in several steps. The `Vendor`'s four fields represent the current inventory, the price, the currently deposited amount and the change from the last sale. `Vendor`'s constructor sets the price and the initial inventory. `Vendor` also has one <u>static</u> field, `totalSales`, that holds the total amount of sales for <u>all</u> vendors. It is incremented appropriately after each successful sale. The `getTotalSales` static method returns the total amount of sales and at the same time zeroes out the `totalSales` field.

Vendor's other methods work as follows:

- The `addMoney` method adds a specified number of cents to the already deposited amount.

- The `makeSale` method is called when the buyer tries to complete the transaction. If the vendor is not out of stock and if the buyer has deposited enough money, then a sale takes place: the `totalSales` field is updated, the stock is decreased, the change is calculated, and `makeSale` returns `true`. Otherwise the sale fails: `totalSales` remains unchanged, the stock remains unchanged, the whole deposit is returned to the buyer (by transferring it to the change amount), and `makeSale` returns `false`.

- The `getDeposit` accessor simply returns the value of the current deposit (not the money itself!) to the caller. A vending machine calls this method when it needs to display the deposited amount on its display panel.

- The `getChange` method completes the transaction: it returns the change due to the buyer after a sale and at the same time (well, almost at the same time) sets the `change` field to 0. You have to be a little careful here: save the return value in a temporary local variable before setting `change` to 0.

- The `getStock` accessor returns the current stock.

- The `setStock` method sets the new inventory quantity.

Copy the `SnackBar.java`, `VendingMachine.java`, and `Vendor.java` files from the `Ch08\SnackBar` ⊞ folder to your work folder. Complete the `Vendor` class and test the applet thoroughly.

8.13 Summary

Methods are always defined within a class. Methods can take a number of arguments of specific types and return a value of a specific type. The syntax for defining a method is:

```
public [or private]
returntype methodName(sometype1 argName1, ..., sometypeN argNameN)
{
    < method body (code) >
}
```

The arguments and the return value can be of any primitive type (`int`, `double`, etc.) or any type of objects defined in the program. The return type can be `void`, which indicates that a method does not return any value.

Two methods of the same class can have the same name as long as they have different numbers or types of arguments. Such methods are called overloaded methods.

Constructors work like methods for building objects of a class. Like methods, constructors may take arguments of specified types. A constructor always has the same name as the class. If a class has several constructors, they are overloaded and must have different numbers or types of arguments. Constructors do not return any type of values, not even `void`. Usually constructors are not called explicitly; instead, objects are created using the `new` operator:

```
SomeClass someVar;
...
someVar = new SomeClass(<arguments>);
```

or

```
SomeClass someVar = new SomeClass(<arguments>);
```

A class may have some non-static fields (instance variables) that can hold different values for each object of the class and some static fields that are shared by all objects of the class. Likewise, a class may have non-static (instance) methods that work for a specific object of the class and static (class) methods that work for the class as a whole. Static fields are useful for sharing universal settings or for collecting statistics from all active objects of the class. Static methods cannot access non-static fields or call non-static methods.

Methods and fields of an object are accessed using "dot" notation: if `o` is an object and `meth` is its method, it can be called as `o.meth(<arguments>)`. However, an object can call its own methods without any prefix, just `meth(<arguments>)`. The same applies to fields.

Static methods are called using the class's name as opposed to the individual object:

```
SomeClass.staticMeth(<arguments>);
```

All arguments of primitive data types are always passed to methods and constructors by value, which means a method or a constructor works with copies of the variables passed to it and cannot change the originals. Objects of class types, on the other hand, are always passed as references. A method can change the original object using the supplied reference.

A method specifies its return value using the `return` statement. `return` tells the method what value to return to the caller. When a `return` statement is executed, the program immediately quits the method's code and returns control to the caller. A method can have several `returns`, but all of them must return a value or expression of the specified type, and all but one must be inside a conditional statement (or in a switch). All primitive types are returned by value, while objects (class types) are returned as references. A `void` method can also have a `return`, but without any value, just as a command to quit the method.

Public fields and methods are accessible to all methods and constructors of the same class and of any other class. Private fields and methods are accessible only to methods of the same class. In OOP, all fields are usually private. If necessary, the programmer provides accessor "get" methods that return the values of private fields and modifier "set" methods that update private fields.

Exercises

Sections 8.1-8.5

1. Mark true or false and explain:

   (a) A method is always defined inside a class. _____
   (b) A method returns a value unless its return type is `void`. _____
   (c) A method can have several arguments of different types. _____
   (d) Overloaded methods belong to the same class. _____ ✓
   (e) Two overloaded methods may have one `int` argument each and different return types. _____

2. Write a header line for a public method `replace` that takes two arguments, a `String` and a `char`, and returns another `String`. ✓

3. Will the class below compile? If not, suggest a way to fix it. ✓

```
public class Pair
{
  private double first;
  private double second;

  public Pair(double a, double b)
  {
    first = a;
    second = b;
  }

  public void swap()
  {
    double temp = first;
    first = second;
    second = temp;
  }

  public Pair swap()
  {
    return new Pair(second, first);
  }
}
```

4.   If a class `Complex` has constructors `Complex(double a, double b)` and `Complex(double a)`, which of the following statements are valid ways to construct a `Complex` object?

   (a)   `Complex z = new Complex();` _____ ✓
   (b)   `Complex z = new Complex(0);` _____ ✓
   (c)   `Complex z = new Complex(1, 2);` _____
   (d)   `Complex z = new Complex(0.0);` _____
   (e)   `Complex z = new Complex(1.0, 2);` _____
   (f)   `Complex z = new Complex(1.0, 2.0);` _____

5.   Which of the following constructors of a class `Date` are in conflict?

   I.   `Date(int month, int day, int year)`
   II.   `Date(int julianDay)`
   III.   `Date(int day, String month, int year)`
   IV.   `Date(int day, int month, int year)`

   A.   I and II
   B.   II, III, and IV
   C.   I and IV
   D.   I, III, and IV
   E.   There is no conflict — all four can coexist

6.   Find out in the Java API specification (available at `http://java.sun.com/j2se/1.3/docs/api/index.html` or on your computer if you have installed "docs") whether the `String` and `Color` classes have copy constructors. ✓

7.■   Java's class `Color` has a constructor that takes three integers, the color's red, green, and blue components, as arguments. A class `Balloon` has two fields: `double radius` and `Color color`. Write a constructor for the `Balloon` class that takes no arguments and sets the balloon's radius to 10 and its color to "sky blue" (with RGB values 135, 206, and 250).

Sections 8.6-8.13

8.   Find and fix a syntax error in the following program:

```
public class Problem
{
  private String message = "Hello, World";

  public void hello()
  {
    System.out.println(message);
  }

  public static void main(String[] args)
  {
    hello();
  }
}
```
✓

9.   The applet *Temperature* (Ch08\exercises\Temperature.java 🖫 on the student disk) converts degrees Celsius to Fahrenheit and vice-versa using the FCConverter class. Examine how this class is used in the actionPerformed method in the Temperature class and write and test the FCConverter class. ⸮ Hint: 0°C is 32°F; one degree Celsius is 5/9 degree Fahrenheit. For example, 68°F is $5/9 \cdot (68 - 32) = 20°C$ ⸮

10.   Rewrite the FCConverter class from Question 9, eliminating the fields and all constructors and providing two static methods:

```
public static double cToF(double degrees)
public static double fToC(double degrees)
```

Adjust the Temperature class accordingly and retest the applet.

11.▪   Add an integer argument size to the RollingDie's constructor and set dieSize to size in the constructor. Change the avoidCollision method to compare the horizontal and vertical distances between the centers of this and other dice to the arithmetic mean of their sizes instead of dieSize. Change the CrapsTable class to roll two dice of different sizes in the applet.

12.   A class `Circle` below has a constructor that builds a circle with a given radius.

```
public class Circle
{
  private double myRadius;

  public Circle(double radius)
  {
    myRadius = radius;
  }

  < ... Other methods >
}
```

(a)   Add a public method to this class that returns the area of this circle. ⸖ Hint: the public static constant `Math.PI` (in the `Math` class) is defined in Java documentation as "the `double` value that is closer than any other to π, the ratio of the circumference of a circle to its diameter." ⸖ ✓

(b)▪   Write a program or an applet that uses the `Circle` class to calculate the area of a circle with a radius entered by the user.

13.   Add `subtract` and `divide` methods to the `Fraction` class and test them. If the argument for the `divide` method is a zero fraction, display an error message and return a copy of the fraction for which the method was called.

14.   (a)   A class `Point` has private fields `double x` and `double y`. Write a copy constructor for this class.

(b)   A class `Disk` has private fields `Point center` and `double radius`. Write a copy constructor for this class. ✓

15.   The class `Time` represents the time of day in hours and minutes in the 24-hour format for hours (e.g., 7 p.m. is 19):

```
public class Time
{
  private int hours;
  private int mins;
  < ... etc. >
}
```

Continued ⇨

(a)   Write a constructor `Time(int h, int m)` that checks that its arguments are valid and sets `hours` and `mins` appropriately. If the arguments are invalid, print an error message to `System.err` and set `hours` and `mins` to 0.

(b)   Write a private method `toMins` that returns the time in minutes since the beginning of the day for this `Time` object.

(c)■   Write a public `boolean` method `equals(Time other)` that returns `true` if this time equals `other` and `false` otherwise. ✓

(d)■   Write a method `elapsedSince(Time t)` that returns the number of minutes elapsed from `t` to this time. Assume that `t ≤ ` *this time* ` < t+24h`. For example, if this time is 8:30 and `t` is 22:45, the method assumes that `t` is on the previous day and returns 585 (minutes). ⸞ Hint: use `toMins`. ⸟

(e)   Test your `Time` class using the provided `TestTime` console application class (`Ch08\exercises\TestTime.java` ▣) that uses the `EasyReader` class.

16.   (a)   Write a class `Rectangle` that represents a rectangle with integer width and height. Include a constructor that builds a rectangle with a given width and height and another constructor (with one argument) that builds a rectangle that is actually a square of a given size. Make sure these constructors check that the width and height are positive. Add a constructor that takes no arguments and builds a square of size 1.

(b)   Add a `boolean` method `isSquare` that returns `true` if and only if the rectangle is a square. Add a method `quadratize` that converts this rectangle into a square with approximately the same area — the closest possible for a square with an integer side.

(c)   Test all your constructors and methods in a simple console application. Define several rectangles, check which ones among them are squares and print appropriate messages. "Quadratize" one of the rectangles, verify that it becomes a square, and print an appropriate message.

17.   (a)   Implement the `Complex` class (which represents a complex number $a + b·i$) with two fields of the type `double` and two constructors as described in Question 4. `Complex(a)` should make the same complex number as `Complex(a, 0.0)`.

(b)   Add a method `abs` to your class that returns $\sqrt{a^2 + b^2}$ for a complex number constructed as `Complex(a, b)`. ✓

(c)■   Recall that if $a + b·i$ and $c + d·i$ are two complex numbers, their sum is defined as $(a + c) + (b + d)·i$. Fill in the blanks in the code for a method `add` in the `Complex` class that builds and returns the sum of this number and another number, its argument:

```
public Complex add(Complex other)
{
  < ... missing statements >
}
```

(d)■   Add the following `toString` method to your `Complex` class:

```
public String toString()
{
  return myA + " + " + myB + "i";
}
```

where `myA` and `myB` are the names of the fields that correspond to a and b in $a + b·i$. Test your `abs` and `add` methods in a console application that calls `toString` and `System.out.println` to generate output. ✓

(e)◆   Find the rule for multiplying two complex numbers. ⸮ Hint: you can derive this rule yourself knowing that $i·i = -1$. ⸮ Implement and test a method `multiply` for multiplying this complex number by a another complex number. As with the `add` method, the `multiply` method should not change this object; it should build and return a new complex number, the product. Can you pass a `double` rather than a `Complex` to this method as an argument or do you need an overloaded version of `multiply` for that? If you need an overloaded version, then write it, too.

18.■   Consider the following class (Ch08\exercises\Pair.java ⊞ on your student disk):

```java
public class Pair
{
  public double first;
  public double second;

  public Pair(double a, double b)
  {
    first = a;
    second = b;
  }

  public static void swap(double a, double b)
  {
    double temp = a;
    a = b;
    b = temp;
  }

  public static void swap(Pair p)
  {
    double temp = p.first;
    p.first = p.second;
    p.second = temp;
  }

  public Pair swap()
  {
    return new Pair(second, first);
  }
}
```

(a)   What is the output of the following program?

```java
public static void main(String[] args)
{
  double a = 3, b = 4;
  Pair p;
  System.out.println("a = " + a + " b = " + b);

  // Swap attempt 1:
  double temp = a;
  a = b;
  b = temp;
  System.out.println("a = " + a + " b = " + b);
```

Continued ⇨

```
    // Swap attempt 2:
    Pair.swap(a, b);
    System.out.println("a = " + a + " b = " + b);

    // Swap attempt 3:
    p = new Pair(a, b);
    Pair.swap(p);
    a = p.first;
    b = p.second;
    System.out.println("a = " + a + " b = " + b);

    // Swap attempt 4:
    p = new Pair(a, b);
    p.swap();
    a = p.first;
    b = p.second;
    System.out.println("a = " + a + " b = " + b);

    // Swap attempt 5:
    p = new Pair(a, b);
    p = p.swap();
    a = p.first;
    b = p.second;
    System.out.println("a = " + a + " b = " + b);
  }
```

(b)   The purpose of the program is obviously to test different swap attempts. Which of the proposed five swap attempts work and which fail? Explain why. Which one of the five methods is the simplest way to swap the values of two variables? ✓

19.   Write a class `Coins` with one constructor that takes a number of cents as an argument. Supply four public methods, `getQuarters`, `getNickels`, `getDimes`, and `getPennies`, that return the number of corresponding coins that add up to the amount (in the optimal representation with the smallest possible number of coins).

(a)   Test your class in a small console application that takes a change amount from the command line or reads it from the console (with `EasyReader`).

(b)■ Integrate your class into the *SnackBar* applet, so that the applet reports the amount of change received by the customer in specific coin denominations (e.g. `"Change 65c = 2q + 1d + 1n"`). ⋜ Hint: modify statements in the `actionPerformed` method of the `VendingMachine` class after `vendor.getChange` is called. ⋝

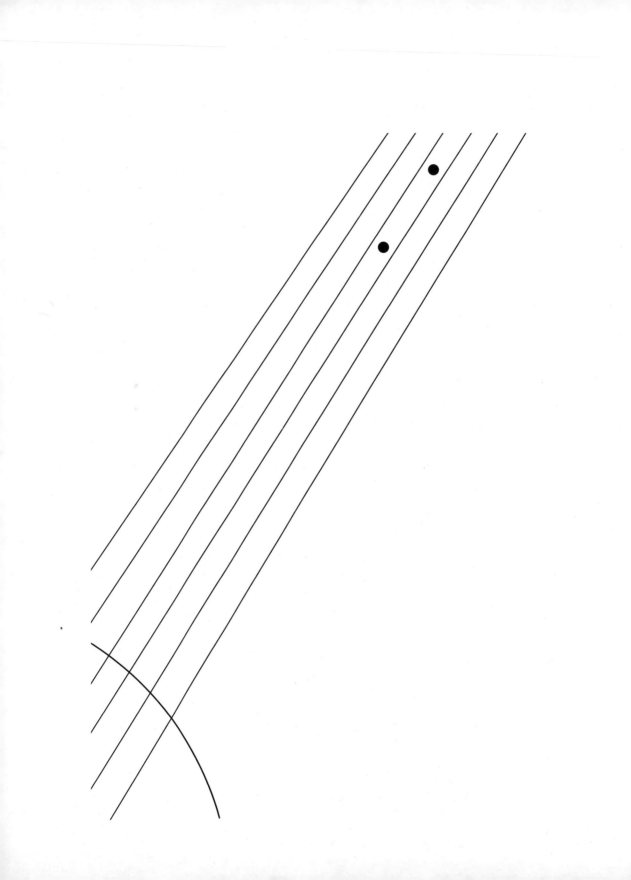

"Chapter 9"

Strings

9.1   Prologue

In Java, a string of characters is represented by an object of the `String` type. `String` objects are treated pretty much like any other type of objects: they have constructors and methods, and they can be passed to other methods (always as references, see Section 8.8) or returned from methods. But their status is somewhat privileged because the `String` data type is basically built into Java. The Java compiler knows how to deal with two special properties of strings: *literal strings* (represented by text in double quotes) and the + and += operators for concatenating strings with other strings and numbers.

In this chapter we will cover some string properties and methods that help us use strings in our programs. In particular, we will discuss:

- How to declare and use literal strings

- `String` constructors

- The immutability property

- Commonly used `String` methods

- How to convert numbers into strings and strings into numbers

- A few methods of the `Character` class that identify digits and letters

9.2   Literal Strings

Literal strings represent string constants. They are written as text in double quotes. The text may contain escape characters (see Section 6.4). Recall that the backslash character '\' is used as the "escape" character: \n stands for "newline," \" is used when you need to represent a double quote, and \\ represents a backslash inside a literal string. A literal string can be empty, too, if there is nothing between the quotes. Figure 9-1 shows some examples.

Literal strings act as `String` objects, but they do not have to be created — they are "just there" when you need them. The compiler basically treats a literal string as a reference to a `String` object with the specified value that is stored somewhere in memory. If you want, you can actually call that object's methods (e.g., `"Internet".length()` returns 8). A declaration

```
String s = "Sunshine";
```

sets the reference s to a String object "Sunshine". Note that Sunshine here is not the <u>name</u> of the object but its <u>value</u>.

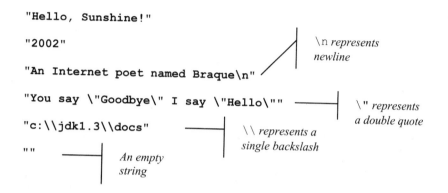

Figure 9-1. Examples of literal strings

9.3   Immutability of Strings

The String class has nine constructors, but it is less common to use constructors for strings than for other types of objects. Instead, we can initialize String variables to either literal strings or to strings returned from String methods.

One of the constructors, String(), takes no arguments and builds an empty string; rather than invoking this constructor with the new operator, we can simply write:

```
String str = "";   // str is initialized to an empty string
```

Another constructor is a copy constructor String(String s) that builds a copy of the string s. But in most cases we do not need to make copies of strings because, as we'll explain shortly, strings, once created, never change; so instead of copying a string we can just copy a reference. For example:

```
String str = "Foo Fighters";
```

This is not exactly the same as

```
String str = new String("Foo Fighters");
```

but, as far as your program is concerned, these two declarations of `str` act identically.

The other seven constructors create strings from character and byte arrays and they are potentially useful, but not before we learn about arrays (Chapter 10).

> **Note that there is a big difference between an empty string and an uninitialized `String` reference.**

Empty strings are initialized to `""` or created with the empty string constructor, as in

```
String s1 = "";            // s1 is set to an empty string
String s2 = new String();  // s2 is set to an empty string
```

An uninitialized `String` reference is `null`:

```
String s3;                 // s3 is set to null
```

You can call methods for an empty string, and they will return the appropriate values (e.g., `s1.length()` returns 0, and `s2.equals("")` returns `true`), but calling methods for a `null` reference will cause a run-time error.

❖   ❖   ❖

Once a string is constructed, it cannot be changed! If you look carefully at `String`'s methods, summarized in Figure 9-3, you will notice that none of these methods changes the content of the string.

> **A string is what is called an *immutable* object: none of its methods can change the content of a `String` object.**

For example, you can get the value of a character at a given position in the string using the `charAt` method. But there is no method to <u>set or replace</u> one character in a string. If you want to change, say, the first character of a string from upper to lower case, you have to build a whole new string with a different first character. For example:

```
String bandName = "Foo Fighters";
char c = bandName.charAt(0);
bandName = Character.toLower(c) + bandName.substring(1);
        // bandName now refers to a new string
        //   with the value "foo Fighters"
```

This code changes the <u>reference</u> — bandName now refers to your new string with the value "foo Fighters" — but the old string is thrown away. Java's automatic garbage collector releases the memory from the old string and returns it to the free memory pool. This is a little wasteful — like pouring your coffee into a new mug and throwing away the old mug each time you add a spoonful of sugar or take a sip.

The immutability of strings makes it easier to follow what's going on and to avoid bugs. In particular, it is possible to have two String variables refer to the same string (Figure 9-2) without the danger of changing the string contents through one variable without the knowledge of the other. This way you don't have to create several copies of the same string. You can use

```
String s2 = s1;  // s2 refers to the same string as s1
```

rather than

```
String s2 = new String(s1); // s2 refers to a new copy of s1
```

But because you have to build a new string for every little change, a program that manipulates a lot of long strings using String objects may become very slow.

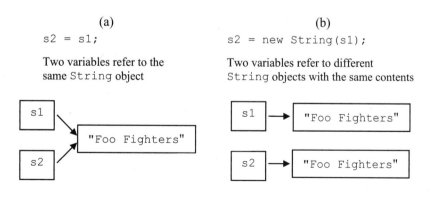

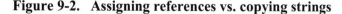

Figure 9-2. Assigning references vs. copying strings

Java provides another class for representing character strings, called StringBuffer. StringBuffer objects are not immutable: they have the setCharAt method and other methods that change their contents. With the StringBuffer class we can easily change one letter in a string without moving the other characters around. For example:

```
StringBuffer bandName = new StringBuffer("Foo Fighters");
char c = bandName.charAt(0);
bandName.setCharAt(0, Character.toLower(c));
    // bandName still refers to the same object, but its first
    //   character is now 'f';
```

If some text applications run rather slowly on your fast computer, it may be because the programmer was too lazy to use (or simply never learned about) the StringBuffer class. Strings may be easier to understand and they are considered safer in student projects. We have summarized StringBuffer constructors and methods in Appendix D. Make sure you've read it before writing commercial applications!

9.4   String **Methods**

The more frequently used String methods are summarized in Figure 9-3. There are methods for returning the string's length, for getting the character at a specified position, for building substrings, for finding a specified character or substring in a string, for comparing strings alphabetically, and for converting strings to upper and lower case.

length and charAt

The length method returns the number of characters in the string. For example:

```
String s = "Internet";
int len = s.length();   // len gets the value of 8
```

The charAt method returns the character at the specified position.

> **Character positions in strings are counted starting from 0.**

This convention goes back to C, where elements of arrays are counted from 0. So the first character of a string is at position (or index) 0, and the last one is at position *length*-1. For example:

```
String s = "Internet";
int len = s.length();         // len gets the value of 8
char c1 = s.charAt(0);        // c1 gets the value 'I'
char c2 = s.charAt(7);        // c2 gets the value 't'
```

If you call `charAt(pos)` with `pos` less than 0 or `pos` greater than or equal to the string length, the method will report an `IndexOutOfBounds` error and your program will stop working properly.

Always make sure that when you refer to the positions of characters in strings, they fall in the range from 0 to string's length − 1.

```
int n      = s.length();
char ch    = s.charAt(pos);
String s2 = s.substring(fromPos);
String s2 = s.substring(fromPos, toPos);
String s2 = s.concat(str);
```

```
int result    = s.compareTo(s2);
int result    = s.compareToIgnoreCase(s2);
boolean match = s.equals(s2);
boolean match = s.equalsIgnoreCase(s2);
```

```
int k = s.indexOf(ch);
int k = s.indexOf(ch, fromPos);
int k = s.indexOf(str);
int k = s.indexOf(str, fromPos);
int k = s.lastIndexOf(ch);
int k = s.lastIndexOf(ch, fromPos);
int k = s.lastIndexOf(str);
int k = s.lastIndexOf(str, fromPos);
```

```
String s2 = s.trim();
String s2 = s.replace(oldChar, newChar);
String s2 = s.toUpperCase();
String s2 = s.toLowerCase();
```

Figure 9-3. Commonly used `String` methods

Substrings

The `String` class has two (overloaded) `substring` methods. The first one, `substring(fromPos)`, returns the tail of the string starting from `fromPos`. For example:

```
String s = "Internet";
String s2 = s.substring(5);  // s2 gets the value "net"
```

The second one, `substring(fromPos, toPos)` returns the segment of the string from `fromPos` to `toPos-1`. For example,

```
String s = "Internet";
String s2 = s.substring(0, 5);  // s2 gets the value "Inter"
String s3 = s.substring(2, 6);  // s3 gets the value "tern"
```

Note: the second argument is the position of the character following the substring, and that character is <u>not</u> included into the returned substring. The length of the returned substring is always `toPos - fromPos`.

Concatenation

The `concat` method concatenates strings; it works exactly the same way as the string version of the + operator. For example:

```
String s1 = "Sun";
String s2 = "shine";
String s3 = s1.concat(s2);  // s3 gets the value "Sunshine"
String s4 = s1 + s2;        // s4 gets the value "Sunshine"
```

There is also a += operator, which concatenates the operand on the right to the string on the left. For example:

```
String s = "2*2 ";
s += "= 4";  // s gets the value "2*2 = 4"
```

It may appear at first that the += operator violates the immutability of strings. This is not so. The += first forms a new string concatenating the right-hand operand to the original s. Then it changes the reference s to point to the new string. The original string is thrown away. So s += s2 is as inefficient as s = s + s2.

You can also concatenate characters and numbers to strings using the + and += operators, as long as the compiler can figure out that you are working with strings, not numbers. For example,

```
String s = "Year: ";
s += 2003;   // s gets the value "Year: 2003";
```

But if you write

```
String s = "Year:";
s += ' ' + 2003;  // is interpreted as s += (' ' + 2003);
```

it won't work as expected because neither ' ' nor 2003 is a string. Instead of concatenating them it will add 2003 to the Unicode (ASCII) code for space (32) and then append the sum to s! So s would get the value "Year:2035". On the other hand,

```
String s = "Year:";
s += " " + 2003;
```

does work because the result of the intermediate operation is a string.

<u>Finding characters and substrings</u>

The indexOf(char c) method returns the position of the first occurrence of the character c in the string. Recall that indices are counted from 0. If c is not found in the string, indexOf returns −1. For example:

```
String s = "Internet";
int pos1 = s.indexOf('e');  // pos1 gets the value 3
int pos2 = s.indexOf('x');  // pos2 gets the value -1
```

You can also start searching from a position other than the beginning of the string by using another (overloaded) version of indexOf. It has a second argument, the position from which to start searching. For example:

```
String s = "Internet";
int pos = s.indexOf('e', 4);  // pos gets the value 6
```

You can search backward starting from the end of the string or from any other specified position using one of the two lastIndexOf methods for characters. For example:

```
String s = "Internet";
int pos1 = s.lastIndexOf('e');     // pos1 gets the value 6
int pos2 = s.lastIndexOf('e', 4);  // pos2 gets the value 3
int pos3 = s.lastIndexOf('e', 2);  // pos3 gets the value -1
```

`String` has four similar overloaded methods for searching for a specified substring instead of a single character. For example:

```
String s = "Internet", s2 = "net";
int pos1 = s.indexOf("net");        // pos1 gets the value 5
int pos2 = s.indexOf(s2, 6);        // pos2 gets the value -1
int pos3 = s.lastIndexOf(s2);       // pos3 gets the value 5
int pos4 = s.lastIndexOf("net", 6); // pos4 gets the value 5
```

Comparisons

You cannot use relational operators (==, !=, <, >, <=, >=) to compare strings.

Recall that relational operators when applied to objects compare <u>references</u> to objects (i.e., their addresses), not the <u>values</u> of objects; strings are no exception. The `String` class provides `equals`, `equalsIgnoreCase`, and `compareTo` methods for comparing strings. `equals` and `equalsIgnoreCase` are `boolean` methods; they return `true` if the strings have the same length and the same characters (case-sensitive or case-blind, respectively), `false` otherwise. For example:

```
String s = "OK!";
boolean same1 = s.equals("Ok!");           // same1 is set to false
boolean same2 = s.equals("OK");            // same2 is set to false
boolean same3 = s.equalsIgnoreCase("Ok!"); // same3 is set to true
```

Occasionally the string in the comparison may not have been created yet. If you call its `equals` method (or any other method) you will get a run-time error. For example:

```
String s;                         // s is a null reference
boolean same = s.equals("Ok!");   // ==> run-time error
```

To avoid errors of this kind you can write

```
boolean same = (s != null && s.equals("Ok!"));
```

The above statement always works due to short-circuit evaluation (see Section 7.7). However, real Java pros may write

```
boolean same = "Ok!".equals(s);  // Strange but works!
```

This always works, whether `s` is initialized or `null`, because you are not calling methods of an uninitialized object. The same applies to the `equalsIgnoreCase` method.

The `compareTo` method returns an integer that describes the result of a comparison. `s1.compareTo(s2)` returns a negative integer if `s1` lexicographically precedes `s2`, 0 if they are equal, and a positive integer if `s1` comes later than `s2`. (To remember which argument should come first you can mentally replace "compareTo" with a minus sign.) The comparison starts at the first character and proceeds until different characters are encountered in corresponding positions or until one of the strings ends. In the former case, `compareTo` returns the difference of the Unicode codes of the characters, so the string with the first "smaller" character (i.e., the one with the smaller ASCII or Unicode code) is deemed smaller; in the latter case `compareTo` returns the difference in lengths, so the shorter string is deemed smaller. This is called "lexicographic ordering," but it is not exactly the same as used in a dictionary because `compareTo` is case-sensitive, and uppercase letters in Unicode come <u>before</u> lowercase letters. For example:

```
String s = "ABC";
int result1 = s.compareTo("abc");
        // result1 is set to a negative number:
        //   "ABC" is "smaller" than "abc"

int result2 = s.compareTo("ABCD");
        // result2 is set to a negative number:
        //   "ABC" is "smaller" than "ABCD"
```

Naturally, there is also a `compareToIgnoreCase` method.

Conversions

Other useful methods include `toUpperCase`, which builds and returns a new string in which all the letters are converted to the upper case; `toLowerCase`, which rebuilds a string in lowercase letters; and `replace(c1,c2)`, which builds and returns a new string in which all occurrences of the character `c1` are replaced with `c2`. The `trim` method builds and returns a new string in which all the "whitespace" characters (spaces, tabs, and newline characters) are trimmed from the beginning and end of the string. For example:

```
String s1, s2, s3, s4;

s1 = " <u>String Methods</u>  ";

s2 = s1.trim();  //  s2 becomes "<u>String Methods</u>"
                 //  s1 remains " <u>String Methods</u>  "

s3 = s2.toUpperCase();
                 //  s3 becomes "<U>STRING METHODS</U>"
                 //  s2 remains "<u>String Methods</u>"

s4 = s3.replace('U', 'B')
                 //  s4 becomes "<B>STRING METHODS</B>"
                 //  s3 remains "<U>STRING METHODS</U>"
```

> **None of these methods (nor any other String methods) change the String object for which they are called. They build and return a new string instead.**

This is a source of tricky bugs. The names of these methods might imply that they change the string, and it is easy to call them but forget to put the result anywhere. For example:

```
String s1 = " <code>  ";
s1.trim();       // A useless call: s1 remains unchanged!
                 // You probably meant s1 = s1.trim();
```

9.5   Converting Strings into Numbers and Numbers into Strings

Java offers two equivalent ways for converting an `int` into a string of digits (with a minus sign if the number is negative). The first way is to use the static method `toString` of the `Integer` class. For example:

```
int n = -123;
String s1 = Integer.toString(n);  // s1 gets the value "-123";
```

The `Integer` class belongs to the `java.lang` package that is automatically imported into all programs. It is called a ***wrapper class*** because it "wraps" around a primitive data type `int`: you can take an `int` value and construct an `Integer` object from it. The reason for "wrapping" is to treat a value of a primitive type as an object, for instance, if you want to add it to a list that holds objects. The `Integer` class also has several "public service" static methods, and `toString` is one of them.

The second way is to use the static method `valueOf` of the `String` class.

```
String s2 = String.valueOf(n);     // s2 gets the value "-123";
```

A third way is to concatenate an integer with a string. For example:

```
int n = -123;
String s3 = "" + n;       // s3 gets the value "-123";
String s4 = "n = " + n;   // s4 gets the value "n = -123";
```

Similar methods work for `double` values (using the `Double` wrapper class). For example:

```
double x = 1.5;
String s1 = Double.toString(x);   // s1 gets the value "1.5";
String s2 = String.valueOf(x);    // s2 gets the value "1.5";
String s3 = "" + x;               // s3 gets the value "1.5";
```

For doubles, though, the number of digits in the resulting string may vary depending on the value, and a `double` may even be displayed in scientific notation. So it is better to convert a double into a string using a specified format. This can be accomplished by using an object of the `DecimalFormat` library class and its `format` method. First you need to create a new `DecimalFormat` object that describes the format. The format is described as a string in the form `"000.0000"`, indicating the number of leading zeroes and the number of digits after the decimal point. Then you use that format object to convert numbers into strings. We won't go too deeply into this here, but your programs can imitate the following examples:

```
import java.text.DecimalFormat;

// Create a DecimalFormat object specifying 2 digits after
//    the decimal point:
DecimalFormat moneyFormat = new DecimalFormat("0.00");

// Create a DecimalFormat object specifying 2 digits
//    (with a leading zero, if necessary):
DecimalFormat timeFormat = new DecimalFormat("00");

// Convert totalSales into a string using moneyFormat:
double totalSales;
String s1 = moneyFormat.format(totalSales);
    // if totalSales holds the value 123.5,
    //   s1 gets the value "123.50"

// Convert minutes into a string using timeFormat:
int minutes;
String s2 = timeFormat.format(minutes);
    // if minutes holds the value 7,
    //   s2 gets the value "07"
```

If, for example, `totalSales` is 123.5 and you need to print something like

```
Total sales are $123.50
```

you could write

```
System.out.print("Total sales are $" +
                        moneyFormat.format(totalSales));
```

If `hours` = 3 and `minutes` = 7 and you want the time to look like `3:07`, you would write

```
System.out.print(hours + ":" + timeFormat.format(minutes));
```

❖   ❖   ❖

The reverse operation — converting a string of digits (with a sign, if necessary) into an `int` value — can be accomplished by calling the static `parseInt` method of the `Integer` class. For example:

```
String s = "-123";
int n = Integer.parseInt(s);   // n gets the value -123
```

What happens if the string argument to `parseInt` does not represent a valid integer? This question takes us into the subject of Java *exception handling*, which is outside the scope of this book. In a nutshell, `parseInt` with a bad argument "throws" a `NumberFormatException`. Your program should call `parseInt` "tentatively," within a `try` block, and "catch" this particular type of exception within the `catch` block that follows. If you don't catch the exception, your program may crash or continue running with incorrect results. The `catch` block is executed only when an exception is thrown. It may be followed by the `finally` block that is always executed and therefore can perform the necessary clean-up. `try`, `catch`, and `finally` are Java reserved words. Figure 9-4 shows how all this may be coded.

A similar method, `parseDouble` of the `Double` class, can be used to extract a `double` value from a string. For example:

```
String s = "1.5";
double x = Double.parseDouble(s);   // x gets the value 1.5
```

```
JTextField display = new JTextField(); // declare an input field
                                       //    display
< ... etc. >

String text = display.getText();         // read text from display
int n;

try
{
  n = Integer.parseInt(text);
}
catch (NumberFormatException ex)
{
  JOptionPane.showMessageDialog(this,
      "Invalid number " + text,    // message
      "Input Error",               // dialog window title
      JOptionPane.ERROR_MESSAGE);  // message type
}
finally
{
  display.selectAll();  // prepare for new input --
                        //    highlight display field
}

// Process n if no exception:
long factorial = 1;

for (int i = 2; i <= n; i++)
  factorial *= i;

display.setText(n + "! = " + factorial);
< ... etc. >
```

Figure 9-4. Converting a string into an `int` with exception handling

9.6   Character Methods

When you work with characters and strings, you often need to find out whether a particular character is a digit, a letter, or something else. The `Character` wrapper class has several static `boolean` methods that test whether a character belongs to a particular category. All of these take one argument, a `char`, and return `true` or `false`. For example:

```
boolean result = Character.isDigit(c);
                        // result is set to true if c is a digit,
                        //    false otherwise
```

Other character "category" methods include isLetter, isLetterOrDigit, isUpperCase, isLowerCase, and isWhitespace (space, tab, newline, etc.).

There are also two methods that return the uppercase and lowercase versions of a character, if these are available. These are called toUpperCase and toLowerCase. For example:

```
char c1 = Character.toUpperCase('a');   // c1 is set to 'A'
char c2 = Character.toUpperCase('*');   // c2 is set to '*'

String firstName = console.readLine();
char c = firstName.charAt(0);
firstName = Character.toUpperCase(c) + firstName.substring(1);
```

9.7   *Case Study and Lab: Equation Solver*

In this case study we discuss a toy interpreter of arithmetic expressions of the form a + b or a - b, where a and b are integers. Our applet, called *Equation Solver*, parses the expression, extracts the operands and the operation sign (+ or -), and displays the result in the form a + b = c or a - b = c.

The applet only works with integers. It does not include exception handling, so the user must enter the numbers correctly and separate the numbers from the operation sign by spaces.

The complete code for the applet is implemented in one class, EquationSolver, shown in Figure 9-5. Copy the file EquationSolver.java 🖫 and the companion HTML file that runs the applet from the Ch09\Equations folder to your work folder. Compile and run the applet to see how it works.

Our applet uses a JTextField GUI component from the Swing package to both enter the input and display the result. This "widget" (GUI components are sometimes called "widgets") allows you to display, input, and edit one line of text. In our applet we call this object display. display's getText method returns a string with the current text from display. Pressing the <Enter> key on a JTextField object ends the input and generates an action event. Our EquationSolver object also serves as an ActionListener for display, so this event triggers a call to its actionPerformed method. actionPerformed obtains the input string from `display`, processes it, and shows the result back in the `display` field. `display`'s `setText` method sets `display`'s text to a specified string. `actionPerformed` also calls `display`'s `selectAll` method, which "selects" (highlights) the whole text in `display`. This is done to automatically clear the input field when the user starts typing in it again.

We can use this set-up or a similar set-up with separate input and display fields in applets to display the results of simple calculations or string transformations.

To interpret arithmetic expressions entered in *Equation Solver* we need to implement four steps:

1. Split the input string into three terms
2. Extract the operation sign and integer operands from the terms
3. Perform the arithmetic
4. Convert the result into a string and display it

We use the `StringTokenizer` class from the `java.util` package to extract individual words from a string. An object of the `StringTokenizer` class is constructed with a string as an argument. The string contains a sentence or an expression with several "tokens." Tokens are individual words or terms separated by spaces or other "whitespace" characters (tabs, newline, etc.). The `StringTokenizer` object's constructor extracts all the tokens and places them into a queue. Its `countTokens` method returns the number of tokens in the queue. Successive calls to the `nextToken` method retrieve and return the next token from the queue, in the same order that they were placed there, from left to right.

In our toy interpreter we expect three terms: the first operand, the operation sign, and the second operand. The applet reports a syntax error if we get a different number of tokens. We then pass these three strings to the `evaluate` method, which extracts the operation sign into a `char` and the operands into two `int`s from the respective strings:

```
private String evaluate(String term1, String op, String term2)
{
  String result;

  if (op.length() != 1)
    return ARROW + "Syntax error";

  char opSign = op.charAt(0);
  int a = Integer.parseInt(term1);
  int b = Integer.parseInt(term2);
  < ... etc. >
}
```

```
/**
 *  This program evaluates arithmetic expressions
 */

import java.awt.*;
import java.awt.event.*;
import javax.swing.*;
import java.util.StringTokenizer;

public class EquationSolver extends JApplet
        implements ActionListener
{
  private JTextField display;
  private static final String ARROW = "==> ";

  public void init()
  {
    display = new JTextField(40);
    display.setFont(new Font("Monospaced", Font.BOLD, 14));
    display.setBackground(Color.white);
    display.setForeground(Color.blue);
    display.addActionListener(this);
    display.setText("Equation Solver");
    Container c = getContentPane();
    c.setLayout(new FlowLayout());
    c.add(display);

    // Select the whole display text:
    display.selectAll();

    // Prepare for typing:
    display.requestFocus();
  }

  public void actionPerformed(ActionEvent e)
  {
    // Skip if display has any selected text:
    if (display.getSelectedText() != null)
      return;

    String text = display.getText();
    display.setText(text + " " + process(text));
    display.selectAll();
  }
```

Figure 9-5 EquationSolver.java *Continued* ➲

```java
  private String process(String s)
  {
    String term1, op, term2;
    s = s.trim();

    StringTokenizer terms = new StringTokenizer(s);
    if (terms.countTokens() == 3)
    {
      term1 = terms.nextToken();
      op = terms.nextToken();
      term2 = terms.nextToken();
      return evaluate(term1, op, term2);
    }
    else
      return ARROW + "Syntax error";
  }

  /**
   *  Evaluates an arithmetic expression in the form
   *  "a +/- b" and returns the result
   *  in the form "= c" or an error message.
   */
  private String evaluate(String term1, String op, String term2)
  {
    String result;

    if (op.length() != 1)
      return ARROW + "Syntax error";

    char opSign = op.charAt(0);
    int a = Integer.parseInt(term1);
    int b = Integer.parseInt(term2);

    switch (opSign)
    {
      case '+':
        result = "= " + (a + b);
        break;

      case '-':
        result = "= " + (a - b);
        break;

      default:
        result = ARROW + "Invalid operation";
        break;
    }
    return result;
  }
}
```

Figure 9-5. `Ch09\Equations\EquationSolver.java` ⌸

We then perform the required arithmetic operation inside a `switch` statement (based on the operation sign) and append `"= "` and the resulting number to the `result` string.

Implement one or more of the following extensions to *Equation Solver*:

1. add `*` and `/` operations. For division, display the "Divide by 0 error" message if the second operand is 0. Display an "`<a>` is not evenly divisible by `<b>`" message if exact integer division cannot be performed. (`<a>` and `<b>` should be replaced in the message by the actual operands.) For example:

    ```
    6 / 2 = 3
    6 / 0 ==> Divide by 0 error
    3 / 2 ==> 3 is not evenly divisible by 2
    ```

2. Allow input expressions with no spaces between the operation sign and the operands. ⸰ Hint: find the operation sign in the expression using the `String`'s `indexOf` method and <u>insert</u> the spaces around it if they are missing (using the `substring` method and concatenation); then proceed as before. This is how programmers solve problems! ⸰

3. Add to *Equation Solver* the capability to solve equations in the form `x op b = c`, where `x` is any name of a variable, `op` can be an arithmetic operation of the user's choice, and `b` and `c` are integers. The result should be displayed as

    ```
    x op b = c ==> x = a
    ```

    For example:

    ```
    num * 2 = 6 ==> num = 3
    z * 2 = 7 ==> No solutions
    ```

4. Make *Equation Solver* solve equations with the variable either in the first operand or the second operand, as in

    ```
    5 + x = 8 ==> x = 3
    ```

9.8   Summary

Text in double quotes represents a literal string. Literal strings are treated as string objects, and you can assign them to `String` references without explicitly creating a string with the `new` operator. Literal strings may include escape characters, such as \n, \t, and \".

Once a string is constructed, there is no way to change it because objects of the `String` class are immutable: no `String` method can change its object. However, you can reassign a `String` reference to another string. The old string will be released by Java's garbage collection mechanism. This may be quite inefficient; professional programmers often use the `StringBuffer` class instead of `String`.

Figure 9-3 summarizes the most commonly used string methods. The positions of characters in strings are counted from 0, so the `charAt(0)` method returns the first character of a string. Java supports the + and += operators for concatenating strings. If several + operators are combined in one expression for concatenation, you have to make sure that at least one of the arguments in each intermediate operation is a string.

You cannot use == or != or other relational operators to compare strings because these operators compare the <u>references</u> to (addresses of) strings, not their contents. Use the `equals`, `equalsIgnoreCase`, and `compareTo` methods instead.

The `Integer` class is what is called a wrapper class for the primitive data type `int`. It provides some methods that let you operate on integers as though they were objects. `Integer.toString(int n)` or `String.valueOf(int n)` convert n into a string — its representation as a string of digits (possibly with a sign) and return that string. The same can also be accomplished as `""` + n. With `doubles` it is better to use a `DecimalFormat` object for conversion into strings. For example:

```
DecimalFormat moneyFormat = new DecimalFormat("0.00");
...
String s1 = moneyFormat.format(totalSales);
```

To convert a string of decimal digits into an `int` value, call the static `parseInt` method of the `Integer` class. For example:

```
String s = "-123";
int n = Integer.parseInt(s);    // n gets the value -123
```

This method "throws" a `NumberFormatException` if s does not represent a number. Your program should be able to catch the exception, correct it in time, and keep running correctly (see Figure 9-4).

The Character class (a wrapper class for char) has useful boolean static methods isLetter, isDigit, isWhitespace, and a few others that take a char as an argument and return true or false. The Character's other two methods, toUpperCase and toLowerCase, return a char value equal to the argument converted to the appropriate case.

Exercises

Sections 9.1-9.4

1.   Find a bug in the following declaration: ✓

```
String fileName = "c:\dictionaries\words.txt";
```

2.   (a)   Write a method that returns true if a given string is not empty and ends with a star ('*'), false otherwise. ✓

   (b)   Write a method that returns true if a given string has at least two characters and ends with two stars, false otherwise.

3.   (a)   A string dateStr represents a date in the format "mm/dd/yyyy" (e.g., "05/31/2003"). Write a statement or a fragment of code that changes dateStr to the format "dd-mm-yyyy" (e.g., "31-05-2003"). ✓

   (b)   Use the applet provided (Ch09\exercises\StringTest.java 💾) to test this code and for other exercises:

```
import java.awt.*;
import java.awt.event.*;
import javax.swing.*;

public class StringTest extends JApplet
        implements ActionListener
{
  private JTextField input, result;

  public void init()
  {
    input = new JTextField(20);
    input.setBackground(Color.white);
    input.addActionListener(this);
    input.selectAll();
```

Continued ➪

```
        result = new JTextField(20);
        result.setBackground(Color.white);
        result.setEditable(false);
        <... etc.  See Ch09\Exercises\StringTest.java 🖫 >
    }

    public void actionPerformed(ActionEvent e)
    {
        String str = input.getText();

        // ... insert code to process str or call
        // a method here. For example:
        // str = process(str);

        result.setText(str);
        input.selectAll();
    }
}
```

4. Write a method that eliminates two dashes from a social security number in the format "ddd-dd-dddd" and returns a 9-character string of digits. For example, `removeDashes("987-65-4321")` returns a string equal to `"987654321"`.

5. A credit card number is represented as a `String ccNumber` that contains four groups of four digits. The groups are separated by one space. For example:

```
String ccNumber = "4111 1111 1111 1111";
```

(a) Write a statement that declares a string `last4` and sets it to the last four digits in `ccNumber`. ✓

(b) Write a statement that sets `String last5` to a string that holds the last five digits in `ccNumber`.

6. Write a `scroll` method that moves the first character to the end of the string and returns the new string.

7.■   Suppose a string holds a person's first and last name, separated by one or several spaces. Assume that the string does not have leading spaces and that the first name does not contain spaces. Write a method `convertName` that takes a string with these properties and returns a string where the last name is placed first, followed by a comma, one space, and the first name. For example:

```
String lastfirst1 = convertName("Grace   Hopper ");
    // lastfirst1 is set to "Hopper, Grace"

String lastfirst2 = convertName("John von Neumann");
    // lastfirst2 is set to "von Neumann, John"
```

⟨ Hint: `trim` helps get rid of extra white space. ⟩

8.   Write a method that removes the first occurrence of a given substring (if found) from a given string. For example,

```
String result = cutOut("Hi-ho, hi-ho", "-ho");
    // result is set to "Hi, hi-ho"
```
     ✓

9.   The `String` class has `boolean` methods `startsWith(String prefix)` and `endsWith(String suffix)`. `startsWith` tests whether this string starts with a given substring and `endsWith` tests whether this string ends with a given substring. Pretend that these methods do not exist and write them using other string methods (but no iterations or recursion).

10.■   Write your own <u>recursive</u> implementation of `indexOf(ch, fromPos)`. ✓

11.■   Write a method that checks whether a given string starts with an HTML tag (or what looks like one: a word in angular brackets) and ends with a matching closing HTML tag. If yes, the method removes both tags and returns the result; otherwise the method returns the original string unchanged.

Sections 9.5-9.8

12.   If two strings, `s1` and `s2`, represent positive integers `n1` and `n2` in the usual way, as sequences of decimal digits, is it true that the sign of `s1.compareTo(s2)` is always the same as the sign of `(n1 - n2)`? Write a simple console application that takes two strings from the command line to experiment with this "hypothesis."

13.◆   In *MS DOS*, a file name consists of up to eight characters (excluding `'.'`, `':'`, backslash, `'?'`, and `'*'`), followed by an optional dot (`'.'` character) and extension. The extension may contain zero to three characters. For example: `1STFILE.TXT` is a valid file name. File names are case-blind. Write and test a method

```
String validFileName(String fileName);
```

that validates the input, appends the default extension `".TXT"` if no extension is given (i.e., no `'.'` appears in `fileName`), converts the name to the upper case, and returns the resulting string to the caller. If `fileName` ends with a dot, remove that dot and do not append the default extension. If the name is invalid, `validFileName` should return `null`.

14.   Write a method that returns `true` if a given string ends with a digit, `false` otherwise. ✓

15.◆   Write a method that determines whether all the characters in a string are the same, using only library `String` methods, but no loops or recursion.
    ⸓ Hint: there are several approaches. For example, see Question 6 above. ⸓

```
double chapter10[] =
  {10.1, 10.2, 10.3,
   10.4, 10.5, 10.6};
```

Arrays

10.1 Prologue

Java programmers can declare several consecutive memory locations of the same data type under one name. Such memory blocks are called ***arrays,*** and the individual memory locations are called the ***elements*** of the array. The number of elements is called the ***size*** or ***length*** of the array. Your program can refer to an individual element of an array using the array name followed by the element's number (called its ***index*** or ***subscript***) in brackets. An index can be any integer constant, variable, or expression.

There are many good reasons for using arrays. Suppose your program requires you to enter a number of integers, say test scores, and calculate their average. Theoretically you could try to hold the entered values in separate variables, `score1`, `score2`, ... But this would not work very well. First, since you might not know in advance how many scores would be entered, you would have to declare as many variables as the maximum possible number of inputs. Then you would have to read each score individually:

```
score1 = input.readInt();
score2 = input.readInt();
...
```

This could get tedious. And then adding the scores up would require a separate statement for each addition:

```
sum += score1;
sum += score2;
...
```

Now suppose you wanted to enter a test number, *k*, and see the score for that test. Imagine programming it like this:

```
if (k == 1)
   System.out.print(score1);
else if (k == 2)
   System.out.print(score2);
else if < ... etc. >
```

Fortunately, arrays make coding of such tasks much easier. You can write

```
for (k = 0; k < scores.length; k++)
  sum += scores[k];
```

and

```
System.out.print(scores[k]);
```

Here `scores[0]` refers to the first score, `scores[1]` to the second, and so on.

This chapter is only a brief introduction to arrays. We will get into more detail about important algorithms associated with arrays in the next two chapters, after we learn how to use Java's iterative statements. Here we will discuss how to

- Declare and create arrays
- Access array's elements using indices
- Access array's length
- Pass arrays to methods
- Declare and create two-dimensional arrays

10.2 One-Dimensional Arrays

Java treats arrays as objects of the type "array of `ints`," "array of `doubles`", "array of `Strings`," and so on. You can have an array of elements of any type. Use empty brackets after the name to indicate that a name refers to an array, as follows:

```
sometype someName[];
```

For example:

```
int scores[];
```

You can put the brackets <u>before</u> the first array name; then all the variables declared in that statement will be arrays. In other words,

```
String [] words1, words2;
```

is equivalent to

```
String words1[], words2[];
```

But we will use only the latter form to avoid confusion, and we recommend you do the same. (We'll make an exception for `main(String[] args)`, which has become accepted Java style.)

▌ Arrays in Java are treated as objects.

In particular, you need to declare an array then create it using the `new` operator. You can declare and create an array in the same statement. For example, the following statement declares an array of integers, called `scores`, and creates that array with 10 elements:

```
int scores[] = new int[10];
```

An array of 5000 strings and an array of 16 "colors" can be declared and created as follows:

```
String words[] = new String[5000];
Color colors[] = new Color[16];
```

The number in brackets, as in `new int[10]` or `new String[5000]`, indicates the size (length) of the array. Note that brackets, not parentheses, are used here with the `new` operator.

▌ When an array is created, its elements are initialized to default values. Numeric elements are initialized to 0, `boolean` to `false`.

If array elements are of a <u>class</u> type, then the array contains <u>references</u> to objects of that type and they are initialized to `null`.

If elements are object references, you have to initialize each element before it is used by setting it to a valid reference. For example:

```
colors[0] = new Color(207, 189, 250);
colors[1] = Color.blue;
```

and so on.

❖   ❖   ❖

▌ Another way to declare and create an array is to list explicitly, between braces, the values of all its elements. The `new` operator is not used in this form.

For example:

```
int scores[] = {95, 97, 79, 99, 100};
String names[] = {"Vikas", "Larisa", "Nick"};

Color rainbowColors[] =
{
  Color.red, Color.yellow, Color.green,
  Color.cyan, Color.blue, Color.magenta
};
```

The first statement creates an array of five integers; the second creates an array of three strings; the third creates an array of six colors. The initial values within braces can be any constants, initialized variables, or expressions.

> **Once an array is declared and initialized, either with the new operator or with a list of values, it is not possible to change its size. You can only reassign its name to another array and throw away the first one.**

10.3 Accessing Array Elements

> **A program can access individual elements of an array using *indices* (also called *subscripts*). An index is an integer value placed in square brackets after the array name to indicate the consecutive number of the element. In Java (as in C and C++), the elements of an array are numbered starting from 0.**

In the above example of the array `scores`, the five scores can be referred to as `scores[0]`, `scores[1]`, `scores[2]`, `scores[3]`, and `scores[4]`, respectively.

The following statements declare an array of 100 integer elements:

```
final int MAXCOUNT = 100;
int a[] = new int[MAXCOUNT];
```

The elements of this array can be referred to as `a[0]`, `a[1]`, ... , `a[99]`.

The power of arrays lies in the fact that an index can be any integer variable or expression. A program can refer, for example, to `a[i]`, where `i` is an integer variable. When the program is running, it interprets `a[i]` as the element of the array whose index is equal to whatever value `i` currently has. For example, if variable `i` gets the value 3 and the program accesses `a[i]` at that point, `a[i]` will refer to `a[3]`, which is the fourth element of the array (`a[0]` being the first element).

The index can be any expression with an integer value. For example:

```
double coordinates[] = new double[12]; // holds 6 points
int i;

< ... other statements >

coordinates[2 * i] = console.readInt();
coordinates[2 * i + 1] = console.readInt();
i += 2;
```

❖   ❖   ❖

In Java, every array "knows" its own size (length). Java syntax allows you to access the length of an array by using the expression *arrayName*.length. In terms of syntax, length acts as a public field that holds the size of the array.

> **In arrays, `length` is not a method (as in the `String` class). It is accessed like a field, without parentheses.**

For example:

```
double samples[] = new double[10];
...
if (i >= 0 && i < samples.length)
   ...
```

> **All indices must fall in the range from 0 to *length* – 1, where *length* is the number of elements in the array. If an index happens to be out of this range, your program will report a run-time error — an `IndexOutOfBoundsException`.**

❖   ❖   ❖

Arrays are not immutable objects: you can set any element in an array with a simple assignment statement:

```
a[k] = < ... constant, variable, or expression >;
```

> **Like other Java objects, arrays are always passed to methods as references.**

If an array is passed to a method, the method gets the address of the original array and works with the original array, not a copy. Therefore, a method can change an array passed to it. For example:

```
/**
 *  Swaps a[i] and a[j]
 */
public void swap(int a[], int i, int j)
{
  int temp = a[i];
  a[i] = a[j];
  a[j] = temp;
}
```

A method can also create a new array and return it (as a reference). For example:

```
int[] readScores()   // return type is an integer array
{
  int scores = new int[10];
  int k;

  for (k = 0; k < 10; k++)
    scores[k] = readInt();

  return scores;
}
```

10.4 *Lab*: *Fortune Teller*

The applet in Figure 10-1 is a "fortune teller." When the user presses the "Next" button, the applet displays a message randomly chosen from an array of messages. The applet is implemented in one class, `FortuneTeller` (Figure 10-2).

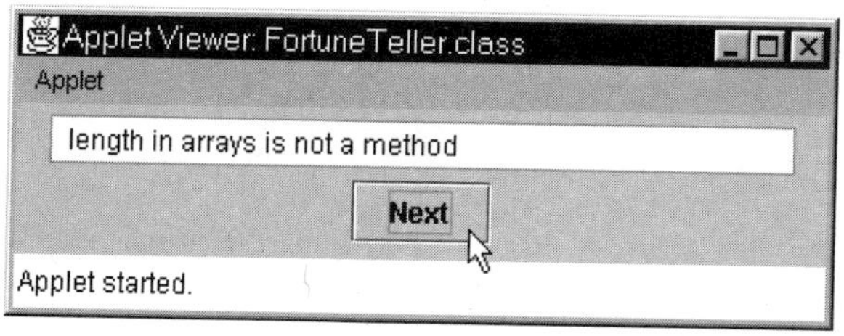

Figure 10-1. The *Fortune Teller* applet

Copy `FortuneTeller.java` and `TestFortune.html`, the HTML file that runs it, from the `Ch10\Fortunes` 🖫 folder to your work folder. Fill in the blanks in the applet's code, adding an array of a few "fortunes" (strings) and the code to randomly choose and display one of them. Recall that the static `Math.random` method returns a random `double` value $0 \leq x < 1$. We have used it in earlier programs (e.g.,

Ch07\Craps2\RollingDie.java). Scale the value returned by `Math.random` appropriately to obtain a random value for an index within the range of your array. Use `display`'s `setText` method to show the chosen message.

```java
import java.awt.*;
import java.awt.event.*;
import javax.swing.*;
import java.applet.AudioClip;

public class FortuneTeller extends JApplet
    implements ActionListener
{

    < ... missing "fortunes" ...>

    private JTextField display;
    private AudioClip ding;

    public void init()
    {
        ding = getAudioClip(getDocumentBase(), "ding.wav");

        display = new JTextField(
                " Press \"Next\" to see your fortune...", 30);
        display.setBackground(Color.white);
        display.setEditable(false);

        JButton go = new JButton("Next");
        go.addActionListener(this);

        Container c = getContentPane();
        c.setLayout(new FlowLayout());
        c.add(display);
        c.add(go);
    }

    public void actionPerformed(ActionEvent e)
    {
        ding.play();

        // Display a random fortune:

        < ... missing statements >

        display.setText( ... );
    }
}
```

Figure 10-2. Ch10\Fortunes\FortuneTeller.java 🖫

10.5 Two-Dimensional Arrays

Two-dimensional arrays are used to represent rectangular tables of elements of the same data type. A 2-D array may hold positions in a board game, a table of spreadsheet cells, elements of a matrix, or pixel values in an image.

The following example shows two ways to declare and initialize a 2-D array of doubles:

```
int rows = 2;
int cols = 3;

double a[][] = new double[rows][cols]; // Declares a 2 by 3 array of
                                       //   doubles, all set to 0.

double b[][] =                         // Declares a 2 by 3 array of
{                                      //   doubles
  {0.0, 0.1, 0.2},
  {1.0, 1.1, 1.2}
};
```

> **We access the elements of a 2-D array with a pair of indices, each placed in square brackets. We can think of the first index as a "row" and the second as a "column." Both indices start from 0.**

In the above example,

```
b[0][0] = 0.0;    b[0][1] = 0.1;    b[0][2] = 0.2;
b[1][0] = 1.0;    b[1][1] = 1.1;    b[1][2] = 1.2;
```

In Java, a 2-D array is represented essentially as a 1-D array of 1-D arrays, its rows. Each row is an array. In the example above, `b[0]` is the first row that contains the values 0.0, 0.1, and 0.2. `b[1]` is the second row of values 1.0, 1.1, and 1.2. Strictly speaking, different rows in a 2-D array may have different numbers of "columns." We will deal only with rectangular 2-D arrays that have the same number of columns in all rows.

> **If `m` is a 2-D array, then `m.length` is the number of rows in the array, `m[0]` is the first row (a 1-D array), and `m[0].length` is the number of columns (in the first row).   `m[r][c]` is the element in row `r` and column `c`.**

❖   ❖   ❖

You can also declare three-dimensional and multi-dimensional arrays in a manner similar to two-dimensional arrays. Arrays in three or more dimensions are not used very often. In this book we never go beyond two dimensions.

10.6 Summary

Java allows programmers to declare arrays — blocks of consecutive memory locations under one name. An array represents a collection of related values of the same data type or objects of the same class.

You can refer to any specific element of an array by placing the element's index (subscript) in brackets after the array name. An index can be any integer constant, variable, or expression. In Java the index of the first element of an array is 0 and the index of the last element is *length* – 1, where *length* is the array's length. An index must always be in the range from 0 to *length* – 1, otherwise a run-time error occurs.

In Java, arrays are objects. If a is an array, a.length acts as a public field of a that holds the number of elements in a. Arrays are passed to methods as references, so a method can change the contents of an array passed to it.

Programmers can also declare and use two-dimensional and multi-dimensional arrays. We can refer to an element in a 2-D array by placing two indices, each in brackets, after the array's name. Think of the first index as a "row" and the second as a "column." Both indices start from 0. In Java, a 2-D array is treated basically as a 1-D array of 1-D arrays, its rows. If m is a 2-D array, m.length is the number of rows and m[0].length is the number of columns (assuming that all rows have the same number of columns).

Exercises

Sections 10.1-10.4

1. (a) Write a statement that declares an array of three integers, initialized to 1, 2, and 4. ✓

    (b) Write an expression that represents the sum of the three elements of the above array (regardless of their current values).

2. Mark true or false and explain:

    (a) The following array has 101 elements:

    ```
    int x[] = new int[100];  _____   ✓
    ```

    (b) Java syntax allows programmers to use any expression of the `int` data type as an array subscript. _____

    (c) The program, when running, verifies that all array subscripts fall into the valid range. _____ ✓

    (d) Any one-dimensional array object has a `length` method that returns the size of the array. _____ ✓

3. Write a method that takes an array of integers and swaps the first element with the last one. ✓

4. Write a method that takes an array of `chars` and replaces the middle element with an asterisk (`'*'`). (Assume that the length of the array is an odd number.)

5. An array of integers `scores` has at least two elements and its elements are arranged in ascending order (i.e. `scores[i]` ≤ `scores[i+1]`). Write a condition that tests whether all the elements in `scores` have the same values. ≼ Hint: you do not need iterations. ≽

6.■ Write a method `getRandomRps` that returns a character `'r'`, `'p'`, or `'s'`, chosen randomly with odds of 3 : 5 : 6 respectively. ≼ Hint: declare an array of `chars` and initialize it with values `'r'`, `'p'`, and `'s'`, with each value occurring a number of times proportional to its desired odds. Return a randomly chosen element of the array. ≽ ✓

7.■   Change the SnackBar class from the lab in Chapter 8
(Ch08\SnackBar\SnackBar.java 🖫) to hold the three vending machine
objects in an array instead of three separate variables machine1, machine2,
machine3.

Sections 10.5-10.6

8.   Mark true or false and explain:

(a)   As opposed to one-dimensional arrays, the elements of a
two-dimensional array cannot be initialized in its declaration. _____

(b)   The elements in a two-dimensional array are accessed with two
subscripts placed in square brackets and separated by a comma. _____

9.   A two-dimensional array matrix represents a square matrix with the number
of rows and the number of columns equal to n. Write a condition to test that
an element matrix[i][j] lies on one of the diagonals of the matrix. ✓

10.   Suppose a two-dimensional array m has five rows and all are the same length.
Mark those of the following expressions that represent the number of
columns.

(a)   m.length;   _____
(b)   m.length[0];   _____   ✓
(c)   m.length(0);   _____
(d)   m[0].length;   _____
(e)   m[0].length();   _____
(f)   m[4].length;   _____
(g)   m[4].length();   _____
(h)   m[5].length();   _____   ✓

11.■   The String class has a constructor that takes an array of chars as an
argument and places its elements into a string. If you need to compare the
contents of char arrays or perform some other tests on them, it may be
convenient (although perhaps not as efficient) to convert the arrays into
strings and apply String methods. Using this approach, write a boolean
method that determines whether a given array of ten characters has five 'H's
followed by five 'T's. ✓

12.■   If you take any two positive integers m and n ($m > n$), then the numbers a, b, and c, where

$$a = m^2 - n^2; \quad b = 2mn; \quad c = m^2 + n^2$$

form a Pythagorean triple:

$$a^2 + b^2 = c^2$$

You can use algebra to prove that this is always true.

Write a method `makePythagoreanTriple` that takes two integer arguments, m and n, calculates the Pythagorean triple using the above expressions, places the resulting values a, b, and c into a new array of three elements, and returns that array. Test your method in a simple applet or console application.

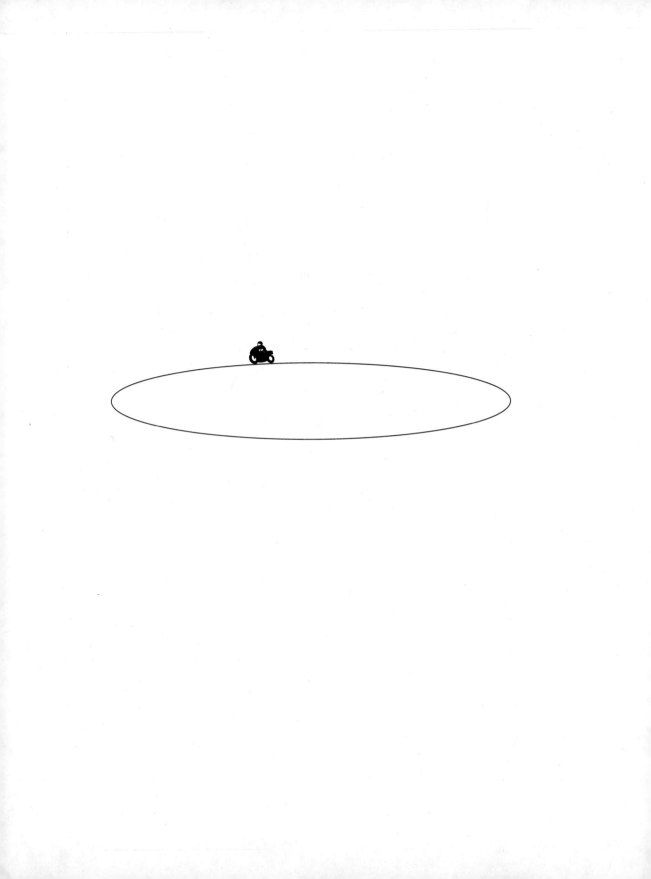

```
while (chapter < 11)
   chapter++;
```

Iterative Statements: `while`, `for`, `do-while`

11.1 Prologue

Loops or *iterative statements* tell the program to repeat a fragment of code several times for as long as a certain condition holds.   Java provides three convenient iterative statements: `while, for,` and `do-while`. Strictly speaking, any iterative code can be implemented using only the `while` statement, but the other two add flexibility and make the code more concise and idiomatic.

Iterations are often used in conjunction with arrays or files. We can use iterations to process all the elements of an array in turn (useful for finding a particular element in an array or calculating the sum of all the elements) or read and process lines of text from a file.

In this chapter we will learn the Java syntax for loops and examine how iterations work on one- and two-dimensional arrays.   After that we will implement the `LetterGrid` class for the *Ramblecs* applet.

11.2 The `while` and `for` Loops

The general form of the `while` statement is:

```
while (condition)
{
  statement1;
  statement2;
  ...
  statementN;
}
```

condition can be any logical expression; it is evaluated exactly as in `if` statements.

Informally the `while` statement is often called a ***while loop***. The statements within braces are called the ***body*** of the loop. If the body consists of only one statement, the braces surrounding the body can be dropped:

```
while (condition)
  statement1;
```

It is important <u>not</u> to put a semicolon after while(*condition*). With a semicolon, the loop would have no body, only an empty statement; *statement1* would be left completely out of the loop.

❖   ❖   ❖

The following method of the MyMath class (Ch11\MyMath\MyMath.java 🖫 on your student disk) returns the sum of all integers from 1 to *n*:

```
/**
 * Returns the sum of all integers from 1 to n, if n >= 1,
 * and 0 otherwise.
 */
public static int sumUpTo(int n)
{
  int sum = 0;
  int i = 1;

  while (i <= n)
  {
    sum += i;
    i++;          // increment i
  }
  return sum;
}
```

We can discern three elements that must be present, in one form or another, with any while loop: an initialization, a test of the condition, and an increment.

1. Initialization

The variables tested in *condition* must be initialized to some values before the loop. In the above example, i is initially set to 1 in the declaration int i = 1.

2. Testing

The condition is tested <u>before</u> each pass through the loop. If it is false, the body is not executed, the iterations end, and the program continues with the next statement after the loop. If the condition is false at the very beginning, the body of the while loop is <u>not executed at all</u>. In the sumUpTo example, the condition is i <= n. If n is zero or negative, the condition will be false on the very first test (since i is initially set to 1). Then the body of the loop will be skipped and the method will return 0.

3. Increment

At least one of the variables tested in the condition must change within the body of the loop. Otherwise, the loop will be repeated over and over and never stop, and your program will **hang**. The change of a variable is often implemented with increment or decrement operators, but it can come from any assignment or input statement. In any case, the tested variables must at some point get values that will make the condition false. Then the program jumps to the next statement after the body of the loop.

The sumUpTo method achieves this change by incrementing the variable i:

```
    ...
    i++;          // increment i
    ...
```

These three elements — initialization, testing, and incrementing (change) — must be present, explicitly or implicitly, with every while loop.

❖ ❖ ❖

The for loop is a shorthand for the while loop that combines the initialization, condition, and increment in one statement. Its general form is:

```
for (initialization; condition; increment)
{
  statement1;
  statement2;
  ...
}
```

where *initialization* is a statement that is <u>always executed once</u> before the first pass through the loop, *condition* is tested <u>before each pass</u> through the loop, and *increment* is a statement executed <u>at the end of each pass</u> through the loop.

A typical for loop for processing elements of a string or an array of length n is:

```
for (i = 0; i < n; i++)
{
  < ... statements >
}
```

For instance, if we want to zero out all the elements of an array a we might write:

```
for (i = 0; i < a.length; i++)
{
   a[i] = 0;
}
```

The braces can be dropped if the body of the loop has only one statement, but many people like to have braces even around one statement because that way it is easier to add statements to the body of the loop. We don't feel strongly about either style, so we will use both, depending on the situation or our mood.

The MyMath.sumUpTo method can be rewritten with a for loop as follows:

```
static public int sumUpTo(int n)
{
   int sum = 0, i;

   for (i = 1; i <= n; i++)
      sum += i;

   return sum;
}
```

The following method (also in the MyMath class) calculates *n*! (***n factorial***), which is defined as the product of all numbers from 1 to *n*:

```
/**
 *  Returns 1 * 2 * ... * n, if n >= 1 (and 1 otherwise)
 */
static public long factorial(int n)
{
   long f = 1;
   int k;

   for (k = 2; k <= n; k++)
      f *= k;

   return f;
}
```

If *n* < 2, the body of the loop is not executed at all and factorial returns 1.

11.3 *Lab*: Fibonacci Numbers

Find a few informative web sites dedicated to *Fibonacci numbers*. Copy MyMath.java ⊟ from the Ch11\MyMath folder on your student disk to your work folder. MyMath uses our EasyReader class for console input, so copy EasyReader.java or EasyReader.class to your work folder, too.

Add a method to the MyMath class that returns the *n*-th Fibonacci number. Add a line to main that calls fibonacci(n) and prints out the result. The MyMath class is a console application. You can run it from the command prompt:

```
C:\Mywork> java MyMath
```

11.4 The do-while Loop

> The do-while loop differs from the while loop in that the condition is tested <u>after</u> the body of the loop. This ensures that the program goes through the loop at least once.

The do-while statement's general form is:

```
do
{
  ...
} while (condition);
```

The program repeats the body of the loop as long as *condition* remains true. It is better always to keep the braces, even if the body of the loop is just one statement, because the code is hard to read without them.

do-while loops are used less frequently than while and for loops. They are convenient when the variables tested in the condition are calculated, entered, or initialized within the body of the loop. The following example comes from main in the MyMath class (Ch11\MyMath\MyMath.java ⊟):

```
public static void main(String[] args)
{
  EasyReader console = new EasyReader();
  int n;

  do
  {
    System.out.print("Enter an integer from 4 to 20: ");
    n = console.readInt();
  } while (n < 4 || n > 20);

  System.out.println();
  System.out.println("1 + ... + " + n + " = " + sumUpTo(n));
  System.out.println(n + "! = " + factorial(n));
}
```

In this code the `do-while` loop calls `EasyReader`'s `readInt` method to get the value of n from the user's input. The iterations continue until the user enters a number within the requested range.

If for some reason you do not like `do-while` loops, you can easily avoid them by using a `while` loop and initializing the variables in such a way that the condition is true before the first pass through the loop. The `do-while` loop in the above code, for example, can be rewritten as follows:

```
int n = -1;

while (n < 4 || n > 20)
{
  System.out.print("Enter an integer from 4 to 20: ");
  n = console.readInt();
}
```

11.5 break and return in Loops

We saw in Section 7.11 that `break` is used inside a `switch` statement to end a case and break out of the switch. `break` can be also used in the body of a loop. It instructs the program to break out of the loop immediately and go to the next statement after the body of the loop. `break` must always appear inside a conditional (`if` or `else`) statement — otherwise you will just break out of the loop on the very first iteration.

The following method checks whether a positive integer n is a prime. (If you'd like, you can add it to the `MyMath` class in `Ch11\MyMath\MyMath.java` ▣.) A prime is an integer that is greater than 1 and does not have any factors besides 1 and itself. Our algorithm has to check all potential factors m, but only as long as $m^2 \le n$ (because if m is a factor, then so is n/m, and one of the two must be less than or equal to the square root of *n*). The isPrime method below employs break to reduce the number of iterations:

```
/**
 *  Returns true if n is a prime, false otherwise.
 */
public static boolean isPrime(int n)
{
  boolean noFactors = true;
  int m;

  if (n <= 1)
    return false;

  for (m = 2; noFactors; m++)
  {
    if (m * m > n)
      break;

    if (n % m == 0)
      noFactors = false;
  }
  return noFactors;
}
```

Another way to break out of the loop (and out of the method) is to put a return statement inside the loop. For example:

```
public static boolean isPrime(int n)
{
  int m = 2;

  if (n <= 1)
    return false;

  while (m * m <= n)
  {
    if (n % m == 0)
      return false;
    m++;
  }
  return true;
}
```

Either version is acceptable, but the latter is a little shorter. You will find programmers, though, who like to have only <u>one</u> return in each method and who find a break or return inside a loop objectionable.

11.6 Iterations and Arrays

Iterations are indispensable for handling arrays for two reasons. First, if an array is large and we want to access every element (for example, to find the sum of all the elements), it is not practical to repeat the same statement over and over again in the source code:

```
sum = 0;
sum += a[0];
sum += a[1];
...
...
sum += a[999];
```

A simple `for` loop saves 998 lines of code:

```
sum = 0;
for (i = 0;  i < 1000;  i++)
  sum += a[i];
```

Second, a programmer may not know the exact size of an array in advance. The actual number of elements may become known only when the program is running. For example, an array may be filled with data read from a file, and we may not know in advance how many elements are stored in the file. The only way to deal with such a "variable-length" array is through iterations.

❖ ❖ ❖

If we want to process all the elements of a two-dimensional array, it is convenient to use **nested** `for` loops. For example:

```
int rows = 12; cols = 7;
char grid[][] = new char[rows][cols];
int row, col;
...
// Set all elements in grid to '*':
for (row = 0; row < rows; row++)
{
  for (col = 0; col < cols; col++)
  {
    grid[row][col] = '*';
  }
}
```

Braces are optional here since the body of each loop consists of only one statement. You could just as well write

```
for (row = 0; row < rows; row++)
  for (col = 0; col < cols; col++)
    grid[row][col] = '*';
```

> **Be careful when using `break` in nested loops: a `break` statement inside a nested loop will only break out of the inner loop.**

For example, suppose you have a 2-D array of characters `grid` and you want to find the first occurrence of the letter 'A' in it (scanning the first row left to right, then the next row, etc.). You might try to use the following code:

```
int rows = grid.length, cols = grid[0].length;
int r, c, firstArow, firstAcol;

for (r = 0; r < rows; r++)
{
  for (c = 0; c < cols; c++)
  {
    if (grid[r][c] = 'A')
      break;
  }
}
firstArow = r;
firstAcol = c;
```

Unfortunately, it will only find the first occurrence of 'A' in the <u>last</u> row (if any).

11.7 *Case Study and Lab:* **LetterGrid** *for Ramblecs*

Now that we are equipped with essential knowledge about arrays and loops, it is time to revisit and update our *Ramblecs* game project. Our prototype in Chapter 6 had one "letter cube" falling and always landing in the same place. In the real game, the cubes can land one on top of another, and the program must somehow keep track of the cubes' current configuration. In this lab we will add this functionality to our *Ramblecs* applet.

Let's implement it in the form of a class `LetterGrid`. Now our applet will consist of five classes with one object of each class (Figure 11-1).

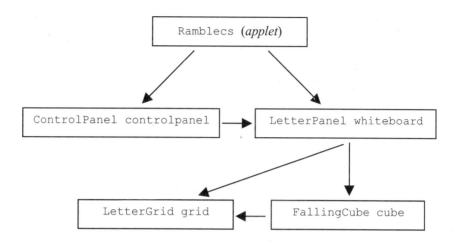

Figure 11-1. *Ramblecs* classes and objects after adding LetterGrid

The new LetterGrid class will have one constructor that takes two arguments, the number of rows and the number of columns in the grid. It creates an "empty" grid: a 2-D array of chars, filled with spaces. The class will have seven methods: numRows, numCols, charAt, setCharAt, isEmpty, lastRowToString and dropDown (Figure 11-2).

The first five are general-purpose methods; these are self-explanatory. The last two, lastRowToString and dropDown, are specific to the *Ramblecs* game.

lastRowToString converts the last (bottom) row of the grid into a string, "trims" the spaces on both sides, and returns the resulting string. Later *Ramblecs* will try to look up this string in its dictionary of words. In this method you could use a for loop that appends individual characters to a string one by one, but there is a much quicker way. The String class has a constructor that builds a string from a character array. Recall that each row in a 2-D array is a 1-D array. All you have to do is create a string using that constructor, then trim it and return.

The dropDown method will be called when the player hits the space bar or <Enter>. It throws away the bottom row in the grid, shifts all rows down by one, and fills the top row with spaces. Let us agree that "down" means in the direction of <u>increasing</u> row number: the "top" row index is 0 and the bottom row index is numRows() - 1. The dropDown method sounds like a candidate for using nested loops followed by one simple loop to fill the top row with spaces.

```java
/**
 *   Implements a 2-D array of characters with lastRowToString
 *   and dropDown methods for the Ramblecs applet
 */
public class LetterGrid
{
  < ... Missing fields >

  /**
   *  Constructor:
   *  Creates a grid with dimensions rows, cols, and fills
   *  it with spaces
   */
  public LetterGrid(int rows, int cols)
  {
    < ... Missing code >
  }

  /**
   *  Returns the number of rows in grid
   */
  public int numRows()
  {
    < ... Missing code >
  }

  /**
   *  Returns the number of columns in grid
   */
  public int numCols()
  {
    < ... Missing code >
  }

  /**
   *  Returns the character at row, col position
   */
  public char charAt(int row, int col)
  {
    < ... Missing code >
  }

  /**
   *  Sets the character at row, col position to ch
   */
  public void setCharAt(int row, int col, char ch)
  {
    < ... Missing code >
  }
```

Figure 11-2 `LetterGrid.java` *Continued* ➥

```
/**
 *  Returns true if the character at row, col is a space,
 *  false otherwise
 */
public boolean isEmpty(int row, int col)
{
  < ... Missing code >
}

/**
 *  Returns the string formed by characters in the last row
 *  after trimming white space on both ends
 */
public String lastRowToString()
{
  < ... Missing code >
}

/**
 *  Shifts all rows down by one and fills the top row
 *  with spaces
 */
public void dropDown()
{
  < ... Missing code >
}
}
```

Figure 11-2. `Ch11\Ramblecs\LetterGrid.java` ⊟

Note how this class combines a few general-purpose methods with a couple of application-specific methods. The general methods could potentially be useful in other applications, so we might want to eventually reuse this class. Unfortunately, the *Ramblecs*-specific methods would be there, too. We don't necessarily want to clutter another application with unused code from *Ramblecs*. A proper OOP solution to this dilemma would be to split the functionality of the LetterGrid class between two classes. The first class, a ***superclass*** (let's call it, say, CharMatrix) would have only the general-purpose methods, such as numRows, numCols, charAt, setCharAt. Perhaps, with an eye to future use, we would generalize lastRowToString into a rowToString method that would convert <u>any</u> specified row into a string. CharMatrix's constructor might take three arguments, the grid dimensions and a "fill" character used to initialize all the elements of the array.

This class would be reusable. It would ***encapsulate*** the functionality associated with <u>any</u> 2-D array of characters. The second class, the ***subclass*** LetterGrid, would <u>extend</u> CharMatrix, inheriting all its methods. It makes sense to do this because a

LetterGrid object is "a kind of" CharMatrix object, with a few additional methods specific to the *Ramblecs* game. The LetterGrid class would add the isEmpty method and the lastRowToString and dropDown methods. Inheritance and related object-oriented design principles are explained in more detail in Chapter 17.

You can use either the one-class approach or the superclass-subclass approach in your implementation. In Ch11\Ramblecs\LetterGrid.java 🖫 we have it set up for one class, but it is relatively easy to cut and paste it into two classes. While you are working on LetterGrid, I have modified the other classes to support the new functionality. This is teamwork at its best: you get the easy part! I have made the following changes:

LetterPanel

The LetterPanel class in its constructor creates one LetterGrid object. That object is passed to the FallingCube constructor as an argument because now the falling cube has to check its position against the grid and land on top of other cubes:

```
grid = new LetterGrid(ROWS, COLS);
cube = new FallingCube(grid, CUBESIZE);
```

LetterPanel's paintComponent method needs to draw the falling cube plus the whole grid, so I added a method drawGrid:

```
public void paintComponent(Graphics g)
{
  super.paintComponent(g); // call JPanel's paintComponent
  drawGrid(g);
  cube.draw(g);
}
```

We also need a method getWord that returns the string from the bottom row of the grid. This method simply calls grid.lastRowToString() and returns the result:

```
public String getWord()
{
  return grid.lastRowToString();
}
```

A few other minor cosmetic changes make it easier to integrate the new functionality into the project.

FallingCube

The biggest change is in the moveDown method. The falling cube now has to check its position against the letter grid before it moves, and the grid has to be updated when the cube lands:

```
public boolean moveDown()
{
  int col = cubeX / cubeSize;
  int row = (cubeY + cubeSize + yStep) / cubeSize;
  if (row < grid.numRows() && grid.isEmpty(row, col))
  {
    cubeY += yStep;
    return true;
  }
  else  // land this cube:
  {
    row--;
    if (row >= 0 && row < grid.numRows())
      grid.setCharAt(row, col, randomLetter);
    return false;
  }
}
```

I have added means to draw the letter grid conveniently. The FallingCube class already had code to draw a cube, and there is no reason to duplicate this code. It is better to keep it in only one place in case we want to change the appearance of the cubes later. So instead of having two separate but similar methods for drawing the falling cube and a cube in the grid, I added a general static method drawCube that draws a cube with a specified letter at specified coordinates. This method can be used both for drawing the falling cube and drawing a cube in the grid:

```
public void draw(Graphics g)
{
  drawCube(g, xLeft + cubeX, cubeY, cubeSize, randomLetter);
}

public static void drawCube(Graphics g, int x, int y,
                                        int size, char letter)
{
  g.setColor(Color.red);
  g.fill3DRect(x, y, size-1, size-1, true);
  g.setColor(Color. white);
  g.fillRoundRect(x + 5, y + 5, size - 10, size - 10,
                                      size/2 - 5, size/2 - 5);
  g.setColor(Color.darkGray);
  String s = String.valueOf(letter);
  g.drawString(s, x + size/2 - 6, y + size/2 + 5);
}
```

ControlPanel

I have made `ControlPanel` a "key listener" to capture keyboard events. We will discuss mouse and keyboard handling in detail in Chapter 16; meanwhile, if you are anxious to start using keyboard input in your own applets you can use this as an example. When the user strikes `<Enter>`, the string returned by `whiteboard.getWord()` will show up in the applet's status line; when the user strikes the space bar, the program will call `whiteboard.dropRow()` which in turn calls `grid.dropDown()` and repaints `whiteboard`.

When you finish your part, put together the updated *Ramblecs* applet and test it. It now has five classes: `Ramblecs`, `LetterPanel`, `ControlPanel`, `FallingCube`, and `LetterGrid`. It's beginning to look a little like a real game: multiple letter cubes are supported and stacked one on top of another, and there is even some keyboard action. All we have left to do is enable cursor keys for moving and turning the falling cube and add a dictionary and some methods for keeping and displaying the score.

11.8 Summary

Java offers three iterative statements:

```
while (condition)
{
   . . .
}

for (initialization; condition; increment)
{
   . . .
}

do
{
   . . .
} while (condition);
```

In a `while` loop, the variables tested in *condition* must be initialized before the loop, and at least one of them has to change inside the body of the loop. The program tests *condition* before each pass through the loop. If *condition* is false on the very first test, the `while` loop is skipped, and the program jumps to the first statement after the body of the loop. Otherwise the program keeps iterating for as long as *condition* holds true.

The for loop combines *initialization, condition,* and *increment* (change) in one statement. The *initialization* statement is executed once, before the loop. *condition* is tested before each pass through the loop, and if it is false, the loop is skipped and the program jumps to the next statement after the body of the loop. The *increment* statement is executed at the end of each pass through the loop.

The do-while loop is different from the while loop in that *condition* is tested <u>after</u> the body of the loop. Thus the body of a do-while loop is always executed at least once.

A break statement inside the body of a loop tells the program to jump immediately out of the loop to the first statement after the body of the loop. break should appear only inside an if or else statement; otherwise it will interrupt the loop on the very first iteration. A break statement inside a nested loop will only break out of the inner loop. A return statement inside a loop immediately quits the loop and the whole method, too.

Exercises

Sections 11.1-11.5

1. The population of Mexico in 1990 was 89.2 million. Write a program that calculates and prints out the year in which the population of Mexico will reach 120 million, assuming a constant growth rate of 2.3% per year. Use a while loop.

2. Write a method int addOdds(int n) that calculates and returns the sum of all odd integers from 1 to *n*. Your method should use exactly one for loop and no other iterative statements. (Do not use the formula for the sum of odd numbers.) ✓

3. Write a program to test the algorithms from Questions 2 and 3 in Chapter 3 (page 88).

4. Using the `EasyReader` class, write a program that supports the following dialog with the user:

```
Enter quantity: 75
You have ordered 75 floppies -- $19.50

Next customer (y/n): y

Enter quantity: 97
Floppies can be ordered only in packs of 25.

Next customer (y/n): n

Thank you for using Floppy Systems.
```

(Define the unit price of a floppy as a <u>constant</u> equal to 26 cents.)

5. Write a program that produces the following output (where the user may enter any positive integer under 10): ✓

```
Enter a positive integer under 10: 6
1 + 2 + 3 + 4 + 5 + 6 = 21
```

6. Write a method that tests whether a given string contains only digits.

7. Write a program that prompts the user to enter a string of characters. The program reads one character at a time (using `EasyReader`'s `readChar` method) and counts 'H's (for "heads") and 'T's (for "tails"). The program skips all other characters and stops reading when it encounters a '.' (period). It then reports the ratio of "heads" to "tails" as a decimal number (or "All heads" if the number of "tails" is zero). Your program may use only one iterative statement: a `do-while` loop. ✓

8. (a) Modify the `isPrime` method on page 304 so that if the argument is not 2 it tests only odd numbers as potential factors of *n*. ✓

(b) Make `isPrime` even more efficient by testing only potential factors that are relatively prime with 6 (i.e., factors that are not evenly divisible by either 2 or 3). ✓

9.▪   Given a positive number a, the sequence of values

$$x_0 = \frac{a}{2}$$

$$x_{n+1} = \frac{1}{2}\left(x_n + \frac{a}{x_n}\right) \quad (n \geq 0)$$

converges to $\sqrt{a}$. Fill in the blanks in the following method that uses iterations to estimate the square root of a number:

```
/**
 *   @precondition a is a positive number.
 *   @return an estimate r of the square root of a,
 *   such that |r^2 - a| < 0.01 .
 */
public static double sqrtEst(double a)
{
  double r = a/2;
  double diff;

  do
  {
    _____;

    ...

  } while (diff > .01 || diff < -.01);

  return r;
}
```

10.▪   Recall that $1 + 3 + \ldots + (2p - 1) = p^2$ for any integer $p \geq 1$. Write a "simple" method

```
public static boolean isPerfectSquare(int n)
```

which tests whether a given number is a perfect square. A "simple" method cannot use arrays, nested loops, math functions, or arithmetic operations except addition (see Question 5 for Chapter 3 on page 88). ✓

11.◆   Consider all fractions with positive denominators that do not exceed 100. Write a program that finds the two such fractions that are closest to 17 / 76: one from above and one from below.

Sections 11.6-11.8

12.   Fill in the blanks in the following method that sets the elements of an array to the integers 1 through n, where n is the length of the array: ✓

```
private void setSequence(int v[])
{
   int i, n = _____;

   for (_____)

   _____;
}
```

13.■   Write a method that determines whether a given number is a median for values stored in an array:

```
/**
 *   Returns true if m is a median for values in the array
 *   <code>sample</code>, false otherwise.
 *   (Here we call m a median if the number of elements that are
 *   greater than m is the same as the number of elements that
 *   are less than m)
 */
public boolean isMedian(double sample[], double m)
```

14.■   (a)   Write and test a method that computes a value of a polynomial
$P(x) = a_0 + a_1 x + \ldots + a_n x^n$ for a given x: ✓

```
/**
 *   Returns the value of the n-th degree polynomial
 *   P(x) = a[0] + a[1]*x + a[2] * x^2 + ... + a[n] * x^n
 *   where the length of a is n + 1
 */
public double polynomial(double a[], double x)
```

(b)   The same polynomial can be rewritten as:

$$P(x) = a_0 + x(a_1 + x(a_2 + (\ldots + x(a_n))\ldots)$$

The latter representation is more efficient because it needs the same number of additions but fewer multiplications. Modify the method your wrote in Part (a) for the second implementation.

15. What does the `mysteryCount` method count?

```
private int mysteryCount(int v[])
{
  int i, n = v.length, count = 0;

  for (i = 0; i < n; i++)
  {
    if (v[i] != 0) break;
    count++;
  }
  return count;
}
```

16. Write a method

```
public void fillCheckerboard(Color[][] board)
```

that fills `board` with alternating black and white colors in a checkerboard pattern. For example:

✓

17. Fill in the blanks in the following method:

```
/**
 *  Returns an array filled with values
 *    1, 2, ..., n-1, n, n-1, ..., 2, 1.
 */
public static int[] fillWedge(int n)
{
  int w[] = _____;

  int i = 1;

  while (i <= n)
  {
    w[ _____ ] = i;

    w[ _____ ] = i;

    i++;
  }

  return _____;
}
```

18.   Let us say that a matrix (a 2-D array of numbers) m1 "covers" a matrix m2
(with the same dimensions) if m1[i][j] > m2[i][j] for at least half of
all the elements in m1. Fill in the blanks in the following method: ✓

```
/**
 *   Assumes that m1 and m2 have the same dimensions.
 *   Returns true if m1 "covers" m2, false otherwise.
 */
private static boolean covers(double m1[][], double m2[][])
{
  int count = 0;
  int nRows = _____, nCols = _____;
  int r, c;

  _____
  ...
}
```

19.♦   The applet *Cooney* (Ch11\exercises\Cooney.class 🖫) plays a game in
which the player tries to guess which words Cooney "likes" and which ones
Cooney "doesn't like." After five correct guesses in a row Cooney
congratulates the player and the game stops. Play the game and guess the
rule; then write the Cooney applet. ⟨ Hint: use
Ch09\exercises\StringTest.java 🖫 as a basis for your applet. ⟩

20.■   Fill in the blanks in the following method that takes a square matrix
(2-D array) of integers m as an argument and returns a 1-D array of integers
that holds the values from the main diagonal of m. (The main diagonal
connects the upper-left and the lower-right corners.) ✓

```
_____ getDiagonal (_____m_____)
{
    int i, len = _____ ;

    _____ ; // declare the resulting array

    for (i = 0; i < len; i++)

        _____ ;

    return _____ ;
}
```

21.■   (a)   Write a method

```
boolean isPalindrome(String word)
```

that tests whether word is a palindrome (the same when read forward or backward, as in "madam"). Test isPalindrome using the appropriately modified *String Test* applet (Ch09\exercises\StringTest.java ▣).

(b)◆   Upgrade isPalindrome so that it can handle any phrase (as in "Madam, I'm Adam"). In testing for a palindrome, skip all spaces, punctuation marks, apostrophes, and other non-alphanumeric characters and consider lower- and uppercase letters the same. ⸖ Hint: recall that the Character class has static methods
boolean isLetterOrDigit(ch) and
char toUpperCase(ch). ⸖

22.◆   Write your own implementation of the Integer.parseInt(String s) method.

23.■   In the Fraction class in Section 8.11, we used a recursive version of the Euclid's Algorithm that finds the greatest common factor (gcf) of two positive integers:

```
public static int gcf(int n, int d)
{
  int r = n % d;

  if (r == 0)
    return d;
  else
    return gcf(d, r);
}
```

Write and test an iterative implementation of this algorithm.

24. ▪ A non-negative "large integer" is represented as an array of *N* digits. The value of each digit is an integer from 0 to 9. The most significant digits are at the beginning of the array; zero values at the beginning indicate leading zeroes.

(a) Fill in the blanks in the following method that calculates and returns the sum of two "large integers" *a* and *b*: ✓

```
private final int N = 100;

/**
 *   Calculates the sum of two "large integers" <code>a</code>
 *   and <code>b</code>, represented as arrays of digits,
 *   and places the result into the array <code>sum</code>.
 *   Assumes that the length of <code>sum</code> is N
 *   and that the result fits into N digits: the overflow
 *   condition is ignored.
 */
public static int[] add(int a[], int b[])
{
    int sum[] = _____;
    int i, d, carry = 0;

    for ( _____ )

    {
       d = a[i] + b[i] + carry;

       sum[i] = _____;

       carry = _____;
    }
    return _____;
}
```

(b) Write a test program that defines and initializes (or lets the user enter) two arrays of digits and displays their "large" sum.

25. ▪   An ISBN (International Standard Book Number) has ten digits. The first nine digits may have values from '0' to '9'; they identify the country in which the book was printed, the publisher, and the individual book. The tenth digit is a "check digit" assigned in such a way that the number $d_1d_2d_3d_4d_5d_6d_7d_8d_9d_{10}$ has the property:

$$(10d_1 + 9d_2 + 8d_3 + 7d_4 + 6d_5 + 5d_6 + 4d_7 + 3d_8 + 2d_9 + d_{10}) \mod 11 = 0$$

"mod" stands for modulo division (same as % in Java). If d_{10} needs the value 10 to balance the check digit equation, then the character 'X' is used. For example, 096548534X is a valid ISBN.

Note that if we simply took the sum of all the digits, the check digit would remain valid for any permutation of the digits. Different coefficients make the number invalid when any two digits are swapped, catching a common typo.

Write a method

```
public static boolean isValidISBN(String isbn)
```

that returns true if isbn represents a valid ISBN, false otherwise. Test your method in a simple applet or application. ⸮ Hint: the Character class has the static int method digit(char ch, int base) that returns the numeric value of the digit in the specified base. For example, Character.digit('7',10) returns 7. ⸮

26.◆   Change the `SnackBar` class from the lab in Chapter 8
(`Ch08\SnackBar\SnackBar.java` 🖫) to be able to support any number
of vending machines. Assume that the number of machines is specified in a
`<param>` tag in the HTML file that runs the applet. For example:

```
<param name="N_MACHINES" value="5">
```

⸮ Hint: the `JApplet` class has a method `getParameter` that obtains the
value (a string) for a specified parameter. For example:

```
String s = getParameter("N_MACHINES");
```

⸮

Assign brand names and colors to the machines randomly from the three
names and colors specified in the `SnackBar` class.

12ACEHPRT

Searching, Sorting, and Other Array Algorithms

12.1 Prologue

Searching and ***sorting*** are vast and important subjects. At the practical level they are important because they are what many large computer systems do much of the time. At the theoretical level they help to distill the general properties and interesting theoretical questions about algorithms and data structures and offer rich material on which to study and compare them. We will consider these topics in the context of working with arrays, along with other common algorithms that work with arrays.

Searching tasks in computer applications range from finding a particular character in a string of a dozen characters to finding a record in a database of 100 million records. In the abstract, searching is a task involving a set of data elements represented in some way in computer memory. Each element includes a ***key*** that can be tested against a target value for an exact match. A successful search finds the element with a matching key and returns its location or some information associated with it: a value, a record, or the address of a record.

Searching refers to tasks where matching the keys against a specified target is straightforward and unambiguous. If, by comparison, we had to deal with a database of fingerprints and needed to find the best match for a given specimen, that application would fall into the category of ***pattern recognition*** rather than searching. It would also be likely to require the intervention of some human experts.

To ***sort*** means to arrange a list of data elements in ascending or descending order. The data elements may be numeric values or some records ordered by keys. In addition to preparing a data set for easier access (e.g., Binary Search), sorting has many other applications. One example is matching two data sets. Suppose we want to merge two large mailing lists and eliminate the duplicates. This task is straightforward when the lists are alphabetically sorted by name and address but may be unmanageable otherwise. Another use may be simply presenting information to a user in an ordered manner. A list of the user's files on a personal computer, for example, may be sorted by name, date, or size. A word processor sorts information when it automatically creates an index or a bibliography for a book. In large business systems, millions of transactions (e.g., bank checks or credit card charges) are sorted daily before they are posted to customer accounts or forwarded to other payers.

In this chapter we consider and compare two searching methods, Sequential Search and Binary Search, and three common sorting algorithms: Selection Sort, Insertion

Sort, and, a faster one, Mergesort. Question 17 in the exercises introduces another sorting algorithm, called Quicksort. In addition to searching and sorting algorithms we discuss other common algorithms for working with arrays: finding the largest or the smallest element, inserting an element in the middle of an array, and rotating an array.

12.2 Sequential and Binary Search

Suppose we have an array of a certain size and we want to find the location of a given "target" value in that array (or ascertain that it is not there). If the elements of the array are in random order, we have no choice but to use *Sequential Search*, that is, to check the value of each consecutive element one by one until we find the target element (or finish scanning through the whole array). For example:

```
String words[] = { < ... some words> };
String target = < ... a word >;
int k;

for (k = 0; k < words.length; k++)
  if (target.equals(words[k]))
    return k;
```

This may be time-consuming if the array is large. For an array of 1,000,000 elements, we will examine an average of 500,000 elements before finding the target (assuming that the target value is always somewhere in the array). This algorithm is called an $O(n)$ ("order of n") algorithm because it takes an average number of operations roughly proportional to n, where n is the size of the array.

It turns out that if the elements of the array are arranged in ascending or descending order (or, as we say, the array is *sorted*), there is a much faster searching algorithm, the *Binary Search*. Let's say our array is sorted in ascending order and we are looking for a target value x. Take the middle element of the array and compare it with x. If they are equal, the target element is found. If x is smaller, the target element must be in the left half of the array, and if x is larger, the target must be in the right half of the array. In any event, each time we repeat the same procedure we narrow the range of our search by half (Figure 12-1). This sequence stops when we find the target or get down to just one element, which happens very quickly.

Using the Binary Search method, an array of 3 elements requires at most 2 comparisons. An array of 7 elements requires at most 3 comparisons. An array of 15 elements requires at most 4 comparisons, and so on. In general, an array of $2^n - 1$ (or fewer) elements requires at most n comparisons. So an array of 1,000,000 elements will require at most 20 comparisons ($2^{20} - 1 = 1,048,575$) which is much better than

500,000. That is why such methods are called "divide and conquer." Binary Search is an $O(\log n)$ algorithm because the number of operations in it is roughly proportional to $\log_2 n$.

The `binarySearch` method in Figure 12-2 implements the Binary Search algorithm for an integer array sorted in ascending order.

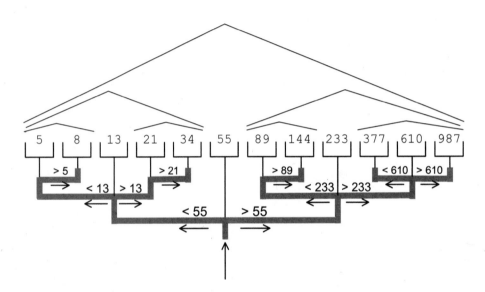

Figure 12-1. Binary Search

```java
/**
 * Performs Binary Search on the array
 * a[0] < a[1] < ... < a[size-1].
 * Looks for an element a[k] equal to target.
 * Returns k if the target is found; -1 otherwise.
 */
static public int binarySearch(int a[], int target)
{
  int left = 0, right = a.length - 1, middle;
  int k = -1;

  while (left <= right)
  {
    // Take the index of the middle element between
    //   "left" and "right":

    middle = (left + right) / 2;

    // Compare this element to the target value
    //   and adjust the search range accordingly:

    if (target > a[middle])
      left = middle + 1;
    else if (target < a[middle])
      right = middle - 1;
    else
    {      // target must be equal to a[middle]
      k = middle;
      break;
    }
  }
  return k;
}
```

Figure 12-2. Binary Search Implementation in Java

One way to understand and check code is to *trace* it manually on some representative examples. Let us take, for example:

```
Given:
    a[] = {8, 13, 21, 34, 55, 89}
      (a[0] =  8; a[1] = 13; a[2] = 21; a[3] = 34;
       a[4] = 55; a[5] = 89);
    target = 34

Initially:
    left =  0; right = a.length-1 = 5

First iteration:
    middle = (0+5)/2 = 2;
    a[middle] = a[2] = 21;
    target > a[middle] (34 > 21)
      ==> Set left = middle + 1 = 3; (right remains 5)

Second iteration:
    middle = (3+5)/2 = 4;
    a[middle] = a[4] = 55;
    target < a[middle] (34 < 55)
      ==> Set right = middle - 1 = 3; (left remains 3)

Third iteration:
    middle = (3+3)/2 = 3;
    a[middle] = a[3] = 34;
    target == a[middle] (34 = 34)
      ==> Set k = middle = 3; break

Return: 3
```

A more comprehensive check should also include tracing special situations (e.g., when the target element is the first or the last element, or is not in the array) and "degenerate" cases, such as when a.length is equal to 1.

We also have to make sure that the method terminates — otherwise, the program may hang. This is better accomplished by logical or mathematical reasoning than by tracing specific examples, because it is hard to foresee all the possible paths of an algorithm. Here we can reason as follows: our binarySearch method must terminate because on each iteration the difference right - left decreases by at least 1. So eventually we either break out of the loop via break (when the target is found), or reach a point where right - left becomes negative and the condition in the while loop becomes false.

12.3 Finding the Largest or the Smallest Element

A variation of searching is looking for the array's largest or smallest element. To find the maximum value we can set an initial value of a variable representing the maximum to, say, the first element of the array, then compare it with all the other elements and update its value when we encounter a larger element. For example:

```
/**
 *  Returns the value of the largest element in the array a
 */
static public double findMax(double a[])
{
  int i;
  double aMax = a[0];

  for (i = 1; i < a.length; i++)
    if (a[i] > aMax)
      aMax = a[i];

  return aMax;
}
```

Alternatively we can keep track of the <u>position</u> of the maximum:

```
/**
 *  Returns the position of the largest element in the array a
 */
static public int findMaxPos(double a[])
{
  int i, iMax = 0;

  for (i = 1; i < a.length; i++)
    if (a[i] > a[iMax])
      iMax = i;

  return iMax;
}
```

To find the minimum we can proceed in a similar way but update the current minimum value (or its position) when we encounter a smaller element.

12.4 Inserting a New Element into an Array

In some applications you may need to add elements to an array as you go. You have to make sure that the array has room to add an element to it. When you create your array, you have to allocate sufficient space for the <u>maximum possible</u> number of elements. In this case the array's `length` will refer to the maximum capacity of the array. You need a separate variable to keep count of the elements actually stored in it. For example:

```
final int maxCount = 5000;        // Maximum number of words
String dictionary[] = new String[maxCount];
int count = 0;                    // Start with an empty dictionary
< ... etc. >
```

To add an element at the end of an array you need to check that there is still room and, if so, store the element in the first vacant slot and increment the count. For example:

```
String word;

<... other statements >

if (count < maxCount)
{
  dictionary[count] = word;
  count++;
}
```

If you want to keep an array sorted in ascending or descending order, it may be necessary to insert a new element <u>in the middle</u> of the array. To do that, you first need to shift a few elements toward the end of the array to create a vacant slot in the desired position. You have to start shifting from the last element — otherwise you may overwrite an element before you get it out of the way. Figure 12-3 illustrates the process. The following code serves as an example:

```
String word;
int i, insertPos;

<... other statements >

if (count < maxCount)  // count is the number of words
{
  for (i = count; i > insertPos; i--)
    dictionary[i] = dictionary[i-1];
  dictionary[insertPos] = word;
  count++;
}
```

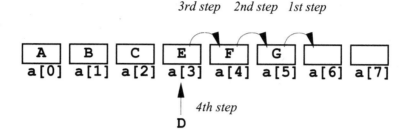

3rd step   2nd step   1st step

A	B	C	E	F	G		
a[0]	a[1]	a[2]	a[3]	a[4]	a[5]	a[6]	a[7]

4th step

D

Figure 12-3. Inserting an element in the middle of an array

12.5 *Lab*: Rotate an Array

In the *Ramblecs* game, a letter cube has six faces with a letter on each face. The player must be able to turn the cube to display one of the letters using cursor keys. To keep things simple, we can implement this functionality by placing the six letters in a 1-D array and rotating the array one step "left" or "right" when necessary. (The program will always display the first element of the array on the visible face of the cube.)

We have prepared a little applet that tests array rotations (`RotateArray.java` in the `Ch12\Rotate` folder). The applet lets the user enter a string of characters. When the "<<" or ">>" button is pressed, the applet converts the input string into an array, rotates the array in the appropriate direction, then converts the result back into a string and displays it.

Your task is to supply and test the `void rotateLeft(char buffer[])` and `void rotateRight(char buffer[])` methods.

12.6 Selection Sort

The task of rearranging the elements of an array in ascending or descending order is called *sorting*. We are looking for a general algorithm that works for an array of any size and for any values of its elements. There exist many sorting algorithms for accomplishing this task, but the most straightforward one is probably *Selection Sort*. It involves the following steps:

Selection Sort

1. Initialize a variable *n* to the size of the array.
2. Find the largest among the first *n* elements.
3. Make it swap places with the *n*-th element.
4. Decrement *n* by 1.
5. Repeat steps 2 - 4 while $n \geq 2$.

On the first iteration we find the largest element of the array and swap it with the last element. The largest element is now in the correct place, from which it will never move again. We decrement *n*, pretending that the last element of the array does not exist anymore, and repeat the procedure until we have worked our way through the array. The iterations stop when there is only one element left, because it has already been compared with every other element and is guaranteed to be the smallest.

The `SelectionSort` class in Figure 12-4 implements this algorithm for an array of the type `double`.

A similar procedure will sort the array in descending order; instead of finding the largest element on each iteration, we can simply find the smallest element among the first *n*.

Sorting is a common operation in computer applications and a favorite subject on which to study and compare algorithms. Selection Sort is an $O(n^2)$ algorithm because the number of comparisons in it is $n \cdot (n-1)/2$, which is roughly proportional to n^2. It is less efficient than other sorting algorithms considered here, but more predictable: it always takes the same number of comparisons.

```
public class SelectionSort
{
  /**
   * Sorts a[0], ..., a[size-1] in ascending order
   *    using Selection Sort
   */
  public static void sort(double a[])
  {
    int i, iMax, n;
    double aTemp;

    for (n = a.length; n >= 2; n--)
    {

      // Find the index iMax of the largest element
      //    among a[0], ..., a[n-1]:

      iMax = 0;
      for (i = 1; i < n; i++)
        if (a[i] > a[iMax])
          iMax = i;

      // Swap a[iMax] with a[n-1]:

      aTemp = a[iMax];      // Save a[iMax] in a temporary location.
      a[iMax] = a[n-1];     // Copy a[n-1] to a[iMax].
      a[n-1] = aTemp;       // Copy saved value to a[n-1].

      // Decrement n (accomplished by n-- in the for loop).
    }
  }
}
```

Figure 12-4. `Ch12\Benchmarks\SelectionSort.java` 💾

12.7 Insertion Sort

The idea of the ***Insertion Sort*** algorithm is to keep the beginning part of the array sorted and insert each next element into the correct place in it. It involves the following steps:

Insertion Sort

1.   Initialize a variable n to 1 (keep the first n elements sorted).
2.   Save the next element and find the place to insert it among the first n so that the order is preserved.
3.   Shift the elements as necessary and insert the saved one in the created vacant slot.
4.   Increment n by 1.
5.   Repeat steps 2 - 4 while n < array length.

```java
public class InsertionSort
{
  /**
   * Sorts a[0], ..., a[size-1] in ascending order
   *    using Insertion Sort
   */
  public static void sort(double a[])
  {
    int i, iMax, n;
    double aTemp;

    for (n = 1; n < a.length; n++)
    {
      // Save the next element to be inserted:

      aTemp = a[n];

      // Going backwards from a[n-1], shift elements to the
      //    right until you find an element a[i] <= aTemp:

      i = n;
      while (i > 0 && aTemp < a[i-1])
      {
        a[i] = a[i-1];
        i--;
      }

      // Insert the saved element after a[i]:
      a[i] = aTemp;

      // Increment n (accomplished by n++ in the for loop).
    }
  }
}
```

Figure 12-5. `Ch12\Benchmarks\InsertionSort.java` 🖫

The `InsertionSort` class in Figure 12-5 implements this algorithm for an array of `doubles`.

Insertion Sort is also on average an $O(n^2)$ algorithm, but it can do better than Selection Sort when the array is already nearly sorted. In the best case, when the array is already sorted, Insertion Sort becomes an $O(n)$ algorithm.

12.8 Mergesort

The tremendous difference in efficiency between Binary Search and Sequential Search hints at a possibility of faster sorting, too, if we could find a "divide and conquer" algorithm for sorting. Mergesort is one such algorithm. It works as follows:

Mergesort

1. If the array has only one element, do nothing.
2. (Optional) If the array has two elements, swap them if necessary.
3. Split the array into two approximately equal halves.
4. Sort the first half and the second half.
5. Merge both halves into one sorted array.

This recursive algorithm will allow us to practice our recursive reasoning. Step 4 tells us to sort half of the array. But how will we sort it? Shall we use Selection Sort or Insertion Sort for it? Potentially we could, but then we wouldn't get the full benefit of faster sorting. For best performance we should use Mergesort again!

This makes the method that implements Mergesort a recursive method — it has to call itself. This fact may seem odd at first, but there is nothing paradoxical about it. Java and other high-level languages use a *stack* mechanism for calling methods. When a method is called, a new frame is allocated on the stack to hold the return address, the arguments, and all the local variables of a method. With this mechanism there is really no difference whether a method calls itself or any other method.

All recursive methods must recognize two possibilities: a ***base case*** and a ***recursive case***. In the base case, the task is so simple that there is little or nothing to do, and no recursive calls are needed. In Mergesort, the base case occurs when the array has only one or two elements. The recursive case must reduce the task to similar but smaller tasks. In Mergesort, the task of sorting an array is reduced to sorting two smaller arrays. This ensures that after several recursive calls the task will fall into the base case and recursion will stop. If an erroneous recursive algorithm has no base case or if the recursive case does not reduce the size of the task, then the recursive calls may go on and on until they cause a "stack overflow" error.

Figure 12-6 shows a `Mergesort` class that can sort an array of `doubles`. This straightforward implementation uses a temporary array into which the two sorted halves are merged. The `sort` method calls a recursive helper method that sorts a particular segment of the array.

```java
public class Mergesort
{
  private static double temp[];

  /**
   * Sorts a[0], ..., a[size-1] in ascending order
   *    using Mergesort
   */
  public static void sort(double a[])
  {
    int n = a.length;
    temp = new double[n];
    recursiveSort(a, 0, n-1);
  }

  private static void recursiveSort(double a[], int from, int to)
  {
    if (to - from < 2)          // Base case: 1 or 2 elements
    {
      if (to > from && a[to] < a[from])
      {
        double aTemp = a[to];   // swap a[to] and a[from]
        a[to] = a[from];
        a[from] = aTemp;
      }
    }
    else                        // Recursive case
    {
      int middle = (from + to) / 2;
      recursiveSort(a, from, middle);
      recursiveSort(a, middle + 1, to);
      merge(a, from, middle, to);
    }
  }
```

Figure 12-6 `Mergesort.java` *Continued* ⟹

```java
/**
 *   Merges a[from] ... a[middle] and a[middle+1] ... a[to]
 *   into one sorted array a[from] ... a[to]
 */
private static void merge(double a[], int from, int middle, int to)
{
  int i = from, j = middle + 1, k = from;

  // While both arrays have elements left unprocessed:
  while (i <= middle && j <= to)
  {
    if (a[i] < a[j])
    {
      temp[k] = a[i];    // Or simply temp[k] = a[i++];
      i++;
    }
    else
    {
      temp[k] = a[j];
      j++;
    }
    k++;
  }

  // Copy the tail of the first half, if any, into temp:
  while (i <= middle)
  {
    temp[k] = a[i];      // Or simply temp[k++] = a[i++]
    i++;
    k++;
  }

  // Copy the tail of the second half, if any, into temp:
  while (j <= to)
  {
    temp[k] = a[j];      // Or simply temp[k++] = a[j++]
    j++;
    k++;
  }

  // Copy temp back into a
  for (k = from; k <= to; k++)
      a[k] = temp[k];
}
}
```

Figure 12-6. `Ch12\Benchmarks\Mergesort.java` ⊟

The `merge` method is not recursive. To understand how it works, imagine two piles of cards, each sorted in ascending order and placed face up on the table. We want to merge them into the third, sorted, pile. On each step we take the smaller of the two exposed cards and place it face down on top of the destination pile. When one of the original piles is gone, we take the remaining cards in the other one (the whole pile or one by one — it doesn't matter) and place them face down on top of the destination pile. We end up with the destination pile sorted in ascending order.

Mergesort is an $O(n \log n)$ algorithm — much better than the $O(n^2)$ performance of Selection Sort and Insertion Sort.

12.9 *Lab:* Benchmarks

A benchmark is an empirical test of performance. The applet in Figure 12-7 is designed to compare running times for several sorting methods. Enter the array size, select one of the three sorting methods in the "combo box" (pull-down list) and click the "Run" button. The program fills the array with random numbers and sorts them. This test is repeated many times for more accurate timing. (The number of repetitions is set in the HTML file that loads the applet in the

```
<param name="RUNS" value="20">
```

tag.) Then the applet displays the time it took to run all the tests.

Figure 12-7. The *Benchmarks* applet

The code for this applet is shown in Figure 12-8. The tests are performed by the `runSort` method, which returns the elapsed time. Your task is to write this method.

First you need to learn how to generate a sequence of random numbers. We have already used the `Math.random` method, but this time we won't use it because we want to have more control over how the random number generator is "seeded." A "seed" is a value that is used to initialize the random number generator. If you seed the random number generator with the same seed, you will get the same sequence of random numbers. If you want different sequences on different runs of your program, you need different seeds. A common technique is to use the current system time as a seed. In our applet we call the `currentTimeMillis` method of the `System` class to obtain a value for the seed. (Recall that `System` is imported into all programs and has only static fields and methods.) Once we obtain a seed value we initialize the random number generator with this seed in each call to `runSort` because, to be fair, we want to run all the sorting methods on exactly the same data.

Java's `util` package provides a class `Random` that has a constructor with one argument, seed. For example:

```
Random generator = new Random(seed);
```

You should create a `Random` object at the beginning of `runSort` using this constructor. After that you can generate the next random `double` by calling this object's `nextDouble` method. For example:

```
    a[k] = generator.nextDouble();
```

The `runSort` method fills the array with random numbers and then sorts it. This is repeated RUNS times and `runSort` returns the total time it took in milliseconds. Call the system time before and after the tests and return the difference.

Collect `Benchmarks.java`, `SelectionSort.java`, `InsertionSort.java`, `Mergesort.java`, and `TestBenchmarks.html` in your work folder and fill in the blanks in the `Benchmarks` class. Once your applet is working, run the benchmarks for each sorting algorithm for arrays of various sizes ranging, say, from 1,000 to 50,000 elements. Plot the running time vs. the array size for each of the three sorting methods. You can do this manually or by entering the results into a spreadsheet, another data analysis program, or a graphing calculator. Try to see how well your experimental results fit with parabolas for Selection Sort and Insertion Sort and with an *n* log *n* curve for Mergesort.

```java
/**
 *  This program compares benchmarks for Selection Sort,
 *  Insertion Sort, and Mergesort
 */
import java.awt.*;
import java.awt.event.*;
import javax.swing.*;
import java.util.Random;

public class Benchmarks extends JApplet
       implements ActionListener
{
  private JTextField arraySizeInput, timeDisplay;
  private String sortMethodNames[] =
    {"Selection Sort", "Insertion Sort", "Mergesort"};
  private JComboBox chooseSortMethod;
  private static int RUNS = 10;
  private long seed;

  public void init()
  {
    // Try to get the number of runs from the <param> tag:
    String runsStr = getParameter("RUNS");
    if (runsStr != null)        // if successful
      RUNS = Integer.parseInt(runsStr);
    System.out.println("Testing with number of runs = " + RUNS);

    <... etc.  See Ch12\Benchmarks\Benchmarks.java 💾 >

    // Use the same random number generator seed for all benchmarks
    //   in one run of this applet:
    seed = System.currentTimeMillis();
  }

  public void actionPerformed(ActionEvent e)
  {
    String inputStr = arraySizeInput.getText();
    int n = Integer.parseInt(inputStr);
    if (n <= 0)
      return;
    showStatus("Testing...");
```

Figure 12-8 `Benchmarks.java` *Continued* ➷

```
    int sortMethod = chooseSortMethod.getSelectedIndex() + 1;
    double a[] = new double[n];
    long time = runSort(a, sortMethod);
    showStatus("  " + time);

    <... etc.  See Ch12\Benchmarks\Benchmarks.java 💾 >
  }
  /**
   *  Fills array a with random numbers and sorts
   *  it using the sorting method specified in sortMethod:
   *       1 -- Selection Sort
   *       2 -- Insertion Sort
   *       3 -- Mergesort
   *  This is repeated RUNS times for better accuracy
   *  Returns the time it took in milliseconds
   */
  private long runSort(double a[], int sortMethod)
  {
    < ... missing code >
  }
}
```

Figure 12-8. `Ch12\Benchmarks\Benchmarks.java` 💾

12.10   The Arrays Class

No matter what you do in Java, it has been done before. Sure enough, Java's API (Applications Programming Interface) has an `Arrays` class, with methods that implement Binary Search and sorting (using a version of the Quicksort algorithm). `Arrays` is part of Java's `util` package; your class needs to import `java.util.Arrays` in order to use it. All of `Arrays`'s methods are static. For example, its `binarySearch` method is called as follows:

```
    int pos = Arrays.binarySearch(a, target);
```

`Arrays` has overloaded versions of `binarySearch` for arrays of `chars`, `ints`, and other primitive data types. There is also a version for any objects that have "natural order," i.e., for which a `compareTo` method is defined. In particular, it can be used with strings.

`Arrays.sort` methods can sort an array of `chars`, `ints`, `doubles`, `strings`, and so on, either the whole array or a segment within specified limits. For example:

```
String dictionary[] = new String[maxWords];
int wordsCount;
< ... other statements >

Arrays.sort(dictionary, 0, wordsCount - 1);
```

Add Arrays's sorting method to the *Benchmarks* applet to see how it compares to our own sorting classes.

The Arrays class also offers fill methods that fill an array or a portion of an array with a specified value.

12.11   Summary

Sequential Search is used to find a target value in an array. If the array is sorted in ascending or descending order, Binary Search is a much more efficient searching method. It is called a "divide and conquer" method because on each step the size of the searching range is cut in half.

The three sorting algorithms discussed in this chapter work as follows:

Selection Sort
  Set n to the size of the array. While n is greater than 2: find the largest element among the first n, swap it with the n-th element of the array, and decrement n.

Insertion Sort
  Keep the first n elements sorted. Starting at $n=2$, for each element a[n] find its place in order among the first $n-1$ elements, shift the required number of elements to the right to make room, and insert a[n].

Mergesort
  If the array size is less than or equal to 2, just swap the elements when necessary. Otherwise, split the array into two halves. Recursively sort the first half and the second half, then merge the two sorted halves.

Selection Sort is the slowest and most predictable of the three: each element is always compared to every other element. Insertion Sort works quickly on arrays that are almost sorted. Mergesort is a "divide and conquer" algorithm. It is by far the quickest of the three on random arrays.

Java's Arrays class from the java.util package has binarySearch and sort methods for primitive types, strings, and other "comparable" objects.

Exercises

Sections 12.1-12.5

1.   Describe the difference between searching and pattern recognition.

2.   Describe a situation where the performance of Sequential Search on average is better than $O(n)$. ⋜ Hint: different target values do not have to come with the same probability. ⋝ ✓

3.   What is the number of comparisons in Binary Search required in the worst case to find a target value in a sorted array of 80 elements? Consider two scenarios:

   (a)   we know for sure that the target is always in the array; ✓
   (b)   the target may be not in the array. ✓

4.   Find and fix the bug in the following code:

```
char hello[] = {' ', 'h', 'e', 'l', 'l' 'o'};
int i = 0;

// Shift to the left and append '!':
while (i < 6)
{
  hello[i-1] = hello[i];
  i++;
}
hello[5] = '!';
```

5.   Write a method that returns the value of the largest positive element in a 2-D array, or 0 if all its elements are negative: ✓

```
/**
 *  Returns the value of the largest positive element in
 *  the matrix m, or 0, if all its elements are negative.
 */
private static double positiveMax(double m[][])
```

6.▪   A string contains several X's followed by several O's. Devise a divide-and-conquer method that finds the number of X's in the string in log(n) steps, where n is the length of the string.

7. A divide-and-conquer algorithm can be used to find a zero (root) of a function. Suppose a function $f(x)$ is a continuous function on the interval $[a, b]$. Suppose $f(a) < 0$ and $f(b) > 0$:

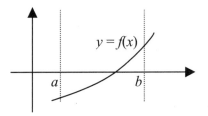

The graph of the function must cross the x-axis at some point. We can split the segment into two halves and continue our search for a zero in the left or the right half, depending on the value of $f(x)$ in the middle point $x = (a + b) / 2$.

Write a program that finds x (to the nearest .001), such that $x = \cos(x)$.
⸠ Hint: consider the function $f(x) = x - \cos(x)$ on the interval $[0, \pi/2]$. ⸠ ✓

8. Write a method that rotates an array by a given number of positions d:

```
public static void rotate(int a[], int d)
```

A positive d rotates the array forward; a negative d, backward. For example, if a holds elements 1, 4, 9, 16, 25, 36, after `rotate(a, -2)` the values in a are 9, 16, 25, 36, 1, 4. ✓

9. An array originally contained different numbers in ascending order but may have been subsequently rotated by a few positions. For example, the resulting array may be:

```
21 34 55 1 2 3 5 8 13
```

Is it possible to adapt the Binary Search algorithm for such data?

10. ■ Fill in the blanks in the following method that returns the average of the two largest elements of an array: ✓

```
/**
 *   Finds the two largest elements in scores
 *   and returns their average.
 *   Precondition: the size of the array is >= 2.
 */
public static double averageTopTwo(int scores[])
{
    int i, size = scores.length;
    int iMax1 = 0;          // index of the largest element
    int iMax2 = 1;          // index of the second largest element

    // if scores[iMax2] is bigger than scores[iMax1] --
    //    swap iMax1 and iMax2
    if (scores[iMax2] > scores[iMax1])
    {
        i = iMax1;

        _____

        ...
    }

    for (i = 2; i < size; i++)
    {
        if (scores[i] > scores[iMax1])
        {

            _____

        }
        else if ( _____ )
        {

            _____

            ...
        }
    }
    return _____;
}
```

11. In *SCRABBLE,*® different letters are assigned different numbers of points:

A – 1	E – 1	I – 1	M – 3	Q – 10	U – 1	X – 8
B – 3	F – 4	J – 8	N – 1	R – 1	V – 4	Y – 4
C – 3	G – 2	K – 5	O – 3	S – 1	W – 4	Z – 10
D – 2	H – 4	L – 1	P – 3	T – 1		

Write a method computeScore(String word) that returns the score for a word without using either if or switch statements. ⸮ Hint: in Unicode, codes for the letters of the English alphabet have consecutive values. The Character class has a static method getNumericValue(ch) that returns the Unicode numeric value of the character as a positive integer. ⸮

12.■   Neural networks are non-linear statistical models that learn from experience; they are used in pattern recognition systems. Neural network algorithms need to calculate the "sigmoid" function over and over again:

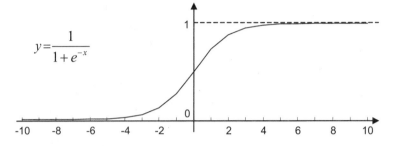

Write a class `Sigmoid` that tabulates the sigmoid function and provides a method to return its value from the table.

(a)   Provide a constructor

```
public Sigmoid(double step)
```

that tabulates the values of sigmoid for $-10 \leq x \leq 10$ with the given step and places the values into a private field `double myValues[]`. For example, if `step` is 0.01, `myValues` will hold 2001 elements. ⸢ Hint: your constructor may call `Math.exp(x)`. ⸥

b)   Write a method

```
public double getValue(double x)
```

that fetches and returns the sigmoid value for $-10 \leq x \leq 10$ from the table. The method should return 0 if $x < -10$, and 1 if $x > 10$.

(c)   Write an applet or an application to test your class.

Sections 12.6-12.11

13.   Mark true or false and explain:

   (a)   If the original array was already sorted, 190 comparisons would be
          performed in a Selection Sort of an array containing 20 elements.
          _____ ✓

   (b)   Mergesort works faster than Insertion Sort on any array. _____ ✓

14.   An array of six integers — 6, 9, 74, 10, 22, 81 — is being sorted in ascending
          order. Show the state of the array after two iterations through the outer `for`
          loop in Selection Sort (as implemented in Figure 12-4).

15.   What are the values stored in the array `a` after five iterations in the `for` loop
          of the Insertion Sort (as implemented in Figure 12-5) if the initial values are:
          3, 7, 5, 8, 2, 0, 1, 9, 4, 3? ✓

16.■   The following method rearranges the elements in an array in such a way that
          it ends up partially ordered: all the negative numbers appear to the left of all
          the non-negative numbers. Fill in the blanks and test your method.

```
private static void swapPosNeg(double v[])
{
  int size = v.length, i = 0, j = size - 1;
  double temp;

  while (i < j)
  {
    if (v[i] < 0)                   // Skip it

      _____

    else if ( _____ ) // Skip it


      _____

    else
    {       // if both out of place -- swap them

      _____
      . . .
    }
  }
}
```

17.♦   A sorting algorithm, called **Quicksort**, involves partitioning the array. Partitioning means rearranging the array's elements in such a way that all elements to the left of one marked position are less than or equal to the element in the marked position (called the **pivot** element) and all the elements to the right of the pivot are greater than or equal to the pivot. Once the array is partitioned, Quicksort can be applied recursively to the segment to the left of the pivot and to the segment to the right of the pivot, which results in a sorted array. The pivot element can be chosen randomly among the elements of the array.

(a)   Write a method that implements partitioning of an array. ⋜ Hint: proceed from both sides of the array as long as the element on the left is not greater than the pivot value or the element on the right is not less than the pivot value. When you reach a deadlock, swap the elements and continue. This is very similar to the algorithm in Question 16. Once the left and the right side meet at a certain position, swap the pivot element correctly to place it into that position. ⋝

(b)   Complete a recursive Quicksort method.

Self-Test: Word Search

Figure W-1 shows a *Word Search* in which a player looks for words in a grid of letters. Words may be found vertically, horizontally, or diagonally in any direction and may overlap. Your task is to write the WordSearch class that represents a grid of letters and has methods for searching for words in it.

Figure W-1. A *Word Search* puzzle

1. Provide a constructor that takes three arguments: the number of rows in the grid, the number of columns in the grid, and a string of letters. The letters from the string are used to fill the grid, starting in the first row, left to right, then the next row, and so on. The length of the string should be the number of rows times the number of columns. Convert all letters to upper case before placing them into the grid.

2. Write a method

   ```
   private boolean isInside(row, col)
   ```

   that returns true if the row, col position is inside the grid array and false otherwise.

3. Write a method

```
private boolean match(String word, int row, int col,
                              int rowStep, int colStep)
```

that returns `true` if a `word` placed at a particular position and in a particular direction matches the letters in the grid and `false` otherwise. The `row`, `col` arguments indicate the position of the first letter in the word. `rowStep` and `colStep` define the direction of the word: they indicate how `row` and `col` change when we go from one letter to the next. For example, if `rowStep` is 0 and `colStep` is −1, it means that we are going in the direction from east (right) to west (left), and if `rowStep` is 1 and `colStep` is 1 it means that we are going in the direction from north-west (upper-left) to south-east (lower-right). Therefore, with the grid in the picture above, both `match("TWO",0,4,0,-1)` and `match("ONE",2,2,1,1)` would return `true`.

4. Write a method `find(String word)` that looks for a given word in the grid. This method returns a string. For each occurrence of `word` in the grid `find` should append the description of the match to the result in some reasonable format. The description should include the word itself, the position and the direction of the match, and the newline character. If there are no matches, `find` returns `word + " not found"`. So if you execute the statements

```
System.out.println(ws.find("ONE"));
System.out.println(ws.find("TWO"));
System.out.println(ws.find("THREE"));
System.out.println(ws.find("FOUR"));
```

(where `ws` is the `WordSearch` object holding letters shown in Figure W-1) you would see something like:

```
ONE E to W starting at row = 1 column = 3
ONE W to E starting at row = 3 column = 3
ONE NW to SE starting at row = 3 column = 3
ONE SW to NE starting at row = 5 column = 3

TWO E to W starting at row = 1 column = 5
TWO SW to NE starting at row = 5 column = 1

THREE S to N starting at row = 5 column = 1
THREE E to W starting at row = 6 column = 5

FOUR not found
```

Add to your class a main method that creates one WordSearch object and tries to find a few words in it. For one of the tests use the same grid as in Figure W-1 and the same search words and see if you get the same results.

You can find a solution in WordSearchSolution.java 🖫 in the WordSearch folder on your student disk.

```
System.out.println
    ("Chapter 13");
```

Streams and Files

13.1 Prologue

Any program that processes a considerable amount of data has to read the data from a file (or several files). Any program that produces a lot of data is likely to write that data into a file. A file is a software entity supported by the operating system. The operating system provides commands for renaming, copying, moving, and deleting files, as well as low-level functions, callable from programs, for opening, reading, and writing files. A file has to be opened before it can be read. To open a file the program needs to know its pathname in the system (the path to the folder that holds the file and the file's name). A new file has to be created before we can write into it. To create a new file, a program needs to know its path and what name to give it.

> **Data files are not a part of the program source code, and they are not compiled. The same executable program can work on different sets of data as long as it can handle the particular format of the data in the files and knows the file names (or receives them from the user at run time).**

A computer user distinguishes two kinds of files: binary files and ASCII (text) files. (Actually, the term ASCII has become obsolete because the Internet requires different coding schemes for different alphabets and uses Unicode encoding of characters.) A binary file can contain any kind of information: images, sound clips, binary numbers, or any other information. The format of data in a file is determined by the program that created that file. There are many standardized file formats that allow different programs to understand the same files. A standard format is usually designated by the file name's extension. For example, standard formats for representing compressed images may have the .gif or .jpg extensions, music files may have the .mp3 extension, and so on. A text file often has the .txt extension.

> **Each line in a text file is marked by a terminating end-of-line character or combination of such characters (e.g., CR+LF, "carriage return" + "line feed").**

If necessary, a program can treat a text file as a binary file, reading the line terminators as data bytes like any others. But most programming languages provide special functions for reading a line of text from a text file or writing a line to a file or to the screen.

An application may treat a file as a ***stream*** or as a ***random-access file***. The term "stream" has its origins in operating systems, such as *UNIX* and *MS DOS*. It refers to the abstract model of an input or output device in which an input device produces a stream of characters and an output device receives a stream of characters. Some input/output devices, such as a keyboard and a printer, are rather close to this abstract model. Ignoring the technical details we can say that a keyboard produces an input stream of characters and a printer receives and prints an output stream.

Other devices, such as graphics adapters, hard drives, CD-ROM drives or floppy disk drives, are actually random-access devices, not stream devices: software can transfer a whole block of bytes to or from any sector on a disk or set the values of pixels anywhere on a screen. Still, the operating system software lets us implement input/output from/to a disk text file as a <u>logical</u> stream. For example, when we read from a disk file, the input is ***buffered*** so that characters are read into the program not directly from the disk but from an intermediate buffer in memory. Likewise, a console window on the screen can be thought of as a <u>logical</u> output stream of characters positioned line by line from left to right.

A stream can be opened for input (reading) or for output (writing), but not for both at the same time. Bytes are read sequentially from an input stream, although Java input streams have a method to skip several bytes. Bytes are written to an output stream sequentially, without gaps. If an output stream represents an existing file, a program can open it in the "create" mode and start writing from the beginning, destroying the old contents, or it can open it in the "append" mode and start adding data at the end of the file.

In a random-access file, the program can start reading or writing at any place. In fact, a random-access file can be opened for both input and output at the same time.

It is more common to treat text files as streams. A binary file with fixed-length records can be opened as a random-access file.

This is so because text lines may have different lengths, and it is hard to keep track where each line begins. So random access may not be very useful for a text file. In a binary file, if all the records have the same length, we can easily calculate the position of the *n*-th record. Then we can go directly to that place and read or write that record.

Programming languages usually include library functions or classes for opening, reading, creating, and writing files. These functions call low-level operating system functions. Programming languages and operating systems also support "standard input" and "standard output" streams for reading keyboard input and writing text to the screen. These streams are implemented in a manner similar to file streams, but they are automatically open when a program is running.

In this chapter we present a case study that demonstrates a small subset of Java's I/O package and provides cookbook recipes for reading a string of text from the console and for reading and writing lines of text from/to a text file. Appendix E* describes our own `EasyReader` and `EasyWriter` classes, which implement reading numbers, characters, and strings from the keyboard and reading and writing these types of data from/to a file without the need to deal with exceptions.

13.2   Java's I/O Package

Java's classes for handling input and output streams and files are rather hard to use. Java's I/O package offers two separate implementations of streams: one based on `InputStream` and `OutputStream` classes, the other based on `Reader` and `Writer` classes. Each of these four branches has a few classes of its own, with similar methods. Most of these classes are implemented as **wrapper** classes where a constructor of one class uses an object of another class as an argument. There is also a separate class for handling random-access files.

Amid all this complexity, there is no really convenient method that reads a number from the console or a file. The object that represents the standard input stream, `System.in`, has to be "wrapped" a couple of times (with `InputStreamReader` and `BufferedReader` objects) before you can get a method to read a line of text from it.

Java I/O reports errors by "throwing exceptions." An exception is a type of event that can be either "caught" inside a method using the `try-catch-finally` syntax or left unprocessed and passed up to the calling method (or to the Java run-time environment). In the latter case, you have to declare up front that your method can `throw` a particular type of exception. An exception that is not caught by any method in your program is reported in a run-time error message and, depending on the type of exception, may abort the program.

Exception handling in itself is not too complicated, but we don't really want to go into it in this book. If a hardware or system error occurs while your program is trying to read valid data from a file, an exception is justified. But if an error occurs when your program is trying to open a file because the user mistyped its name, it would make more sense to handle such an error without throwing exceptions. For example, the I/O package could set the status of the stream to "bad" and provide a method for checking the status after the program tries to open the file, as our `EasyReader` class does.

Similarly, if your program is trying to read all the data from a file, it often tries reading beyond the end of file. This is not really an error, just an honest attempt (because the program does not know in advance when the file ends). The read method should just tell you in some way that it encountered the end of file. When the method throws an `EOFException`, it makes programming more difficult. Java's I/O package itself makes a little concession to the friendlier approach: the `readLine` method in the `BufferedReader` class does not throw `EOFException` but returns a `null` string when the end of file is reached.

Applets may be forbidden to access files for security reasons. An applet can come to your computer from an unknown source on the World Wide Web, and you do not want to give it access to your files. A web browser can usually set different levels of security for applets, and reading or writing files on your computer would be disabled. Console output and especially input are not as common because Java applications are intended to be GUI applications.

You can find a detailed description of Java's I/O classes in Java's API documentation or in technical reference books. In this book we present only a simplified example: a case study that uses Java's `BufferedReader` and `PrintWriter` classes. Our `EasyReader` and `EasyWriter` classes can serve as another example for using Java's I/O if you examine their source code.

13.3 *Case Study:* a Dictionary for *Ramblecs*

In this section we will discuss a stand-alone console application that creates a dictionary for *Ramblecs*. We start with a text file that contains about 20,000 English words. Each word is written on a separate line. For *Ramblecs*, we want to find all the three-, four-, and five-letter words, convert them into the upper case, and write them to an output file.

Here we only prepare a *Ramblecs* dictionary file. We are not yet ready to integrate it into the game. Eventually we will want to create a `RamblecsDictionary` class that will have the dictionary words coded in an array of strings and allow us to match a word against the dictionary words. That class will be compiled and integrated into the *Ramblecs* project. We do not want the *Ramblecs* applet to load dictionary words from a separate text file because of security concerns about reading files in applets. For now, let's make our output file here use the syntax of a Java class, as shown in Figure 13-1. In Chapter 17, we will add to this class a method for matching a word against the dictionary and add this class to the *Ramblecs* project.

```
public class RamblecsDictionary
{
  private String words[] =
  {
    "ABACK",
    "ABASE",
    "ABASH",
    "ABATE",
    . . .
    . . .
    "ZIPPY",
    "ZLOTY",
    "ZONE",
    "ZOO",
    "ZOOM",
  };
}
```

Figure 13-1. The output file format for the `MakeDictionary` application

At first glance, our plan seems to contradict our earlier statement that data files are different from program source files. In fact there is no contradiction. In this case study, both the input file and the output file are data files. It just so happens that the output file uses Java syntax. The same thing happens when you create Java source with a program editor: for the editor the resulting file is just some output text. Later, in Chapter 17, the text file generated here becomes a source file for a Java class used in another project.

Our Java console application for generating a dictionary is shown in Figure 13-2. It is coded as one class, `MakeDictionary`. The input text file is called `words.txt`. It contains about 20,000 words. The output file created by the program is called `RamblecsDictionary.java`. It contains about 4,800 words. Our application uses the `BufferedReader` class to open and read the input file and the `PrintWriter` class to create and write the output file. We need to import Java's I/O package `java.io.*` into our program to use these classes and other library classes used in declarations of the `BufferedReader` and `PrintWriter` streams.

```java
import java.io.*;

public class MakeDictionary
{
  private static final int MINLENGTH = 3, MAXLENGTH = 5;
  private static BufferedReader fileIn;
  private static PrintWriter fileOut;

  public static void main(String[] args) throws IOException
  {
    BufferedReader console =
            new BufferedReader(new InputStreamReader(System.in));

    System.out.println();
    System.out.print("Enter input file name: ");
    String fileName = console.readLine();

    openInputFile(fileName);
    if (fileIn == null)
    {
      System.out.println("*** Can't open " + fileName + " ***");
      return;
    }

    createOutputFile("RamblecsDictionary.java");
    if (fileOut == null)
    {
      fileIn.close();
      System.out.println("*** Can't create RamblecsDictionary.java ***");
      return;
    }

    int count = copyWords();
    System.out.println("Done: " + count + " words.");

    fileIn.close();
    fileOut.close();
  }

  /**
   *  Opens a file fileName (in the current folder)
   *  and places a reference to it into fileIn
   */
  private static void openInputFile(String fileName)
  {
    try
    {
      fileIn = new BufferedReader(new FileReader(fileName));
    }
    catch (FileNotFoundException e)
    {
    }
  }
```

Figure 13-2 `MakeDictionary.java` **Continued** ⇗

```java
/**
 *  Creates a new file fileName (in the current folder)
 *  and places a reference to it into fileOut
 */
private static void createOutputFile(String fileName)
{
  try
  {
    fileOut = new PrintWriter(new BufferedWriter(
                            new FileWriter(fileName)));
  }
  catch (IOException e)
  {
  }
}

/**
 *  Reads all words from fileIn, selects the words that have
 *  from MINLENGTH to MAXLENGTH letters, converts them
 *  into upper case and writes the words into fileOut in
 *  Java syntax
 */
private static int copyWords() throws IOException
{
  String word;
  int count = 0;

  fileOut.println("public class RamblecsDictionary");
  fileOut.println("{");
  fileOut.println("  private String words[] =");
  fileOut.println("  {");
  while ((word = fileIn.readLine()) != null)
  {
    word = word.trim();        // In case there are extra spaces
                               //   in words.txt
    int len = word.length();
    if (len >= MINLENGTH && len <= MAXLENGTH)
    {
      word = word.toUpperCase();
      fileOut.println("    \"" + word + "\",");
      count++;
    }
  }
  fileOut.println("  };");
  fileOut.println("}");

  return count;
}
```

Figure 13-2. `Ch13\Dictionary\MakeDictionary.java` 💾

MakeDictionary's main method first prompts the user to enter the input file name, then calls the methods that open the input file and create the output file. If both are successful, it calls the method that reads all the words from the input file and writes some of them to the output file. It then closes both files.

Compile and run the MakeDictionary application (you can find it along with the words.txt file on your student disk in the Ch13\Dictionary folder). Examine the RamblecsDictionary.java file generated from words.txt.

This program gives the following examples:

1. How to read a line from the console.

2. How to open an input file and create an output file.

3. How to read and write one line from/to a file.

Let's look at them one by one.

13.3.1   Reading Text from the Console

Java's System class provides two public objects, System.out for writing to the screen and System.in for reading from the keyboard. These objects are called *standard output* and *standard input*.

System.out is an object of the PrintStream class. It has several overloaded print and println methods for displaying primitive data types and strings. println appends the newline character at the end of the output. There is also a println method that takes no arguments — it just prints the newline character. We have already used System.out in many programs. Here our program uses it to display a prompt at the beginning of the program and to display a report line at the end:

```
System.out.print("Enter the input file name: ");
...
System.out.println("Done: " + count + " words.");
```

In the last statement we use string concatenation to incorporate the word count into the message. We could also do this through separate calls to print and println. For example:

```
System.out.print("Done: ");
System.out.print(count);   // calls print with an integer argument
System.out.println(" words.");
```

❖   ❖   ❖

Using `System.in` is a little trickier. `System.in` is an object of the `InputStream` type, a class that only offers methods for reading a few "raw" bytes. We need to "wrap" `System.in` first with an `InputStreamReader` object and then with a `BufferedReader` object to use a `readLine` method. The statement

```
BufferedReader console =
        new BufferedReader(new InputStreamReader(System.in));
```

does just that. It first constructs an anonymous `InputStreamReader` object, passing `System.in` to it as an argument. Then it passes the newly constructed `InputStreamReader` object to `BufferedReader`'s constructor as an argument and constructs `console`, a `BufferedReader` object. (`console` is a name we chose.) If we want to, we can split the above statement into two separate statements. For example:

```
InputStreamReader tempISR = new InputStreamReader(System.in);
BufferedReader console = new BufferedReader(tempISR);
```

All of this is necessary just to use the `console`'s `readLine` method, which returns an entered string. (Neither `BufferedReader` nor any of Java's other I/O classes have methods for reading separate words or numbers.) Our program calls this method to obtain the input file name from the user:

```
String name = console.readLine();
```

13.3.2   Opening Text Files for Reading and Writing

`MakeDictionary`'s `openInputFile` method opens the input file. We pass the file name, a `String` object, to this method as an argument. The file is actually opened by the constructor to an object of the `FileReader` type. Again, we want to "wrap" a `BufferedReader` object around it in order to use `BufferedReader`'s `readLine` method and in general to make the reading more efficient. For this we pass the newly constructed anonymous `FileReader` object to the `BufferedReader` constructor as an argument. All of it happens in one statement:

```
fileIn = new BufferedReader(new FileReader(fileName));
```

Unfortunately, these constructors throw `FileNotFoundException` if the file with the specified name does not exist. If this exception is not caught, the program will be aborted.

We do not necessarily want to "hardcode" the file name in the program because eventually our program might need to work on other input files (e.g., a file of Spanish words). But we do want to give the user a second chance if he mistypes the file name. For this we need to catch the exception. The syntax for exception handling is to place the statement that may cause an exception inside a `try` statement, and to supply a `catch` statement that immediately follows `try`. The syntax for `try-catch` is somewhat similar to `if-else`.

We have chosen to deal with this exception by simply letting `main` worry about it. `main` checks whether `inFile` has been successfully opened or not. If not, the `inFile` reference remains `null`. Accordingly, the `catch` statement in our `openInputFile` method does nothing. Alternatively, we could make `openInputFile` a `boolean` method that returns `true` if the file is opened successfully and `false` otherwise. Then we would put `return false` inside the `catch` statement:

```
private static boolean openInputFile(String name)
{
  try
  {
    fileIn = new BufferedReader(new FileReader(fileName));
  }
  catch (FileNotFoundException e)
  {
    return false;
  }
  return true;
}
```

Then `main` should check the returned value.

❖   ❖   ❖

You have to be careful when creating files. If a file with the given name already exists, your new file will wipe it out and all the data in it will be lost.

Therefore we do not want to let the user choose a name for the output file — instead of prompting the user, we'll just hard code the name into the program.

The output file is created in our `createOutputFile` method. We prefer to work with a `PrintWriter` object because it has useful `print` and `println` methods. So we use three "wrappers":

```
fileOut = new PrintWriter(new BufferedWriter(new
                                 FileWriter(fileName)));
```

If the file cannot be created, this statement causes an `IOException`. This may happen if the output device is write-protected or not ready, or if a read-only file with the same name already exists. As with `openInputFile`, we leave it to `main` to handle this error, leaving the `catch` statement empty. It would also be acceptable not to catch this exception at all. Then we would not use `try-catch`, but would add `throws IOException` to the `createOutputFile` header. Java syntax requires that we announce explicitly any exceptions that a method might throw and not catch.

Note that if we fail to create the output file, we should close the input file that we opened earlier. It is a good idea to release all resources back to the system as soon as we no longer need them.

Other I/O operations, such as reading from standard input and reading and writing to files, can cause exceptions. We have chosen to leave them to the system and added the `throws IOException` clause to all methods that potentially can cause exceptions and to all methods that call such methods. For instance, `main` has `throws IOException` because it has several potentially offending statements:

```
String fileName = console.readLine();
...
int count = copyWords();  // copyWords throws IOException
...
fileIn.close();
...
```

The compiler checks at compile time that all possible exceptions of this type (called ***checked exceptions***) are either inside a `try-catch` block or inside a method that has a `throws` declaration.

13.3.3   Reading and Writing Lines of Text

You can read a line of text from a `BufferedReader` by calling its `readLine` method. This method returns a reference to a string if successful or `null` if there is no more data left in the file. The statement

```
while ((str = fileIn.readLine()) != null)
{
  ... // process str
}
```

reads a line, assigns it to `str`, and processes it if the return is not `null`. An alternative would be:

```
do
{
  str = fileIn.readLine();
  if (str != null)
  {
    ... // process str
  }
} while (str != null)
```

or

```
while (true)  // i.e. repeat until break
{
  str = fileIn.readLine();
  if (str == null)
    break;
  ... // process str
}
```

There are no methods in `BufferedReader` to read numbers or separate words from a file. You can use a `StringTokenizer` object to split the string returned by `readLine` into tokens; then you can convert the individual tokens into numbers or words (see Section 9.5 and 9.7). Or you can parse the string yourself.

❖   ❖   ❖

We use `PrintWriter`'s `println` method to write lines of text to a file. For example:

```
fileOut.println("    \"" + word + "\",");
```

This statement writes a word in double quotes with a comma after it. `PrintWriter` also has `print` and `println` methods for primitive data types and a `println()` method for writing the newline character. `println()` can be used to print a blank line.

13.4 Summary

Java's I/O classes are complicated to use. Initially it may be better to avoid them altogether and use one of the many simplified I/O packages developed by schools or organizations and available free on the Internet. Our `EasyReader` and `EasyWriter` classes (see Appendix E)※ are one such package. Their source code includes simple examples of their use and their complete documentation in HTML format can be generated with *javadoc*.

`EasyReader` includes `readChar`, `readInt`, `readDouble`, `readWord`, and `readLine` methods for reading input from the console and from files. `EasyWriter` can create a new output file or open an existing file for appending text to it. It has several overloaded `print` and `println` methods for writing characters, numbers, and strings to a file. The `EasyReader` and `EasyWriter` classes let you read and write data from/to streams in a manner somewhat similar to C++, without having to deal with exceptions. `EasyReader` and `EasyWriter` of course rely on Java's stream I/O package and therefore their source code provides another example of how Java's I/O classes can be used.

Exercises

1.   Which of the following is true? ✓

   A.   Any file can be opened for reading either as a stream or as a random-access file.
   B.   All files in *UNIX* are streams, while in *Windows* some may be random-access files.
   C.   Both in *Windows* and *UNIX*, all text files are streams and all binary (non-text) files are random-access files.
   D.   When a file is first created, an attribute is set that designates this file as a stream or as a random-access file for all future applications.

2.   Explain why random-access files usually contain fixed-length records.

3.   Many methods in Java stream I/O classes throw an exception whenever an I/O error occurs. It would be perhaps more convenient for a programmer to handle certain errors by making the program check the return value or the stream status after the operation rather than letting it throw an exception. Which errors among the following would be good candidates for such no-exception treatment?

(a)   Failure to open a file because it does not exist _____ ✓
(b)   Failure to open a file that is already opened by another application _____ ✓
(c)   Failure to create a file because a read-only file with the same name already exists _____ ✓
(d)   Device is not ready for reading (e.g., a CD-ROM drive is empty) _____

(e)   System error reading from a device (e.g., a damaged sector on disk) _____

(f)   System write error (e.g., disk full) _____
(g)   Device is not ready for writing (e.g., a floppy disk is write-protected) _____

(h)   End of file is encountered while trying to read data _____

4.   Using `EasyReader`, write a program that checks whether braces are balanced in a Java source file. ⑀ Hint: read the file one character at a time. When you encounter an opening brace, increment the count and when you encounter a closing brace, decrement the count. The count should never be negative and should be zero at the end. ⑂ ✓

5.   Rewrite the `MakeDictionary` class (`Ch13\Dictionary\MakeDictionary.java` 🖫) using `EasyReader` and `EasyWriter` classes.

6.   Write a program that compares two files for exactly matching data. ✓

7.■   *GREP* is an old utility program from *UNIX* that scans a file or several files
for a given word and prints out all lines in which that word occurs.
(According to *The New Hacker's Dictionary*, the name "GREP" comes from
the "qed/ed" editor commands g/re/p — globally search for a regular
expression and print the lines.)

Write a simplified version of *GREP* that looks for a word in one file. A
"word" is defined as a contiguous string of non-whitespace characters. For
every line that contains the word, print out the line number and the text of the
line in brackets. For example:

```
Line  5: [  private static PrintWriter fileOut;]
```

Take the target word and the file name from the command line.

The search for a matching word can be accomplished by using `String`'s
method `indexOf`. This method will find the target word even if it occurs as
part of another word in the line. If you want to find only matches between
complete words, write your own method. ⸨ Hint: search for all occurrences
of the word in the line and then check that the matching substring is
surrounded by whitespace characters wherever it doesn't touch the beginning
or the end of the line. ⸩

8.■   Write a class that represents a picture: a 2-D array of characters with values
of `'x'` or `'.'`. Supply a constructor that loads the picture from a file with a
specified name. The first line in the file contains two integers, the number of
rows and the number of columns in the picture. The following lines, one for
each row, contain strings of x's and dots. The length of each string is equal
to the number of columns in the picture. For example:

```
3 4
x.xx
xx.x
....
```

⸨ Hints: (1) Use `EasyReader`. (2) After reading the numbers from the first
line, don't forget to skip the remainder of the line (even if only the newline
character is left) before reading the rest of the lines. ⸩

Supply a method to print a picture object to `System.out` and test your
class. ✓

9.♦   Write and test a program that merges two sorted files into one sorted file. The files contain lines of text that are sorted lexicographically (the same ordering used by `String`'s `compareTo` method). Your program should read each file only once and should not use arrays.

10.♦   In the *Mad Libs*™ party game, the leader has the text of a short story with a few missing words in it. The missing words are tagged by their function: <noun>, <verb>, <place>, etc. For example:

```
It was a <adjective> summer day.
Jack was sitting in a <place>.
```

The leader examines the text and prompts the players for the missing words:

```
Please give me an/a:
adjective
place
...
```

She then reads the text with the supplied words inserted into their places.

Write a program that acts as a *Mad Libs* leader. It should prompt the user for a file name, read the text from the file, find the tags for the missing words (anything within <...>), prompt the user for these words and save them. It should then reopen the file and display the completed text, inserting the saved words in place of the corresponding tags. ≾ Hint: you can read the text line by line and assume that tags are not split between lines, but it may be easier to read the text character by character. ≿

11.♦   A word is said to be an ***anagram*** of another word if it is made of the same letters arranged in a different order. Write a program that finds all anagrams of a given word in a file of words, sorted alphabetically. Follow these steps:

(a)   Write a method or constructor to load words from the file into an array of strings. (The maximum possible number of words in the file is 25,000.)

(b)   Implement Binary Search in the array of words (see Section 12.2).

(c)   Generate all arrangements of letters in a given word, match each of them against the dictionary of words, and print out all the anagrams you find.

Continued ⇒

⸺ Hint: in mathematics, the operation of rearranging the order of objects or symbols, as well as any resulting arrangement, is called **permutation**. A String object is not very suitable for generating all permutations because it is immutable; it is easier to use a StringBuffer or an array of chars. The method for generating all permutations of an array can be implemented recursively. The trick is to formulate a slightly more general task, to generate all permutations of the first k elements in the array, then call it for the whole array:

```
processAllPermutations(letters, letters.length);
```

Consider the following implementation

```
private static void processAllPermutations
                              (char letters[], int k)
{
  if (k <= 1)
  {
    ...   // process this permutation (convert to string,
          //   search the dictionary, etc.
  }
  else
  {
    int i;
    char temp;

    for (i = 0; i < k; i++)
    {
      // Swap letters[i], letters[k-1]:
      temp = letters[i];
      letters[i] = letters[k-1];
      letters[k-1] = temp;

      processAllPermutations(letters, k-1);

      // Swap back:
      temp = letters[i];
      letters[i] = letters[k-1];
      letters[k-1] = temp;
    }
  }
}
```

⸺

(d)   See if you can find any anagrams for RAMBLECS.

Height | Ascent | Baseline | Descent

Graphics

14.1 Prologue

What you see on your computer screen is ultimately determined by the contents of the video memory (**VRAM**) on the graphics adapter card. The memory represents a rectangular array of **pixels** (picture elements). Each pixel has a particular color which can be represented as a mix of red, green, and blue components, each with its own intensity. A typical graphics adapter may use eight bits to represent each intensity (in the range from 0 to 255), so each color is represented in 24 bits or three bytes. This allows for $2^{24} = 16,777,216$ different colors. With a typical screen resolution of 1024 by 768 pixels, your adapter needs $1024 \cdot 768 \cdot 3$ bytes — a little over 2 MB — to hold the picture for one screen. The picture is produced by setting the colors of pixels in VRAM. The video hardware scans the whole video memory frequently (many times per second) and refreshes the image on the screen.

A graphics adapter is what we call a **raster** device: each individual pixel is changed separately from other pixels. (This is different from a **vector** device, e.g., a plotter, which can draw a line directly from point *A* to point *B*.) To draw a red line or a circle on a raster device, you need to set just the right group of pixels to the red color. That's where a graphics package can help: you certainly don't want to program all these routines for setting pixels yourself.

A typical graphics package has functions for setting drawing attributes, such as color, line style and width, fill texture or pattern for filled shapes, and font for text, and another set of functions for drawing simple shapes: lines, arcs, circles and ovals, rectangles, polygons, text, and so on. Java's graphics capabilities are based on the `Graphics` class and the `Graphics2D` package. The `Graphics` class is pretty rudimentary: it lets you set the color and font attributes and draw lines, arcs, ovals (including circles), rectangles, rectangles with rounded corners, polygons, polylines (open polygons), images, and text. There are "draw" and "fill" methods for each basic shape (e.g., `drawRect` and `fillRect`).

The `Graphics2D` package is a later addition to Java. It includes the `Graphics2D` class and a few other classes. The `Graphics2D` class is derived from `Graphics` and inherits all its methods. The package also defines the `Stroke` interface and one implementation of it, `BasicStroke`, which represents in a very general manner the line width and style for drawing lines. The `Paint` interface and its implementations `Color`, `GradientPaint`, and `TexturePaint` represent a color, a color gradient (gradually changing color), and a texture for filling in shapes, respectively.

`Graphics2D` also adds methods for various coordinate transformations, including rotations.

A more important feature of `Graphics2D` is its ***polymorphic*** capability. In the `Graphics` class implementation, contrary to the OOP spirit, shapes are not represented by objects and there is a separate special method for drawing each shape. Suppose you are working on a drawing editor program that allows you to add different shapes to the picture. You keep all the shapes already added to the picture in some kind of a list. To redraw the picture you need to draw all the shapes from the list using a loop. With `Graphics` you have to store each shape's identification (e.g., "circle," "rectangle," etc.) together with its dimensions and position and use a `switch` statement to call the appropriate drawing method for each shape. With `Graphics2D` you can define different objects of types derived from `Shape` and store references to them in your list. The `draw` method called for each shape will automatically draw each shape properly. If you derive your own class from `Shape` and supply a `draw` method for it, then your "shapes" will be drawn properly, too. This type of behavior is called ***polymorphism***. More precisely, polymorphism lets objects of different types, derived from the same base class *X*, automatically execute their own methods when accessed through a reference to *X*. (See Section 17.6 for a more detailed explanation of polymorphism.)

Like any package with very general capabilities, `Graphics2D` is not easy to use. We will stay mostly within the limits of the `Graphics` class, but the adventurous among you can examine the `Graphics2D` API and learn to use some of its fancy features.

In the following sections we will examine Java's event-driven graphics model and review the basic drawing attributes and methods. We will then use Java's graphics capabilities to implement a simple *Puzzle* applet in which a player rearranges the pieces of a scrambled picture.

14.2 `paint`, `paintComponent`, and `repaint`

In Java the hardest thing may be figuring out <u>when</u> and <u>where</u> to draw, rather than <u>how</u>. Java graphics must be event-driven because applets and applications run under multitasking operating systems. Suppose you are playing *Ramblecs* when all of a sudden you decide to check your e-mail. You bring up your e-mail and its window overlaps a part of the *Ramblecs* window. When you close or minimize your e-mail application, the operating system has to redisplay the *Ramblecs* window. The operating system sends *Ramblecs* a message that its window has been partially wiped out and now needs to be "repainted." *Ramblecs* must be ready to dispatch a single method in response to this "repaint" message.

In Java, this method is called `paint`. `paint` is a `void` method that receives one argument of the type `Graphics`, usually named g:

```
public void paint(Graphics g)
{
  ...
}
```

g defines the graphics context: the size and position of the picture, the current attributes (color, font), the clipping area for the picture, and so on.

A `JApplet` or `JFrame` object has a default `paint` method that just paints the background with the default color (or with the background color set earlier by the `setBackground` method). It then calls the `paintComponent` method for each of the components (buttons, labels, text edit fields, etc.) in its "contents pane" container. If you derive your main class from `JApplet` or `JFrame`, which is usually the case, and you want to do some drawing on your window, you can override the inherited `paint` method by defining your own. The first statement in your `paint` most likely will be a call to the base class's `paint`:

```
public void paint(Graphics g)
{
  super.paint(g);
  ...
}
```

After that you can add your own statements. That's exactly what we did in `Ch03\HelloGui\HelloGraphics.java` 🖫 (see Figure 3-11 on page 83):

```
public void paint(Graphics g)
{
  super.paint(g);     // Call JFrame's paint method
                      //  to paint the background
  g.setColor(Color.red);
  g.drawRect(75, 25, 150, 50);  // draw a rectangle 150 by 50
  g.setColor(Color.blue);
  g.drawString("Hello, World!", 120, 50);
}
```

Naturally `paint` does not have to define all the drawing in its own code. It can call other methods, passing g to them as one of the arguments.

`paint` is called automatically in response to certain messages received from the operating system. Sometimes your program needs to repaint the window itself after changing its appearance. It can't call `paint` directly because it does not have a valid `Graphics` argument, a g, to pass to it. Instead your applet or application calls the `repaint` method, which does not take any arguments. `repaint` recovers or recreates the graphics context stored internally and passes it to `paint`.

`paint` is the central drawing method for your application window, where all drawing originates. Therefore, it must handle all the different drawing requirements for all the different situations in which the application might find itself. This is not easy. Fortunately in Swing you can redefine painting of individual components. Each type of component (a `JButton` object, a `JTextField` object, etc.) has its own default `paintComponent` method. `paintComponent` also takes one argument, `Graphics g`. You can derive a class from any of these classes and redefine `paintComponent` for it. It is not very common, though, to draw on top of buttons or text edit fields. But one type of objects, `JPanel`, is particularly suitable for painting on. The default `paintComponent` method for an empty `JPanel` just paints its background. You can derive your own class from `JPanel` and add your drawing in your own `paintComponent` method. Again, it will usually start by calling the base class's `paintComponent`.

That is precisely what we did in *Ramblecs*, *Craps*, *SnackBar*, and other applets. In *Ramblecs*, for instance, we defined a class `LetterPanel` derived from `JPanel` (`Ch11\Ramblecs\LetterPanel.java` 🖫):

```
public class LetterPanel extends JPanel
  . . .
```

We then provided our own `paintComponent` method for it:

```
public void paintComponent(Graphics g)
{
  super.paintComponent(g); // call JPanel's paintComponent
  drawGrid(g);
  cube.draw(g);
}
```

When you need to repaint a component, you call its `repaint` method. (A component's `repaint` is different from an applet's `repaint`: it calls `paintComponent` only for this particular component.) In *Ramblecs*, when the cube moves, we adjust its position and call `whiteboard`'s `repaint`:

```
public void actionPerformed(ActionEvent e)
{
  if (!cube.moveDown())
  {
    stopCube();
  }
  repaint();
}
```

> Note that `repaint` just sends a request message to repaint the window or a component and this request goes into the event queue. The actual call may be postponed until your program finishes processing the current event.

By painting individual components in Swing you can implement smooth animations. Without this capability you would have to repaint the whole window when any little thing on it changed. We will return to the subject of using `JPanels` and see another example later in this chapter, in the *Pieces of the Puzzle* case study.

❖   ❖   ❖

An insightful reader may wonder at this point, how can we call `Graphics2D` methods if all we get is a reference to `Graphics g`? The truth is that `g` is a `Graphics2D` reference in disguise. It is presented as `Graphics` simply for compatibility with earlier versions of Java. To use it for calling `Graphics2D` methods you simply have to cast it into `Graphics2D`. For example:

```
Graphics2D g2D = (Graphics2D)g;
g2D.setPaint(new GradientPaint(0, 0, Color.red,
                               100, 100, Color.blue, true));
< ... etc. >
```

14.3 Coordinates

The graphics context `g`, passed to `paint` and `paintComponent`, defines the coordinate system for the drawing. As in most computer graphics packages, the *y*-axis points down, not up as in math (Figure 14-1).

> By default, the `Graphics` class places the origin at the <u>upper</u> left corner of the content area of the application window (for `paint`) or in the upper left corner of the component (for `paintComponent`). The coordinates are <u>integers</u> and the units are pixels.

The `translate(x,y)` method shifts the origin to the point `(x,y)`. In the `Graphics2D` class, there are methods to scale and rotate the coordinates.

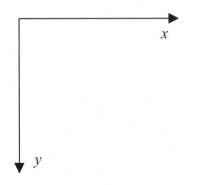

Figure 14-1. Graphics coordinates: *y*-axis points down

`Graphics` also sets the ***clipping rectangle*** to the window drawing area or the component drawing area. Anything outside the clipping rectangle does not show. Therefore, one component's `paintComponent` method usually can't paint over other components that do not overlap with it. `Graphics` has a method `setClip` for redefining the clipping rectangle.

This leaves you responsible for scaling your drawing. You decide what happens when the application window is resized. In some applications (like *Ramblecs*) you may want to leave all the graphics unchanged. In other situations (like *SnackBar*) you may adjust the approximate <u>positions</u> of your graphics objects, but not their sizes. Or you may want everything scaled, like in the *Puzzle* applet later in this chapter. You may lose some precision when scaling coordinates, but the high resolution (number of pixels per unit length) of modern graphics adapters makes these inaccuracies hardly visible.

> **Each component provides `getWidth` and `getHeight` methods that return the current width and height of the component in pixels. You can scale the coordinates based on these values.**

Suppose you want to draw a filled red rectangle with its center at the center of the panel and its size equal to 75 percent of the panel's size. On top of it you want to draw a filled blue oval inscribed into the rectangle (Figure 14-2). This can be accomplished as follows:

```java
public void paintComponent(Graphics g)
{
  super.paintComponent(g); // call JPanel's paintComponent

  int width = getWidth();
  int height = getHeight();
  int xSize = (int)(.75 * width);
  int ySize = (int)(.75 * height);
  int x0 = width/2 - xSize/2;    // Coordinates of the
  int y0 = height/2 - ySize/2;   //   upper left corner

  g.setColor(Color.red);
  g.fillRect(x0, y0, xSize, ySize);
  g.setColor(Color.blue);
  g.fillOval(x0, y0, xSize, ySize);
}
```

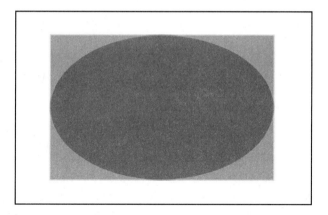

Figure 14-2. A filled oval inscribed into a filled rectangle

The above example shows not only how drawings can be scaled, but also how the positions of simple shapes (rectangles, ovals) are passed to drawing methods. The position and size of a rectangle are described by the x and y coordinates of its upper left corner and by its width and height. In the above example we subtract half the size of the rectangle from the coordinates of the center of the panel to determine where the upper left corner should be.

The position and size of a rounded rectangle, an oval, and even an arc are described by the position of the rectangle in which those shapes are inscribed (Figure 14-3).

In the above code the same arguments are passed to `fillRect` and `fillOval` because the oval is inscribed into the rectangle.

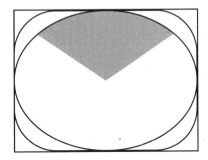

Figure 14-3. Positioning of ovals, arcs, and rounded rectangles

14.4 Colors

We have already used the `setColor` method whose argument is a `Color` object. The `Color` class has thirteen predefined constants for colors (`white`, `black`, `gray`, `lightGray`, `darkGray`, `blue`, `green`, `cyan`, `red`, `magenta`, `pink`, `orange`, and `yellow`). You can also construct your own color by specifying its red, green, and blue components:

```
int r = 18, g = 50, b = 255;
Color c = new Color(r, g, b);
g.setColor(c);
```

or simply:

```
g.setColor(new Color(18, 50, 255));
```

> **You can set the background color for a component by calling that component's `setBackground` method. This method only specifies the new background color but does not automatically repaint the component. If you set the background inside your `paintComponent` method, do it before calling `super.paintComponent`. If you do it elsewhere, call `repaint`.**

Paint and imaging applications and color choosing tools on the web[rgbcolors] can help you obtain RGB numbers for different colors and tints.

14.5 Drawing Shapes

Figure 14-4 summarizes the drawing methods of the `Graphics` class.

The `drawLine(x1,y1,x2,y2)` method draws a straight line from `(x1,y1)` to `(x2,y2)`.

There are eleven methods for drawing and filling rectangles, ovals and arcs: `clearRect`, `drawRect`, `fillRect`, `drawRoundRect`, `fillRoundRect`, `draw3DRect`, `fill3DRect`, `drawOval`, `fillOval`, `drawArc` and `fillArc`. We have already used most of them in one project or another, so they should look familiar. The first four arguments in each of these methods are the same: the *x* and *y* coordinates of the upper left corner, and the width and height of the bounding rectangle (as explained in Section 14.3). The `clearRect` method fills the rectangle with the component's current background color. The `drawRoundRect` and `fillRoundRect` methods take two additional arguments: the horizontal and vertical diameters of the oval used to round the corners. The `draw3DRect` and `fill3DRect` methods add a shadow on two sides to hint at a 3-D effect. Their fifth argument can be either `true` for a "raised" rectangle or `false` for a "lowered" rectangle.

The `drawArc` and `fillArc` methods respectively draw and fill a fragment of an oval inscribed into the bounding rectangle. `fillArc` fills a sector of the circle (a slice of the pie) bound by the arc. The fifth and sixth arguments in these methods are the beginning angle (with the 0 at the easternmost point) and the measure of the arc in degrees (going counterclockwise).

❖   ❖   ❖

The `drawPolygon` and `fillPolygon` methods take three arguments: the array of *x*-coordinates of the vertices, the array of *y*-coordinates of the vertices, and the number of points:

```
drawPolygon(int xCoords[], int yCoords[], int n)
```

The number of points n should not exceed the smaller of `xCoords.length` and `yCoords.length`. As you can see, the `xCoords` and `yCoords` arrays do not have to be filled to capacity: they may hold fewer points than their size allows. This is convenient if you are adding points interactively or if you are reading them from a file and don't know in advance how many points you will end up with.

```
g.drawLine(x1, y1, x2, y2);

g.clearRect(x, y, width, height);
g.drawRect(x, y, width, height);
g.fillRect(x, y, width, height);

g.drawOval(x, y, width, height);
g.fillOval(x, y, width, height);
g.drawRoundRect(x, y, width, height, int horzDiam, int vertDiam);
g.fillRoundRect(x, y, width, height, int horzDiam, int vertDiam);

g.draw3DRect(x, y, width, height, isRaised);
g.fill3DRect(x, y, width, height, isRaised);

g.drawArc(x, y, width, height, fromDegree, measureDegrees);
g.fillArc(x, y, width, height, fromDegree, measureDegrees);

g.drawPolygon(xCoords, yCoords, nPoints);
g.fillPolygon(xCoords, yCoords, nPoints);
g.drawPolyline(xCoords, yCoords, nPoints);

g.drawString(str, x, y);

g.drawImage(image, x, y, this);
```

Figure 14-4. The drawing methods of the Graphics class

drawPolygon and fillPolygon automatically connect the last point to the first point and draw or fill a closed polygon, respectively.

```
g.drawPolygon(xCoords, yCoords, n);
```

is basically the same as:

```
for (int i = 0; i < n - 1; i++)
{
  g.drawLine(xCoords[i], yCoords[i], xCoords[i+1]; yCoords[i+1]);
}
g.drawLine(xCoords[n-1], yCoords[n-1], xCoords[0]; yCoords[0]);
```

The drawPolyline method works the same way as drawPolygon, but it does not connect the last point to the first.

14.6 Fonts and Text

The `setFont` method lets you set the font for drawing text. Java uses an object of the `Font` class to describe a font. `Font` objects are used for graphics text displayed with `g.drawString` and for text in various GUI components (`JLabel`, `JTextField`, `JTextArea`, `JButton`, etc.). The `Graphics` method for setting a font and the methods for setting a font in Swing components share the same name, `setFont`.

> **A font is described by its name, its style, and its size.**

Font names are system-dependent, but Java guarantees that at least three font names are always recognized: `"Serif"` (a proportional font, in which letters may have different widths, with serifs, or little decorative strokes, like "Times Roman"), `"SansSerif"` (a proportional font without serifs, like "Arial"), and `"Monospaced"` (a fixed-width font where all characters have the same width, like "Courier"). The `GraphicsEnvironment` class has a `getAllFonts()` method that returns an array of all the fonts available in the system.

Styles are `Font.PLAIN`, `Font.BOLD`, `Font.ITALIC`, or
`Font.BOLD | Font.ITALIC` (the bit-wise combination of the two attributes, meaning both bold and italic).

The font size is specified in *points*. In typography, a point is 1/72 of an inch, but this measure loses its meaning when the text is scaled to a computer screen. For default coordinates, Java assumes that one point is equal to one pixel.

You can create all the fonts you need ahead of time (e.g., in the constructor for your drawing panel). For example:

```
Font font1 = new Font("Monospaced", Font.PLAIN, 20);
Font font2 = new Font("Serif", Font.BOLD, 30);
```

Then you set the font with `setFont`. For example:

```
g.setFont(font2);
```

If you intend to use a font only once, you can create an anonymous font:

```
g.setFont(new Font("Serif", Font.BOLD, 30));
```

For very precise text positioning, Graphics has a method getFontMetrics that returns a FontMetrix object. This object, in turn, has getAscent, getDescent, and getHeight methods that return font's vertical measurements (Figure 14-5).

Figure 14-5. Font metrics

The Graphics class's drawString(text, x, y) method draws the text string. This method positions the left end of the text's baseline at the point (x, y).

14.7 *Case Study and Lab:* Pieces of the Puzzle

In this section we will create an applet *Puzzle* to implement a simple puzzle that involves rearranging pieces of a picture. The applet first shows a picture made of nine pieces on a 3 by 3 grid. After two seconds, it scrambles the pieces randomly and shows the scrambled picture. The player has to restore the picture by moving the pieces around. There is an extra empty cell below the picture for holding a piece temporarily (Figure 14-6). The player can move a piece by "picking it up," then "dropping" it into the empty cell. To pick up a piece the player clicks on it. This is acknowledged by some feedback; for example, the picked-up piece gets a different background color. To "drop" the picked piece the player clicks on the empty cell.

Play with this applet (Ch14\RunPuzzle\TestPuzzle.html ⊞) to get a feel for how it works. In this version the initial picture is not very creative: it simply shows a circle and the numbers of the pieces (numbered from left to right and top to bottom like a telephone keypad). Examine the code for the Puzzle class in the Ch14\Puzzle folder. As you can see, the applet processes one timer event and after that is driven by mouse events. The Puzzle class implements a MouseListener interface by providing its five required methods. Of them only mousePressed is used. There is a way to not include unused methods (using a so-called *adapter class*, see Section 16.2), but we won't go into that here.

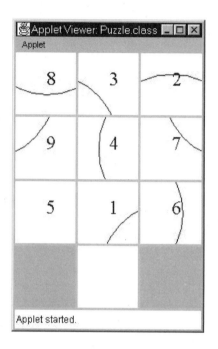

Figure 14-6. The *Puzzle* applet

The pieces of the puzzle are numbered from 1 to 9, and number 0 represents the empty cell. Before scrambling the pieces are arranged as follows:

```
1 2 3
4 5 6
7 8 9
  0
```

The applet uses an array of cells that hold the pieces. Each cell in the puzzle "knows" which piece it is currently holding. That number is returned by the cell's getPieceNumber method and can be set by the cell's setPieceNumber(k) method. In the initial non-scrambled picture, the index of each cell in the array matches the number of the piece displayed in it.

The logic for moving the pieces is pretty straightforward. When a mouse clicks on the applet, the `mousePressed` method is called:

```
public void mousePressed(MouseEvent e)
{
  int x = e.getX();
  int y = e.getY();

  // Figure out the index of the cell that was clicked:
  int col = 3 * x / getWidth();
  int row = 4 * y / getHeight();
  int i = 3 * row + col;
  if (i >= 0 && i < 9)
    i++;
  else if (i == 10)
    i = 0;
  else
    return;

  if (pickedIndex < 0)
    pickPiece(i);
  else
    dropPiece(i);
}
```

It gets the coordinates of the click and figures out in which cell i it occurred. Then it can go two different ways, depending whether there is already a picked-up piece "hanging in the air" or not. The `Puzzle` class has a field `pickedIndex` that holds the index of the cell whose piece has been picked up. If there is no picked piece, `pickedIndex` is set to −1. Then if the player has clicked on a non-empty cell, the puzzle piece is (logically) "lifted" from that cell. The cell is highlighted, and its index i is saved in `pickedIndex` for future use. The `pickPiece` method implements this:

```
private void pickPiece(int i)
{
  if (cells[i].getPieceNumber() != 0) // pick only non-empty cells
  {
    pickedIndex = i;
    cells[i].setPicked(true);
    cells[i].repaint();
  }
  else
  {
    bzz.play();
  }
}
```

If, on the other hand, there is already a piece "in the air" (pickedIndex >= 0) and the player has clicked on the empty cell (the cell holding the 0 piece), then the piece that was picked up earlier is "dropped" into that cell. The cell is updated to reflect that it now holds a piece with a particular number while the previously picked cell is set to empty. This is implemented in the dropPiece method:

```
private void dropPiece(int i)
{
  if (cells[i].getPieceNumber() == 0) // drop only on the empty cell
  {
    // Set the empty cell's number to the picked piece
    int k = cells[pickedIndex].getPieceNumber();
    cells[i].setPieceNumber(k);

    // Set the piece number for the source cell to "empty"
    cells[pickedIndex].setPieceNumber(0);
    cells[pickedIndex].setPicked(false);

    cells[i].repaint();
    cells[pickedIndex].repaint();

    pickedIndex = -1;    // nothing picked now
    if (allSet())
      bells.play();
    else
      drop.play();
  }
  else
  {
    bzz.play();
  }
}
```

Figure 14-7 shows a little state machine with two states that represents this logic. A *state machine* is a model that uses nodes to represent different possible states (of a system or a program) and connecting arrows to represent the rules for changing states.

❖   ❖   ❖

The trickier part is to display different pieces of the puzzle in different cells. The question is: how can we show a particular piece in a cell? One approach would be to have a separate method draw each of the nine pieces of the puzzle. This might work, but only for very simple pictures. In the real puzzle we want to use drawings whose lines cut across the grid lines; to draw separate fragments of them would be a nightmare.

A better approach would be to use <u>one</u> method to draw the whole picture, but show only one piece of it in each cell. You can envision this as a cell being a little "window" into the bigger picture. The picture slides below that window so that different pieces of it show. Since the `Graphics` class has methods for setting the clipping rectangle and for moving the origin of the coordinate system, this should be possible. The `paint` method would draw all cells within a loop, setting the appropriate clipping limits and the horizontal and vertical offsets for each cell. But this approach would create too much work: dealing with the `setClip` method and writing a loop for drawing the cells.

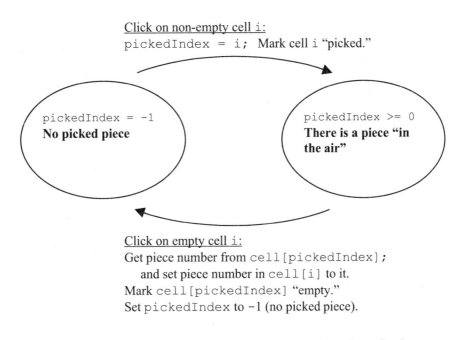

Click on non-empty cell i:
pickedIndex = i; Mark cell i "picked."

pickedIndex = -1
No picked piece

pickedIndex >= 0
There is a piece "in the air"

Click on empty cell i:
Get piece number from `cell[pickedIndex]`;
   and set piece number in `cell[i]` to it.
Mark `cell[pickedIndex]` "empty."
Set `pickedIndex` to -1 (no picked piece).

Figure 14-7. State machine diagram for moving pieces in the
***Puzzle* applet**

The solution that we will pursue is to use a separate panel for each of the ten cells. Each panel can be an object of the same class that we derive from `JPanel`. Each panel will use the same `paintComponent` method to draw the whole big picture, but only a part of it will be visible on the panel. Each panel object will take care of its own clipping automatically. All we have to do is <u>shift the origin</u> of the coordinate system appropriately for each panel, depending on what puzzle piece it currently holds. Then `JApplet`'s default `paint` method will automatically paint all the panels for us.

Now our plan of action is clear. Our applet will use two classes. The first one, `Puzzle`, is the main class derived from `JApplet`. The second class, let's call it `PuzzleCell`, will be derived from `JPanel`. The applet declares and initializes an array of ten `PuzzleCell` objects, one for each cell on the 3 by 3 grid and an extra empty cell. The applet's layout actually uses a 4 by 3 grid, with the extra cell placed in the middle of the fourth row. The cells are indexed 0, 1, 2, ..., 9. We first place cells 1 through 9 on the puzzle grid starting from the upper left corner, then we place cell 0 in the middle of the fourth row.

Each `PuzzleCell` object holds a number representing the piece of the picture it currently displays. When a cell is created, the piece number is passed as an argument to its constructor. At the beginning, before the picture is scrambled, the piece number is set to the cell index in each cell. The code in the `init` method creates the cells and adds them to the applet's content pane:

```
private PuzzleCell cells[];

<... etc.  See Ch14\Puzzle\Puzzle.java 🖫 >

public void init()
{
<... etc.  See Ch14\Puzzle\Puzzle.java 🖫 >

  Container c = getContentPane();
  c.setLayout(new GridLayout(4, 3, 1, 1)); // 4 by 3; horz gap 1,
                                           //   vert gap 1
  cells = new PuzzleCell[10];

  int i;
  for (i = 1; i <= 9; i++)
  {
    cells[i] = new PuzzleCell(i);
    c.add(cells[i]);
  }
  c.add (new JPanel()); // must put something in row 4 col 1
  cells[0] = new PuzzleCell(0);
  c.add(cells[0]);        // put empty cell in row 4 col 2

<... etc.  See Ch14\Puzzle\Puzzle.java 🖫 >
}
```

After showing the original picture we need to scramble it. To do that, we initialize a temporary array with values 1 through 9 and shuffle it, then assign the shuffled numbers to cells 1 through 9:

```
// Scramble the puzzle by setting shuffled numbers 1 through 9
//    to the puzzle cells:
int numbers[] = {1, 2, 3, 4, 5, 6, 7, 8, 9};
shuffle(numbers);
int i, k;
for (i = 1; i <= 9; i++)
{
  k = numbers[i-1];
  cells[i].setPieceNumber(k);
}
```

Copy the `Puzzle.java` and `PuzzleCell.java` files from the `Ch14\Puzzle` 💾 folder, as well as `TestPuzzle.html` and three audio clip `.wav` files from the `Ch14\RunPuzzle` folder, to your work folder.

As a warm-up exercise, write the code for the `Puzzle` class's `shuffle` method. This method rearranges the elements of an array in random order. The algorithm is very similar to Selection Sort, only instead of choosing the largest among the first *n* elements, you choose an element randomly among the first *n* elements and swap it with the *n*-th element. This algorithm produces all possible arrangements with equal probabilities.

As another little exercise, write the `Puzzle` class's `allSet` method, which returns `true` if all pieces have been returned to their proper places and `false` otherwise. Call the `getPieceNumber` method for each of the cells and compare its returned value with the cell number.

And now to the serious business. Fill in the blanks in the `PuzzleCell` class's `paintComponent` method. First set the background color — white for a non-picked piece and yellow for a picked piece — and call `super.paintComponent`. Then shift the origin appropriately based on the value of `PuzzleCell`'s `pieceNumber` field, which represents the number of the piece this panel (cell) is supposed to show. Recall that the panel's `getWidth` and `getHeight` methods return the dimensions of the panel. You need to adjust them slightly to compensate for the gaps between panels. Finally, call a method that paints your picture.

Test your code first with the simple picture (a circle and cell numbers) provided. It will also help you test your `shuffle` method and your coordinate offsets. The purpose of the circle is to test how the pieces fit together — make sure your circle looks smooth. After you get it working, create a different picture <u>of your choice</u> for the puzzle. For instance you can draw circles, polygons, or letters of different sizes and colors that intersect the grid. Make sure your picture is <u>fully scalable</u>, so that if the applet's window shrinks or stretches, the picture shrinks or stretches with it. Find several five- to seven-year-olds and test your working puzzle on them.

14.8 Summary

Java provides a straightforward but limited class `Graphics` for drawing simple shapes and graphics text. The `Graphics2D` package is much more powerful but harder to use.

Since Java applets and applications are event-driven, all drawing must originate either in the `paint` method of the applet or application window or in the `paintComponent` method of one of the Swing components (usually a `JPanel` object or an object of some class derived from it). `paint` and `paintComponent` take one argument, `Graphics g`, which defines the graphics context for this component. If the application needs to repaint its window or component, it calls `repaint`, which takes no arguments.

The Java coordinate system has the origin in the upper left corner of the window or panel, with the *y*-axis pointing down. The coordinates are integers and their units are pixels. The `drawLine` method draws a line segment described by the coordinates of its beginning and end. Rectangles are described by their upper-left-corner coordinates, width, and height. Ovals, rounded rectangles, and even arcs are defined by the position of the bounding rectangle into which they are inscribed. Besides filled or hollow rectangles, rounded rectangles, ovals, and arcs, `Graphics` can draw polygons and polylines.

You can set the current drawing color by calling the component's `setColor` method, which takes a `Color` object as its argument. To set the background color, call the `setBackground` method.

You can display graphics text by calling the `drawString` method; choose a desired font by calling `setFont`.

Exercises

1. The applet below (`Ch14\Exercises\Drawings.java` ▣) displays a red rectangle in the middle of the content pane:

```
import java.awt.*;
import javax.swing.*;

public class Drawings extends JApplet
{
  public void init()
  {
    Container c = getContentPane();
    c.setBackground(Color.white);
  }

  public void paint(Graphics g)
  {
    super.paint(g);
    int w = getWidth();
    int h = getHeight();
    g.setColor(Color.red);
    g.drawRect(w/4, h/4, w/2, h/2);
  }
}
```

Add code to display a message inside the red rectangle. ✓

2.   Modify the applet in Question 1 to display the following designs:

(a) ✓   (b)   (c)   (d)

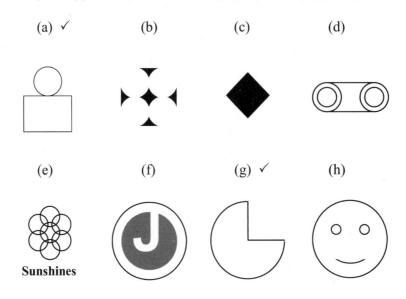

(e)   (f)   (g) ✓   (h)

Sunshines

≶ Hint: (b) is a black rounded rectangle with four white circles; (c) is a polygon. ≷

Make your applet scalable and use any colors you want.

3.   Define a class `MyPanel` that extends `JPanel`. Make it show one of the designs from Question 2 (or your own design) by redefining its `paintComponent` method. Change the *Drawings* applet in Question 1: eliminate the `paint` method and instead create one object of the `MyPanel` type and add it to the center region of the content pane as follows:

```
Container c = getContentPane();
c.add(myDrawingPanel, BorderLayout.CENTER);
```

4.   (a)   Adapt the applet from Question 1 to show the NGAA logo:

(b)■   Now take a different approach to showing the same logo. Add a
constructor to the `MyPanel` class from Question 3 that takes a letter
and a background color as arguments and saves them. Make
`MyPanel`'s `paintComponent` method draw the letter on the specified
background. Set the 2 by 2 grid layout for the applet's content pane as
follows:

```
Container c = getContentPane();
c.setLayout(new GridLayout(2, 2));
```

Add four `MyPanel` objects to it, one for each letter in the logo.

5.◆   Write methods that draw AND, OR, and NOT gates of given sizes (see
Figure 1-1 on page 3).

6.■   The applet *Boxes* (`Ch14\Exercises\Boxes.java` ▣) can display
different types of boxes (rectangles) in different colors. The user chooses the
color of the box from a "combo box" that shows all 13 predefined colors
from the `Color` class. He sets the box type by checking option boxes for
filled, rounded, and 3-D rectangles. The box type is represented in the
program as an integer in which individual bits indicate the three attributes:
bit 0 for filled, bit 1 for rounded, and bit 2 for 3-D. For example, the value 5
(binary 101) indicates a filled 3-D box.

The *Boxes* applet relies on a `BoxDrawer` class derived from `JPanel`. It has
additional methods `setBoxType(int boxType)`,
`setBoxColor(Color color)`, and `drawBox(Graphics g)`.
`BoxDrawer` also redefines the `paintComponent` method to repaint the
background and call `drawBox`. Implement the `BoxDrawer` class.

⋛ Hints: (1) Use a `switch` on the box type in `drawBox`. (2) Set the
background to gray or black in `paintComponent` if the white color is
chosen. (3) Display an error message instead of a box if both rounded and
3-D attributes are selected. ⋛

7.◆   (a)   Change the applet from Question 4-b to display a checkerboard pattern of the given dimensions. The dimensions should be specified in the `<param>` tags in the HTML file that runs the applet. For example:

```
<param name="ROWS" value="8">
<param name="COLS" value="8">
```

Use the grid layout with the given dimensions and add panels with alternating colors. ⅋ Hint: see Question 16 in exercises for Chapter 11 (page 317). ⅌

(b)   Change the `MyPanel` class again to show conditionally a picture of a chess queen figure. Add a constructor or a method that sets a `boolean` flag to indicate whether the panel should be empty or show a queen.

(c)◆   Change the applet to show a solution to the "Eight Queens" problem (see Question 12 in Chapter 2, page 56). Create an 8 by 8 array of `MyPanels` and set the `showQueen` flags appropriately in eight of them to show the queens. Set the content pane's layout to an 8 by 8 grid and add the panels to the grid.

(d)◆◆ Provide a method to find your own solution to the "Eight Queens" problem. ⅋ Hint: make it a recursive method `addQueens` with two arguments: a list of queens already placed (to hold up to eight positions) and the number of queens currently in the list. Start with an empty list. If the list has eight queens, save the list and return `true` (the problem is solved). If not, try to add the remaining queens to the list. Mark all spaces in an 8 by 8 array that are covered by the queens that are currently in the list. Scan the array trying to add a queen in each unmarked spot, then calling `addQueens` recursively. If all such attempts fail, return `false`. ⅌

GUI Components and Events

15.1 Prologue

In this chapter we finally get to the strongest points of Java and object-oriented programming: ***graphical user interfaces***, ***event-driven programming***, and ***multimedia***. Event-driven GUI is what made the OOP concept popular, and it remains the area where it's most relevant. While you can write console applications in Java, such programs won't take full advantage of Java or OOP; in most cases such programs might just as well be written in C or Pascal. The style of modern user interfaces — with many different types of control components such as menus, buttons, pull-down lists, checkboxes, radiobuttons, and text edit fields — provides an arena where OOP and event-driven programming naturally excel.

The Swing package in Java 2 has introduced a new implementation of GUI components, which is written entirely in Java and is therefore more portable. By default these components (sometimes called ***lightweight*** components) have their own ***look and feel*** (i.e., appearance and interaction style). This, probably for its cool appearance, is known as a "metal" look and feel. In the older `java.awt` (Abstract Windowing Toolkit) package, GUI components were tied directly into the corresponding GUI components of the host operating system. This enforced the look and feel of the operating system. For example, when a Java application developed in `awt` runs under *Windows*, its menus look exactly like any other *Windows* menus and its buttons look exactly like *Windows* buttons. You get the standard *Windows* look and feel. This in itself is not such a bad thing, but it could make an application a little less portable: some of the conventions accepted in *Windows* may be different, say, under a Macintosh *OS*.

Swing makes the interface platform-independent, with the exception of `JFrame` objects, which must look and behave like "native" windows under a particular operating system. As a compromise, Swing supports ***pluggable look and feel***, giving you the option to choose a native look and feel instead of its default "metal." Look and feel in general is a touchy subject that involves marketing considerations, competition among major software vendors, and legal issues of intellectual property rights and patents. This competition may well be what produced Swing.

Our task in this chapter is to more formally organize the bits and pieces of Swing and multimedia that you have managed to grasp from examples so far. Overall the Java 2 API (Applications Programming Interface) lists over 1,500 classes and interfaces, with thousands of constructors and methods. It would take several volumes to document them all in conventional books. The online documentation in HTML format gives you convenient access to these detailed specifications. Still, it is not very easy to find what you need unless you know exactly what to look for. Some descriptions of constructors and methods or their arguments may be sketchy and give you incomplete information. It would be impossible to learn the details of the whole API; by the time you finished, it would have been replaced by Release 17.

A sizable portion of the API — more than 100 classes — deals with Swing GUI components, events handlers and multimedia. Even this smaller portion is a significant challenge. You can claim to have learned how to use a component only when you have tried its most common methods yourself. So in many cases it may be easier to look up an example of how a particular type of object is used than to read about it in the API spec file. In most cases you need only the most standard uses of classes and their methods, and there are thousands of examples of these in SDK demos, books, online tutorials, and other sources.

This is the approach our book has taken, too. While introducing Java's fundamental concepts, basic syntax and control structures, and other elements, we have sneaked in a variety of commonly used GUI widgets and methods. We have added some decorative "bells" and "listeners" here and there, just so you could see, if you cared to, how such things might be done. This chapter summarizes what you have seen and fills some gaps. Appendix C presents a synopsis and an index of the more commonly used GUI components that appear in the code examples of previous chapters.

Knowing all the details of the latest GUI package still does not guarantee that the GUI in your application will "work." In addition to working the way you, the programmer, expect it to work, it must be also intuitive and easy to use. Designing a good user interface is a matter of experience, good sense, trial and error, paying attention to your software users, developing prototypes, and in some cases, relying on more formal "human factors" research. A good user interface designer should gain experience with a wide range of applications, observe what works and what doesn't, and absorb the latest styles from cyberspace. You should be aware that, strictly speaking, this skill may not be directly related to programming skills.

In this chapter we will discuss the basic Swing components:

- `JLabel` — displays an icon or a line of text
- `JButton` — triggers an "action event" when pressed
- `JToggleButton` and `JCheckBox` — toggle an option
- `JComboBox` and `JRadioButton` — choose an option out of several possibilities
- `JSlider` — adjusts a setting

- `JTextField`, `JPasswordField`, and `JTextArea` — allow the user to display and enter or edit a line of text, a password, or a multi-line fragment of text, respectively

We will discuss some of their methods and the events they generate. We will also get familiar with four layout managers that help to arrange GUI components on the application's window.

15.2 Basic Swing Components and Their Events

Each of these GUI objects is created using one of its constructors. For example, one of `JLabel`'s constructors takes one `String` argument — the line of text to be displayed. Another constructor takes one `Icon` argument — an image to be displayed. After an object is created, you can add or change its features by calling its methods. For example, `JLabel`'s `setText` method can be used to change the line of text it displays. A GUI object must be added to your application's or applet's "content pane" or to one of its components. We'll discuss placement of GUI components on windows or panels in Section 15.5.

❖   ❖   ❖

A GUI component (with the exception of `JLabel`) generates certain types of events. Your program can capture these events using an appropriate type of event "listener," an object of a class that **_implements_** a particular "Listener" **_interface_**.

> An _interface_ **lists a number of methods and their arguments but does not include any code for them. A class is said to** _implement_ **an interface if it supplies <u>all</u> the methods specified in that interface.**

The keyword `implements` is somewhat similar to `extends`, but instead of a base class there are only method headers. A class can "extend" only one base class, but it can "implement" several interfaces. For example:

```
public class ControlPanel extends JPanel
    implements ActionListener, ChangeListener, KeyListener
{
   ...
}
```

To capture events from a component you need to add the appropriate type of listener object to that component. For example, a `JButton` object generates "action" events.

These events can be captured by an `ActionListener` object (i.e. an object of a class that implements the `ActionListener` interface). The `ActionListener` interface requires one method:

```
public void actionPerformed(ActionEvent e)
```

To add an "action listener" to a button you have to call that button's `addActionListener` method. All of this may look as follows:

```
// MyApplet.java
// =============
import < ... required import statements >

public class MyApplet extends JApplet
{
  AudioClip bells = getAudioClip(getDocumentBase(), "bells.wav");

  void init()
  {
    JButton button = new JButton("Click here to hear bells");
    button.addActionListener(new MyOwnButtonListener());
    Container c = getContentPane();
    c.add(button);
  }

  < ... other methods >

  private class MyOwnButtonListener
            implements ActionListener
  {
    public void actionPerformed(ActionEvent e)
    {
      bells.play();
    }
  }
}
```

Embedded private class

Here, the `MyOwnButtonListener` class is embedded into `MyApplet` as a ***private class***. We have tried to avoid embedded classes in this book (in order not to confuse you more than necessary), and we could have made `MyOwnButtonListener` a separate public class here, too. However, with many GUI components and a separate listener class for each of them, the number of source files may become quite large. Also, a listener may need access to fields in the class or object that creates it (e.g., `bells` in the above example). So

when implementing an event listener, programmers often use a private embedded class that has access to all the fields in the surrounding public class.

In simple cases, the object that creates a GUI component can also serve as its listener. Then you can just use `this` as an argument to the `addActionListener` (or `add<Whatever>Listener`) method. For example:

```
// MyApplet.java
// =============
import < ... required import statements >

public class MyApplet extends JApplet
    implements ActionListener
{
  AudioClip bells = getAudioClip(getDocumentBase(), "bells.wav");

  void init()
  {
    JButton button = new JButton("Click here to hear bells");
    button.addActionListener(this);
    Container c = getContentPane();
    c.add(button);
  }

  < ... other methods >

  public void actionPerformed(ActionEvent e)
  {
    bells.play();
  }
}
```

The advantage of the latter approach is simpler code. The disadvantage is that if your object has created several buttons, then its `actionPerformed` method has to sort them out and take different actions depending on which one was clicked. For example:

```
  public void actionPerformed(ActionEvent e)
  {
    JButton button = (JButton)e.getSource();
    if (button == myButton1)
      < ... do one thing >
    else if (button == myButton2)
      < ... do another thing >
  }
```

A listener for a particular component is an object, not a class.

The *SnackBar* applet, for example (Section 8.12), creates three similar objects of the `VendingMachine` class, and each machine becomes the action listener for its own buttons. Very convenient.

❖   ❖   ❖

You do not have to capture every event from GUI components. With the exception of `JButton`, an event signals that the state of the component has changed. Sometimes you may prefer to retrieve the current state of the component later, when you need it, not right at the moment when it changes. (For instance, you may not care what options a user has chosen until he clicks "OK.") All components provide methods for getting state information from them. For example, `JTextField` and `JTextArea` have the `getText` method, `JComboBox` has the `getSelectedItem` and `getSelectedIndex` methods, and `JCheckBox` has the `isSelected` method. In the *Benchmarks* applet in Chapter 12, `JComboBox`'s and `JTextField`'s events are ignored while `JButton`'s events are captured and processed by an "action listener." Then the listener's `actionPerformed` method retrieves the information from the `JComboBox` and `JTextField` components. For `JButtons` you pretty much have to capture their events (unless it's just a clicking exercise) because a button's state does not change after it is clicked.

> **If you want to capture a GUI object's events, don't forget to attach a listener to it.**

In a Java program, events are represented by objects of special types: `ActionEvent`, `ItemEvent`, `KeyEvent`, `MouseEvent`, and so on. If you do capture an event, the event itself carries information that the listener's method can use. You can find out who caused the event by calling the event's `getSource` method. It returns an `Object`, a reference to the object that caused the event. You can cast this returned `Object` into whatever type of component this listener is processing events for (see the example for `JButton` above).

For action events you can also retrieve an "action command" by calling the event's `getActionCommand` method. It returns a string associated with the component. By default it returns the text written on the button or in a `JTextField` component, but you can set it yourself by calling your component's `setActionCommand` method. This may be useful, for instance, if the same button should trigger different actions at different times (e.g., "Go" / "Stop").

> **The same component may generate different types of events captured by different types of listeners. Your program may choose to capture a certain type of events and ignore other types. Most components generate `ActionEvents` that are captured by an action listener.**

Appendix C summarizes the basic Swing components, their event listeners, and their most commonly used constructors and methods. Most importantly, it gives references to some examples of their use.

15.3 *Case Study and Lab:* Speed Control

In this lab we will add a "slider" to the *Ramblecs* applet to control the speed of the falling cubes. The first question, as usual, is where to put the slider (that is, both where to display it and where to add code for it). Let us consider the options.

Our `Ramblecs` class is the top-level class and we want to keep it that way — we don't want to burden it with details about speed sliders.

> **In general, one of the main principles of sound OOP design is that each object should know as little as possible about how other objects work. Classes should form layers, and more detailed responsibilities should be assigned to lower levels.**

Our `LetterPanel` class controls and paints the falling cube and paints the letter grid, so it is already quite busy with other functions.

But the control panel, which already displays the speed gauge, is the natural place for the slider.

> **If possible, the dependencies between objects of two different classes (called *coupling*) should be reduced.**

In this case it is convenient to have the slider and the gauge in the same place because they have to work together.

Note that `controlpanel` doesn't really want to know <u>how</u> the speed parameter is used. It knows how to adjust and display it, but it doesn't use or store it because a more natural place for the `speed` field is in the `whiteboard` object. It is `whiteboard` that talks to the falling cube and sets it in motion. So we need to add the `speed` field and accessor and modifier methods `getSpeed` and `setSpeed` to the `LetterPanel` class. We have done it for you (see `LetterPanel.java` 🖫 in the `Ch15\Ramblecs1` folder). `setSpeed` converts our arbitrary speed units into pixels per timer cycle and calls `cube`'s method to set its `yStep` parameter:

```
public void setSpeed(int v)
{
  speed = v;
  int dy = v * delay / 1000;
      // dy is displacement in pixels per timer cycle
  if (dy < 1)
    dy = 1;
  cube.setStep(dy);
}
```

Now back to the slider. We have decided that it goes on the control panel, but where on the control panel? Note that the control panel uses a "border" layout (we will discuss different layouts in Section 15.5) and its east and west sides are still vacant. Why don't we add it on the east side? The panel may be a little narrow for the slider, especially if the slider has tick marks and labels on it. We have extended the control panel's width by calling its `setPreferredSize` method in its constructor. (The vertical size doesn't matter because the panel extends through the whole height between the north and south regions of the applet's window.)

The tasks left for you are as follows:

1. Read Appendix C to learn about `JSliders`. Note that this component uses `javax.swing.event` package, which must be imported in addition to `java.awt.event`.

2. Add a vertical slider to the control panel on its east side using the `minSpeed`, `maxSpeed`, and `avgSpeed` constants. We have added a `minSpeed` field set to 50. Implement a `ChangeListener` in the `ControlPanel` class itself and add `this` as the slider's "change listener."

3. Make each "change" event call `whiteboard`'s `setSpeed` method and also change the appearance of the speed gauge on the control panel. Hints: (1) recall the `repaint` method discussed in the previous chapter. (2) A technical detail: add a `requestFocus()` call in the slider event handler to return the keyboard focus from the slider to the control panel. (3) In `controlpanel`'s `paintComponent`, instead of showing `avgSpeed` now obtain the actual speed from `whiteboard`.

4. As long as you're fiddling with the `ControlPanel` class, go ahead and (for "extra credit") change the way the "Go" button works. Currently when a player clicks "Go," one cube falls and stops. Make it work so that cubes start falling and keep falling until the player clicks the same button to stop. You can toggle

the <u>text</u> on the button between "Go" and "Stop" after each click using the button's `setText` method. You can retrieve the button's text in the `actionPerformed` method by calling the button's `getText` method. So the `actionPerformed` method can find out what state the button was in when it was clicked. Don't move too much code around in the `LetterPanel` class; all you need to do is add one line to call `dropCube` again after `stopCube`. The "Stop" button should simply call `whiteboard`'s `stopCube` method.

15.4 Pull-Down Menus

Any self-respecting program should have a menu bar with pull-down menus. If nothing else, that's where the copyright message goes, under "Help / About..."

You can add a menu bar to a `JApplet` or a `JFrame` object, or any object of a class derived from one of them. A menu bar is a `JMenuBar` class object; it is added by calling the `setMenuBar` method. You can add `JMenu` objects to your menu bar. To `JMenu` objects you can add `JMenuItems`, `JRadioButtonMenuItems`, `JCheckBoxMenuItems`, and more `JMenus` (submenus). You can split a menu into groups by calling `JMenu`'s `addSeparator` method. You can add "action listeners" to `JMenuItems`, checkboxes and radiobuttons. All of this is quite straightforward but verbose and repetitive. Visual development tools let programmers design menus and other GUI components interactively, then generate most of the Java code automatically. Still, you have to know what's going on, and the best way to learn it is by working through a simple example.

Our example is to add a menu bar to the *Ramblecs* applet. It will have only two menus, the "File" menu and the "Help" menu. The "File" menu has a "Preferences" submenu and a "New game" menu item. The preferences submenu has one option: sound on or off. (In the updated version of the applet each cube makes a clacking sound when it lands — a feature that some players have found really cool but others consider super-annoying. As a compromise, we have made it an option under the "Preferences" menu.) The "Help" menu has the items "How to Play" and "About."

Since this code is bulky, we have decided to put it into a separate class, `RamblecsMenu`, derived from `JMenuBar`. Our `Ramblecs` project is growing: now it will have six classes, with one object of each class created (Figure 15-1). As before, the arrows in this figure connect objects that are "aware" of each other: there is an arrow from one object to another if the first object constructs another or calls its methods. We have added the `menuBar` object under `Ramblecs` because the applet has to incorporate the menu bar. We have also added a connection from `whiteboard` back to `Ramblecs` because `whiteboard` consults the applet on whether to play a sound when the cubes land, and the applet in turn consults the "Preferences" menu setting in `menuBar`. It is getting a little complicated — the price we pay for encapsulation. But we are still maintaining functional layers that keep the structure orderly. For example, we know that if we make changes to the `FallingCube` class, we might need to adjust `LetterPanel` above it, but we don't have to worry about `ControlPanel` or other classes.

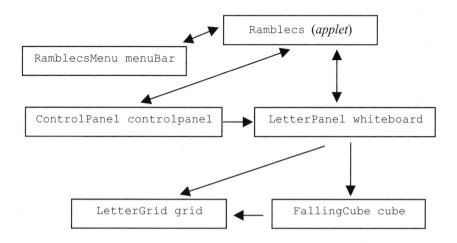

Figure 15-1. *Ramblecs* classes and objects after adding a menu bar

The updated code for the `Ramblecs` class is shown in Figure 15-2. We have added the `menuBar` field and statements to create it and add it to the applet in the `init` method. We have also added a `reset` method called from `menuBar`'s action listener when the "New game" menu command is selected, as well as the audio clip and a `playSound` method to play it from `whiteboard` when a cube lands.

`RamblecsMenu` code is shown in Figure 15-3.

```java
/**
 *   This is the applet class for the Ramblecs game.
 *   Author: B. Speller
 *
 *   See Help for rules
 */
import java.awt.*;
import javax.swing.*;
import java.applet.AudioClip;

public class Ramblecs extends JApplet
{
  private AudioClip drop;
  private RamblecsMenu menuBar;
  private ControlPanel controlpanel;
  private LetterPanel whiteboard;

  public void init()
  {
    drop = getAudioClip(getDocumentBase(), "drop.wav");

    menuBar = new RamblecsMenu(this);
    setJMenuBar(menuBar);

    whiteboard = new LetterPanel(this);
    whiteboard.setBackground(Color.white);
    controlpanel = new ControlPanel(whiteboard, this);
    Container c = getContentPane();
    c.add(whiteboard, BorderLayout.CENTER);
    c.add(controlpanel, BorderLayout.EAST);
  }


  public void reset()
  {
    controlpanel.reset();
  }

  public void playSound()
  {
    if (menuBar.isSoundEnabled())
      drop.play();
  }
}
```

Figure 15-2. `Ch15\Ramblecs2\Ramblecs.java` 🖫

```
/**
 *  A menu bar for the Ramblecs applet
 */
import java.awt.*;
import java.awt.event.*;
import javax.swing.*;

public class RamblecsMenu extends JMenuBar
    implements ActionListener
{
  private Ramblecs game;
  private JCheckBoxMenuItem sound;
  private JMenuItem newgame, howtoplay, about;

  public RamblecsMenu(Ramblecs applet)
  {
    game = applet;

    // "File" menu:

    JMenu fileMenu = new JMenu("File");
    fileMenu.setMnemonic('F');

    // Second level menu under "Preferences":
    JMenu preferences = new JMenu("Preferences");
    preferences.setMnemonic('P');
    sound = new JCheckBoxMenuItem("Play sound", true);
    sound.setMnemonic('S');
    preferences.add(sound);

    newgame = new JMenuItem("New game");
    newgame.setMnemonic('N');
    newgame.addActionListener(this);

    fileMenu.add(preferences);
    fileMenu.addSeparator();
    fileMenu.add(newgame);

    add(fileMenu);

    // "Help" menu:

    JMenu helpMenu = new JMenu("Help");
    helpMenu.setMnemonic('H');

    howtoplay = new JMenuItem("How to play...");
    howtoplay.setMnemonic('p');
    howtoplay.addActionListener(this);
    about = new JMenuItem("About...");
    about.setMnemonic('A');
    about.addActionListener(this);

    helpMenu.add(howtoplay);
    helpMenu.add(about);
```

Figure 15-3 `RamblecsMenu.java` *Continued* ⇗

```java
    add(helpMenu);
  }

  public void actionPerformed(ActionEvent e)
  {
    JMenuItem src = (JMenuItem)e.getSource();

    if (src == newgame)
      game.reset();
    else if (src == howtoplay)
      showHelp();
    else if (src == about)
      showAbout();
  }

  private void showHelp()
  {
    JOptionPane.showMessageDialog(null,
        "Make complete words (3 to 5 letters) in the bottom row.\n" +
        "Use cursor keys <- and -> to move the" +
        " falling cube left or right.\n" +
        "Use up and down cursor keys to rotate the cube.\n" +
        "Press Ctrl+F or Ctrl+S for faster or slower falling cube.\n" +
        "Press <Enter> to enter the word.\n" +
        "Press spacebar to flush the bottom row without entering.\n" +
        "Scoring:\n\n" +
        "  Entered valid word: " +
        "  3 letters -- 3 pts; 4 letters -- 6 pts;" +
        " 5 letters -- 12 pts\n" +
        "  15 points penalty for misspelled entered word\n" +
        "  3 points penalty for each flushed row\n",
        "How to Play",        // Dialog title
        JOptionPane.PLAIN_MESSAGE);
  }

  private void showAbout()
  {
    JOptionPane.showMessageDialog(null,
        "This game serves as a case study for \"Java Methods\"\n" +
        "by Maria Litvin and Gary Litvin\n" +
        "Copyright (C) 2001 by Skylight Publishing, Andover, MA\n" +
        "ISBN 0-9654853-7-4.\n" +
        "You are allowed to copy and use this game and its code\n" +
        "for teaching and educational purposes only.\n" +
        "You are not allowed to change or remove this message.\n",
        "About",         // Dialog title
        JOptionPane.PLAIN_MESSAGE);
  }

  public boolean isSoundEnabled()
  {
    return sound.isSelected();
  }
}
```

Figure 15-3. `Ch15\Ramblecs2\RamblecsMenu.java` 💾

Now let's put the *Ramblecs* applet back together again.

Copy the updated `Ramblecs.java` and `LetterPanel.java` ⊟ files and the new `RamblecsMenu.java` file provided in the `Ch15\Ramblecs2` folder to your work folder. Note that we have added the `reset` method to the `LetterPanel` class:

```
public void reset()
{
  grid.makeEmpty();
  stopCube();
}
```

Add a `makeEmpty` method that fills the grid with spaces to your latest version of the `LetterGrid` class (your solution to the lab in Section 11.7). Then add the following `reset` method to your latest version of the `ControlPanel` class (your solution for the lab in Section 15.3):

```
public void reset()
{
  speedSlider.setValue(avgSpeed);
  repaint();
  requestFocus();
  whiteboard.reset();
  go.setText("Go");
}
```

The `FallingCube` class from `Ch15\Ramblecs1` remains unchanged.

Note how one unforeseen change, the addition of the "New game" menu command, has propagated through many classes: we had to add `reset` methods to `Ramblecs`, `ControlPanel`, and `LetterPanel`, and a `makeEmpty` method to `LetterGrid`. More careful design at the beginning would have helped us avoid this. But it is impossible to foresee all future needs; that is why your code has to be readable so that someone else can modify it.

Finally, copy the `drop.wav` and `TestRamblecs.html` ⊟ files from the `Ch15\Ramblecs2` folder and compile and test the applet.

15.5 Layouts

Learning about GUI components is only half the trick. The second half is learning how to place them on your application window.

▌ **In AWT and Swing, GUI components are added to containers.**

A *container* is an object of the Java class `Container`. One container is the main window's "content pane." A reference to it can be obtained by calling the `getContentPane` method. Other containers include boxes (objects of the `Box` class) and panels (objects of the `JPanel` class). In fact, all Swing components are eventually derived from the `Container` class, so all of them are "containers." But it is boxes and panels to which other components are usually added. You can have nested containers: boxes within boxes and boxes within panels and panels within boxes, and so on.

Repainting all the components in an application is a perfect opportunity to use recursion: for each component, first its picture is repainted, then (recursively) all components contained in it are repainted. In general, recursion is a very useful tool for dealing with nested structures and branching processes.

Java applications try to be platform-independent and to some extent scalable. To achieve this, Java gives up the possibility of precise placement of components based on specified pixel coordinates. Instead, components are placed with the help of "layout managers." In this section we will consider four kinds of layout managers: `FlowLayout`, `GridLayout`, `BorderLayout` and `BoxLayout`. (You can look up other layouts in the Java's tutorials and API specs.) Each type of container has a default layout manager, but you can choose a different one by calling the container's `setLayout` method. A layout manager is an object; as such it must be created before it can be used in a container. A typical idiom for setting a layout manager may look like this:

```
Container c = getContentPane();
c.setLayout(new FlowLayout());
c.add(...);      // Add a component
< ... etc. >
```

▌ **By default, the content pane has `BorderLayout`, a `Box` has `BoxLayout`, and a `JPanel` has `FlowLayout`.**

Let us consider these three plus `GridLayout`, usually used with panels.

Flow Layout

`FlowLayout` is the most automatic and the least precise of layout managers. It places components in the order they are added, starting from the top row of the container area and filling it as long as components fit, then starting a next row, and so on. There is a way to center the components or left- or right-justify them. For example:

```
Container c = getContentPane();
FlowLayout layout = new FlowLayout();
layout.setAlignment(FlowLayout.LEFT);
c.setLayout(layout);
c.add(...);      // Add a component
< ... etc. >
```

A `FlowLayout` manager spaces the rows and the components within them in a reasonable way. We have used `FlowLayout` several times:

```
Ch03\HelloGui\HelloGui.java
Ch07\Craps1\CrapsStats.java
Ch07\Exercises\Mail.java
Ch07\Exercises\Rps.java
Ch09\Equations\EquationSolver.java
Ch09\Exercises\StringTest.java
Ch12\Rotate\RotateArray.java
```

It is convenient to use `FlowLayout` when you want to put together a little applet with a couple of GUI components quickly.

Grid Layout

`GridLayout` is the opposite of `FlowLayout`: it is the most rigidly controlled. The grid occupies the whole area of the container, and all grid cells are the same size. `GridLayout`'s constructor takes two arguments, the number of rows and the number of columns in the grid. There are no gaps between the grid cells. Another constructor takes the number of rows and the number of columns in the grid plus two more arguments, the horizontal gap and the vertical gap between the grid cells (in pixels). Components are added starting from the upper left corner of the grid filling the first row, then the next row, and so on. There is no way to skip a cell unless you put a dummy object into it (e.g., an empty panel). We have used `GridLayout` in the following examples:

```
Ch06\Exercises\Bmi.java
Ch07\Craps2\Craps.java
Ch07\Exercises\Wages.java
Ch08\SnackBar\VendingMachine.java
Ch08\Exercises\Temperature.java
Ch12\Benchmarks\Benchmarks.java
Ch14\Puzzle\Puzzle.java
```

Border Layout

BorderLayout splits the area into five regions (Figure 15-4) and lets you add one component to each region. A border region expands to reasonably fit the component in that region. If necessary, you can set the size of the component by calling its setPreferredSize method (as we did when adding a slider to the ControlPanel class in Section 15.3). When you add a component to a container with a "border" layout, you have to specify explicitly which region it goes into. For example:

```
Container c = getContentPane();
c.add(whiteboard, BorderLayout.CENTER);
c.add(controlpanel, BorderLayout.EAST);
```

We have used BorderLayout in the following examples:

```
Ch04\Ramblecs\Ramblecs.java
Ch04\Exercises\Welcome.java
Ch06\Poll\Poll.java
Ch06\Ramblecs\ControlPanel.java
Ch06\Exercises\Bmi.java
Ch07\Craps2\Craps.java
Ch07\Exercises\Wages.java
Ch08\SnackBar\SnackBar.java
Ch14\Exercises\Boxes.java
```

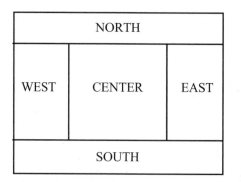

Figure 15-4. The border layout

Box Layout

`BoxLayout` can be used with panels, but it is usually used with boxes, in which it is the default layout. You can create a `Box` container using a constructor with one `int` argument with the value `BoxLayout.X_AXIS` or `BoxLayout.Y_AXIS`. For some reason, there are also two static methods `Box.createHorizontalBox()` and `Box.createVerticalBox()` that return a reference to a new box, and it is common to use them instead of the constructors. In general, the idiom for working with boxes is different: it relies more on `Box`'s static methods.

The "horizontal" and "vertical" boxes are not defined by their dimensions but rather by how components are placed in them. In a horizontal box, components are added left to right. Stretchable components, such as panels, take the full height of the box. You can also add a horizontal "strut," an invisible spacer that inserts a fixed amount of space between components. For example:

```
Box b = Box.createHorizontalBox();
b.add(...);  // add a component
b.add(Box.createHorizontalSrtrut(10)); // unused space, 10 pixels
b.add(...);  // add another component
< ... etc. >
```

In a vertical box, components are added starting from the top and fill the whole width if they can. For a vertical box you can add a vertical "strut" If you add a horizontal strut to a vertical box, it will set the minimum width of the box. We have used both horizontal and vertical boxes in:

```
Ch08\SnackBar\SnackBar.java
Ch08\SnackBar\VendingMachine.java
```

15.6 Summary

The Java 2 specification includes the `javax.swing` package, which has introduced a new, platform-independent implementation of GUI components. Swing components have their own "look and feel," which is known as the "metal" look and feel. However, a programmer can opt for a "native" look and feel (one that looks like *Windows*, or Mac *OS* or *UNIX Motif*) using Swing's pluggable look and feel feature. Appendix C presents a synopsis of several Swing GUI components and an index of their use in the case studies, labs, and exercises in previous chapters.

Events generated by Swing components are captured by different event "listeners." Most components generate "action events" that can be captured by the `actionPerformed` method of an "action listener." `JToggleButton`, `JCheckBox`,

JRadioButton, and JComboBox components also generate "item events" that can be captured by the itemStateChanged method of an "item listener." JSlider components generate "change events" that can be captured by the stateChanged method of a "change listener." An event listener is an object that can be added to a Swing component by calling its addActionListener, addItemListener, or addChangeListener method. An object that creates a component can also be its event listener, in which case the argument to the component's add<Whatever>Listener method is this.

To add a menu bar (a JMenuBar object) to an applet or application, call its setMenuBar method. You can add JMenu objects to the program's menu bar and JMenuItems, JCheckBoxMenuItems, JRadioButtonMenuItems, or JMenus (submenus) to any JMenu. You can split a menu into groups of items by calling JMenu's addSeparator method. To make the menu work, add "action listeners" to JMenuItems, checkboxes and radiobuttons.

Swing components are added to **containers** with the help of **layout managers**. One container is the main window's "content pane." To obtain a reference to it, call JApplet's or JFrame's getContentPane method. Its default layout manager has the BorderLayout type. Examples of other containers are boxes (objects of the Box class) and panels (objects of the JPanel class). For boxes, the default layout manager type is BoxLayout; for panels, FlowLayout. You can choose a different layout by calling the container's setLayout method.

In FlowLayout, components are added in one row as long as they fit, then in the next row, and so on. Components are reasonably spaced and can be centered (default), right aligned, or left aligned. In GridLayout, components are placed on a rectangular grid that covers the container's area and has all cells of the same size. You can specify horizontal and vertical gaps between the cells. Components are added starting at the upper left corner of the grid and filling the first row, then the next row, and so on. BorderLayout can accommodate up to five components, one for each of the five regions: north, south, east, west, and center. In BoxLayout, components fill a horizontal or vertical box. In a horizontal box, components are placed left to right, each filling the entire height of the box. In a vertical box, components are placed top to bottom, each filling the entire width of the box.

In all layouts, a component can be a panel or a box with its own components in it. There is no easy uniform way of placing components in Java, and one has to resort to a bag of tricks to get the layout right.

Exercises

1. For the following Swing GUI components in column one, mark the listeners from column two and "status accessors" from column three that are commonly used with them. ✓

    (a) JPanel   < *none* >   < *none* >
    (b) JLabel   ActionListener   isSelected
    (c) JButton   ItemListener   getSelectedIndex
    (d) JCheckBox   ChangeListener   getSelectedItem
    (e) JRadioButton   getText
    (f) JComboBox   getValue
    (g) JTextField
    (h) JSlider
    (i) JMenuItem

2. Mark true or false and explain:

    (a) An object's `actionPerformed` method can be called directly in the program by other methods. _____ ✓

    (b) The same object can serve as action listener for one component and item listener for another component. _____ ✓

    (c) A button can have several different action listeners attached to it. _____ ✓

    (d) An object can serve as its own action listener. _____

3. (a) In the `Boxes` applet (`Ch14\Exercises\Boxes.java` 🖫) from Question 6 in Chapter 14 (page 393), add a menu bar with only one menu of two items: "Increase size" and "Decrease size." When clicked, these items should increase or decrease the current size of the box by 10%. Modify the `BoxDrawer` class to support this functionality.

    (b) Unite the `rounded` and `threeD` checkboxes in one group (a `ButtonGroup` object), so that they cannot be both selected at the same time. Usually such groups are used with radiobuttons (see Appendix C), but they can work for checkboxes as well.

4.■ Write an applet that serves as a GUI front end for the code you created for Question 11 in Chapter 6 (page 167), the quadratic formula.

5.■ Rewrite the `MakeDictionary` program (Ch13\Dictionary\MakeDictionary.java 🖫) as a GUI application. Provide a field for entering the file name or learn about the `JFileChooser` class and use it for choosing the input file. Add two fields for entering the minimum and maximum lengths of words that you want to select. ⸘ Hint: use the following "empty" application (Ch15\Exercises\Nothing.java 🖫) as a starting point:

```
< ... import statements >

public class Nothing extends JFrame
{
  public Nothing()
  {
    super("An empty application");
    Container c = getContentPane();
    c.setBackground(Color.white);
  }

  public static void main(String[] args)
  {
    Nothing w = new Nothing();
    w.addWindowListener(new ExitButtonListener());
    w.setSize(200, 200);
    w.show();
  }
}
```

6.■ Write an applet that adds several "large integers" as described in Question 24 for Chapter 11 (page 320).

7.■ Rewrite the *Mad Libs* program described in Question 10 for Chapter 13 (page 369) as a GUI application. ⸘ Hint: use a `JTextArea` component to display the final text. ⸘

8.■   (a)   Create the following GUI layout:

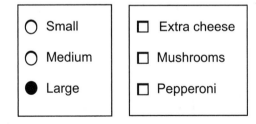

ફ Hint: put all the radiobuttons into a panel and all the checkboxes into another panel, each with a 3 by 1 grid layout. Add a border to each panel by calling its setBorder method. For example:

```
import javax.swing.border.*;
< ... other statements >
    CompoundBorder border = new CompoundBorder(
        new LineBorder(Color.black, 1),
        new EmptyBorder(6, 6, 6, 6));
    // outside: black, 1 pixel thick
    // inside: empty, 6 pixels on
    //    top, left, bottom, right

    panel.setBorder(border);
```

Put both panels into a horizontal box with struts between them and on the left and right sides. Unite the radiobuttons into a group (see Appendix C). ફ ✓

(b)   Add a JToggleButton "To Go" to the right, initially set to "false." ✓

9.◆   Create the following GUI layout:

≷ Hint: Put the two labels on a panel with a 2 by 1 grid layout. Use right-justified labels `JLabel(<text>, null, SwingConstants.RIGHT)`. (Instead of `null` you can put an icon showing the flag or an emblem of a country that speaks the language.) Put input fields on another 2 by 1 panel. Put both panels into a horizontal box with a strut between them; put this box and the "Translate" button into a vertical box with struts around them. This is only one way of doing it. ≷

10.◆   Create a *Keypad* applet. This applet class can serve as a basis for calculators of different models. First run a compiled version (`Ch15\Exercises\TestKeypad.html` ▣). The applet consists of two classes: `Keypad` and `DigitalDisplay`. `Keypad` is the applet class. Its `init` method creates an object `display` of the `DigitalDisplay` type. Write a class `DigitalDisplay` by extending `JTextField`. Make `DigitalDisplay` implement `ActionListener` and make `display` serve as an action listener for all the buttons. The "C" button clears the display; any other button appends the text from the button to the current display text. For example:

```
JButton b = (JButton)e.getSource();
String str = b.getText();
< ... etc. >
```

Let `display`'s constructor configure the display: dark green background (e.g., RGB 50, 200, 50), white or yellow foreground. Make it non-editable to prevent extraneous keyboard input. Set text alignment to the right:

```
setHorizontalAlignment(RIGHT);
```

Continued ⇨

Set the preferred size of the display in the applet and add an empty border on the left and right to make it look better. For example:

```
import javax.swing.border.*;
< ... etc. >

    display.setPreferredSize(new Dimension(width, width/6));
    display.setBorder(new EmptyBorder(0, 10, 0, 10));
                                // top left bottom right
```

Also set `display`'s font to a fairly large fixed-pitch font (in proportion to `width`). Is it a good idea to set display's size, border, and font in `DigitalDisplay`'s constructor? Explain.

In the `Keypad` class, place all the buttons on a 4 by 3 grid on a panel with some space between them. Add the `display` field above the buttons. ⸘ Hint: place the display and the buttons panel into a vertical box. You can add the box directly to the content pane or you can add it to a panel with a border, as we did. ⸘

Chapter

Mouse, Keyboard, Sounds, and Images

16.1 Prologue

Java's VM (virtual machine) has a "virtual" mouse that rolls on an *x-y* plane and uses one button. Mouse coordinates are actually graphics coordinates of the mouse cursor; they are in pixels and they are relative to the upper left corner of the component that captures mouse events. Mouse events can be captured by any object designated as a `MouseListener` (i.e. that belongs to a class that implements `MouseListener` interface).

Keyboard events can be captured by any object designated as a `KeyListener`. Handling keyboard events in an object-oriented application is complicated by the fact that a computer has only one keyboard and different objects need to listen to it at different times. There is a fairly complicated system of passing the *focus* (the primary responsibility for processing keyboard events) from one component to another and of passing keyboard events from nested components up to their "parents." Handling mouse events is easier than handling keyboard events because the concept of "focus" does not apply.

In this chapter we will discuss the technical details of handling the mouse and the keyboard in a Java applet or a GUI application. We will also learn how to load and play audio clips and how to display images and icons.

16.2 Mouse Events Handling

The `MouseListener` interface defines five methods: `mousePressed`, `mouseReleased`, `mouseClicked`, `mouseEntered`, and `mouseExited`. Each of these methods receives one argument, a `MouseEvent e`. `e.getX()` and `e.getY()` return the *x* and *y* coordinates of the event, relative to the upper left corner of the object (usually a panel) whose listener captures the event. You add a mouse listener to a panel by calling the panel's `addMouseListener` method. It is often convenient to make a panel its own mouse listener. To do that, the panel's constructor can call `addMouseListener(this)`. You have a simple example of how to use a mouse listener in `Ch14\Puzzle\Puzzle.java` 🖫.

A class that implements the `MouseMotionListener` interface adds `mouseMoved` and `mouseDragged` methods for processing events that report changes in the mouse coordinates without a change in the button state. These methods are usually used together with `MouseListener` methods. `mouseMoved` is called when the mouse is moved with its button up; `mouseDragged` is called when the mouse is moved with its button held down.

❖   ❖   ❖

Implementing an interface in Java requires the programmer to implement each method in the interface, even those that are never used. In our *Puzzle* applet, for example, only the `mouseClicked` method of the mouse listener interface is used — the remaining four are empty. To eliminate these empty methods, Java designers came up with **adapter classes**, which implement <u>all</u> interface methods as empty methods. Then a programmer can extend the adapter class, overriding only the methods he or she needs. Often this is done using **inline** classes. For example, the following code adds a mouse listener to an object:

```
public class MyPanel extends JPanel
{
  public MyPanel() // constructor
  {
    ...
    addMouseListener
    (
      new MouseAdapter()
      {
        public void mouseClicked(MouseEvent e)
        {
          ... // process click at e.getX(), e.getY()
        }
      }
    );  // Yes, these are parentheses, not braces!
    ...
  }
}
```

(In an inline class, the definition of the whole class is written as an argument to the `addMouseListener` method and goes inside parentheses.) Unfortunately, adapter classes undo the discipline of interfaces. If, for instance, you accidentally type `mouselicked` instead of `mouseClicked`, the code will compile but events won't be processed.

16.3 Keyboard Events Handling

Any object, designated as a `KeyListener` can capture keyboard events. But first it must request *focus* — the responsibility for handling the keyboard events. At different times different GUI components obtain focus. Some GUI components, such as buttons or text field objects, receive the focus automatically when they are clicked.

Other types of objects you have to explicitly activate in your program by passing the focus to them. A `JPanel` component, for instance, does not get the focus automatically. So our `controlpanel` object in *Ramblecs* will never "hear" any keystrokes unless we call its `requestFocus` method.

When you click a button in your application, Swing automatically shifts keyboard focus to that button because the spacebar on the keyboard is normally programmed to click the button. If you want another component to get the focus back, the button's action listener's `actionPerformed` method has to call that other component's `requestFocus`. For example:

```
// ControlPanel.java
// =================
  /**
   *  Processes Go button events.
   *  Toggles the button between "Go" and "Stop" states
   */
  public void actionPerformed(ActionEvent e)
  {
    < ... other statements >

    requestFocus(); // tells control panel to listen to keystrokes
  }
```

In this example, `controlpanel` is the "Go" button's action listener. `controlpanel` is also a `KeyListener` — it captures keyboard commands that move and spin the falling cube. When the "Go" button is clicked, Swing automatically passes keyboard focus to it. In its last statement, `actionPerformed` returns the focus back to `controlpanel`.

As we have seen in the example in `Ch11\Ramblecs\ControlPanel.java`, an object that wants to process keyboard events must have a "key listener" object attached to it. Call the object's `addKeyListener` method to attach a key listener to it. A "key listener" can be another object, or an object can be its own key listener. In *Ramblecs*, for example, `controlpanel`'s constructor calls

```
addKeyListener(this);
```

making `controlpanel` its own key listener.

A "key listener" object must belong to a class that implements the `KeyListener` interface. This class must have three public `void` methods: `keyPressed`, `keyReleased`, and `keyTyped`. Each of these methods receives one argument, `KeyEvent e`. In the *Ramblecs* applet, control panel is its own key listener and the `ControlPanel` class implements the `KeyListener` interface.

The `KeyEvent` class distinguishes "character keys," such as letters, digits, and so on, from "action keys," such as cursor keys, function keys, `<Enter>`, and so on. Action keys do not have characters associated with them. These keys are identified by their "virtual codes." These virtual codes are defined as static `int` constants in the `KeyEvent` class. Table 16-1 shows the names of several commonly used action keys. The `VK` prefix stands for "virtual key." For instance, `KeyEvent.VK_LEFT` refers to the left-arrow cursor key.

`VK_F1` through `VK_F24`	Function keys
`VK_LEFT, VK_RIGHT,` `VK_UP, VK_DOWN`	Cursor arrow keys
`VK_KP_LEFT, VK_KP_RIGHT,` `VK_KP_UP, VK_KP_DOWN`	Cursor arrow keys on the numeric keypad
`VK_HOME, VK_END,` `VK_PAGE_UP, VK_PAGE_DOWN,` etc.	As implied by the names

Table 16-1. `KeyEvent`'s symbolic constants for virtual keys

The relationships between what happens on the keyboard, what methods are called in response, and what is passed to them in the `KeyEvent` are rather convoluted. For instance, if you press the shift key and then 'a', then release 'a' and release shift, this will result in two calls to `keyPressed`, two calls to `keyReleased`, and one call to `keyTyped`.

To keep things simple, use the `keyTyped` method to capture characters and use either the `keyPressed` or `keyReleased` method to capture action keys. Pressing an action key does not call the `keyTyped` method.

In the `keyTyped` method, `e.getKeyChar()` returns the typed character. In the `keyPressed` and `keyReleased` methods, `e.getKeyCode()` returns the virtual code.

A `KeyEvent` object also has the `boolean` methods `isShiftDown`, `isAltDown`, and `isControlDown` that return `true` if the respective "modifier" key was held down when the key event occurred.

❖   ❖   ❖

A more general `getModifiers` method returns an integer whose individual bits, when set, represent the pressed modifier keys: `Shift`, `Ctrl`, `Alt`, and so on. These bits can be tested by using bit masks defined as static constants in `KeyEvent`.

Let's take this opportunity to review the use of Java's bit-wise logical operators. For example, we would use the bit-wise "and" operator to test whether a particular bit is set in an integer:

```
if ((e.getModifiers() & KeyEvent.ALT_MASK) != 0)
   // if ALT is down ...
```

Here `&` is bit-wise "and." A bit in the result is set to 1 if <u>both</u> corresponding bits in the operands are 1. `KeyEvent.ALT_MASK` is an integer constant with only one bit set in it. The condition tests whether this bit is also set in the value returned by `getModifiers` (Figure 16-1).

```
getModifiers()       0010...0011001
                   &
KeyEvent.ALT_MASK    0000...0001000
                     =============
                     0000...0001000
```

Figure 16-1. `&` operator used to test a particular bit in an integer

You can use a combined mask to test whether two modifier keys are held down at once. For example:

```
int mask = KeyEvent.SHIFT_MASK | KeyEvent.CTRL_MASK;
```

Here `|` is the bit-wise "or" operator: a bit in the result is set to 1 if <u>at least one</u> of the corresponding bits in the operands is 1. So the above statement sets both `Shift` and `Ctrl` bits in `mask` (Figure 16-2). Then

```
if ((e.getModifiers() & mask) == mask)
```

tests whether the two bits "cut out" by `mask` from the value returned by `getModifiers` are both set (Figure 16-3).

Be very careful not to misuse bit-wise operators in `boolean` expressions. They are allowed, but they don't follow short-circuit evaluation rules.

```
KeyEvent.SHIFT_MASK  |  0000...0000001
KeyEvent.CTRL_MASK      0000...0000010
                        ==============
                        0000...0000011
```

Figure 16-2. | operator used to combine bits in two integers

```
getModifiers()   &  0010...0010110
mask                0000...0000011
                    ==============
getModifiers() & mask  0000...0000010
```

Figure 16-3. & operator used to "cut out" mask bits from an integer

16.4 *Case Study and Lab: Drawing Editor*

In this lab we will create a *Drawing Editor* applet in which the user can add several filled circles of different colors and sizes to the picture and drag and stretch or squeeze them with the mouse or cursor keys. The applet's "control panel" has two buttons: one for choosing a color, another for adding a "balloon" (a filled circle) to the picture. The user can "grab" any balloon by pressing and holding the mouse on it. The grabbed balloon changes from a solid (filled) shape to the outline only. If the user grabbed the balloon somewhere inside it, then he can drag it with the mouse to a new location (while its size remains unchanged); if the user grabbed the balloon in the vicinity of its border, then he can stretch or squeeze the balloon while its center remains in the same location. When the mouse button is released, the balloon goes back to the solid shape.

The last balloon added or "grabbed" becomes the "active balloon." The user can move it using cursor (arrow) keys and stretch or squeeze it using the up/down cursor keys with the `Ctrl` key held down.

Run the applet to see how it all works. Use the `TestDraw.html` 🖫 and compiled Java classes in the `Ch16\RunDraw` folder.

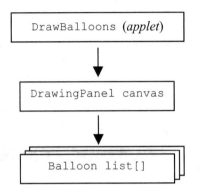

Figure 16-4. Classes and objects in the *Drawing Editor* applet

The applet consists of three classes (Figure 16-4): `DrawBalloons` (derived from `JApplet`) represents the applet, `DrawingPanel` (derived from `JPanel`) represents the canvas on which balloons are drawn, and `Balloon` represents balloon objects.

In the previous labs, we provided the GUI and "front-end" classes while you implemented the "back end" — the details of arithmetic or logic. Here we'll switch roles: we provide the lower-level `Balloon` class and your task is to write the "front end" — the `DrawBalloons` and `DrawingPanel` classes. You will be a "client" of the `Balloon` class: while you are welcome to look at its code at your leisure, for this lab you only need to have the documentation for its constructors and public methods. These are summarized in Table 16-2.

Constructor:	
`Balloon(int x, int y,` `        int radius, Color color)`	Creates a balloon with the center at (x,y) with the specified radius and color.
Methods:	
`int getX()`	Returns the x-coordinate of the center.
`int getY()`	Returns the y-coordinate of the center.
`int getRadius()`	Returns the radius.
`int distance(int x, int y)`	Returns the distance from the point (x, y) to the center of this balloon (rounded to an integer).
`void move(int x, int y)`	Moves the center of this balloon to (x, y).
`void setRadius(int r)`	Sets the radius of this balloon to r.
`boolean isInside(int x, int y)`	Returns `true` if the point (x, y) lies inside this balloon (and not on the border), `false` otherwise.
`boolean isOnBorder(int x, int y)`	Returns `true` if the point (x, y) lies approximately on the border of this balloon, `false` otherwise.
`void draw(Graphics g,` `          boolean filled)`	Draws this balloon. Draws a filled circle if `filled` is `true`, and a hollow circle otherwise.

Table 16-2. Class `Balloon`: the constructor and public methods

The `DrawBalloons` class configures the applet's window: it places the "canvas" in the center and a control panel with "Set color" and "Add balloon" buttons at the bottom. The class `DrawingPanel` describes an object `canvas` where all the action takes place. The `DrawingPanel` class extends `JPanel` and implements `MouseListener`, `MouseMotionListener`, and `KeyListener`. The main applet creates one object, `canvas`, of the type `DrawingPanel`; `canvas`'s constructor makes it its own listener for all the mouse and keyboard events.

We suggest the following steps for writing and testing this applet:

1. Start with a very simple applet without buttons and a very simple `canvas` object. Make `canvas`'s constructor create just one blue balloon of a reasonable size and make `canvas`'s `paintComponent` method call this balloon's `draw` method.

2. Add code to make `canvas` its own mouse listener and implement the `mousePressed` and `mouseReleased` methods so that the balloon changes into a hollow circle (outline only) when the mouse is clicked inside it, and changes back into a solid circle when the mouse is released. (Here a "click" means a "mouse pressed" event.) You might need a `boolean` field `picked` to mark that the balloon is selected (i.e., the mouse button is down) and a statement that checks the value of this field in the `paintComponent` method.

3. Make `canvas` a mouse motion listener as well, and add code to drag the balloon when the balloon is "picked" and the mouse is dragged. In `canvas`'s constructor call `addMouseMotionListener(this)` to make canvas its own mouse motion listener.

    The secret for smooth dragging action is to keep the *x-y* offsets from the current mouse position to the current balloon's center constant as the mouse moves. Save these offsets when the mouse button is first pressed down, then set the balloon's coordinates in `mouseDragged` so that these offsets remain the same.

4. If the initial click happens in the vicinity of the border of the balloon (i.e., `isOnBorder(x,y)` returns `true`), then instead of dragging the balloon make the mouse motion stretch or squeeze it. You might need a `boolean` field in `canvas` to mark whether you will be moving or stretching the picked balloon.

    The same principle as for moving applies for smooth stretching action, only this time the distance from the current mouse position to the balloon's <u>border</u> must remain constant. (This distance is equal to the distance from the balloon's center, returned by `balloon.distance(x,y)` minus the balloon's radius.)

5. Modify the `DrawingPanel` class to support a list of balloons. Keep the list in an array of a fixed maximum size. For example:

    ```
    private final int maxBalloons = 20;
    private int numBalloons = 0;
    private Balloon list[];
    < ... etc. >
    list = new Balloon[maxBalloons];
    ```

Start with an empty list and provide an `addBalloon` method to add a balloon of random color and size to the list if there is room. Balloons in the drawing may overlap. If that's the case, the new balloon should be shown on top of other balloons, so add it at the end of the list if you draw the list starting from the beginning. Don't forget to call `repaint` after adding each balloon. Add a control panel with the "Add balloon" button on it to the applet's content pane. Make the applet the action listener for the "Add balloon" button and make its `actionPerformed` method call `canvas.addBalloon()`.

When the mouse is pressed on balloons, make sure it selects the <u>topmost</u> balloon that contains the coordinates of the click. (You need to scan the list from the end <u>backwards</u> to achieve that.)

Add code to keep track of the "active balloon." This is the balloon that was last created or touched with the mouse. Change `canvas`'s `paintComponent` method to draw the whole list. Note that if the active balloon is picked (mouse button is down), it has to be drawn separately as the outline only, on top of other balloons.

6. Enable cursor keys to move the "active balloon" and to stretch or squeeze it with up / down arrow cursor keys when the `Ctrl` key is held down.

7. Learn about the `JColorChooser` class from the "How to Use Color Choosers" section in Sun's *Java Tutorial*. Its static method `showDialog` is really easy to use. For example:

```
public void pickColor()
{
  Color pickedColor = JColorChooser.showDialog(this,
                                "Pick a color", color);
  if (pickedColor != null) // if user didn't click "Cancel"
    color = pickedColor;
}
```

Add a "Set color" button to the applet's control panel. Keep this button's background color the same as the current drawing color. (You need to add an accessor method `getColor` to the `DrawingPanel` class to achieve that.)

8. Thoroughly test all the mouse and keyboard action in your applet.

9. Consider what it would take to support balloons of two different shapes.

16.5 *Lab: Ramblecs* Keyboard Support

We have already implemented the `<Enter>` and spacebar keys in *Ramblecs*'s `ControlPanel` class. Now let's add action to all four cursor keys (also duplicated on the four arrow keys of the numeric pad). Make the left and right arrows move the falling cube, if there is room, left or right by the distance of its size (which corresponds to one column in the letter grid). Make the up and down arrow keys "rotate" the cube.

Left and right movement

You need to add `moveLeft` and `moveRight` methods to the `FallingCube` class. Your code must take into account the borders of the grid and also its current configuration, so that a cube does not bump into cubes that have landed earlier. For example:

```
// FallingCube.java
public boolean moveLeft()
{
  int row = (cubeY + cubeSize) / cubeSize;
  int col = cubeX / cubeSize;
  if (row >= 0 && row < grid.numRows() &&
      col >= 1 && grid.isEmpty(row, col - 1))
  {
    cubeX -= cubeSize;
    return true;
  }
  else
  {
    return false;
  }
}
```

You also need to add `moveLeft` and `moveRight` methods to `whiteboard`. These methods simply call `cube.moveLeft` and `cube.moveRight` respectively and, if necessary, `repaint`. For example:

```
// LetterPanel.java
public void moveLeft()
{
  if (cube.moveLeft())
    repaint();
}
```

`whiteboard`'s `moveLeft` and `moveRight` methods should be called from `ControlPanel`'s `keyPressed` method when a left or right arrow key is pressed.

Rotation

The cube's rotations are "virtual" rotations — they simply cycle through all six letters on the cube in one or another direction. It is time to replace `char randomLetter` in the `FallingCube` class with a `randomLetters` array of six `char`s filled with random letters, one for each face of the cube. To keep things simple we can just rotate the whole array, left or right, and display `randomLetters[0]` on the cube. Borrow the code from the `rotateLeft` and `rotateRight` methods you implemented in the lab in Section 12.5 and adapt it to rotate the `randomLetters` array.

You also need to add a method or methods to `whiteboard` to rotate the cube. Let's use one method, `rotateCube`, with one integer argument: `rotateCube(1)` rotates the cube in one direction and `rotateCube(-1)` rotates it in another direction. For example:

```
// LetterPanel.java
public void rotateCube(int dir)
{
  if (dir < 0)
    cube.rotateLeft();
  else
    cube.rotateRight();
  repaint();
}
```

`ControlPanel`'s `keyPressed` method should call `whiteboard`'s `rotateCube` with an appropriate argument.

Other enhancements

While you are working with the `FallingCube` class, change the frequencies with which letters are likely to show up. Use for example the same frequencies as in *SCRABBLE*® (see page 345). Hint: One simple way to change the odds for selecting different letters is to make the string `letters` longer, adding multiple copies of different characters according to the desired odds.

For "extra credit" enable the `Ctrl-F` key to increase the speed (say, by 25) and the `Ctrl-S` key to decrease the speed. Basically all you have to do is set a new value for `speedSlider` — the rest happens automatically.

16.6 Sounds and Images

An applet's or application's `getAudioClip` method can be used to load an audio file into your program. The file can be a `.wav` file; some other popular formats (`.au`, `.mid`, etc.) are supported, too. The file is actually loaded only when your program attempts to play it for the first time.

You need to import Java's `AudioClip` class to use this method:

```
import java.applet.AudioClip;
```

One overloaded form of the `getAudioClip` method takes one argument: the URL (or pathname) of a file. The URL must be an <u>absolute</u> URL. Use the <u>forward</u> slash to separate directories in the string that represents a path — it works on all systems.

A more convenient form of `getAudioClip` takes two arguments: the path and file names separately. In this form, you can use as the first argument the string returned by the applet's method `getDocumentBase()`, which returns the path of the HTML file that runs the applet. The second argument is usually a literal string, the file name. For example:

```
AudioClip bells;

< ... other code >

bells = getAudioClip(getDocumentBase(), "bells.wav");
```

Alternatively, you can use as the first argument `getCodeBase()`, which returns the URL or path of the applet's compiled code.

Once loaded, the clip can be played using its `play` method. For example:

```
...
bells.play();
```

We have already played audio clips in *Puzzle* (Section 14.7), *Ramblecs*, and other applets.

❖   ❖   ❖

Java has two types of objects that represent images: `Image` and `ImageIcon`. Either of these objects can be created by loading a picture from an image file. The two most common formats for image files are `.gif` (***Graphics Interchange Format***, pronounced "giff") and `.jpg` (***Joint Photographic Experts Group***, pronounced "jay-peg") format.

You can use an applet's `getImage` method to load an `Image`. This method is analogous to the `getAudioClip` method discussed above. There are two forms of `getImage` that take the same kinds of arguments as `getAudioClip`: the absolute URL (or pathname) of a file, or a path and a file name as two separate arguments. In the latter form, the first argument is often `getDocumentBase()`.

The image file is actually loaded only when your program attempts to show it for the first time. You need to import Java's `awt` package or the `awt.Image` class to use `getImage`.

You display an `image` object by calling `drawImage` from any `paint` or `paintComponent` method. For example:

```
import java.awt.*;
import javax.swing.*;

public class ImageTest extends JApplet
{
  private Image picture;

  public void init()
  {
    picture = getImage(getDocumentBase(), "wintertrack.jpg");
    if (picture == null)
    {
      System.out.println("Can't load wintertrack.jpg");
    }
  }

  public void paint(Graphics g)
  {
    int x = 5, y = 10;
    if (picture != null)
    {
      g.drawImage(picture, x, y, this);
    }
  }
}
```

In the `drawImage` call, the first argument is a reference to the image; the second and third are the *x* and *y* coordinates of the upper left corner of the displayed image, relative to the applet or panel on which it is drawn; and the fourth is a reference to an `ImageObserver` object, usually `this`.

❖   ❖   ❖

Another way to load and show images uses the `ImageIcon` class defined in the Swing package. An `ImageIcon` object can be constructed directly from a file or a relative URL. For example:

```
ImageIcon coin = new ImageIcon("coin.gif");
```

In this example, the `coin.gif` file is located in the same folder as the applet's code.

An `ImageIcon` can be also constructed from an `Image` object. For example:

```
private Image coinImage;
< ... load this image, etc. >
ImageIcon coin = new ImageIcon(coinImage);
```

You can display an `ImageIcon` object by calling its `paintIcon` method from any `paint` or `paintComponent` method. For example:

```
import java.awt.*;
import javax.swing.*;

public class IconTest extends JApplet
{
  private ImageIcon coin;

  public void init()
  {
    coin = new ImageIcon("coin.gif");
  }

  public void paint(Graphics g)
  {
    int x = 5, y = 10;
    coin.paintIcon(this, g, x, y);
  }
}
```

In the `coin.paintIcon` call, the first argument is a reference to the component on which the icon is displayed; the second is a reference to `Graphics`; and the third and fourth are the *x* and *y* coordinates of the upper left corner of the displayed image, relative to the applet or panel on which it is drawn.

Many Swing classes, such as `JButton`, `JLabel`, `JCheckBox`, `JRadioButton`, have convenient constructors and methods that allow you to add icons to these components (see Appendix C).

16.7 Summary

Mouse events on a component can be captured and processed by a "mouse listener" object attached to that component. A mouse listener is added to a component (usually a panel) by calling its `addMouseListener` method. It is not uncommon for a panel to be its own mouse listener. A class that implements a mouse listener interface must have five methods: `mousePressed`, `mouseReleased`, and `mouseClicked`, called upon the corresponding button action, and `mouseEntered` and `mouseExited`, called when the mouse cursor enters or leaves the component. Each of these methods takes one argument, a `MouseEvent e`. `e.getX()` and `e.getY()` return the *x* and *y* coordinates of the event in pixels, relative to the upper left corner of the panel whose listener captures it.

For more detailed mouse tracking you can use a "mouse motion listener" which adds two more methods, `mouseMoved` and `mouseDragged`. These methods are called when the mouse moves with the button up or down, respectively.

Adapter classes allow a programmer to supply only those listener methods that the program actually uses, inheriting the other (empty) methods from the adapter class.

Keyboard events can be captured and processed by a "key listener" object: an object of a class that implements the `keyPressed`, `keyReleased`, and `keyTyped` methods. You add a key listener to a component by calling its `addKeyListener` method. An object can be its own key listener, in which case the argument to `addKeyListener` is `this`. A component must obtain "focus" (by calling the `requestFocus` method) to enable processing of keyboard events.

The `keyPressed` and `keyReleased` methods are used to process "action" keys (e.g., `<Enter>`, "Left Arrow," and "Home"). The `keyTyped` method is called for "typed" keys that represent a character. Each of these methods takes one argument of the `KeyEvent` type. `KeyEvent`'s `getKeyCode` method returns the virtual code of the key, such as `VK_ENTER`, `VK_LEFT`, `VK_HOME`, and so on. `KeyEvent`'s `getKeyChar` returns the typed character. For example, `Shift+'a'` triggers a call to `keyTyped` and `e.getKeyChar` returns `'A'`. `KeyEvent`'s boolean methods `isShiftDown`, `isControlDown`, `isAltDown` return `true` if the corresponding modifier key, `Shift`, `Ctrl`, `Alt`, was held down when the event occurred. The `getModifiers` method returns an integer that holds a combination of bits representing the pressed modifier keys. `KeyEvent` has static constants defined for different modifier bits: `KeyEvent.SHIFT`, `KeyEvent.CTRL`, and so on.

You can load an audio file (a .wav file or a file in one of several other popular formats) into your applet by calling the applet's getAudioClip method. To play it, call AudioClip's play method. For example:

```
import java.applet.AudioClip;
. . .
AudioClip bells = getAudioClip(getDocumentBase(), "bells.wav");
. . .
bells.play();
```

Similarly, an Image object can be loaded from a .gif or .jpg file by calling the applet's getImage method; to display it, call Graphics's drawImage method.

The ImageIcon class in Swing provides another way to represent an image in your program. ImageIcon's constructor loads an icon from a file, and ImageIcon's paintIcon method displays the image. An ImageIcon object can be added to any JLabel, JButton, JCheckBox, or JRadioButton object.

Exercises

1.   Write a *Four Seasons* applet that changes the background color (from white to green to dark green to gold to white again, etc.) each time a mouse is clicked on it. ⸵ Hints: (1) Increment an index into an array of colors with wraparound. (2) Don't forget to repaint after each click. ⸴ ✓

2.   Write a DrawingPanel class that extends JPanel and implements MouseListener. Redefine paintComponent to draw a filled circle or another shape. Make mousePressed change the shape's size or color when the mouse is pressed anywhere on the applet. Test your class with a simple applet that creates one DrawingPanel object and makes it its own mouse listener. ✓

3. Adapt the `DrawingPanel` class from Question 2 to draw polygons. Each time the mouse is pressed, add the coordinates to a list of points. ⸘ Hints: (1) Use `mousePressed`, not `mouseClicked`, because a mouse "click" (in the Java definition) requires that pressed and released locations be the same, so "clicks" do not always register. (2) It is easier to hold *x*- and *y*-coordinates in separate lists for the sake of the `drawPolyline` method. (3) Don't forget to repaint after adding a point to the list. ⸘

Consider a polygon finished when the number of points reaches some maximum number (e.g., 20) or when it has three or more points and the last one is close to (e.g., is within 5 pixels of) the first one. ⸘ Hint: Java's `Point` class has a static method

```
static double distance(int x1, int y1, int x2, int y2)
```

that returns the distance between the points (x_1, y_1) and (x_2, y_2), and a method

```
static double distanceSq(int x1, int y1, int x2, int y2)
```

that returns the squared distance. The latter is more efficient because it does not need to calculate a square root. ⸘

Draw an unfinished polygon as a polyline and a finished one as a filled polygon. Once a polygon is finished, mark that state and empty the list of points before starting a new polygon.

4. Modify the `Boxes` applet (`Ch14\Exercises\Boxes.java` ▤) from Question 6 in Chapter 14 (page 393) to make the `BoxDrawer` class implement `KeyListener`. Make `canvas` its own key listener. Make the cursor keys move the box and the cursor keys with the `Ctrl` key held down stretch or squeeze the box. ⸘ Hint: pass the focus to `canvas` in applet's `actionPerformed` method. ⸘

5. Write an applet that displays the name of the key when that key is pressed. ⸘ Hint: the `KeyEvent` class has a static method `getKeyText(int keyCode)` that returns a string that describes the key. ⸘

6. (a) Create an applet that shows a specified image in a panel added to its content pane. Take the image file name from a `<param>` tag and pass it to your panel's constructor. ✓

    (b) Change the applet to show four different images.

7.▪   Create an applet that shows a series of images as a "slide show." Add a combo box for choosing an image directly as well as "Next" and "Back" buttons (with appropriate icons on them) for going to the next or the previous slide. When the sequence reaches the end it should start over from the beginning. The same for the "Back" button: when the sequence reaches the beginning it should start over from the end. Place these controls on a control panel at the bottom and display the images on a separate panel located above the controls. Test your applet with a few image files.

```
public class Chapter17
    extends Chapter4
```

OOP Concepts and Object-Oriented Design

17.1 Prologue

Over the years, software development methodologies have followed the evolution of computer hardware and applications. At the dawn of the computer era, it was not at all obvious that software needed a design methodology! At that time, the top concerns in software design were the efficiency, economy, and reliability of programs: a good design meant a program that ran faster, used less memory, and did not crash.

As larger systems were developed it became important to define software specifications more formally. Corporations also had to face the huge costs of software maintenance: making modifications, adding features, fixing mistakes as they surfaced over time, and making programs run on upgraded systems. The focus shifted to formal system analysis techniques and to methodologies for writing more readable and better documented code. Structured programming gained prominence as one such methodology.

When inexpensive microprocessors and personal computers appeared, the criteria for well-designed software gradually changed again. As the speed of microprocessors started doubling roughly every two to three years and the price of memory dropped at roughly the same rate, major software vendors started anticipating faster and bigger hardware every year. They adopted the attitude that software efficiency and economy were no longer an issue. Faster hardware never failed to appear in time to accommodate the bulkier applications, packed with new features, that forced consumers to throw away their perfectly working but obsolete PCs and replace them with new ones every few years.

At the same time, a rapidly growing group of less technically savvy computer users demanded "user-friendly" GUI applications. And while software maintenance remained a priority, new priorities came to the fore: reducing software development time and cost through powerful "visual" (interactive) prototyping and development tools, team development, and reusable software components. Developing distributed client-server systems and platform-independent software on the Internet required new tools. Object-oriented programming is one attempt to answer those needs.

This chapter will review the more theoretical concepts of object-oriented software design and development methodology. You already have some idea of what OOP feels like; here we will sum it up and discuss the main OOP concepts in a more systematic way.

17.2 Objects as Independent Agents

OOP is based on several intertwined concepts that together produce a unique approach to programming. One of these concepts is ***event-driven computations***. The von Neumann computer architecture, with one CPU that controls all operations and has exclusive access to memory, imposes a particular view of programming: a program is thought of as a set of instructions to be performed in sequence. Research in artificial intelligence (or AI, a branch of computer science that strives to model intelligent systems and rational behaviors) and in cognitive science has drawn attention to models where many autonomous agents perform meaningful tasks by working together in parallel without rigid centralized control. Such models allow for the kind of parallelism and autonomy that scientists consider more typical of the cognitive activity in the human brain. In event-driven models, independent agents can communicate with each other by sending signals or messages. Many things can be taking place at the same time without synchronization of activities that do not have to be synchronized.

The event-driven computational model does not have to be implemented in hardware. Although research continues on various types of parallel computers and distributed systems, models based on active objects can run as simulations on conventional computers. One such model was implemented in the Simula programming language, developed in the mid-1960s (before Smalltalk) by Ole-Johan Dhal and Kristen Nygaard at the Norwegian Computing Center (NCC) in Oslo. This model perhaps pioneered the OOP approach. Other well-known and influential models for concurrent OOP computations are known as ***Actors*** models. They originate from the work of Carl Hewitt at the Massachusetts Institute of Technology's AI Laboratory in the early 1970s.

A more recent metaphor for a distributed system of active agents is the Internet itself. It has millions of independent users exchanging messages and data asynchronously and without any centralized control. Yet things get done. There are even examples of mathematical computations that would take too much time on a single computer but which are making progress with the work divided among a large number of volunteers on the Internet.★mersenne

In the OOP model, each agent, an active object, has its own memory and a set of methods that allow it to recognize and process certain types of messages. An object responds to a message by sending messages to other objects. An object can create other objects. Its memory can contain other objects. Different mechanisms for distributing messages can be included in the model. For example, messages can be directed to one specific object (somewhat like an e-mail message) or they can be broadcast to many objects at once (like newsgroups or e-mail lists). In the latter case, only those objects that can recognize a message and find it "relevant" respond to it. For example, Java's "key listeners" may intercept and process certain keyboard events while ignoring other events, leaving them to other components. This model is particularly suitable for event-driven applications, where messages can come not only from other objects in the same program but also from the operating system and from the "real world."

In Java, events handling is an important part of GUI development. We discussed different types of listeners for Swing components and for mouse and keyboard events in Chapters 15 and 16. As for other objects, sending messages to them is represented by direct calls to their methods. (Some people still occasionally say that a "message is passed" from one object to another.)

Parallelism in Java is implemented through **multithreading**, support for multiple threads of program execution. A **thread** is a part of the program that can run independently and "concurrently" with other parts. Threads can be synchronized at key points if necessary: one thread may have to wait for a certain signal from another thread to continue. For example, loading an image file into an applet launches a separate thread so the applet can keep running without waiting for the whole image to completely download. On a sequential computer, the "concurrency" of threads is simulated through **timeslicing**: allocating small segments of CPU time to each thread. The details of multithreading in Java are outside the scope of this book. Beyond Java, on a truly parallel computer, it is possible to envision a model in which each object has its own thread of execution.

17.3 *Case Study and Lab:* Actors' World

After a skiing trip, Kitty, Tommy, and Lizzy discovered that they had misplaced some of their gloves. Some of their hats were missing, too. It turns out nothing was lost: they had simply grabbed in a hurry some random items that didn't belong to them. Kitty ended up with three right gloves and one hat; Tommy got only one left glove; Lizzy got two left gloves and two hats. (They all wear the same type and size of gloves and hats.) But, thanks to e-mail, they were able to quickly figure out who got what and swap, so that each ended up with a complete set.

In this case study we will examine and experiment with the *Actors* applet, which simulates an event-driven world of "actors." Our actors will be implemented as objects of a class Actor. Each actor has "possessions": a number of items out of a small list of items. In this example we have three actors and three types of items. The `init` method in the `ActorsWorld` class (`ActorsWorld.java` 🖫 in the `Ch17\Actors` folder) initializes the actors:

```
public class ActorsWorld extends JApplet
{
  private static final int numItems = 3;
  ... < other fields >

  public void init()
  {
    < ...GUI setup >

    int possessions1[] = {0, 3, 1};
    int possessions2[] = {1, 0, 0};
    int possessions3[] = {2, 0, 2};
    Actor actors[] =
      { new Actor("Kitty", possessions1),
        new Actor("Tommy", possessions2),
        new Actor("Lizzy", possessions3) };

    <... etc.  See Ch17\Actors\ActorsWorld.java 🖫 >
  }
```

Each actor can send or receive messages, either privately to another actor, or to the whole list (all three actors). A message is an object of a class `Message` (`Ch17\Actors\Message.java` 🖫) and it has the following fields:

```
public class Message
{
  public Actor sender;
  public Actor recipient;
  public String subject;
  public int item;

  <... etc.  See Ch17\Actors\Message.java 🖫 >
}
```

If the `recipient` field is `null`, the message is intended for the whole list.

The subject of a message can be any `string`, but our actors recognize and react only to the following three subject lines:

> `"need"` — someone is missing a particular item;
> `"have"` — someone has an extra item;
> `"ship"` — someone is asking for a particular item to be sent over.

Polite as they are, our actors also send thank-you messages. But the protocol doesn't call for a "you are welcome" response — thank-you messages are sent but ignored by their recipients.

A message also has a `toString` method that converts it into a readable message, such as

```
From: Kitty
To: Tommy
Subject: ship LEFT GLOVE
```

Messages between actors do not have to be synchronized in any way. It is possible to envision a distributed computing environment in which our three actors would be implemented as three programs (or rather three copies of the same program) running on computers in different cities; the programs would be connected to e-mail so that they could send and receive messages automatically.

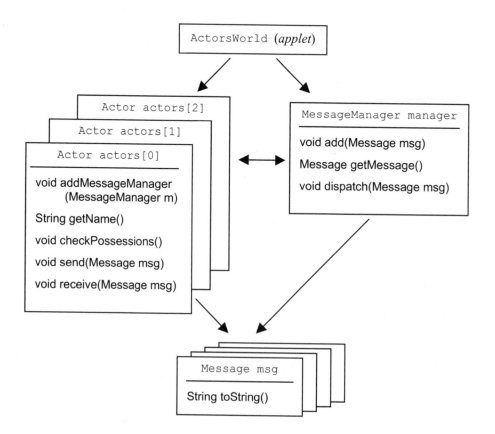

Figure 17-1. Classes, objects, and public methods in the *Actors* applet

When we run the program on one computer, however, we need a mechanism to simulate a distributed environment, some kind of a manager that handles dispatching of messages. The event-driven applets and applications we have seen so far also had event managers, but these were hidden from us. Events were handled by the operating system and by Java's run-time support code. All we had to do was supply different event listeners. Here we have made the event manager explicit so that you can see how it works. In fact our implementation here is conceptually not so far from what goes on behind the scenes in Java programs and other applications under GUI event-driven operating systems.

We have implemented the manager as an object of the `MessageManager` class (`Ch17\Actors\MessageManager.java` 🔖). A message manager maintains its own list of messages (not to be confused with the list of actors). It has three methods: `add`, `getMessage` and `dispatch`. The `add` method appends a message at the end of the list and the `getMessage` method removes and returns the first message in the list (or returns `null` if the list is empty). This type of a list, in which data is handled in the FIFO (First-In-First-Out) manner, is called a *queue*. We have used the Java library class `LinkedList` to implement a queue of messages. The `dispatch` method either sends a message to the specific recipient, or, if the recipient is `null`, to all actors.

Figure 17-1 summarizes the four classes of the *Actors* applet and their methods.

After the `ActorsWorld`'s `init` method has created the actors and a message manager, it notifies the actors who their manager is. This is analogous to signing them up for e-mail service or to adding a listener to an object in Java. Then the actors check their initial possessions. Each actor's `checkPossessions` method takes stock of what this actor has and announces to the list what items are still needed. This results in several messages added to the manager's queue. The rest of the exchanges are driven by one loop in the applet's `init` method (Figure 17-2). This loop simply gets the next message from the queue, displays it for the benefit of idle bystanders, like us, and then dispatches this message to its recipient(s) by calling the manager's `dispatch` method.

```
public void init()
{
    <... etc.   See Ch17\Actors\ActorsWorld.java 🖫 >

    MessageManager manager = new MessageManager(actors);
    actors[0].addMessageManager(manager);
    actors[1].addMessageManager(manager);
    actors[2].addMessageManager(manager);

    // All actors check their possessions and send messages about
    //   items they need:
    for (int k = 0; k < actors.length; k++)
      actors[k].checkPossessions();

    display.append("The following exchanges have taken place:\n\n");

    Message msg;
    while((msg = manager.getMessage()) != null)
    {
      display.append(msg.toString() + '\n');
      manager.dispatch(msg);
    }
    display.append("Everyone is all set\n");
}
```

Figure 17-2. `Ch17\Actors\ActorsWorld.java` 🖫

As a lab exercise, complete the following tasks:

1. Examine the code in the `Actor` class and supply the missing `receive` method. This method receives a message addressed to this actor and reacts to it either by sending a reply or by giving the specified item directly to the sender of the message. If the subject of the message is `"need"` (someone needs an item) and this actor has an extra one, it replies with a `"have"` message. If the subject is `"have"` and this actor needs this item, it replies with a `"ship"` message requesting that item. Finally, if the subject is `"ship"` and this actor still has this item available, it calls the sender's `take` method. Note that the "take" message is implemented as a direct call to the `take` method from one actor to another as opposed to sending a message because we want this message to be received instantaneously, at the same time when it is sent — like a courier delivery or another form of quick exchange. Otherwise we would have to keep track of who promised what to whom, which would make the program more complicated.

2. Run the applet, trace the order of exchanges, and verify that everyone ends up with a complete set of items.

3. In this application we have defined a precise protocol of exchanges. For example, an actor doesn't send a "have" message to someone until it receives a "need" request from that actor first. In these controlled exchanges messages can be handled asynchronously. In a truly parallel setup, actors can send their messages at any time, as long as they follow the protocol. In our sequential simulation, instead of always taking the first message from the list we could take and dispatch <u>any</u> message.

    Rewrite `MessageManager`'s `getMessage` method to take the <u>last</u> message from the list of messages instead of the <u>first</u> one. The FIFO method will become a LIFO (Last-In-First-Out) method. (Such a structure is called a *stack*.) ⸘ Hint: use `LinkedList`'s `removeLast` method, which is similar to `removeFirst`. ⸘ Trace all the exchanges again. The order may be different, but the final result should be the same: everyone ends up with a complete set of items.

4. Change `MessageManager`'s `getMessage` again, this time removing and returning a random message from the list. Use `LinkedList`'s `size()` method, which returns the number of elements in the list, and its `remove(n)` method, which removes and returns the *n*-th element. Make sure all actors are still able to recover their missing possessions.

17.4 Inheritance and Class Hierarchies

Another fundamental concept of OOP is *class hierarchies and inheritance*. This concept can also be traced to AI research: in particular, to studies of models for representing knowledge using hierarchical *taxonomies*. Taxonomy is a system of classification in which an object can be defined as a special case, "a kind of" another object. In Linnaeus' zoological taxonomy, for example, a person is a kind of primate which is a kind of mammal which is a kind of animal. Taxonomies have been one of the main ways of thinking in natural science for centuries, and they undoubtedly reflect an inclination of the human mind toward descriptive hierarchies.

In OOP all instances of a class have the same features: the same methods and the same fields. The <u>values</u> of fields may be different, of course, but their configuration is the same. An object with even slightly different methods or a different configuration of fields has to belong to a different class. Inheritance allows a programmer to define one class (called a *subclass* or a *derived class*) as an extension of another class (called a *superclass* or a *base class*).

> **Objects of the derived class** *inherit* **the methods and fields of the base class and may add a few of their own. A derived class can also redefine some of the methods of the base class.**

Thus a derived class usually offers a superset of the methods of a base class.

A derived class can in turn serve as the base class for another class, and so on. You can create an inheritance line in which a class inherits all the methods of all the classes above it. Figure 17-3 shows the derivation line for Swing's `JPasswordField` class. This class has a few of its own methods, such as `setEchoChar` and `getEchoChar`, that are specific to password entry, but it also inherits more than 300 methods from different "ancestors." Other inheritance lines may branch off at different levels, resulting in a tree that represents an inheritance hierarchy. In fact, in Java all classes belong to one huge inheritance tree rooted at the `Object` class. Figure 17-4 shows one small branch of that tree that starts at the `JTextComponent` class.

As you know, Java's syntax indicates inheritance with the keyword `extends`. A class can extend only one other class. (Attempts to introduce ***multiple inheritance*** in programming languages led to confusion and ultimately failed. A Java compromise allows a class to `implement` multiple ***interfaces***.)

One question that comes up with inheritance concerns access privileges to class methods and fields. A derived class can treat all the <u>public</u> methods and fields of the base class as its own. Should it also have access to the <u>private</u> methods and fields of the base class? Java's answer is no, but it offers a special access level designated by the keyword `protected`. A `protected` method or field is accessible to all the derived classes further down in the inheritance hierarchy. For all other classes `protected` methods and fields work like `private` ones.

One exception to inheritance is constructors.

> **In Java, constructors are not inherited from superclasses. Each class must define its own constructors if it needs them. These constructors can call constructors of the superclass using the keyword `super`:**
>
> ```
> super(<arguments>);
> ```

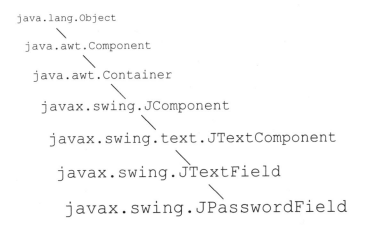

Figure 17-3. **JPasswordField's derivation line**

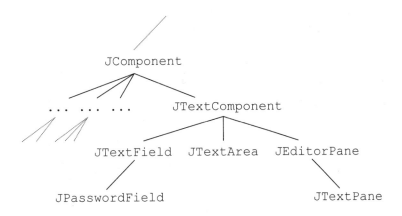

Figure 17-4. **JTextComponent's inheritance tree**

`super` is a Java reserved word. It refers to the object of the superclass from which the current object is derived. As we have seen earlier, `super` is also used to call the base class's methods, as in

```
super.paintComponent(g);
```

If you derive a class from a Java library class, you can consult the vast Java documentation to find out what inherited methods and fields are at your disposal. Or you can simply rely on examples.

❖ ❖ ❖

Inheritance is a great tool, but a very dangerous one, too. You have to choose names for methods in your class very carefully when you derive your class from another class, especially from a class in one of the Java packages.

> **Be very careful not to override a method of the superclass (or of one of the superclasses in the inheritance hierarchy) <u>unintentionally</u> by giving your own method the same name and arguments.**

For example, suppose you decide to derive your own class from `JTextField` and supply a method `contains(int m, int n)` for it that determines, say, whether the input field contains stars in positions `m` and `n`:

```
private class StarTextField extends JTextField
{
  StarTextField(String s) // constructor
  {
    super(s);
  }

  public boolean contains(int m, int n)
  {
    String s = getText();
        // the getText method is inherited from JTextField
    return m < s.length() && n < s.length() &&
          s.charAt(m) == '*' && s.charAt(n) == '*';
  }
}
```

Guess what? It turns out that `JTextField` is derived from the following inheritance line:

```
java.lang.Object
   |
   +--java.awt.Component
         |
         +--java.awt.Container
               |
               +--javax.swing.JComponent
                     |
                     +--javax.swing.text.JTextComponent
                           |
                           +--javax.swing.JTextField
```

JTextField has more than 300 methods, most of them inherited from its ancestors. Some of these methods have common names, such as move, resize, remove, getX, getY, list and so on. It happens that one of the ancestors, the Component class, already has a method contains(int, int) that is used to determine whether a point (*x*, *y*) is inside that component. You have accidentally overridden it with your own method in your StarTextField class. You click on your input component, but nothing happens: you don't get its attention, because it cannot figure out that it "contains" the coordinates of the click. It may take you a <u>very</u> long time to figure out what is wrong.

❖　❖　❖

Inheritance is used for organizing classes in a project and for reusing existing classes. A class hierarchy must be designed from more general classes at the top to more specialized classes at the bottom. In fact, closer to the top of the hierarchy, Java programmers can define ***abstract classes*** in which all or some methods are declared abstract: they have only a header, without any code. A program cannot create objects of abstract classes (or, in OOP parlance, abstract classes cannot be ***instantiated***). The purpose of an abstract class is to introduce a general structure and protocol into the design process, to let the programmer derive other classes from it, and to provide a common data type for polymorphic collections (see Section 17.6). An abstract class can have some fully defined methods, but it remains abstract as long as at least one method remains abstract. Eventually, down the inheritance line, all the methods get properly defined and you end up with a ***concrete class*** that can be instantiated and whose objects and methods can be used in the program. For example, in the class hierarchy shown in Figure 17-4, JComponent and JTextComponent are abstract classes, while the classes below them are concrete classes.

Designing a meaningful hierarchy of classes for a project is a tricky task. In the previous chapters we often derived classes from Java's JApplet, JFrame, and JPanel classes, appending our own classes to the Swing class hierarchy. But we have had no opportunity to go much beyond that. In general, simple projects do not require complicated class hierarchies. But in a large project, a neatly laid out hierarchy of classes can save a lot of time and help produce a nicely designed application, whereas a contrived and overly complicated hierarchy of classes can significantly slow down a project.

❖　❖　❖

Inheritance is different from *embedding.* **Embedding is the situation where one type of object is a data member (a field) in another object.**

If inheritance represents the "is a kind of" relationship, embedding represents the "has a" relationship. For example, in the *Craps* applet an object of the class CrapsTable has two dice (objects of the type RollingDie) embedded in it.

In some cases, it may not be so easy to choose between inheritance and embedding. Suppose, for example, that a class Point represents a point on a plane:

```
public class Point
{
  protected int x;
  protected int y;

  < ... Constructors, etc. >

  public int getX()
  {
    return x;
  }

  public int getY()
  {
    return y;
  }

  public void move(int x, int y)
  {
    this.x = x;
    this.y = y;
  }
}
```

A class Balloon represents a filled or hollow circle in a drawing editor. A balloon has a center; accordingly the Balloon class may have a field center of the type Point:

```
public class Balloon
{
  protected int radius;
  protected Point center;  // A Point object is embedded into Balloon

  < ... other fields and methods >
}
```

Then the Balloon class needs its own getX and getY methods for getting the coordinates of its center and perhaps its own move method:

```
public class Balloon
{
  protected int radius;
  protected Point center;   // A Point object is embedded into Balloon

  public int getX()
  {
    return center.getX();
  }

  public int getY()
  {
    return center.getY();
  }

  public void move(x, y)
  {
    center.move(x, y);
  }
  < ... etc. >
}
```

It is possible instead to derive `Balloon` from `Point`:

```
public class Balloon extends Point
{
  protected int radius;
  < ... etc. >
}
```

This would be an expedient solution for putting together the `Balloon` class. Together with the *x* and *y* coordinates of the center, `Balloon` would inherit from `Point` its useful methods, such as `getX`, `getY`, and `move`. However, this solution does not represent "a kind of" relationship because calling a balloon "a kind of" point is a stretch.

Inheritance has the limitation that a class can inherit from only one base class; but a class can have as many fields of different types as you want. If an object of your class has to carry GUI components or you want to paint on it, you have no choice but to derive your class from `JApplet`, `JPanel`, another Java library class, or something derived from one of these. All other potential candidates for a base class have to be ruled out and if our class needs to use them, they are used as fields. For example, the `LetterPanel` class in the *Ramblecs* applet potentially could have been derived from the `LetterGrid` class, which represents a 2-D array of characters. But `LetterPanel` needs to be derived from `JPanel` because we want to be able to paint cubes on it. Therefore, a `LetterGrid` object `grid` is embedded in `LetterPanel` as a field.

17.5 Encapsulation and Information Hiding

In OOP, classes combine fields and methods in one entity. Fields are usually private, and methods that represent a class's internal functions can be private, too. These private fields and methods, which represent the inner mechanics of a class's objects, are hidden from objects of other classes. An object's set of public constructors and methods is what describes this object to the world. These methods define what an object can do for the world; they define the class's *interface* to the rest of the program. This practice of combining data members and methods in one object and hiding the implementation details of a class while representing its functionality through a well-defined set of methods is called *encapsulation*.

An encapsulated class with private fields may provide special methods, called *accessors*, that return the values of its fields. This approach is more independent from the specific representation of data, because an accessor can perform additional calculations or type conversions if necessary. *Modifiers* are methods that set the values of private fields. Modifiers can check that a field always gets a valid value. Occasionally the same method can both return the old value of a field and give it a new value.

Encapsulation helps to limit the amount of information that a class gives its users. It also facilitates maintenance because the inner mechanism of a class can change without affecting the interface or the rest of the program. A general OOP principle is *information hiding*: objects of different classes should know as little about each other as possible. A class's data members in particular are considered to be more prone to redesign, so they are almost always declared `protected` or `private`.

Encapsulation is not unique to object-oriented programming. Before OOP, programmers were writing stand-alone functions or procedures but they were thinking in terms of <u>modules,</u> not individual functions. Each module "encapsulates" a certain functionality. A module in C, for instance, can consist of a set of functions that work on specific data elements and data structures. Some of the functions and data elements are visible only inside the module; other functions are public and can be called from other modules. This is not very different from a class in OOP. Of course, such a procedural module would represent only <u>one</u> object of a certain type. What makes OOP different is that it is so easy to create multiple instances of the same class, each with its own set of fields.

True encapsulation and information hiding depends on the overall design of a software application. A well-designed class must do meaningful work and, at the same time, hide its inner mechanics so that its objects communicate effectively with other objects through a lean, well-defined interface. If a class provides accessors and modifiers for all its private fields but does little else, it encapsulates nothing. But it still may be a good idea to follow the "all-fields-are-private-or-protected" rule if there is a chance that other classes will be derived from this class in the future. For example, in the *Actors* applet in Section 17.3 we defined the `Message` class with all its fields public, just to show that we could. This is all right for a simple class like `Message` that doesn't have any methods to speak of (only `toString`), but this is not a good design idea if you eventually plan to derive other classes from `Message`.

17.6 Polymorphism

There is a tension in modern programming languages between two principles. The first is to use objects of strictly defined types and to check that the types of objects are appropriate in each method call. The second is to treat objects in the same manner regardless of their types. This tension is especially apparent when a program needs to maintain a list or a collection of different objects, as many applications do. Java libraries and other development packages provide special ***container*** classes of different kinds to hold objects. For example, we might want to put a collection of objects into an ordered list or a queue. In Swing, each GUI component is also a container that can hold a number of other components, which creates a branching tree-like structure of nested components.

The functionality of a container class would be very limited if a container could hold only objects of one type or even objects of several predefined types. If you derived your own class from one of the Swing components, you wouldn't be able to add an object of your derived class to a container. And if you did, how would the container know how to deal with it (e.g., how to repaint it)?

A technique called ***polymorphism*** can help resolve this dilemma. Recall that all objects in Java are accessed through references and are passed to all methods <u>as references</u>. Different types of objects are represented by different types of references. But when you get down to it, a reference is an address and its type is a purely logical notion in the language. A more specialized type of object may be represented, if necessary, by a reference of a more generic type, higher in the class hierarchy.

As an example, let us return to the *Drawing Editor* applet from Section 16.4. Suppose instead of drawing only round balloons we now want to make a picture out of different basic shapes: circles, rectangles, polygons. We define an abstract class `BasicShape` and then derive concrete classes `Circle`, `Rectangle`, `Polygon` from it (Figure 17-5).

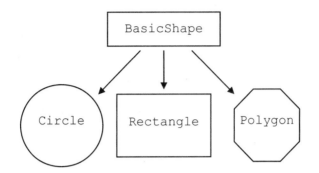

Figure 17-5. Concrete classes derived from the abstract class `BasicShape`

Our editor represents the picture as an array of `BasicShape` objects:

```
private BasicShape list[];
```

but actually each element in this array is a reference to a more specific type of object — a circle, a rectangle, or a polygon (Figure 17-6).

`BasicShape list[]`

Figure 17-6. A list of objects disguised as more general references

Now suppose we want to write the following method that picks from the list an object that contains a given point (*x*, *y*) (e.g., in order to later drag that object with a mouse):

```
public int pick(int x, int y)
{
  int i;
  for (i = numShapes - 1; i >= 0; i--) // last on top
    if (list[i].isInside(x, y))
      return i;
  return -1;
}
```

But `isInside` is different for different shapes. In the `BasicShape` class it is defined only as an abstract method:

```
public abstract class BasicShape
{
  < ... other fields and methods >

  public abstract boolean isInside(int x, int y);
}
```

In the concrete classes derived from `BasicShape` it is redefined properly:

```
public class Circle extends BasicShape
{
  < ... other fields and methods >

  public boolean isInside(int x, int y)
  {
    return (x - xCenter) * (x - xCenter) +
           (y - yCenter) * (y - yCenter) < radius * radius;
  }
}

public class Rectangle extends BasicShape
{
  < ... other fields and methods >

  public boolean isInside(int x, int y)
  {
    return x > xLeft && x < xLeft + width &&
           y > yTop && y < yTop + height;
  }
}
```

and so on.

But how does the compiler know which one of them to call? When the program compiles, the compiler has no way of knowing which shape will be placed into a particular element of `list`.

> **The idea of polymorphism is that each object in a collection knows how to handle itself correctly even if it is disguised as an object of a more generic type.**

When `list[i].isInside` is called, `list[i]` itself knows what kind of shape it is, and its own correct method is called. The same applies to `draw` and other methods that are specific to a particular shape.

To summarize polymorphic behavior:

1. Different classes derived from a common "ancestor" class can have methods with the same name (and argument types) but different code.

2. Objects of these classes (represented by references of the common ancestor type) can be mixed together in one collection.

3. The program automatically calls the correct version of the method for each object in the collection.

Polymorphic behavior is implemented through a technique called *late (or dynamic) method binding*. Even though an object in the code appears to the compiler as an object of some generic ancestor class, the decision of which exact method to call is deferred until run time. Each class has a table of entry points (starting addresses) for its methods, and the correct method is chosen from that table. Instead of calling a generic method for the ancestor class (which may not even exist if this is an abstract class) the program calls the correct method for the specific object. It all happens automatically, so a programmer does not have to worry about different types of objects mixed together in one collection.

17.7 Designing Classes and Methods

The most difficult task in software design is defining software modules and deciding which functions belong in each module. OOP is no exception: identifying the types of objects in an application and deciding what their responsibilities and methods should be is the key design decision. OOP in itself gives little guidance in this process. Designing a software application remains largely an art.

A meaningful discussion of this art would require a large case study, too large for any textbook. Still, some general lessons can be learned even from a small case study. Let us review, for example, the design decisions we made in the *Craps* applet in Chapter 7 and try to examine the main reasons for choosing the particular classes we did.

The applet consists of the four classes shown in Figure 7-2 (page 192). We created each of the four classes for a slightly different reason.

1. The `Craps` class is there because we need a main class, derived from `JApplet`, to hold the applet together. Any Java program needs a main class. In an applet, this class is derived from `JApplet` and must have an `init` method. In a GUI

application, this class may be derived from `JFrame` and may have a `main` method.

In our *Craps* applet, the `Craps` class came out a little too large because we also used it for controlling the game and displaying the results. When we first designed the applet and divided the tasks among the team members, it was not obvious how big this class would become. If we did this project again, perhaps we would put the control and display functions into a separate class. The main applet would only create and position the table and the control panel; the `ControlPanel` class could create and position the display fields and process the "Roll" button events. But Aisha, our virtual consultant who wrote the `Craps` class, did not volunteer to split it into two, and now it's too late (unless you have the time to do it as an exercise).

2. We wrote the `CrapsTable` class, derived from `JPanel`, because we needed a conveniently repaintable object on which to roll the dice. This is a technical reason and has little to do with physical craps tables in casinos. It allows us to make `table`'s background green and to draw rolling dice within its bounds. This is a nice class with one constructor and four simple methods. The whole class fits on one page, which is the preferred size for a class.

3. The `RollingDie` class is there because it represents well-defined functions in the program and because we have two identical dice and each must roll independently from the other. For the same reason, `VendingMachine` must be a class in the *SnackBar* applet (Chapter 8): we want to create three almost identical "vending machines."

    The `RollingDie` class is a little long, with half of its code given over to methods for drawing a die. Could we move the drawing methods into a separate class? Potentially we could isolate the more general moving functions in one class, say, `MovingDie`, then derive the `RollingDie` class from it and add the drawing methods. That would make sense if we hoped to reuse the `MovingDie` class in other applications. But it seems extremely unlikely that such a class could be ever reused without the drawing part. Our verdict: let's leave it as is.

4. Finally, the `CrapsGame` class is there because it encapsulates the rules of the game. Of course we could have scattered the details of the game among the other classes, but that would be a very bad design decision. People writing other classes shouldn't even need to know the rules of the game. If one of them misunderstood the rules and made a mistake, it would be difficult to find. Besides, we can reuse this class in other implementations of the game, or, as we have done, in an applet that runs a statistical trial of the game. For the same reason we separated the `Vendor` class in the *SnackBar* applet in Chapter 8.

Another reusability consideration is that we may eventually want to adapt the *Craps* applet for other games that involve rolling dice. With a separate `CrapsGame` class, it is easy to modify or replace it with only minimal changes to other classes.

In summary, the following reasons may influence your decision to introduce a new class into a project:

- You need a top-level class to hold an application together.
- You need to derive a class from a library class.
- Your program will use multiple instances (objects) of the class type.
- The class will handle events of a particular type or implement a particular interface.
- The class will encapsulate a clearly defined functionality unrelated to GUI.
- You will potentially reuse the class.
- You need to split a class into two to make both more manageable.

If all your classes are arranged into layers, with classes at the higher levels creating objects and calling methods of classes at the lower levels (as, for example, it more or less happens in *Craps* and in *Ramblecs* (see Figure 15-1 on page 405), this is a mark of a good design. If, on the other hand, objects of different classes frequently call each other's methods, this may be a symptom of a design flaw.

17.8 *Lab:* Finishing *Ramblecs*

Completing the game at this stage requires only two minor additions: a dictionary of words and a way to keep score.

Adding a dictionary is not complicated. We already have an array of words generated by the program we wrote in Chapter 13. The words were written into a text file, `RamblecsDictionary.java`, using Java syntax. All we have to do is add a `boolean` method that matches a word against the dictionary. We should use the Binary Search algorithm for speed. We could use our own implementation, discussed in Section 12.2, but it is probably easier to use the static method `binarySearch` from the `Arrays` class. This method takes two arguments, an array of strings and the target string, and returns a non-negative number (the position of the target string in the array) if the target is found or a negative number if the target is not in the array. You need to import `java.util.Arrays` to use the `Arrays` class.

Keeping the score is not a very big problem either. We just have to add methods to `ControlPanel` to update and display the score.

In other words, you are left with the following tasks:

1. Add a `boolean isFound` method to the `RamblecsDictionary` class. Integrate the new class into the *Ramblecs* project and add code that declares and constructs a dictionary. You can simply create the dictionary in `ControlPanel`'s constructor or create it in the `Ramblecs init` method and pass it to `controlpanel`.

2. Add an `int score` field to the `ControlPanel` class and add code to its `paintComponent` method to display the score. Set the initial score value to 100 bonus points. The display may look better if you use `DecimalFormat` with, say, three digits, as follows:

```
private final DecimalFormat scoreFormat =
                            new DecimalFormat("000");
< ... etc. >
public void paintComponent(Graphics g)
{
  < ... other statements >
  g.drawString(scoreFormat.format(score), < coordinates > );
}
```

3. Implement the scoring rules: give three points for each correctly entered three-letter word, six points for each four-letter word, and twelve points for each five-letter word. Give a 15-point penalty for an invalid entered word and a three-point penalty for a row dropped without entering. Supply an `addScore` method that updates the score and repaints the control panel. Call it from `keyPressed` when necessary after testing `dictionary.isFound`.

We can keep the score increments for words of different lengths as well as the penalties in a constant array:

```
private static final int scoreIncr[] = {-15, -3, 0, 3, 6, 12};
```

Then we can get the number we need quickly by using this array as a *lookup table*, going directly to the element we need:

```
len = word.length();
if (len > 0)
{
  if (dictionary.isFound(word))
    addScore(scoreIncr[len]); // reward
  else
    addScore(scoreIncr[0]);   // penalty
  < ... etc. >
```

The first element in the `scoreIncr` array may hold the penalty for a misspelled word and the second element the penalty for a flushed word. Note that we do not want to penalize a player for an entered or dropped empty row (`<Enter>` or spacebar pressed when the grid is empty).

Enjoy the game. We are sure you will add your own features to it when you have time.

17.9 The OOP Appeal

Beyond a doubt, OOP and Java are great tools for implementing reusable code, and they bring order and grace into certain types of projects. But it is also obvious that their appeal goes beyond merely pragmatic considerations. It was inevitable that OOP gain prominence regardless of its practical merits because of its strong theoretical and aesthetic appeal.

Over time, OOP has developed into a strong culture with a large group of true believers, an arcane lingo, rather complex tools, and a particular set of aesthetics. There is no fundamental reason, for instance, why a package should require something like

```
setCursor(Cursor.getPredefinedCursor(Cursor.WAIT_CURSOR));
```

as opposed to, say,

```
setCursor(WAIT_CURSOR);
```

Imagine a surgeon telling the assisting nurse: "Set scalpel scalpel get predefined scalpel." But each discipline has its own culture and tradition.

OOP concepts are basically quite simple. Yet, far from being accessible to every child, as Alan Kay, the inventor of Smalltalk, hoped, OOP has become somewhat formal and complex. Hopefully, if you have gotten this far in this book, you have learned to look past OOP's superficial complexity and appreciate its power, as well as its limitations.

17.10   Summary

OOP applications can be viewed as simulations in which independent objects send messages to each other and respond to messages from each other and from the real world. Each object has its own memory, which may consist of other objects (and, in Java, of fields of primitive data types). In Java, "event" messages are handled by various types of "listeners," while direct messages from object to object are represented as method calls.

Different types of objects in a program are descibed by classes. Inheritance allows a programmer to derive a new class (called a derived class or a subclass) from another class (called a base class or a superclass). A derived class inherits all the data fields and methods (but not constructors) from the base class, and can add its own methods or redefine some of the methods of the base class. (This is convenient, but be extremely careful not to do it unintentionally.) A large application can be designed as a hierarchy of classes, starting with a few general "abstract" classes at the top levels and ending up with more specialized concrete classes at the bottom. An abstract class has some of its methods declared only as headers with no code. Thus no object of an abstract class can be created in the program. In a concrete class, somewhere down the inheritance line, all the methods get defined properly.

Inheritance represents the "is a kind of" relationship between types of objects. In practice it may be used simply to add a few features to an existing class. It is a great tool for reusing your own and standard library classes. Inheritance should not be confused with embedding, where an object of one type is simply a field in another object. Embedding represents the "has a" relationship.

Combining fields and methods into one object and hiding the mechanics of class implementation by making fields and internal helper methods private is called encapsulation. One of the most important OOP principles is "information hiding": in a good design, objects of a particular class know as little as possible about the implementation mechanics of other classes.

Polymorphic behavior overrides strict data type checking and allows objects of different but related types to be combined in the same collection (a list, a "container", etc.). The collection stores references to objects as references of their common ancestor class type. Polymorphism uses the late binding technique to assure that at run time the program calls the appropriate methods for a specific object even if that object is represented by a reference of a more general ancestor type.

Designing a good OOP application may be a daunting task. There are no precise rules for identifying the most useful types of objects and methods. Many considerations determine which classes should be defined and their responsibilities. Manageable size, clear functionality, potential reuse, the need to inherit from a library class, support for multiple instances of the same type of object, and even the particular composition of a development team may all influence these decisions.

Behind terminology and style that seem complicated at times, the concepts of OOP are actually quite simple and straightforward. It's good to remember that they are just a useful way of doing things at this point in time.

Congratulations on getting your first taste of Java and OOP.

Exercises

Sections 17.1-17.4

1. Name three main areas of concern in software development in which OOP is especially helpful.

2. Some programming languages, like C++, support global variables and free-standing functions that do not belong to any class. These are akin to static members of one "universal" class. What are some advantages and disadvantages of the stricter approach in Java, where every method and every variable must belong to a class? ✓

3.■ Write and test a class `MyIntField` derived from `JTextField`. Provide a constructor that calls the superclass's constructor with the same argument and a `getInt` method that returns an integer obtained by trimming and parsing a string returned by `getText`.

4. ▪ Rewrite the class `Complex` from Question 17 in Chapter 8 (page 253), now deriving it from Java's `Point2D.Double` class (that represents a point on a plane with `double` coordinates):

```
public class Complex extends Point2D.Double
```

≤ Hint: the dot in the `Point2D.Double` name indicates that `Point2D.Double` is an inner class inherited from `Point2D`. Just treat it as one name. ≥

The fields of `Point2D.Double` are called `x` and `y`. Make the `Complex` constructors call the `Point2D.Double` constructor that takes two `double` arguments. Eliminate `Complex`'s `toString` method and test the one inherited from `Point2D.Double` instead. ✓

5. Suppose we are working on a "circuit editor" for an interactive PC-board (printed circuit board) design application. The class `LogicElement` (`Ch17\Exercises\LogicElement.java` 🔲, Figure 17-7) is an abstract class that represents a logic element in a circuit. The classes `Signal` and `Gate` are derived from `LogicElement`. A signal represents a true or false input signal. A gate represents an AND, OR, or NOT gate.

Continued ⇗

```
// Ch17\Exercises\LogicElement.java
// ==================================

public abstract class LogicElement
{
  protected static final char UNDEFINED = '?';

  /**
   *   Returns the output value 'T' or 'F' based on the type of
   *   element and the values of inputs, if any.
   *   Returns '?' if required inputs are missing or undefined.
   */
  public abstract char getOutput();
}
```

- -

```
// Ch17\Exercises\Signal.java
// ===========================

public class Signal extends LogicElement
{
  protected char value;

  public Signal(LogicElement input)
  {
    value = input.getOutput();
  }

  public Signal(char v)
  {
    value = v;
  }

  public Signal(boolean b)
  {
    if (b)
      value = 'T';
    else
      value = 'F';
  }

  public char getOutput()
  {
    return value;
  }
}
```

- -

Figure 17-7 LogicElement.java, Signal.java, Gate.java

Continued ➡

```
// Ch17\Exercises\Gate.java
// =========================

public abstract class Gate extends LogicElement
{
  protected LogicElement inputA, inputB;

  public Gate(LogicElement iA, LogicElement iB)
  {
    inputA = iA;
    inputB = iB;
  }

  public void connectA(LogicElement iA)
  {
    inputA = iA;
  }

  public void connectB(LogicElement iB)
  {
    inputB = iB;
  }
}
```

Figure 17-7. `LogicElement`, `Signal`, and `Gate` classes for a circuit editor

(a)   Is `Signal` an abstract or a concrete class? ✓

(b)   Is

```
        Signal sig = new Signal();
```

a valid declaration?

(c)   Explain why defining `TrueSignal` and `FalseSignal` classes, derived from `Signal`, would be a waste of time. ✓

(d)   Explain why a `setValue` method may be handy for the `Signal` class and add it. ✓

(e)   Explain why the `Gate` class is declared `abstract`.

Continued ➩

(f)   Why is the `LogicElement` class necessary in this application? Can we eliminate it and just use the `Signal` and `Gate` classes? ✓

(g)   Implement `AndGate`, `OrGate` and `NotGate` classes, derived from `Gate`. The `AndGate` and `OrGate` constructors should take two arguments: two input `LogicElement`s for `inputA` and `inputB`. The `NotGate` constructor takes one argument: only `inputA` is used. All these constructors must call the superclass's constructor. The `getOutput` method in all three gates must test that the required inputs are not `null`, then get their values by calling their `getOutput` method. If at least one of the required inputs is `null`, or if its value is `UNDEFINED`, `getOutput` returns `UNDEFINED`. Otherwise `getOutput` returns the appropriate logical combination based on the values of the inputs.

(h)   Test your classes in a small applet or console application. "Build" an XOR circuit out of two input signals and five gates (see Figure 1-2 on page 3) and test its output for all combinations of values for the two inputs (including `UNDEFINED` values).

Sections 17.5-17.10

6.   This question continues Question 5 about the `LogicElement` class and its subclasses.

(a)   Explain why all these classes are fully encapsulated.

(b)   Explain why `value` is `private` rather than `protected` in the `Signal` class. Rewrite this class with `value` as `boolean` rather than `char`, but leave all the other classes unchanged. ✓

(c)   How does the `getOutput` method of an `AndGate` object (or of an `OrGate` object) know which type of `LogicElement`s are attached as its inputs when it calls their `getOutput` methods? ✓

(d)   Explain why the `getOutput` method is recursive even though it doesn't seem to directly call itself on the same object.

(e)   If you want to add drawing methods for all types of logic elements (for example for using them in a PC-board layout application) what's the best way of doing it? Discuss alternative approaches to adding drawing methods to the `LogicElement` hierarchy and to making both sets of classes — without drawing capability and with it — reusable. ✓

7.   Rewrite the *Drawing Editor* applet from Section 16.4 to support balloons of two shapes: round and oval. ⸮ Hints: (1) Make `Balloon` an abstract class and derive `RoundBalloon` and `OvalBalloon` classes from it. The constructors in both can just call the superclass's constructor. The `isInside` and `isOnBorder` methods are set up in such a way that they can be the same for `RoundBalloon` and `OvalBalloon`. Only the `distance(x, y)` and `draw` methods have to be redefined for the two new classes. (2) An oval is a circle that has been stretched, say by a factor of 2. So the `distance(x, y)` method for an oval balloon can use the distance formula in which the *y*-coordinate is scaled by a factor of 1/2:

$$d = \sqrt{(x - xCenter)^2 + \frac{1}{4}(y - yCenter)^2}$$

(3) Replace the "Add balloon" button in the applet with two buttons for balloons of different shapes. Add an argument (e.g., a string) to the `addBalloon` method in the `DrawingPanel` class to indicate the shape of a balloon to be added. ⸮

8.   Add a "wildcard" letter to the *Ramblecs* game so that the player can set its value from the keyboard while it is displayed. Reuse the code from the `FallingCube` class by deriving a new class from it.

Appendix A: From C++ to Java

Preprocessor

Java does not use preprocessor directives. The `import` statement is used to access library classes and packages.

Primitive data types, variables, and constants

`int`, `long`, `short`, `float`, and `double` are the same, but their sizes do not depend on the platform. There are no `unsigned` types in Java. `char` takes two bytes but is used the same way as in C++. `bool` is called `boolean`. The keyword `final` is used for `const`; also, `final` fields may get their values assigned in constructors. Literal numeric constants, character constants, and literal strings are written the same way (except the hex escape sequence in characters). There is no `enum` in Java.

Fields (data members of classes) and array elements of numeric data types are by default initialized to 0; `boolean` fields and array elements are by default initialized to `false`, and references to `null`.

Arithmetic, relational and logical operators

The assignment, arithmetic, compound assignment, and increment/decrement operators are the same. A C-style cast operator is used, as in `(double)k`.

Relational and logical operators are the same, but logical operators apply only to the `boolean` type operands. Short-circuit evaluation is used.

Control statements

`if-else`, `switch`, `while`, `for`, `do-while`, `break`, `continue`, and `return` are the same.

473

Functions (methods)

All functions (called "methods" in OOP) belong to classes — there are no free-standing methods. This applies to `main`, too — in a stand-alone application it must be a

```
public static void main(String[] args)
```

in one of the classes. (An applet does not have a `main` — applet's `init` method is called instead.)

All primitive data types are <u>always</u> passed to methods <u>by value</u>. All objects (including strings, arrays, and programmer-defined types) are <u>always</u> passed to methods <u>as references</u> and returned from methods as references. There is no special syntax for that.

Overloaded functions and operators

Overloaded methods work the same way in Java as in C++. No overloaded operators in Java (but there are built-in + and += operators for concatenating strings).

No templates. No inline functions.

Pointers and references

No pointers in Java, only references. There is no special syntax for references: an object is always declared and accessed through a reference. An uninitialized reference is equal to `null` (a reserved word). The same "dot" notation as in C++ is used for accessing data fields and calling an object's methods.

An object (including arrays, strings, programmer-defined types) must be initialized using the `new` operator before it can be used. Exceptions are literal strings and arrays initialized with values — these are allocated automatically. For example:

```
int points[] = {1, 2, 3, 4, 5, 6};
```

A reference to an object can be also returned by a method that creates the object. (Many methods from standard packages return references to objects.)

There is no `delete` in Java — automatic "garbage collection" is used.

Classes

There are no `struct`s in Java. Only one public class can be defined per source file.
No semicolon after the closing brace. Each class's field or method must be
designated `public`, `private`, or `protected` individually. A destructor is
`void finalize()`, but destructors are rarely used because the garbage collector
releases memory automatically.

Inheritance is indicated by the keyword `extends`. There is only one ("public") type
of inheritance in Java. No initializer lists in Java: the base class's constructor can be
called explicitly using the keyword `super`. `super` is also used to call the base
class's methods.

`this` is a <u>reference</u>, not a pointer (e.g., `return this`, not `return *this`).

Static methods are called and static fields are accessed using the class's name with a
dot as a prefix (e.g., `Math.sqrt(x)`, `Color.red`).

There are no `friend` functions or classes in Java, but a private class can be
embedded in a public class. The keyword `abstract` is used instead of `virtual`.

Pitfalls

1. The assignment operator applies to <u>references</u> to objects, not objects themselves.
    For example, in

    ```
    Employee emp1 = new Employee("Geena");
    Employee emp2 = emp1;
    ```

    `emp2` refers to <u>the same</u> object as `emp1`, not to a copy of `emp1`. You need to
    provide a copy constructor or a `clone` method for your class to make copies of
    objects. For example:

    ```
    Employee emp2 = new Employee(emp1);
    ```

    or

    ```
    Employee emp3 = (Employee)emp1.clone();
    ```

2. Relational operators applied to objects, as in

    ```
    if (str1 < str2) ...
    if (obj1 == obj2) ...
    ```

    compare <u>references</u> to (addresses of) objects, not their values. Use special methods `equals` or `compareTo` for strings.

3. Unfortunately, Java's bit-wise `&` and `|` operators may be used with `boolean` variables and expressions, but they do not recognize short-circuit evaluation. It is best to avoid them when working with `boolean` expressions.

Appendix B: The 17 Bits of Style

> The language is perpetually in flux: it is a living stream, shifting, changing, receiving new strength from a thousand tributaries, losing old forms in the backwaters of time. To suggest that a young writer not swim in the main stream of this turbulence would be foolish indeed, and such is not the intent of these cautionary remarks. The intent is to suggest that in choosing between formal and the informal, the regular and the offbeat, the general and the special, the orthodox and the heretical, the beginner err on the side of conservatism, on the side of established usage.
>
> William Strunk Jr. and E.B. White, *The Elements of Style*

Style is a crucial component of professionalism in software development. Clean code that follows stylistic conventions is easier to read, maintain, and share with colleagues. Programmers who code in good style are less likely to have silly bugs and will actually spend less time developing and debugging their code. Finally, good style in programs is a concern because for us, humans, style and aesthetics are a concern in everything we do.

Following stylistic conventions is easy, and, after a little practice, becomes second nature. Occasionally, an especially independent-minded student resists all conventions, arguing, "But it works!" To this person we can point out two things. First, a programmer's product is <u>not</u> an executable program but its source code. In the current environment the life expectancy of a "working" program is just a few months, sometimes weeks. On the other hand, source code, updated periodically, can live for years; to be of any use, it must be readable to others. Second, bad or unconventional style is uncool. It immediately gives away an amateur, a kind of social misfit in the software developers' culture. As nerdy as this culture might be, it has its own sense of aesthetic pride.

In *The Elements of Style*, William Strunk wrote:

> There is no satisfactory explanation of style, no infallible guide to good writing, no assurance that a person who thinks clearly will be able to write clearly, no key that unlocks the door, no inflexible rule by which the young writer may shape his course.

These words, which come in the book's closing chapter, describe (and illustrate) the deeper meaning of style — after the straightforward rules of correct usage have been discussed and illustrated in the previous chapters. In programming, too, style has a deeper meaning: it is that elusive quality which makes one person's code elegant and easy to follow and another person's convoluted and obscure although in line with all the superficial stylistic conventions. The mystery is not as wide open in writing code as in creative writing: there are many firm design principles, and "a person who thinks clearly" usually is able to code clearly. Still, some mystery remains. Here we discuss only the superficial stylistic conventions, leaving the deeper meaning alone.

Bit 0. At the top of each source module, put in a comment that states the purpose of the class, its author, date of completion and other pertinent information, such as a copyright message, special instructions on how to run the program, data files that your program reads or creates, and a history of revisions.

Bit 1. Place all `import` directives at the top of your source module. Start with standard Java packages followed by your own or your organization's packages.

Bit 2. Separate different methods in a class with blank lines and separator comment lines (or more formal documentation comments for *javadoc*). Split your code into "paragraphs" that represent meaningful steps or actions in your program by inserting blank lines and, if necessary, comment lines.

Bit 3. Place each statement on a separate line. Indent.

Java code is usually indented by two character positions in the body of a method, and within braces under `if`, `else`, `switch`, and `for`, `while`, and `do-while` loops.

Bit 4.   Keep braces visible.

There are different styles of placing braces (naturally, this is a subject of heated debates). Many programmers place the opening brace at the end of the previous line, and the closing brace on a separate line. In this book we place both the opening and the closing braces on separate lines.

Bit 5.   Use spaces liberally. Do not cram things together.

There are no clear-cut rules on where to add spaces — different people have different tastes. We use spaces on both sides of the assignment operator and other binary operators: arithmetic, logical, relational. For example, we find

```
for (i=0;i<n;i++)
    sum+=scores[i];
```

less readable than

```
for (i = 0; i < n; i++)
    sum += scores[i];
```

With longer names, spaces become more important. For example:

```
taxAmount=saleAmount*taxRate;
```

appears too crammed. We prefer

```
taxAmount = saleAmount * taxRate;
```

Unary operators, such as - (negation) , ++, --, !, are usually attached to their operands. For example:

```
if (! match)
    count --;
```

is too fancy. People normally write:

```
if (!match)
    count--;
```

Most people do not use spaces around brackets, or the "dot" class member access operators.

```
Color c = Color . white;
```

compiles correctly, but you won't see it in programs.

Some people like to leave spaces on both sides of a parenthesis in expressions and in method calls. We normally leave a space only before an opening parenthesis and after a closing parenthesis.

Bit 6.   Omit needless parentheses.

Java uses a well-defined order of precedence among operators. All unary operators have higher rank than (are applied before) all binary operators. Among the binary operators, arithmetic operators have higher rank than relational operators, which in turn apply before logical operators. There is no need to clutter your code with too many parentheses. For example, instead of

```
if ((!match) && (i < (length - 1)))...
```

you can write

```
if (!match && (i < length - 1))...
```

or even

```
if (!match && i < length - 1)...
```

You have to be a little more careful with `&&` and `||`: the `&&` operator has a higher rank than `||`. For example, you need to keep the parentheses in

```
if (year % 4 == 0 && (year % 100 != 0 || year % 400 == 0))...
```

Occasionally, parentheses facilitate reading long logical expressions:

```
if ((x > -3 && x < - 1) || (x > 1 && x < 3))...
```

Use parentheses whenever you are unsure about the order of operations.

Bit 7. Comment each method: state its purpose, arguments, assumptions ("preconditions"), results ("postconditions"), and return value.

Bit 8. Avoid redundant comments.

```
if (a[i] >= 0)
    count++;   // Increment the count
```

Bit 9. Self-explanatory code is usually better than heavily commented code.

For example, instead of

```
if (s == "MA" && a < 16)  // If state is Massachusetts and
                          //   age is less than Massachusetts
                          //   legal driving age...
```

it is better to write:

```
final int massDrivingAge = 16;
if (stateCode == "MA" && age < massDrivingAge)
```

Bit 10. Explain your intentions ahead of time in difficult algorithms.

```
// Going backwards from a[n-1], shift elements to the
//   right until you find an element a[i] <= aTemp:
i = n;
while (i > 0 && aTemp < a[i-1])
{
  a[i] = a[i-1];
  i--;
}
```

Bit 11. Comment obscure code or unusual usage.

```
int mask = KeyEvent.SHIFT_MASK | KeyEvent.CTRL_MASK;

// If both control and shift are pressed:
if ((e.getModifiers() & mask) == mask)
   . . .
```

Bit 12. Use meaningful names.

```
totalAmt = saleAmt * (1 + taxRate);
```

is better than

```
tot = a * (1 + r);
```

But overly long COBOL-style names will clutter your code:

```
totalAmountDue = totalSaleAmount * (1 + salesTaxRate);
```

In Java, method names should usually sound like <u>verbs</u>. Make names of classes, objects, and variables sound like <u>nouns</u>.

Method names do not have to be too long. The same name may be used for methods that take different numbers or types of arguments (a feature known as *overloading*). Methods in different classes may have the same name, too. In fact, the object-oriented programming approach encourages the use of the same name for methods that perform semantically similar tasks. The object's name often combines with the method's name and the argument's name to create a readable phrase:

```
display.setText(message);
```

Bit 13. It is acceptable to use simple names for loop-control variables and other temporary "throw-away" variables. Declare these variables locally in each method and use the same name where appropriate. Note that longer names, such as `index`, `subscript`, `counter`, `lcv`, or `loopControlVariable` are no more meaningful than `i` or `k`. Likewise, `xCoordinate` is no more expressive than `x`.

If possible, use the same name for similar purposes. For example, the same names for local variables `row` and `col` may be used in different methods to indicate row and column in a 2-D array.

Use names that make sense in context. For example:

```
for (student = 0; student < numStudents; student++)
  sum += gpa[student];
```

Bit 14. Use the upper and lower case consistently.

Java is case-sensitive, and all reserved words are lowercase. Other than that, there are no syntax rules for using the upper or lower case. However, you should follow the Java style:

- Start all class names with a capital letter.
- Start all names of variables and methods with a lowercase letter and capitalize subsequent words.
- Use all caps occasionally for prominent constants.

Bit 15. Code defensively.

```
while (n-- > 0)
{
    . . .
}
```

may save one line of code, but it may also lead to a bug if n is used inside the loop.

```
while (n > 0)
{
    . . .
    n--;
}
```

is safer.

Bit 16. *Non Sibi* ("Not for Self") is the motto of Phillips Academy in Andover. Keep these words in mind when writing code.

Appendix C: Swing GUI Components

> For the complete list of constructors and methods refer to the Swing API documentation.

JButton

Constructors:

```
JButton(String text);
JButton(ImageIcon picture);
JButton(String text, ImageIcon picture);
```

Methods:

```
void addActionListener(ActionListener object)
void setText(String text);
void setActionCommand(String cmd);
void setIcon(ImageIcon icon);
void requestFocus();
```

Events:

```
class ... implements ActionListener
{
  public void actionPerformed(ActionEvent e)
  {
    JButton b = (JButton)e.getSource();
    String s = e.getActionCommand();
  }
}
```

Examples:

```
Ch06\Poll\Poll.java
Ch07\Craps2\Craps.java
Ch08\SnackBar\VendingMachine.java
Ch10\Fortunes\FortuneTeller.java
Ch12\Rotate\RotateArray.java
```

JCheckBox

Constructors:

```
JCheckBox(String text, boolean checked);
JCheckBox(ImageIcon icon, boolean checked);
JCheckBox(String text, ImageIcon icon, boolean checked);
```

Methods:

```
void addActionListener(ActionListener object)
void addItemListener(ItemListener object)
boolean isSelected()
void setSelected(boolean checked)
void setText(String text);
void setIcon(ImageIcon icon);
```

Events:

```
class ... implements ActionListener
{
  public void actionPerformed(ActionEvent e)
  {
    JCheckBox b = (JCheckBox)e.getSource();
    if (b == checkBox1 && b.isSelected())
      ...
  }
}
```

Examples:

```
Ch14\Exercises\Boxes.java
```

JComboBox

Constructors:

```
JComboBox(Object items[]);
( e.g.,
   String items[] = {"One", "Two", "Three"};
   JComboBox cb = new JComboBox(items);
)
```

Methods:

```
void addItemListener(ItemListener object);
void addActionListener(ActionListener object);
int getSelectedIndex();
Object getSelectedItem();
  // e.g. String s = (String)cb.getSelectedItem();
void setSelectedIndex(int itemNum);
void setSelectedItem(String text);
 // finds the item that matches text and
 // makes it selected item
```

Events:

```
class ... implements ItemListener
{
  public void itemStateChanged(ItemEvent e)
  {
    JComboBox cb = (JComboBox)e.getSource();
    int index = cb.getSelectedIndex();
    String item = (String)cb.getSelectedItem();
    ...
  }
}
```

or

```
class ... implements ActionListener
{
  public void actionPerformed(ActionEvent e)
  {
    ...
  }
}
```

Examples:

```
Ch12\Benchmarks\Benchmarks.java
```

JLabel

Constructors:

```
JLabel(String text);
JLabel(ImageIcon icon);
JLabel(String text, ImageIcon icon, SwingConstants.LEFT);
      // or CENTER, RIGHT, LEADING, TRAILING.
```

Methods:

```
void setText(String text);
void setIcon(ImageIcon icon);
```

Events: None

Examples:

```
Ch03\HelloGui\HelloGui.java
Ch04\Exercises\Sign.java
Ch06\Exercises\Bmi.java
Ch06\Ramblecs\ControlPanel.java
Ch07\Craps1\CrapsOne.java
Ch07\Craps1\CrapsStats.java
Ch07\Craps2\Craps.java
Ch08\Snackbar\SnackBar.java
Ch12\Benchmarks\Benchmarks.java
```

JPasswordField

Constructors:

```
JPasswordField(String text);
JPasswordField(int cols);
JPasswordField(String text, int cols);
```

Methods:

```
void addActionListener(ActionListener object)
void setText(String text);
void setBackground(Color c);
void setForeground(Color c);
void setFont(Font font);
void requestFocus();
char[] getPassword();
void selectAll();
```

Events:

```
class ... implements ActionListener
{
  public void actionPerformed(ActionEvent e)
  {
    // When the user strikes <Enter>:
    JPasswordField pf = (JPasswordField)e.getSource();
    String s = new String(pf.getPassword());
    ...
  }
}
```

Examples:

```
Ch08\SnackBar\SnackBar.java
```

JRadioButton

Constructors:

```
JRadioButton(String text);  // default: unselected
JRadioButton(String text, boolean selected);
JRadioButton(ImageIcon icon);
JRadioButton(ImageIcon icon, boolean selected);
JRadioButton(String text, ImageIcon icon, boolean selected);
```

Methods:

```
void addActionListener(ActionListener object)
boolean isSelected()
void setSelected(boolean selected)
void setText(String text);
void setIcon(ImageIcon icon);

...
ButtonGroup gr = new ButtonGroup();
gr.add(radioButton1);
gr.add(radioButton2);
...
```

Events:

```
class ... implements ActionListener
{
  public void actionPerformed(ActionEvent e)
  {
    JRadioButton b = (JRadioButton)e.getSource();
    if (b == radioButton1 && b.isSelected())
      ...
  }
}
```

Examples:

```
Ch07\Exercises\Mail.java
Ch07\Exercises\Rps.java
```

JSlider

Imports:

```
import javax.swing.event.*;   // Not in java.awt.event.* !!!
```

Constructors:

```
JSlider(SwingConstants.VERTICAL, int min, int max, int current);
      // or HORIZONTAL
```

Methods:

```
void addChangeListener(ChangeListener object);
void setInverted(true/false);
void setMajorTickSpacing(int n); // in "slider" units
void setMinorTickSpacing(int n);
void setPaintLabels(true/false);
void setPaintTicks(true/false);
int getValue();
void setValue(int x);
```

Events:

```
class ... implements ChangeListener
{
  public void stateChanged(ChangeEvent e)
  {
    JSlider slider = (JSlider)e.getSource();
    int x = slider.getValue();
    ...
  }
}
```

Examples:

See Section 15.3

JTextArea

Constructors:

```
JTextArea(String text);
JTextArea(int rows, int cols);
JTextArea(String text, int rows, int cols);
```

Methods:

```
void setEditable(true/false);
int getCaretPosition();
void append(String text);
void insert(String text, int pos);
void setText(String text);
void setBackground(Color c);
void setForeground(Color c);
void setFont(Font font);
void requestFocus();
String getText();
void selectAll();
void setCaretPosition(int pos);
void moveCaretPosition(int pos);
```

Examples:

```
Ch17\Actors\ActorsWorld.java
```

JTextField

Constructors:

```
JTextField(String text);
JTextField(int cols);
JTextField(String text, int cols);
```

Methods:

```
void addActionListener(ActionListener object)
void setEditable(true/false);
void setText(String text);
void setBackground(Color c);
void setForeground(Color c);
void setFont(Font font);
void requestFocus();
String getText();
void selectAll();
void setCaretPosition(int pos);
void moveCaretPosition(int pos);
```

Events:

```
class ... implements ActionListener
{
  public void actionPerformed(ActionEvent e)
  {
    // <Enter> is pressed:
    JTextField tf = (JTextField)e.getSource();
    String s = tf.getText();
  }
}
```

Examples:

```
Ch06\Exercises\Bmi.java
Ch07\Craps1\CrapsOne.java
Ch07\Craps1\CrapsStats.java
Ch07\Craps2\Craps.java
Ch08\SnackBar\VendingMachine.java
Ch09\Equations\EquationSolver.java
Ch09\Exercises\StringTest.java
Ch10\Fortunes\FortuneTeller.java
Ch12\Rotate\RotateArray.java
Ch12\Benchmarks\Benchmarks.java
```

JToggleButton

Constructors:

```
JToggleButton(String text, boolean selected);
JToggleButton(ImageIcon icon, boolean selected);
JToggleButton(String text, ImageIcon icon, boolean selected);
```

Methods:

```
addActionListener(ActionListener object)
boolean isSelected()
void setSelected(boolean selected)
void setText(String text);
void setIcon(ImageIcon icon);
```

Events:

```
class ... implements ActionListener
{
  public void actionPerformed(ActionEvent e)
  {
    JToggleButton tb = (JToggleButton)e.getSource();
    if (tb.isSelected())
      ...
  }
}
```

Appendix D: The `StringBuffer` Class

`StringBuffer` objects represent character strings that can be modified. Recall that `String` objects are immutable: you cannot change the contents of a string once it is created, so for every change you need to build a new string. To change one or several characters in a string or append characters to a string, it is usually more efficient to use `StringBuffer` objects.

This is especially true if you know in advance the maximum length of a string that a given `StringBuffer` object will hold. `StringBuffer` objects distinguish between the current <u>capacity</u> of the buffer (i.e., the maximum length of a string that this buffer can hold without being resized) and the current <u>length</u> of the string held in the buffer. For instance, a buffer may have the capacity to hold 100 characters and be empty (i.e., currently hold an empty string). As long as the length does not exceed the capacity, all the action takes place within the same buffer and there is no need to reallocate it. When the length exceeds the capacity, a larger buffer is allocated automatically and the contents of the current buffer are copied into the new buffer. This takes some time, so if you want your code to run efficiently, you have to arrange things in such a way that reallocation and copying do not happen often.

The `StringBuffer` class has three constructors:

```
StringBuffer()          // Constructs an empty string buffer with the
                        //    default capacity (16 characters)
StringBuffer(int n)     // Constructs an empty string buffer with the
                        //    capacity n characters
StringBuffer(String s)  // Constructs a string buffer that holds
                        //    a copy of s
```

Figure D-1 shows some of `StringBuffer`'s more commonly used methods at work. As in the `String` class, the `length` method returns the length of the string currently held in the buffer. The `capacity` method returns the current capacity of the buffer.

In addition to the `charAt(int pos)` method that returns the character at a given position, `StringBuffer` has the `setCharAt(int pos, char ch)` method that sets the character at a given position to a given value.

`StringBuffer` has several overloaded `append(sometype x)` methods. Each of them takes one argument of a particular type: `String`, `char`, `boolean`, `int`, and other primitive types, or char[]. Primitive types are converted into a string using the default conversion method, as in String.valueOf(...). Then the string is appended at the end of the buffer. A larger buffer is automatically allocated if necessary. The overloaded insert(int pos, *sometype* x) methods insert characters at a given position.

The substring(fromPos) and substring(fromPos, toPos) methods work the same way as in the String class: the former returns a String equal to the substring starting at position fromPos, the latter returns a String equal to the substring between fromPos and toPos-1. delete(fromPos, toPos) removes a substring from the buffer and replace(fromPos, toPos, str) replaces the substring between fromPos and toPos-1 with str. Finally, the toString method returns a String object equal to the characters held in the buffer.

```
StringBuffer sb = new StringBuffer(10);  // sb is empty

int len = sb.length();                   // len is set to 0
int size = sb.capacity();                // size is set to 10

sb.append("at");                         // sb holds "at"
sb.insert(0, 'b');                       // sb holds "bat"

char ch = sb.charAt(1);                  // ch is set to 'a'
sb.setCharAt(0, 'w');                    // sb holds "wat"

sb.append("er");                         // sb holds "water"
sb.replace(1, 3, "int");                 // sb holds "winter"

String s1 = sb.substring(1);             // s1 is set to "inter"
String s2 = sb.substring(1, 3);          // s2 is set to "in"
sb.delete(4, 6);                         // sb holds "wint"
sb.deleteCharAt(3);                      // sb holds "win"

sb.append(2004);                         // sb holds "win2004"
String str = sb.toString();              // str is set to "win2004"
```

Figure D-1. Examples of common StringBuffer methods

Index